Active Learning from Infan

Megan M. Saylor • Patricia A. Ganea
Editors

Active Learning
from Infancy to Childhood

Social Motivation, Cognition, and Linguistic Mechanisms

 Springer

Editors
Megan M. Saylor
Department of Psychology
and Human Development
Vanderbilt University
Nashville, TN, USA

Patricia A. Ganea
Department of Applied Psychology
& Human Development
University of Toronto
Toronto, ON, Canada

ISBN 978-3-319-77181-6   ISBN 978-3-319-77182-3   (eBook)
https://doi.org/10.1007/978-3-319-77182-3

Library of Congress Control Number: 2018940664

Printed on acid-free paper

This Springer imprint is published by the registered company Springer International Publishing AG part
of Springer Nature.
The registered company address is: Gewerbestrasse 11, 6330 Cham, Switzerland

This book is dedicated to our collection of children for their persistent question asking.

Contents

Contributors

Ilona Bass Psychology Department, Rutgers University, Newark, NJ, USA

Katarina Begus Cognitive Development Center, Department of Cognitive Science, Central European University, Budapest, Hungary

Elizabeth Bonawitz Psychology Department, Rutgers University, Newark, NJ, USA

Justin T. A. Busch Department of Psychology, The University of Texas at Austin, Austin, TX, USA

Maureen A. Callanan Department of Psychology, University of California, Santa Cruz, CA, USA

Ian L. Campbell Applied Human Development, Boston University, Boston, MA, USA

Kathleen H. Corriveau Applied Human Development, Boston University, Boston, MA, USA

Judith H. Danovitch Department of Psychological and Brain Sciences, University of Louisville, Louisville, KY, USA

Israel Flores Department of Psychology and Human Development, Vanderbilt University, Nashville, TN, USA

Patricia A. Ganea Department of Applied Psychology and Human Development, University of Toronto, Toronto, ON, Canada

Susan A. Gelman Department of Psychology, University of Michigan, Ann Arbor, MI, USA

Sofia Jimenez Department of Psychology and Human Development, Vanderbilt University, Nashville, TN, USA

Jennifer L. Jipson Department of Psychology and Child Development, California Polytechnic State University, San Luis Obispo, CA, USA

Melissa A. Koenig Institute of Child Development, University of Minnesota, Minneapolis, MN, USA

Yana Kuchirko Steinhardt School of Culture, Education, and Human Development, New York University, New York, NY, USA

Danielle Labotka Department of Psychology, University of Michigan, Ann Arbor, MI, USA

Elizabeth Lapidow Psychology Department, University of California, San Diego, CA, USA

Cristine H. Legare Department of Psychology, The University of Texas at Austin, Austin, TX, USA

Susan M. Letourneau New York Hall of Science, Queens, NY, USA

Jeannette Mancilla-Martinez Department of Teaching and Learning, Vanderbilt University, Nashville, TN, USA

Haykaz Mangardich Department of Psychology, Queen's University, Kingston, ON, Canada

Candice M. Mills School of Behavioral and Brain Sciences, The University of Texas at Dallas, Richardson, TX, USA

Annelise Pesch Institute of Child Development, University of Minnesota, Minneapolis, MN, USA

Katherine E. Ridge Institute of Child Development, University of Minnesota, Minneapolis, MN, USA

Mark A. Sabbagh Department of Psychology, Queen's University, Kingston, ON, Canada

Megan M. Saylor Department of Psychology and Human Development, Vanderbilt University, Nashville, TN, USA

David M. Sobel Department of Cognitive, Linguistic, and Psychological Sciences, Brown University, Providence, RI, USA

Victoria Southgate Department of Psychology, University of Copenhagen, Copenhagen, Denmark

Sarah Suárez Institute of Child Development, University of Minnesota, Minneapolis, MN, USA

Daniel D. Suh Steinhardt School of Culture, Education, and Human Development, New York University, New York, NY, USA

Yuyue Sun Department of Psychology and Human Development, Vanderbilt University, Nashville, TN, USA

Catherine S. Tamis-LeMonda Steinhardt School of Culture, Education, and Human Development, New York University, New York, NY, USA

Georgene L. Troseth Department of Psychology and Human Development, Vanderbilt University, Nashville, TN, USA

Aiyana K. Willard Brunel University London, Uxbridge, UK

School of Anthropology and Museum Ethnography, University of Oxford, Oxford, UK

About the Editors

Megan M. Saylor, Ph.D. is an Associate Professor at Vanderbilt University in the Department of Psychology and Human Development. She received her undergraduate degree from UC Berkeley in 1996, where she studied psychology and linguistics. She joined the faculty at Vanderbilt after completing her doctorate at the University of Oregon in 2001. Her research focuses on the social and cognitive mechanisms that support the acquisition of language in infants and preschoolers.

Patricia A. Ganea, Ph.D. is an Associate Professor at the University of Toronto in the Department of Applied Psychology and Human Development. She received her undergraduate degree from the University of Bucharest in 1996, where she studied psychology and philosophy. Following one year at the University of Oxford as a Soros visiting student, she completed her doctorate in developmental psychology at the University of Virginia in 2004. She was Assistant Professor at Boston University from 2007 until 2011, when she joined the University of Toronto. Her research focuses on the social, linguistic, and representational aspects of young children's learning.

Part I
Foundations of Active Learning

Chapter 1
Introduction: How Children Propel Development

Megan M. Saylor and Patricia A. Ganea

Abstract In this chapter, we outline our view of active learning. Active learning involves the ability to identify gaps in one's knowledge, skills for seeking the missing information and the inclination to do so. We consider the treatment of active learning in the context of both classic and contemporary research on cognitive and language development. The probable relation between active learning and children's nascent curiosity is also considered.

> "I wonder why. I wonder why.
> I wonder why I wonder
> I wonder why I wonder why
> I wonder why I wonder."("I wonder why I wonder why" by Richard Feynman)

This book was inspired, in part, by one of our children who has surprised and entertained us with her questions about words and things. She asks questions about the meanings and history of words, the insides and mechanics of living and nonliving things, and the origins of human life. Her questions belie a strong inclination to wonder about meanings and unseen forces and a confidence in her ability to extract whatever facts or information she might be lacking. As one example, while watching an unrelated cooking show, in late December of 2016 she asked, "What does grope mean?" Given that this question occurred on the heels of a very adult themed presidential election, the two grown-ups in the room eyed each other and asked, "Where'd you hear that honey?" Much to their relief, she clarified that she had been wondering about it because a character in a book she was reading had been described as "groping around in the dark." We believe this example stands as a clear example

M. M. Saylor (✉)
Department of Psychology and Human Development, Vanderbilt University,
Nashville, TN, USA
e-mail: m.saylor@vanderbilt.edu

P. A. Ganea
Department of Applied Psychology and Human Development, University of Toronto,
Toronto, ON, Canada

© Springer International Publishing AG, part of Springer Nature 2018
M. M. Saylor, P. A. Ganea (eds.), *Active Learning from Infancy to Childhood*,
https://doi.org/10.1007/978-3-319-77182-3_1

3

of active learning: she had identified a gap in her knowledge, had been wondering about it, and when unable to sort out the meaning on her own sought out the information from trusted sources. Additionally, her interest in this incidence was clearly independent of her caregivers' attentional focus in the moment; her inquiry was driven at least in part by what was going on in her mind, rather than what was happening in the world in that moment.

In our view, active learning is characterized by a goal directed search for information. At its base, active learning involves the ability to identify gaps in one's knowledge, skills for seeking the missing information and the inclination to do so. Active learning can occur in the context of interactions with parents, teachers, and peers and hence involves children's elicitation and evaluation of verbal information (e.g., attention bids, questions, explanations testimony). This elicitation can occur through nonverbal means, such as when a child points to an object to elicit information from a caregiver. Active learning can also occur during children's experimentation during play and exploration. At some point in development, active learning involves evaluating the information that is obtained: is it from a trusted source, is it adequate, is additional information necessary? As children develop their awareness of the process of active learning, metacognitive judgments about the need for missing information and the variability in potential information sources likely become a guiding force in the process.

There are clear benefits to a child who guides their own learning process, as Baldwin and Moses (1996, p. 1915) point out, "A learner capable of actively gathering information through social channels need not passively rely on the chance that needed information will be supplied. Rather, he or she can spontaneously seek out others in pursuit of social input regarding areas of particular interest or significance and will be better at evaluating when this input is relevant." Active learning sets children free of the constraints of their caregivers' interests and attention and enables interest driven information seeking. Among other benefits, what active learning may also enable is the timely acquisition of sought after information. Temporal congruency between wondering about something and information attainment may lead to more robust representations of the acquired knowledge.

Active learning can take many forms. At its most basic, it involves the solicitation of verbal and nonverbal information during interactions with social others. The ability to elicit responses from social others emerges early and relies in part on the ability to engage others' focus of attention. Although the general process of active learning may be goal directed, early in development a central motivation underlying such learning attempts may be sustaining a social interaction rather than seeking a specific piece of information. Early on, infants may not produce their bids for information with the specific intention to fill a knowledge gap. Instead, they may be motivated by the more basic desire to engage their caregivers in sustained interactions. Infants' tendency to elicit contributions from their caregivers with their looks, gestures, and verbal queries may set up both the efficiency of information seeking episodes, as they learn which bids are most successful, and their expectations about the relative quality of information sources, as they learn who is most likely to respond.

The notion that the development of young children is guided in part or entirely by their active exploration of their environments is one of the foundational principles in cognitive development. Both Piaget and Vygotsky proposed models of development and change that included an active child participant seeking information through interaction with their environments and recalibrating their knowledge as a result of these interactions (Piaget, 1926; Vygotsky, 1987). There are, of course, critical differences between the two accounts, including the unit of analysis (individual versus social event), the treatment (or relative neglect) of the role of other people, and the purported importance of variability in development and in contexts of learning (e.g., Rogoff, 1990). Regardless, both theorists shared the view that children were active, rather than passive, agents in knowledge building. As one example, Piaget describes something akin to a compulsion to fill a space left vacant by a previously interesting sight, "...the sight of the rattle created a sufficiently powerful interest for this interest to orient the activity in the direction already following an instant before. In other words, when the rattle stops moving, there ensues *a vacuum which the child immediately tries to fill* and he does so by utilizing the movements which have just been performed," (Piaget, 1952, p. 183). Importantly, for Piaget's infant, the drive to imbue experience with action was the result of infants repeating actions for the sake of action itself, rather than for some external, independent goal or scheme (Flavell, 1963).

An enduring theme in explanations of what supports active learning is a drive to resolve discrepancies between what a child knows and what is possible to be known. A foundation of Piaget's theory was that children were compelled to explore objects to resolve inconsistencies between the contents of their mind and the state of things in the world (Piaget, 1952). This tendency to work toward some resolution between what a child knows or is able to do and more mature skills is also echoed in Vygotsky's sketch of the knowledge that emerges during a child's engagement with a more skilled social partner (Vygotsky, 1978, 1987; Wertsch, 1985). In Vygotsky's view, children were engaged and supported in their knowledge acquisition attempts by social others who both knew more and were motivated to guide children through the process. Whether the discrepancy between what is known and what can be known was thought to be resolved internally, in the child's mind, or externally, in the space that exists between children and their social partners, is an important point of difference between Piaget and Vygotsky (Rogoff, 1990). Determining the relative weight of internal versus external factors as source of the discrepancy between what is known and what is possible is one of the central challenges facing contemporary researchers interested in active learning.

Research on curiosity and the information seeking episodes that result from it also allude to a drive to reduce discrepancies between what is known and what one might want to know (for reviews see Jirout & Klahr, 2012; Kidd & Hayden, 2015; Loewenstein, 1994). Although interest in curiosity as a mechanism supporting information seeking and active learning in children and adults has a long history among psychologists (see, e.g., Berlyne, 1960; James, 1899; Kagan, 1972), both a satisfactory definition of the construct and validated measures that index variability in curiosity await development. Curiosity, it turns out, is a bit of a nebulous construct for researchers and theorists alike.

There are many points of disagreement concerning the best way to define curiosity, the relation between curiosity and information seeking, and as a result, the preferred way to study curiosity. As one brief example, there is some disagreement about whether curiosity is driven purely by internal forces or by a mix of internal and external factors (e.g., Loewenstein, 1994). Furthermore, the affective state that accompanies the drive to acquire information is in dispute: some theorists have described curiosity as being an unpleasant sensation we seek to reduce, while others describe it as being pleasurable and as motivating for its own sake (e.g., see discussions in Litman, 2005; Litman & Jimerson, 2004; Loewenstein, 1994). To complicate things further, although most people are curious, their curiosity can have different levels of intensity and be manifested in different domains.

It is perhaps best to think of curiosity as varying widely on a spectrum, both in terms of the breadth or range of topics that one is curious about and how deeply one goes into a topic of interest (for an engaging discussion of these issues, see Livio, 2017). In the face of these disagreements and open questions, we therefore favor the broad definition offered by Kidd and Hayden (2015), p. 450) who view curiosity as a "drive state for information" in which individuals want information for myriad reasons. In their view, the drive to acquire information can be driven by processes that are "internal or external, conscious or unconscious, slowly evolved or some mixture of the above." Importantly, we view curiosity as a foundation of most types of active learning. Seeking information to fill a gap in one's knowledge or experiences must be supported, at least in part, by the inclination to do so.

One foundational type of active learning involves spontaneous play and exploration. From early in development, children learn about the world, searching for explanations through both language and their own self-initiated exploration of objects. Through play and active exploration children can test their hypotheses and naïve theories about the world around them (Gopnik, 2016; Gopnik, Meltzoff, & Kuhl, 1999). Pretend play, the ability to conjure up alternative representations to current reality, such as when a child pretends to sip tea from an empty cup, is viewed by some as giving the child the opportunity to explore not only real-scenarios learned in their daily interactions but also to consider events that have not yet occurred (Buchsbaum, Bridgers, Weisberg, & Gopnik, 2012; Harris, 2000). In creating alternative representations to reality and generating inferences about possible outcomes, children can use their causal understanding of the world to make sense of new possibilities and in doing so practice skills that are essential for learning (Harris, 2000). Much of children's pretend play is focused on exploring psychological relationships through social dramatic play and the creation of imaginary companions, and in doing so they have the opportunity to practice their understanding of their own and others' minds (Lillard, 2001; Taylor, 1998). Children's pretense and other types of play can be used as tool for active learning: researchers have found that preschoolers will adjust their play and exploration of objects in the face of incongruous or confounding information about objects (e.g., Bonawitz, Schijndel, Friel, & Schulz, 2012; Cook, Goodman, & Schulz, 2011). Play is one of the earliest ways in which children manifest their ability to actively and creatively manipulate current reality to explore new represented worlds and to figure out solutions to puzzles they may wonder about.

Active learning is also revealed in children's question asking. Children are prodigious question askers—in one ambitious monograph, researchers estimated that children between the ages of 1 and 5 ask an average of 107 questions an hour (Chouinard, Harris, & Maratsos, 2007). The nature of children's questions reveals that they are goal directed as they seek information and explanations—children will stop asking questions once a sought-after answer or high quality explanation has been received and continue asking questions (varying the form and perhaps the volume) until they elicit a satisfying answer (Frazier, Gelman, & Wellman, 2009; Kemler Nelson, Egan, & Holt, 2004). Children ask questions about many things including queries about names for things, unseen objects, object functions, and causes for natural events (Callanan & Oakes, 1992; Chouinard et al., 2007; Frazier et al., 2009). Their reasons for asking questions are also varied and include both a quest for satisfying explanations and the delivery of isolated bits of information.

One important lesson from research on children's information seeking in the last decade is that they are not indiscriminate in who they seek information from. Research on selective trust has revealed that preschoolers, and perhaps even infants, make nuanced judgments about both from whom they would like to learn and the quality of information (Harris, 2012). These evaluations of information sources play a critical role in children's ability to incorporate new knowledge based on verbal testimony and provide converging evidence for the importance of active learning processes in children's cognitive and language development.

However, it is worth noting that most of the research on the types of active learning we have outlined above has been conducted on a relatively homogeneous group of Western children with more or less robust language skills. When children with a wider range of demographic backgrounds and language skills are included in studies, the skills that we take to be characteristic appear to be a bit more varied. To illustrate this point, we focus on children's question asking. Seminal research on variation in children's home environments illustrates that both the ability to (repeatedly) ask appropriate questions and the benefits of doing so are not equally distributed across preschoolers (McCarthy, 1930; Tizard & Hughes, 1984). In particular, existing studies indicate that socio-economic differences play a role in the number and type of questions that children ask. Children from middle-class families whose parents model question asking for their children end up asking more questions in general (Hart & Risley, 1992; Kurkul & Corriveau, 2017) and more curiosity-based questions in particular (Tizard & Hughes, 1984) compared to children from working-class families. Harris (2012) suggests that these differences may be part of a more general style of communication in the family: in families where conversation is encouraged and seen as an exploratory device for exchanging knowledge, children tend to emulate their parents' stance, while in families where question asking is not viewed as an opportunity to share information but rather as an opportunity to prohibit and control, children ask fewer questions. Parents' conversational stance may not only affect the overall number of questions, but also the types of questions children ask. Cross-cultural research on children's questions also points to important differences in the relative proportion of questions seeking explanations versus information, with fewer explanation-seeking questions in non-western cultures compared to western cultures (Gauvain, Munroe, & Beebe, 2013). Understanding potential sources of variability in children's active learning, both within and across cultures, is thus an important direction for future study.

In reflecting on sources of variability in the behaviors typical of active learning, we wish to end our discussion with an example of someone who was both remarkably curious and inclined to engage in what we view as super-charged active learning. In 1988 the physicist Richard Feynman gave a wonderful account of his interactions with his father in the essay "The making of a Scientist" published in his book "What do You care what other people think? Further adventures of a curious character." Feynman's father taught him to notice and observe things, to look beyond what is apparent in nature, and to understand its meaning. Feynman describes his father's use of many techniques to scaffold learning. For example, he would trigger Feynman's curiosity by asking a question (e.g., "Why do you think birds peck at their feathers?") or by stopping in the middle of a walk in the woods and wondering out-loud about something. He would not necessarily give the answer immediately but rather he would get Feynman to think of an explanation, devise a little experiment, or provide an explanation and use examples to get him to think of the bigger picture. The point was not in giving the answer but rather in getting Feynman to learn "the difference between knowing the name of something and knowing something" (Feynman & Leighton, 1988, p. 14).

Feynman assumed that the things his father knew and the way he interacted with him were things that all fathers knew and did with their children. Only later did he realize how remarkable his father was and he credited his motivation for science and curiosity to the way his father educated him: "I've been caught, so to speak – like someone who was given something wonderful when he was child, and he's always looking for it again. I'm always looking, like a child, for the wonders I know I'm going to find – maybe not every time, but every once in a while" (Feynman & Leighton, 1988, p. 16). Styles of interacting early in development may set the stage for a prodigious tendency to seek information and find satisfaction in novelty and knowledge.

What factors might determine variability in active learning? Feynman's story about his father illustrates that the way we interact with children can stimulate and nourish a child's curiosity. If curiosity is a core foundation of active learning, understanding what factors determine why some individuals end up being more curious than others and why some individuals experience curiosity with different intensity may be a route to gaining better understanding of how to facilitate the process of active learning. As one example, the way parents talk to their children and model question asking is related to the stance that children take with respect to question asking. But, even within the same family, not all children end up being equally curious, or they end up being curious about different things, or experience their curiosity with different intensity. Are there inherent characteristics that play a role in one's active search for new experiences and new knowledge, or in one's specific interests?

What is the relation between curiosity and other individual characteristics, such as metacognitive skills or information-processing ability? What are the brain mechanisms that are central to active learning? How does growing in different cultures or attending different school environments influence children's active learning behaviors? Discovering the multiple mechanisms that play a role in the genesis of active learning and how they interact over development will shed light on what drives humans to not only seek novel experiences out of boredom but to think beyond the obvious and to wonder why things are the way they are.

To this end, the chapters in this volume trace out the development of mechanisms supporting active learning and raise candidate sources of potential variability in children's ability to seek out information from social others. The chapters are organized into four sections. Part I focuses on foundations of active learning in infancy and factors that influence its development. *Begus and Southgate* (Chap. 2) review the current research on how infants' curiosity is expressed and how responding to their curiosity may affect their learning, and investigate the possible neurological underpinnings of the social and motivational aspects of learning. *Tamis-Lemonda, Kuchirko, and Suh* (Chap. 3) discuss several instances in which general learning mechanisms, such as statistical learning and contingency detection, dovetail with the input infants elicit during everyday activities (e.g., during object play), and how children's language development is shaped by their active role in input seeking during daily interactions with others.

Part II discusses cognitive and linguistic skills that may enable active learning. *Sobel and Letourneau* (Chap. 4) argue that both an understanding of when learning will and will not occur and a metacognitive understanding of how their own learning takes place is necessary to understand how exploration can guide learning to support the acquisition of knowledge. *Jimenez, Sun, and Saylor* (Chap. 5) discuss a set of cognitive, motivational, and language skills that may explain when children seek information about words and why some children are more inclined to do so than others. Chapters 6 and 7 focus on exploration and discovery. *Danovitch and Mills* (Chap. 6) review literature on the role of explanations in learning and discuss when and how different kinds of explanations lead to exploration and discovery. *Busch, Willard, and Legare* (Chap. 7) propose a model of active learning in which inconsistency and ambiguity motivate explanations that lead to exploration, question asking, and information seeking behaviors in children.

Part III focuses on active learning processes in the domain of selective trust. *Ridge, Pesch, Suarez, and Koenig* (Chap. 8) describe evidential and interpersonal reasons that affect whether children trust others as sources of information. Chapters 9 and 10 explore the extent to which internal constraints (in the form of memory processes and belief states) enable selective learning. *Mangardich and Sabbagh* (Chap. 9) provide a compelling case for a semantic gating mechanism that may explain children's selective learning when acquiring novel words. *Campbell and Corriveau* (Chap. 10) argue that children's beliefs about physical possibility affects their acceptance of verbal testimony from adults.

Part IV focuses on information seeking in diverse contexts. *Bonawitz, Bass, and Lapidow* (Chap. 11) focus on children's evaluation of evidence to support their learning. *Jipson, Labotka, Callanan and Gelman* (Chap. 12) discuss ways in which conversations with parents might shape children's learning and understanding. *Mancilla-Martinez, Troseth and Flores* (Chap. 13) discuss active learning during language brokering in bilingual children.

References

Baldwin, D. A., & Moses, L. J. (1996). The ontogeny of social information gathering. *Child Development, 67*(5), 1915–1939.

Berlyne, D. E. (1960). *Conflict, arousal, and curiosity*. New York, NY: McGraw-Hill.

Bonawitz, E. B., van Schijndel, T. J. P., Friel, D., & Schulz, L. (2012). Children balance theories and evidence in exploration, explanation, and learning. *Cognitive Psychology, 64*(4), 215–234. https://doi.org/10.1016/j.cogpsych.2011.12.002

Buchsbaum, D., Bridgers, S., Weisberg, D. S., & Gopnik, A. (2012). The power of possibility: Causal learning, counterfactual reasoning, and pretend play. *Philosophical Transactions of the Royal Society of London B: Biological Sciences, 367*(1599), 2202–2212.

Callanan, M. A., & Oakes, L. M. (1992). Preschoolers' questions and parents' explanations: Causal thinking in everyday activity. *Cognitive Development, 7*(2), 213–233.

Chouinard, M. M., Harris, P. L., & Maratsos, M. P. (2007). Children's questions: A mechanism for cognitive development. *Monographs of the Society for Research in Child Development, 72*, i–129.

Cook, C., Goodman, N. D., & Schulz, L. E. (2011). Where science starts: Spontaneous experiments in preschoolers' exploratory play. *Cognition, 120*(3), 341–349.

Feynman, R. P., & Leighton, R. (1988). *"What do you care what other people think?": Further adventures of a curious character*. New York, NY: WW Norton & Company.

Flavell, J. H. (1963). *The developmental psychology of Jean Piaget*. Princeton, NJ: D. Van Nostrand Company, Inc.

Frazier, B. N., Gelman, S. A., & Wellman, H. M. (2009). Preschoolers' search for explanatory information within adult–child conversation. *Child Development, 80*(6), 1592–1611.

Gauvain, M., Munroe, R. L., & Beebe, H. (2013). Children's questions in cross-cultural perspective: A four-culture study. *Journal of Cross-Cultural Psychology, 44*, 1148–1165. https://doi.org/10.1177/0022022113485430

Gopnik, A. (2016). *The gardener and the carpenter*. New York, NY: Farrar, Straus, and Girout.

Gopnik, A., Meltzoff, A. N., & Kuhl, P. K. (1999). *The scientist in the crib: Minds, brains, and how children learn*. New York, NY: William Morrow & Co.

Harris, P. L. (2000). *The work of the imagination*. Hoboken, NJ: Blackwell Publishing.

Harris, P. L. (2012). *Trusting what you're told: How children learn from others*. Cambridge, MA: Harvard University Press.

Hart, B., & Risley, T. R. (1992). American parenting of language-learning children: Persisting differences in family-child interactions observed in natural home environments. *Developmental Psychology, 28*(6), 1096.

James, W. (1899). *Talks to teachers on psychology: And to students on some of life's ideals*. New York, NY: Henry Holt and Company.

Jirout, J., & Klahr, D. (2012). Children's scientific curiosity: In search of an operational definition of an elusive concept. *Developmental Review, 32*(2), 125–160.

Kagan, J. (1972). Motives and development. *Journal of Personality and Social Psychology, 22*(1), 51.

Kemler Nelson, D. G., Egan, C. L., & Holt, M. B. (2004). When preschoolers ask,"what is it?" what do they want to know about artifacts. *Psychological Science, 15*, 384–389.

Kidd, C., & Hayden, B. Y. (2015). The psychology and neuroscience of curiosity. *Neuron, 88*(3), 449–460.

Kurkul, K. E., & Corriveau, K. H. (2017). Question, explanation, follow-up: A mechanism for learning from others? *Child Development.* https://doi.org/10.1111/cdev.12726

Lillard, A. (2001). Pretend play as twin earth: A social-cognitive analysis. *Developmental Review, 21*(4), 495–531.

Litman, J. (2005). Curiosity and the pleasures of learning: Wanting and liking new information. *Cognition & Emotion, 19*(6), 793–814.

Litman, J. A., & Jimerson, T. L. (2004). The measurement of curiosity as a feeling of deprivation. *Journal of Personality Assessment, 82*(2), 147–157.

Livio, M. (2017). *Why? What makes us curious?* New York, NY: Simon and Schuster.

Loewenstein, G. (1994). The psychology of curiosity: A review and reinterpretation. *Psychological Bulletin, 116*(1), 75–95.

McCarthy, D. (1930). *The language development of the preschool child* (No. 4). Minneapolis, MN: Institute of Child Welfare, Monograph Series.

Piaget, J. (1926). *The language and thought of the child.* New York, NY: Harcourt, Brace.

Piaget, J. (1952). *The origins of intelligence in children.* Madison, CT: International Universities Press.

Rogoff, B. (1990). *Apprenticeship in thinking: cognitive development in a social context.* New York: Oxford University Press.

Taylor, M. (1998). *Imaginary companions and the children who create them.* New York, NY: Oxford.

Tizard, B., & Hughes, M. (1984). *Young children learning: talking and thinking at home and at school.* London, UK: Fontana.

Vygotsky, L. S. (1978). *Mind in society: The development of higher psychological processes.* Cambridge, MA: Harvard University Press.

Vygotsky, L. S. (1987). Problems of general psychology. In R. Rieber & A. Carton (Eds.), *The collected works of L.S. Vygotsky.* New York, NY: Plenum Press.

Wertsch, J. V. (1985). *Vygotsky and the social formation of mind.* Cambridge, MA: Harvard University Press.

Chapter 2
Curious Learners: How Infants' Motivation to Learn Shapes and Is Shaped by Infants' Interactions with the Social World

Katarina Begus and Victoria Southgate

Abstract Most theories of infant social learning focus on how infants learn whatever and whenever the adults decide to teach them. While infants are well equipped to learn from adults, recent research suggests infant social learning is not a passive process but that infants may play an active role in acquiring information and modulating their learning according to their interests. This chapter aims to highlight the importance of investigating young children's intrinsic motivation for learning, particularly in the domain of social learning. It reviews the current research on how infants' curiosity may be expressed through their behaviour while interacting with social partners, and how responding to these expressions of curiosity may affect infants' learning. Finally, through the investigation of the possible neurological underpinnings of the social and motivational aspects of learning, this chapter explores infants' selectivity in social partners and how it can be explained by their motivation to learn.

Introduction

The idea of a child as an active learner, driven by curiosity, is possibly as old as the field of developmental psychology itself, and has been the foundation of some of the most influential theories of early learning (e.g. Piaget, 1952). While children's own independent active exploration could be the principal way of acquiring some skills, others, such as language, for example, could not develop without interaction with the child's social world. It is therefore perhaps not surprising that most research and

K. Begus (✉)
Cognitive Development Center, Department of Cognitive Science,
Central European University, Budapest, Hungary

V. Southgate
Department of Psychology, University of Copenhagen, Copenhagen, Denmark

© Springer International Publishing AG, part of Springer Nature 2018
M. M. Saylor, P. A. Ganea (eds.), *Active Learning from Infancy to Childhood*,
https://doi.org/10.1007/978-3-319-77182-3_2

theories of infant social learning focus on infants' ability to receive and encode the information communicated to them. Accordingly, a vast body of research has demonstrated that infants are very well equipped to learn from others, with attentional biases that ensure they detect when a social partner is transmitting information, and cognitive adaptations that ensure the transmission of information is successful (Csibra & Gergely, 2009). However, to ensure rapid transmission of information by communication, both participants ought to be actively involved in the process (Baldwin & Moses, 1996). If the learner is able to take on an active role in gathering information, they need not passively rely on chance that the information will be supplied. Recent research suggests that even in the field of early social learning, infants are not merely passive consumers of information, but may play an active role in soliciting and selecting the information they learn.

> "I think, at a child's birth, if a mother could ask a fairy godmother to endow the child with the most useful gift, that gift would be curiosity". (Eleanor Roosevelt).

Curiosity

Classically, curiosity has been described in terms of drives. Analogous to other drives, such as the drive for reproduction or food, the feeling of curiosity was suggested to be unpleasant, and the reduction of it, achieved by gathering information about the curiosity-eliciting stimuli, was proposed to be rewarding (Berlyne, 1954, 1966). Later theories proposed that curiosity should instead be understood as an interaction between an individual's knowledge state and the current situation (Lowenstein, 1994). According to this knowledge-gap model, curiosity is aroused when a gap in an individual's knowledge becomes apparent, and the individual becomes motivated to close this gap by acquiring information, which results in subsequent reduction of curiosity. However, interpreting the experience of curiosity as aversive fails to explain why much of human behaviour is in fact geared towards actively seeking curiosity-inducing situations. For example, situations with limited stimulation often lead individuals to explore the environment for something new and interesting, which could help them avoid feelings of boredom (Collins, Litman, & Spielberger, 2004). Furthermore, acquiring information on a topic often leads to even more curiosity and information seeking (Hidi & Renninger, 2006), and not necessarily to satiation, as initially proposed by Lowenstein (1994). These considerations lead to new models of curiosity, according to which individuals seek an optimal level of arousal or stimulation, looking for opportunities to have their curiosity piqued, as much as gathering information to relieve it (Spielberger & Starr, 1994). Furthermore, as opposed to knowledge-gap models, more recent theories of curiosity proposed a mechanism by which an individual tracks their local learning progress, without having to define the starting or desired knowledge state (Gottlieb, Oudeyer, Lopes, & Baranes, 2013; Kaplan & Oudeyer, 2007; Moulin-Frier, Nguyen, & Oudeyer, 2013; Oudeyer & Smith, 2006).

According to these theories, the learning progress is proposed to be tracked by monitoring whether the performed actions (or the information gathered) improve the individual's ability to predict (the consequences of) future actions, or the ability to solve problems and master the environment (Nguyen et al., 2013). The activities an individual performs are intrinsically rewarding in proportion to the decrease of prediction error they produce (Gottlieb et al., 2013). As opposed to the theories viewing curiosity as an unpleasant state, these models propose curiosity induction *itself* can be rewarding, involving emotional states, which are positive and not aversive (Fowler, 1966; Litman, 2005, 2008; Litman & Silvia, 2006). This perspective seems to better account for why humans evolved to be curious, despite the fact that exploring and seeking information frequently appears to serve no immediate purpose in terms of survival. Curiosity and information gathering as a rewarding process likely acquired value through long-term evolutionary selection, by maximising evolutionary fitness in rapidly changing environmental conditions through continuous acquisition of information which, even if not immediately valuable, could become useful in the future (Gottlieb et al., 2013).

As well as its potential role in human evolution, the role of curiosity has long been appreciated and investigated in studies of learning. It has been proposed that interest impacts individuals' attention, goals and levels of learning (Hidi & Renninger, 2006). Situational interests can determine what individuals will attend to and learn at any given moment (Mitchell, 1993), stable interests can determine individuals' career paths and help them overcome low abilities (Hidi & Harackiewicz, 2000), and general levels of curiosity are one of the main predictors of academic success (von Stumm, Hell, & Chamorro-Premuzic, 2011). However, while the function of curiosity in learning has been emphasised in educational settings for decades, true advances in linking states of heightened motivation and curiosity to knowledge acquisition have only been made in recent years.

Neuroimaging studies in adults have confirmed what has long been hypothesised from behavioural and self-report studies; states of curiosity or heightened interest function as an intrinsic reward mechanism, and directly modulate what information will be encoded (Gruber, Gelman, & Ranganath, 2014; Jepma, Verdonschot, van Steenbergen, Rombouts, & Nieuwenhuis, 2012; Kang et al., 2009). For example, in two separate studies, adult participants were presented with trivia questions and were asked to rate how curious they were to find out the answer. Using fMRI recordings, these studies have found that the induction of epistemic curiosity and not (only) the relief of it elicited activity in reward-related areas of the brain (Gruber et al., 2014; Kang et al., 2009), specifically in structures that are most reliably activated by the anticipation and processing of rewards (Knutson, Adams, Fong, & Hommer, 2001). Furthermore, both studies have also found that the magnitude of self-reported curiosity predicted the degree to which the participants encoded information during these tasks, and provided evidence on how states of curiosity can directly affect what information is encoded, by modulating the activity of memory encoding areas of the brain (Gruber et al., 2014; Kang et al., 2009). Kang et al. (2009) investigated how curiosity interacts with prior knowledge and demonstrated enhanced learning for information that participants were most curious about, and the positive effect of curiosity on learning was still observed after a two-week delay. The effects of curiosity on learning were replicated in the study by Gruber et al. (2014), demonstrating enhanced memory for information that participants were curious about in immediate and one-day-delay memory tests. In addition, learning was also enhanced for information that was irrelevant to the curiosity-inducing trivia questions but was presented during states of curiosity, thus highlighting the potential enhancing effect that stimulating curiosity prior to knowledge acquisition could have on learning in educational settings (Gruber et al., 2014).

Curiosity in Early Life

While direct assessments of curiosity are not feasible in infants, several aspects of infant learning suggest that curiosity may drive exploration, and modulate learning, even early in life. Several theories of curiosity-driven learning propose that the information individuals should find most interesting is that which matches an optimal level of complexity or unfamiliarity (Fowler, 1966; Piaget, 1952; Spielberger & Starr, 1994). In trying to reconcile the puzzling tendency of infants to pay greater attention to a novel stimulus in some circumstances, and a familiar stimulus in others, several authors have explained these preferences in terms of infants' changing knowledge states. As infants are encoding features of a stimulus, it is the depth of this encoding that determines their subsequent preferences. While a stimulus is not fully encoded, infants may show a familiarity preference. It is only when the depth of their knowledge is sufficient, that a shift to a novelty preference can be observed (Houston-Price & Nakai, 2004). Infants' tendency to attend to stimuli that are neither too familiar (already encoded) nor too novel (too disparate from existing representations) (Kidd & Hayden, 2015) has also been experimentally demonstrated. Studies showed that 7 and 8-month-old infants preferentially look at event sequences which are moderately predictable, as compared to highly predictable or fully unpredictable sequences (Kidd, Piantadosi, & Aslin, 2012). That infants focus their limited cognitive resources on stimuli of medium predictability, ones that provide the most information for the least cognitive effort, is precisely what would be predicted by the learning-progress models of curiosity, which suggest learning activities that would be most intrinsically rewarding are those that promise the fastest learning progress and greatest decrease of prediction error in the future (Gottlieb et al., 2013; Kaplan & Oudeyer, 2007; Moulin-Frier et al., 2013).

According to the alternative knowledge-gap theory of curiosity, interest arises when attention becomes focused on a gap in one's knowledge (Lowenstein, 1994), leading individuals to seek information that would close this gap. The striking findings that infants structure their exploratory play in a way that resolves uncertainty fits well with this theory. In a series of studies by Stahl and Feigenson (2015), infants were shown events in which common objects (such as a ball or a car) violated basic physical laws, such as object solidity (an object passing through a wall), or object support (an object pushed over the edge of a surface without falling). After demonstrations, infants were allowed to freely explore the objects with the surprising properties, and were found to explore objects qualitatively differently according to which physical law they previously observed the object violate (Stahl & Feigenson, 2015). Following a violation of object solidity, infants engaged in more banging behaviour (presumably testing how the object was able to pass through a solid wall), whereas they spent most of the time dropping objects which have previously violated the expectation of object support (presumably testing the surprising levitation property of the object). While the authors of this study focused on the role of infants' prior knowledge in guiding the acquisition of new information, infants' behaviour in these tasks can be elegantly described in terms of curiosity-driven information seeking. According to the information-gap models, the violation of infants' expectation could be seen as creating or highlighting a knowledge gap, which led to increased curiosity or interest in the surprising object. The interest in turn led to systematic exploration of the objects, aimed at closing the information gap by acquiring more evidence that could explain the surprising properties.

But do these hypothesised states of curiosity or motivation to learn in infants in fact lead to superior learning, as they do in adults (Gruber et al., 2014; Kang et al., 2009)? Indeed, infants in the studies by Stahl and Feigenson (2015) not only systematically explored the objects with surprising properties, but in fact also learned arbitrary additional features of these objects, such as the sounds they produced. In contrast, infants did not learn the same information when its presentation did not follow a surprising event. Nor did they learn the same information when it was presented after a surprising event, but the information was linked to another object, which did not violate infants' expectations. Infants' learning, observed in the studies by Stahl and Feigenson (2015), could therefore be interpreted as the first demonstration of how experimentally inducing infants' curiosity can guide their subsequent information seeking and lead to superior learning. Together, this research suggests that the rewarding mechanisms of information search and consumption may already be in place in infancy and that, like adults', infants' interest or curiosity may directly affect what information they will seek and learn in any given moment.

A question remains as to how infants are able to detect the gaps in their knowledge, or track their own learning progress, which are proposed to be prerequisites to experiencing curiosity and motivating one's learning (Gottlieb et al., 2013; Lowenstein, 1994). In other words, in order to selectively attend to or seek information that one does not yet possess, it is perhaps imperative to possess some level of metacognition—the capacity to reflect upon one's knowledge or uncertainty, and adaptively control one's cognitive processes accordingly (Hampton, 2009). While these computations may seem complex, and the development of metacognitive processes is not fully understood even in older children (see Sobel and Leourneau, this volume), some recent studies arguably provide evidence that suggests infants may already be able to monitor their errors, communicate their uncertainty, and use metacognitive evaluations to regulate subsequent behaviour (Goupil & Kouider, 2016; Goupil, Romand-monnier, & Kouider, 2016, but see Gliga & Southgate, 2016 for a critique, and Carruthers, 2008, for alternative explanations of ostensible metacognitive abilites of non-verbal organisms). Whatever the level of reflection upon their knowledge states, if a gap in knowledge is what piques infants' curiosity, and if the learnability of information determines whether infants will be motivated to obtain it, then infants may indeed be the best moderators of their own learning. It is their knowledge states, interacting with the available information, that would ultimately determine what information they would be interested in and therefore more likely to learn.

However, while the studies discussed above provide some evidence that curiosity guides what infants explore or attend to (Kidd et al., 2012; Stahl & Feigenson, 2015), the importance of understanding the role of curiosity in infant learning is perhaps most pertinent in the domain of social learning. Much of what infants need to learn, they must learn from those around them, and if there were non-verbal infant behaviours that might be communicating, or at least reflecting, infants' motivation or desire for information, awareness of these behaviours in caregivers would be important as such situations may offer special opportunities for facilitated learning. However, infants' interest and motivation for learning has received little attention in the domain of social transmission of knowledge. Most theories of social learning, and studies investigating it, focus on infants' ability to receive and encode the information communicated to them (Csibra & Gergely, 2009), whereas infants' motivation and active contribution to social transmission of knowledge is often neglected. Given the effect that curiosity may have on infant learning, and the fact that learning from people is one of the most prominent ways in which infants acquire knowledge in everyday life, investigating infants' active involvement in the process of social learning seems of particular importance.

Asking Questions Without Words

When observing an infant, who cannot yet speak and has limited means of responding and interacting with others in their environment, it is not easy to determine what information she is processing, let alone which behaviours may be signalling her motivation to obtain information. Yet, systematic investigations of infant behaviour have shown that, even before they can speak, infants can modulate the amount, the content and the timing of information they receive from others.

Social Referencing

One of the earliest behaviours, hypothesised to serve as an information-seeking tool, is social referencing, defined as looking at a social partner with the expectation of eliciting a response. In infant research, social referencing has been predominantly explored in the context of infants looking at another person's emotional cues in ambiguous situations, and has been proposed to serve infants regulating their own behaviour and emotional responses in accordance with others' (Feinman, 1982).

Classically, social referencing has been associated and investigated in the context of attachment and emotional regulation, suggesting that infants, by looking at caregivers in ambiguous situations, are seeking comfort, reassurance, and checking their caregivers' proximity and availability (Ainsworth, 1992; Dickstein, Thompson, Estes, Malkin, & Lamb, 1984).

However, accumulating evidence has since suggested infants' referencing behaviour might be better interpreted as seeking information. For example, infants as young as 6 months of age use social referencing more frequently during unexpected than expected events (Walden, Kim, McCoy, & Karrass, 2007). By 9 months, in an ambiguous situation, such as encountering a novel object, infants looked at the caregiver as much as at the unfamiliar experimenter (Kutsuki et al., 2007), speaking against the hypothesis of seeking comfort. Using a different measure, infants have also been shown to orient their gaze faster and use the information they received about an object to regulate their behaviour more, when the object was ambiguous than when it was not (Kim & Kwak, 2011). These findings suggest that infants not only seek but also utilise given information selectively, based on the level of uncertainty associated with objects at hand. Similarly, in a study where infants were given labels for objects, infants looked at the labeller more in the presence of two objects, when the intended referent of the label was ambiguous, than in the presence of a single object (Vaish, Demir, & Baldwin, 2011). These studies suggest uncertainty, or a need for information, rather than anxiety (Zarbatany & Lamb, 1985), plays a role in how much and how quickly infants use social referencing, and suggests the primary function of referencing may in fact be to seek clarifying information, rather than comfort.

The strongest evidence suggesting infants use social referencing as a means of obtaining information comes from findings that infants appear to take into account the informative potential of the available adults when deciding who to reference. In a study where an ambiguous object was presented either by the experimenter or the parent, 10-month-olds looked more to the person, who has presented the object, and (like 12-month-olds in a previous study; Stenberg, 2009) in fact modulated their behaviour more according to the information received by the experimenter than the parent (Schmitow & Stenberg, 2013). This behaviour is consistent with the "expertise" hypothesis of social referencing, by which infants use social referencing behaviour to seek information from the best source available (Feinman, Roberts, Hsieh, Sawyer, & Swanson, 1992). Accordingly, these studies suggest that infants can discriminate between potential informants, based on who has the relevant information (Schmitow & Stenberg, 2013; Stenberg, 2009), and prioritise seeking and following the information given by the adult who should have more information in the given situation (Stenberg, 2009).

Thus, by controlling their gaze alone, infants can already selectively solicit information transfer from the available social partners. But infants are not limited to the use of their eyes when interacting with the social world. Long before the onset of speech, infants begin utilising another powerful means of attracting attention and interacting with people—their voices.

Babbling

Babbling has been proposed to function as a motor exercise, through which infants develop and practice producing speech-like sounds, eventually leading to language production (Kimbrough, Wieman, Doyle, & Ross, 1976; Locke & Pearson, 1990). Studies have indeed found overlap between preferred babbling sounds and first words (Stoel-Gammon, 1992). Furthermore, the number of syllable types in babbling predicts the onset of first words (Stoel-Gammon, 1992), and speech development more broadly (Kimbrough, Eilers, Neal, & Cobo-Lewis, 1998; Kimbrough, Eilers, Neal, & Schwartz, 1999). However, the interpretation of this relationship and the focus of research on infant vocalisations have recently turned from phonological production to investigating infant vocalisations in the context of a social exchange with their caregivers.

Infant vocalising is sensitive and responsive to social contingency (Masataka, 2003). In the classic still-face paradigm, in which an adult suddenly ceases to interact, while continuing to face the infant, infants have been shown to adapt the frequency and length of vocalisations according to whether or not an adult is responsive (Franklin et al., 2013; Goldstein, Schwade, & Bornstein, 2009). Infants increased their vocalisation during unresponsive periods and returned to turn-taking vocalisations when the responsiveness resumed, suggesting they appreciate the social effect of their vocalisations on their caregivers' behaviour (Goldstein et al., 2009). In turn, caregivers have been shown to adapt their responses in accord with infants' vocalisations, providing responses contingent in time and content to the infants' vocalisations (Bornstein, Tamis-Lemonda, Hahn, & Haynes, 2008; Gros-Louis, West, & King, 2014; Tamis-LeMonda, Bornstein, & Baumwell, 2001). Moreover, how both infants and their caregivers adapt their behaviour to each other in a communicative exchange appears to have an effect on infants' learning.

Infants who modulated their vocalisations to a greater extent when facing an unresponsive adult at 5 months of age had better language comprehension at 13 months (Goldstein et al., 2009), suggesting that using vocalisations instrumentally, to elicit a response, may play a role in infants' knowledge acquisition. Likewise, infants' object-directed vocalisations (vocalising while looking at or holding an object) and parents' contingent responses to those sounds at 9 months of age predict vocabulary size at 15 months (Goldstein & Schwade, 2010). Furthermore, when infants' caregivers respond to their babbling contingently, infants produce linguistically more mature vocalisations, than when the caregivers are instructed to delay their responses (Goldstein & Schwade, 2008). Finally, as well as in experimental settings, the degree to which parents respond to infant prelinguistic vocalisations in everyday life is positively correlated with later receptive and productive vocabulary size (Tamis-LeMonda et al., 2001; Tamis-LeMonda & Bornstein, 2002; see Tamis-LaMonda et al. in this volume for review), as well as with the amount of infants' continued use of vocalisations directed at the parent (Gros-Louis et al., 2014).

The selective way in which infants use their vocalisations when interacting with adults suggests infants are aware that their vocalisations can influence the behaviour of social partners (Goldstein et al., 2009), and speaks against the possibility that vocalisations serve a purely private function of vocal self-stimulation (McCune, 2008). Furthermore, the repeatedly demonstrated effect of parents' responsiveness to babbling on infants' language acquisition provides compelling evidence that, by vocalising, infants can modulate information transfer and consequently their learning from others. However, what motivates infant babbling and what mediates the relationship between responding to babbling and learning remains unclear. It is plausible that infants vocalise because they enjoy interacting with adults and that learning is incidental and merely a result of modulating the amount of verbal input they receive (Hoff, 2003; Huttenlocher, Haight, Bryk, Seltzer, & Lyons, 1991). Infants may therefore boost their vocabulary through babbling by virtue of hearing more words spoken to them in response, without babbling itself being uttered with a communicative or information-seeking motivation. However, some recent findings suggest the link between infant vocalisations and learning might not be fully explained by mere heightened frequency of opportunities for social learning.

Goldstein and Schwade (2010) investigated object-directed vocalisations, defined as non-cry prelinguistic vocalisations, uttered when the infant is looking at an object being held or within reach. They examined the effect of parental responses to infants' spontaneous object-directed vocalisations in a play situation and, as outlined above, found that responses infants received at 9 months predicted their vocabulary size at 15 months of age (Goldstein & Schwade, 2010). However, this effect was only observed when parents labelled the objects infants were attending to at the time of vocalisation. If the parent, instead of labelling the attended object, said words that bore an acoustic resemblance to the babble (e.g. saying "bottle" after infant vocalised "ba"), an opposite relationship was found; parents' responses were negatively correlated with language outcome (Goldstein & Schwade, 2010). This striking dissociation lead the authors to propose that infant babbling, particularly object-directed babbling, might not only serve the modulation of parental input, but may in fact signal that the infant is in a state of focused attention, a state of readiness to learn about the object towards which the babbling was directed (Goldstein, Schwade, Briesch, & Syal, 2010). If this is the case, it follows that infants should learn the information they receive during these states of heightened attention, signalled by vocalisations, better than at other times.

This hypothesis was tested in two further studies by Goldstein et al. (2010). In the first, the number of infant vocalisations, as a potential measure of focused attention, was recorded as infants freely played with individual objects. If vocalisations reflect states of preparedness for learning, the degree of infants' learning should correlate with the number of vocalisations directed at the object. In the second experiment, the experimenter provided labels for the objects infants were exploring. The labels were given contingently on spontaneous object vocalisations during exploration for one group of infants, and non-contingently (at equivalent time points, but irrespective of vocalisations) for the other. Again, if vocalisations signal preparedness to learn new information, the object labels should be better encoded when given contingent on infant babbling. In both studies, infants' learning outcome was in accordance with predictions of the heightened attention hypothesis.

Infants encoded object features better for those objects that they vocalised most than the ones they babbled about least; and infants who received labels contingent on their vocalisations learned the labels of the objects better than infants who heard the same amount of labels non-contingently on their vocalising (Goldstein et al., 2010). The authors conclude that infants' vocalisations in a social interaction can structure parental responses to align, time and content-wise, with the infants' focus of attention, which in turn facilitates infant learning.

In sum, the reviewed research on infant prelinguistic vocalisations suggests infant babbling affects their learning in a broader way than it was first assumed. Not only do infant vocalisations provide the foundation for future language development from a production point of view (Kimbrough et al., 1976; Locke & Pearson, 1990), but, by vocalising, infants create opportunities for social transfer of information that are tailored to their focus of attention and readiness to learn. Infants appear to babble when they need information (such as while exploring an object of interest) and responding to their vocalisations contingently and with appropriate information can lead to superior learning.

While these studies demonstrate that babbling can serve as a powerful mechanism for eliciting information transfer, it remains unclear whether infant babbling is in fact truly communicative and deployed with the intention to obtain information from others. In contrast, when later in development infants begin to use gestures, they appear to be doing just that— communicating and requesting information.

Pointing

The gesture of pointing becomes a part of infants' behavioural repertoire in the months around their first birthday, when they begin to show both comprehension and production of this unique gesture (Tomasello, Carpenter, & Liszkowski, 2007). Although widely studied, the exact function of pointing and the motives driving infants to point are still a matter of debate.

A pointing gesture can be produced communicatively, in the presence of a social partner and with the intention to solicit a response, or privately, for the pointers themselves. The non-communicative type of pointing was proposed in the first theoretical account of pointing (Bates, Camaioni, & Volterra, 1975) and was suggested to serve the function of focusing one's own attention, much like adults do when faced with complex stimuli (Delgado, Gómez, & Sarriá, 2009). Infants highlighting salient events for themselves, might, in addition to enhancing their attention, serve the function of making the infants' focus of attention publicly available, allowing adults to follow-in on infants' attention (Gómez, 2007). Furthermore, by pointing to salient stimuli initially for themselves, infants ensure that the later emerging communicative pointing is already centred around objects and events that infants find interesting (Bates et al., 1975). Although it has been shown that, contrary to the initial proposal (Bates et al., 1975), private pointing is in fact not replaced by emerging social pointing, but can be observed throughout infancy and childhood (Delgado et al., 2009;

Delgado, Gómez, & Sarriá, 2011; Gómez, 2007), it was communicative pointing that received most attention in infant research.

Classically, infant communicative pointing has been conceptualised as a social tool, and categorised as either imperative or declarative (Bates et al., 1975). Infants were proposed to point imperatively, with the intent to use the adult as a tool of obtaining an object of interest; and point declaratively, with the intent to use the referent of the point as a tool of directing the adults' attention (Bates et al., 1975). What motivates infants to attempt to direct adults' attention to an object or event by so-called 'declarative' pointing has been extensively studied.

According to Tomasello and colleagues, infant pointing is a cooperative communicative act from its onset, motivated by the desire either to share interest and align attitudes about a referent with others, or to help others by informing them about a misplaced object (Tomasello et al., 2007). The idea of an altruistic *informative* motive for infant pointing was based on studies in which infants observed an adult perform actions with an object, which subsequently got accidentally misplaced (Liszkowski, Carpenter, Striano, & Tomasello, 2006). Infants in these situations pointed to the object the adult was searching for, without expressing any desire to obtain the object for themselves, which lead the authors to conclude that pointing was altruistically motivated by a wish to provide information (Liszkowski et al., 2006).

Motivation to *share* interest and attitudes about objects or events, on the other hand, was derived from findings that infants were most satisfied when the adult responded to their pointing by attending to both the infants and the referents of their gestures (Liszkowski, Carpenter, Henning, Striano, & Tomasello, 2004). Furthermore, infants' satisfaction with adults' response, as measured by absence of repeated points within the same trial and further instances of pointing in subsequent trials, was particularly high when the adult 'aligned' their attitude with infants' interest (Liszkowski, Carpenter, & Tomasello, 2007). According to Tomasello et al. (2007), these results directly support the proposal that it is a desire to share and align an attitude about a referent with another person, and not only to direct attention, that motivates infants to point declaratively.

However, others have expressed reservations about infants' intention to affect others' mental states, such as their attitude towards a referent or knowledge states about objects, and argue that pointing is more likely aimed at eliciting behavioural responses (Gómez, Sarria, & Tamarit, 1993; Southgate, Maanen, & Csibra, 2007). Furthermore, Southgate et al. (2007) propose that the behaviour infants are most likely aiming to elicit in these situations is provision of information about the referent of infants' interest. They argue that real life situations in which an adult requires an infant's help to locate something are rare, and infants' pointing to share interests, simply for the sake of sharing, has no clear function or obvious benefit. It therefore seems unlikely that this gesture would develop for this purpose. Southgate et al. (2007) proposed a re-interpretation of infant pointing as yet another tool infants possess to ensure fast transmission of cultural knowledge from adults. Indeed, several studies suggest infant pointing plays a role in learning.

Adults' most common spontaneous response to infant pointing is verbally responding and naming the objects that infants are pointing to (Kishimoto, Shizawa,

Yasuda, Hinobayashi, & Minami, 2007), suggesting that adults interpret these gestures in a pedagogical framework, teaching infants about the referent in response to their pointing. Goldin-Meadow, Goodrich, Sauer, and Iverson (2007) explored this relationship further and found that it is the referents of infants' points, about which the adults provide information in response, that are the most likely to enter the infants' vocabulary. It is therefore not surprising that the amount of pointing at 10–11 months of age has been shown to be predictive of infants' vocabulary growth (Brooks & Meltzoff, 2008).

This tight relationship between infant pointing, adults' responses, and their impact on infants' knowledge acquisition supports the hypothesis that, as Southgate et al. (2007) suggested, the function of infant pointing is *interrogative* rather than declarative or informative. This account is also more consistent with recent studies on non-communicative pointing, demonstrating that the frequency of private pointing in young children increases when they are engaged in a cognitively demanding task, and that preventing children from pointing (for themselves) has a negative impact on their problem-solving performance (Delgado et al., 2011). Therefore, both communicative and non-communicative pointing potentially reflect infants' cognitive engagement or motivation to learn and, in the same way as private pointing might be used to enhance one's own attention, thereby facilitating one's cognitive processes (Delgado et al., 2011), communicative pointing might serve the function of bringing a referent to the attention of another with the aim of gaining information about it (Southgate et al., 2007). Combined, this would mean that instead of, or in addition to, communicative pointing being used for informing or sharing with others, pointing may serve as a powerful learning tool by which infants request information from knowledgeable adults about the referents they are interested in (Southgate et al., 2007). A series of recent studies has provided strong support for this proposal.

The hypothesis of interrogative pointing was first tested by Begus and Southgate (2012), reasoning that if infants in fact point to request information, then their pointing should be influenced by the potential of an adult to provide information. To test this, two groups of 16-month-olds were faced with either a knowledgeable or an ignorant source of information (the experimenter), in a situation with unfamiliar and non-graspable objects suddenly appearing out of view of the experimenter—a situation which elicits pointing in infants (Liszkowski et al., 2004).

Whether the experimenter was knowledgeable or ignorant was established by the experimenter correctly or incorrectly labelling familiar objects that her and the infant were playing with (e.g. mislabelling a banana a duck) before and during the appearance of unfamiliar objects behind the experimenter. If the infant pointed to the appearing novel object, the experimenter responded by turning to face the object, and labelling it. Based on the hypothesis that pointing serves an information-gathering or *interrogative* function, infants were predicted to point to novel objects less in the presence of someone who is demonstrably ignorant than someone whom they perceive as knowledgeable. In contrast, if infants' motivation for pointing in this study were to obtain the objects (*imperative*), to share interest and excitement (*declarative*), or to inform an experimenter of the presence of an object that she cannot see (*informative*), there would be no clear reason to predict different rates of pointing between conditions, as the experimenter was responsive, friendly, and demonstrably collaborative in both conditions.

The results revealed that infants pointed to novel objects twice as many times for a knowledgeable than an ignorant informant, despite no other behaviour (infant smiling, willingness to accept objects from the experimenter, etc.) showing any differences between conditions (Begus & Southgate, 2012). These results provide compelling evidence that infants are motivated to share their attention with others because they want to obtain some information about the referent of their gesture, and therefore point more when they perceive that the recipient of their pointing could provide it.

Further supporting evidence for this idea came from a study by Kovács, Tauzin, Téglás, Gergely, and Csibra (2014), in which points, produced by 12-month-old infants, were responded to either with providing information or with sharing the infants' attention. Again, if infants' motivation to share interests through pointing is to merely share attention and align attitudes about the referent with the recipient, then both responses in this study should be equally satisfying. Yet, like in Begus and Southgate (2012), infants were shown to point more frequently when their gestures were responded to with information. The authors concluded that providing information, rather than just sharing attention, was preferred presumably because these responses better matched infants' expectations (Kovács et al., 2014). Both of these studies provide strong evidence that infants indeed point with the motivation and expectation of receiving (reliable) information in response to their gestures, and therefore use the gesture most frequently, when these expectations are met.

The hypothesis of interrogative pointing was then further extended to the prediction that if pointing expresses motivation to learn, it follows that responding to infants' pointing should lead to better assimilation of information. This prediction was first confirmed by Begus, Gliga, and Southgate (2014). In this study, 16-month-olds were introduced to pairs of novel objects and, once they had pointed to one of the objects, were shown a function for either the object they had chosen, or the object they had ignored. Ten minutes later, the objects for which infants had been shown functions were given to the infants, one at a time. Infants replicated the functions of the objects they had pointed to significantly more than those of un-chosen objects. The study provided the first evidence that offering information in response to infants' pointing gestures leads to superior learning, and a control experiment clarified that this difference was due to the learning being *facilitated* when infants' pointing was responded to, and not *hindered* when their pointing was ignored (Begus et al., 2014). A similar paradigm was later also applied to the domain of word learning by Lucca and Wilbourn (2016). In their study, 18-month-olds demonstrated superior mapping of labels to objects when the labels were given to objects that infants had pointed to, compared to ones they did not point to. Furthermore, mapping of labels was more successful when these were provided in response to infant pointing as opposed to other communicative behaviours (Lucca and Wilbourn, 2016).

What drives infants' facilitated learning when information is given in response to their pointing gestures? Regardless of whether infants are pointing communicatively or for themselves, presumably infant pointing reflects their interest in the referent. As reviewed above, it is well established that, in adults, the degree of interest or curiosity for a piece of information is predictive of whether or not this information will be retained (Gruber et al., 2014; Kang et al., 2009) and the findings of Stahl and Feigenson (2015), showing that infants learn more about objects that likely piqued their interest, suggest this relationship may be present early in life. Thus, Begus et al. (2014) proposed that infants direct their points at objects they are interested in, at the time they are prepared to learn about them, and point to them with the intention to solicit information from their social partners. Thus, in addition to infants' pointing modulating their learning by eliciting social interactions (e.g., Petitto, 1988), and by selecting whom to point for (Begus & Southgate, 2012), infant pointing might also facilitate learning directly because it elicits information that is content- and time-contingent to infants' interests and states of preparedness for learning.

Importantly, these findings can have significant implications for infants' learning outside of experimental settings. A closer look at the results of various studies investigating infant pointing behaviour reveals substantial individual variability in how many pointing gestures infants produced under the same circumstances (e.g., Begus & Southgate, 2012). Given the effect that responding to infant (interrogative) pointing has on learning (Begus et al., 2014), and considering that infants' continued deployment of pointing has repeatedly been shown to depend on receiving the desired response (e.g., Begus & Southgate, 2012; Kovács et al., 2014; Liszkowski et al., 2004), variability in the use of, and responsiveness to, this behaviour might have a dramatic effect on infant knowledge acquisition in everyday life.

From Seeking Information to Choosing Social Partners

So far, this chapter outlined how infants' interests and behaviours towards social partners affect when and what information infants learn. But in addition to infants' social interactions affecting their learning and inquisitiveness, infants' drive to acquire information may also directly influence how they perceive social partners, which in turn could influence whom infants prefer to interact with.

Infants selectivity in interactions with other people is well documented. From birth, infants prefer to look at upright, direct-gazing faces (Farroni, Csibra, Simion, & Johnson, 2002; Farroni, Menon, & Johnson, 2006) and faces speaking in infant-compared to adult-directed speech (Cooper & Aslin, 1990). By 6 months of age, infants selectively follow someone's gaze, based on whether or not it was preceded by direct gaze or infant-directed speech (Senju & Csibra, 2008). Later, infants start showing preferences in their behaviour and interactions with social partners based on characteristics such as reliability, conventionality, competence and language. For example, 8-month-olds track how reliably predictive a social partner is when guiding their visual exploration (Tummeltshammer, Wu, Sobel, & Kirkham, 2014); and from infancy to childhood, children consistently copy words produced by a reliable rather than an unreliable labeller (Harris, 2002; Koenig & Echols, 2003; Koenig & Harris, 2007). Furthermore, whether or not infants will imitate a model's actions depends on how competently an adult uses an object (Zmyj, Buttelmann, Carpenter, & Daum, 2010), as well as on the models age (Jaswal & Neely, 2006; Seehagen & Herbert, 2011) and social status (Flynn & Whiten, 2012).

Another widely researched and discussed preference that infants exhibit towards others is their tendency to attend to, imitate, and interact preferentially with social partners that could be described as belonging to the same social group as infants (Buttelmann, Zmyj, Daum, & Carpenter, 2013; Kinzler, Dupoux, & Spelke, 2007; Shutts, Kinzler, McKee, & Spelke, 2009; Soley & Galles, 2015). For example, even before their first birthdays, infants have been shown to exhibit behavioural preferences towards social partners of the same race (Bar-Haim, Ziv, Lamy, & Hodes, 2006), and ones speaking infants' native language (Kinzler et al., 2007).

While infants' selectivity for social partners is well documented, little is known about the role that these preferences play, or whether infants' preferences for different, seemingly unrelated, characteristics of a social partner (e.g. infant-directed speech, competency and native language) might be driven by a common motivation. For example, both infants' preference for direct gaze and for infant-directed speech have been suggested to reflect an adaptation to ensure that infants attend to potential teachers (Csibra & Gergely, 2009, 2011). According to this view, newborns' preference for direct gaze reflects a mechanism dedicated to finding socially relevant information (Farroni et al., 2002). Similarly, infant-directed speech might function as an effective cue for infants to select social partners most likely to provide opportunities for learning (Schachner & Hannon, 2011), and leading infants to expect information from the interlocutor, thus cueing them to attend to the referent of the interlocutor's gaze (Senju & Csibra, 2008).

In contrast, infants' biases towards people speaking the same language or belonging to the same race are usually attributed to highly social motives, such as the desire to affiliate and identify with the chosen social partners (Over & Carpenter, 2012). Because characteristics such as race and language are often seen as indicators of group membership, these early biases have commonly been interpreted as early precursors of our adult tendencies to assign individuals to social groups and, in accordance with the principle of in-group loyalty (Baillargeon et al., 2015), exhibit preferences towards members of one's own group.

It is, however, plausible that both infants' preference for an informative and competent, over an unreliable and incompetent other, and their preference for a native over a non-native speaker, reflect infants' common motivation to focus attention on a social partner who has the most potential to impart useful information. For example, it would seem a sensible learning strategy for infants to attend more to the communication of someone speaking their native language than someone speaking in a foreign tongue. Information communicated in a known language undoubtedly provides more information at lower cognitive effort. A social partner, who demonstrates knowledge of the same language with which infants are already familiar, is likely to provide information that is less discrepant from infants' existing knowledge (Lowenstein, 1994), and that would be easier to embed into infants' existing knowledge, thus enabling better learning progress (Gottlieb et al., 2013).

In sum, many studies have found that infants are selective in their interactions with social partners. However, behavioural data alone cannot disentangle which interpretations best explain infant selectivity; those assuming it arises from a drive for social affiliation, or those hypothesising an underlying motivation to seek information from optimal informants. To address this question directly, Begus, Gliga, and Southgate (2016) exploited a neural measure to test the hypothesis that infants' social preferences reflect a drive for knowledge rather than for affiliation. The neural measure of interest was EEG oscillatory activity in the theta frequency range.

Research investigating neural underpinnings of learning has identified theta rhythmic activity to be associated with, and predictive of, successful information encoding in both adults and infants. For example, in a task where adult participants were asked to learn pairs of words or faces, the amount of theta activity (4–8 Hz) during trials which subsequently resulted in successful recollection, was higher compared to activity during trials which resulted in poor recall performance (Mölle, Marshall, Fehm, & Born, 2002). Similarly, in a study where 11-month-old infants were free to explore novel objects, the power of theta oscillations (3-5Hz in infants) during their object exploration predicted whether or not the infants later recognised the features of the explored objects (Begus, Southgate, & Gliga, 2015). Importantly, adult studies have shown that theta activity is not only recorded during encoding of information, but can be elicited by an expectation to receive information, and that this anticipatory theta activation likewise leads to better retention of the information presented (Fell et al., 2011; Gruber, Watrous, Ekstrom, Ranganath, & Otten, 2013; Guderian, Schott, Richardson-Klavehn, & Düzel, 2009). Furthermore, these anticipatory theta rhythms have been shown to be modulated by whether or not the participants were motivated to encode information, with higher motivation predicting more anticipatory theta activity, and subsequent superior retention of information (Gruber et al., 2013), suggesting theta activity may be indicative of an active preparatory state for learning.

To investigate if an expectation of information is what drives infants' selectivity in their interactions with social partners, Begus et al. (2016) introduced 11-month-old infants to two social partners, one of whom provided infants with information (labels or function demonstrations on known objects), and another who did not (in this case, the person simply pointed at or handled the object while vocalising, 'Oooh'). In subsequent test trials, infants observed the same two people now interacting with novel objects and theta activity was measured at the beginning of each trial, before the person began interacting with the object. The authors reasoned that differences in theta activity during this anticipation period would be most likely to reflect differences in infants' expectation or preparation for learning the information received (or not) at the end of the trials. Infants indeed exhibited heightened anticipatory theta activity selectively, i.e. only in anticipation periods of trials in which they were facing the informant who had previously provided information. Crucially, the same pattern of activation was also found in a further experiment, in which infants were faced with a native and a foreign speaker, both labelling novel objects. Theta rhythms revealed that infants were expecting to learn information from the native speakers, whereas they did not have the same expectations of the foreign speaker (Begus et al., 2016; Begus, Gliga, & Southgate, 2017).

Thus, these findings challenge the theories proposing that infants preferentially attend to, and interact with, someone speaking their native language based on a desire to affiliate and identify with social partners (Over & Carpenter, 2012), specifically with members of one's own group (Baillargeon et al., 2015). Instead, in line with the large body of literature that suggests infants selectively attend to, and preferentially learn from, reliable sources of information (e.g. Begus & Southgate, 2012; Tummeltshammer et al., 2014), this study provided the first direct evidence suggesting that what underlies infants' preferences for native over foreign speakers is likewise their motivation to learn. Consistent with theories of curiosity-driven, intrinsically-motivated learning, infants selectively preparing to learn from the knowledgeable and native speakers can be explained by infants' motivation to obtain information that matches an optimal level of discrepancy from their existing knowledge (Lowenstein, 1994), and one that offers the best learning progress (Gottlieb et al., 2013). Therefore, infants' information-seeking motivation affects not only their learning, but can also systematically influence which social partners they perceive as worthy of attending to, and interacting with. Lastly, while older children demonstrate even more complex and sophisticated social learning strategies (see Bonawitz, Bass, and Lapidow, this volume), infants' selectivity in who to attend to, and ask information from, and what information to ask for and learn, suggests efficient active learning mechanisms are in place already in infancy.

Nurturing Young Children's Curiosity

The research reviewed in this chapter focused on investigating infants' active learning experimentally and has shown that responding to infants' expressions of interest can have an immediate impact on their learning. However, given that studies have shown that whether or not infants continue to express inquisitive behaviours depends on them receiving the intended response (e.g. Begus & Southgate, 2012; Kovács et al., 2014), nurturing infants' interest with informative responses may be crucial not only because it affects immediate learning, but because it may also affect the extent to which young children continue to seek information from social partners. As proposed by Hidi and Renninger (2006), while situational interest can lead to short-term information-seeking and learning, sustained inquisitiveness can be seen as a mental resource that contributes to future endeavours, increased personal knowledge and improved cognitive abilities. It is plausible that recognition of infants' early expressions of interest, and responding to these expressions with the right type of information, is important in fostering an inquisitive mind.

Several studies have suggested that curiosity, or a motivation to learn, does indeed predict individuals' cognitive abilities (reflected in academic success), and that the development of these inquisitive traits may depend on characteristics of a child's early environment. For example, children, whose parents placed more emphasis on academic stimulation and on satisfying children's curiosity (as assessed by interviews and home observations over a period of 2 years), were more likely to develop sustained individual interests, characterised by a relatively enduring predisposition to interact with a target domain (Leibham, Alexander, Johnson, Neitzel, & Reishenrie, 2005). Moreover, other longitudinal studies investigating the relationship between home environment and children's academic motivation have shown that children whose homes had a greater emphasis on learning opportunities and activities were more intrinsically academically motivated (Gottfried, Fleming, & Gottfried, 1998); and that the effect of gene-by-socioeconomic status interaction on academic achievement is mediated by children's learning motivation (Tucker-Drob & Harden, 2013). These studies thus provide strong support for the idea that fostering children's curiosity and interests may have a powerful impact on their learning achievements and might even act as a protective factor against potentially adverse effects of socioeconomic status (Tucker-Drob & Harden, 2013).

But this relationship between home environment and inquisitiveness is likely formed even before children enter formal education. Indeed, characteristics of home environment and parental input have been shown to correlate with frequency of hypothesised inquisitive behaviours even in infancy. For example, the degree to which parents respond to infant prelinguistic vocalisations in everyday life is positively correlated with the amount of infants' continued use of vocalisations directed at the parent (Gros-Louis et al., 2014). Furthermore, aspects of parental responsiveness have been shown to predict the frequency of infant pointing (McGillion et al., 2012), which in turn accounted for the differences in language production between children from families of different socioeconomic status (Rowe & Goldin-meadow, 2009).

In sum, infants' social information seeking, if responded to, could be the cradle of children's curiosity, fostering an inquisitive mind and leading to future academic success. While adults can support their own interests and curiosity by various media, such as literature or inclusion in social networks that involve individuals with similar interests, young children, and especially infants, are dependent on the adult social partners in their environment to provide them with similar types of support (Leibham et al., 2005). Furthermore, as well as nurturing young children's curiosity, it may also be possible to *induce* infants' curiosity. As has been demonstrated in studies exploring effects of violating infants' expectations, highlighting a gap (or inconsistency) in infants' knowledge results in increased theta oscillations (Berger, Tzur, & Posner, 2006), as well as in systematic exploration and facilitated learning (Stahl & Feigenson, 2015). Thus, children's long-term inquisitiveness could plausibly also be encouraged if, for example, formal and informal education included systematically stimulating infants' and young children's curiosity, by exposing gaps in their knowledge or highlighting their learning progress.

Conclusions

Given that our brains appear to be hardwired to experience curiosity and information consumption as rewarding, it seems reasonable to assume every child is born curious. However, as the research reported in this chapter demonstrates, children's expressions of inquisitiveness, as well as its maintenance, can heavily depend on the social environment that children are interacting with. Even before their first birthdays, infants selectively seek and prepare to learn from social partners, who provide them with information that is relevant and learnable. Furthermore, when infants express their interests behaviourally, they appear to expect to receive information in response, and if the appropriate information is conveyed, infants assimilate it better than unsolicited information. Taken together, these studies suggest that even before entering formal education, infants have the motivation and the means to seek information from their environment. Combined with an attentive and responsive social partner, this early inquisitiveness can guide infants' knowledge acquisition and can possibly lay the foundation for life-long curiosity, which is known to be predictive of academic success. Future work on infants' inquisitive behaviours will hopefully lead to better understanding of how the gift of curiosity could be nurtured to ensure it keeps on giving.

References

Ainsworth, M. D. S. (1992). A consideration of social referencing in the context of attachment theory and research. In S. Feinman (Ed.), *Social referencing and the social construction of reality in infancy* (pp. 349–367). New York, NY: Plenum.

Baillargeon, R., Scott, R. M., He, Z., Sloane, S., Setoh, P., Jin, K., … Bian, L. (2015). Psychological and Sociomoral reasoning in infancy. In P. Shaver, M. Mikulincer, J. Borgida, & J. Bargh (Eds.), *APA handbook of personality and social psychology: Vol. 1. Attitudes and social cognition* (Vol. 1, pp. 79–150). Washington, DC: APA. https://doi.org/10.1037/14341-000

Baldwin, D. A., & Moses, L. J. (1996). The ontogeny of social information gathering. *Child Development, 67*(5), 1915. https://doi.org/10.2307/1131601

Bar-Haim, Y., Ziv, T., Lamy, D., & Hodes, R. M. (2006). Nature and nurture in own-race face processing. *Psychological Science, 17*(2), 159–163. https://doi.org/10.1111/j.1467-9280.2006.01679.x

Bates, E., Camaioni, L., & Volterra, V. (1975). The acquisition of performatives prior to speech. *Merrill-Palmer Quarterly of Behavior and Development, 21*(3), 205–226. https://doi.org/10.2307/23084619

Begus, K., Gliga, T., & Southgate, V. (2014). Infants learn what they want to learn: responding to infant pointing leads to superior learning. *PLoS ONE, 9*(10), e108817. https://doi.org/10.1371/journal.pone.0108817

Begus, K., Gliga, T., & Southgate, V. (2016). Infants' preferences for native speakers are associated with an expectation of information. *Proceedings of the National Academy of Sciences, 2016*, 03261. https://doi.org/10.1073/pnas.1603261113

Begus, K., Gliga, T., & Southgate, V. (2017). Reply to Kinzler and Liberman: Neural correlate provides direct evidence that infant's social preferences are about information. *Proceedings of the National Academy of Sciences, 2017*, 03098. https://doi.org/10.1073/pnas.1703098114

Begus, K., & Southgate, V. (2012). Infant pointing serves an interrogative function. *Developmental Science*, 1–8. https://doi.org/10.1111/j.1467-7687.2012.01160.x

Begus, K., Southgate, V., & Gliga, T. (2015). Neural mechanisms of infant learning: Differences in frontal theta activity during object exploration modulate subsequent object recognition. *Biology Letters, 11*(5), 20150041–20150041. https://doi.org/10.1098/rsbl.2015.0041

Berger, A., Tzur, G., & Posner, M. I. (2006). Infant brains detect arithmetic errors. *Proceedings of the National Academy of Sciences of the United States of America, 103*(33), 12649–12653. https://doi.org/10.1073/pnas.0605350103

Berlyne, D. E. (1954). A theory of human curiosity. *British Journal of Psychology, 45*, 3.

Berlyne, D. E. (1966). Curiosity and exploration. *Science, 153*(3731), 25–33. Retrieved from http://www.sciencemag.org/content/153/3731/25.short

Bornstein, M. H., Tamis-Lemonda, C. S., Hahn, C.-S., & Haynes, O. M. (2008). Maternal responsiveness to young children at three ages: Longitudinal analysis of a multidimensional, modular, and specific parenting construct. *Developmental Psychology, 44*(3), 867–874. https://doi.org/10.1037/0012-1649.44.3.867

Brooks, R., & Meltzoff, A. N. (2008). Infant gaze following and pointing predict accelerated vocabulary growth through two years of age: A longitudinal, growth curve modeling study. *Journal of Child Language, 35*(1), 207–220. https://doi.org/10.1017/S030500090700829X

Buttelmann, D., Zmyj, N., Daum, M., & Carpenter, M. (2013). Selective imitation of in-group over out-group members in 14-month-old infants. *Child Development, 84*(2), 422–428. https://doi.org/10.1111/j.1467-8624.2012.01860.x

Carruthers, P. (2008). Meta-cognition in animals: A skeptical look. *Mind and Language, 23*(1), 58–89. https://doi.org/10.1111/j.1468-0017.2007.00329.x

Collins, R. P., Litman, J. A., & Spielberger, C. D. (2004). The measurement of perceptual curiosity. *Personality and Individual Differences, 36*(5), 1127–1141. https://doi.org/10.1016/S0191-8869(03)00205-8

Cooper, R. P., & Aslin, R. N. (1990). Preferences for infant-directed speech in the first month after birth. *Child Development, 61*(5), 1584–1595.

Csibra, G., & Gergely, G. (2009). Natural pedagogy. *Trends in Cognitive Sciences, 13*(4), 148–153. https://doi.org/10.1016/j.tics.2009.01.005

Csibra, G., & Gergely, G. (2011). Natural pedagogy as evolutionary adaptation. *Philosophical Transactions of the Royal Society of London Series B, Biological Sciences, 366*(1567), 1149–1157. https://doi.org/10.1098/rstb.2010.0319

Delgado, B., Gómez, J. C., & Sarriá, E. (2009). Private pointing and private speech: Developing parallelisms. In A. Winsler, C. Fernyhough, & I. Montero (Eds.). Private speech, executive function, and the development of verbal self-regulation (pp. 153–162). Cambridge: Cambridge University Press.

Delgado, B., Gómez, J. C., & Sarriá, E. (2011). Pointing gestures as a cognitive tool in young children: Experimental evidence. *Journal of Experimental Child Psychology, 110*(3), 299–312. https://doi.org/10.1016/j.jecp.2011.04.010

Dickstein, S., Thompson, R. A., Estes, D., Malkin, C., & Lamb, M. E. (1984). Social referencing and the security of attachment. *Infant Behavior and Development, 7*(4), 507–516. https://doi.org/10.1016/S0163-6383(84)80009-0

Farroni, T., Csibra, G., Simion, F., & Johnson, M. H. (2002). Eye contact detection in humans from birth. *Proceedings of the National Academy of Sciences of the United States of America, 99*(14), 9602–9605. https://doi.org/10.1073/pnas.152159999

Farroni, T., Menon, E., & Johnson, M. H. (2006). Factors influencing newborns' preference for faces with eye contact. *Journal of Experimental Child Psychology, 95*(4), 298–308. https://doi.org/10.1016/j.jecp.2006.08.001

Feinman, S. (1982). Social referencing in infancy. *Merrill-Palmer Quarterly of Behavior and Development, 24*, 445–470.

Feinman, S., Roberts, D., Hsieh, K.-F., Sawyer, D., & Swanson, D. (1992). A critical review of social referencing in infancy. In *Social referencing and the social construction of reality in infancy* (pp. 15–54). New York, NY: Plenum.

Fell, J., Ludowig, E., Staresina, B. P., Wagner, T., Kranz, T., Elger, C. E., & Axmacher, N. (2011). Medial temporal theta/alpha power enhancement precedes successful memory encoding: Evidence based on intracranial EEG. *The Journal of Neuroscience: The Official Journal of the Society for Neuroscience, 31*(14), 5392–5397. https://doi.org/10.1523/JNEUROSCI.3668-10.2011

Flynn, E. G., & Whiten, A. (2012). Experimental "microcultures" in young children: Identifying biographic, cognitive and social predictors of information transmission. *Child, 83*(3), 911–925. https://doi.org/10.1063/1.2756072

Fowler, H. (1966). *Curiosity and exploratory behavior.* New York, NY: Macmillan.

Franklin, B., Warlaumont, A. S., Messinger, D., Bene, E., Nathani Iyer, S., Lee, C.-C., ... Oller, D. K. (2013). Effects of parental interaction on infant vocalization rate, variability and vocal type. *Language Learning and Development, 10*(3), 279–296. https://doi.org/10.1080/15475441.2013.849176

Gliga, T., & Southgate, V. (2016). Metacognition: Pre-verbal infants adapt their behaviour to their knowledge states. *Current Biology, 26*(22), R1191–R1193. https://doi.org/10.1016/j.cub.2016.09.065

Goldin-Meadow, S., Goodrich, W., Sauer, E., & Iverson, J. (2007). Young children use their hands to tell their mothers what to say. *Developmental Science, 10*(6), 778–785. https://doi.org/10.1111/j.1467-7687.2007.00636.x

Goldstein, M. H., & Schwade, J. a. (2008). Social feedback to infants' babbling facilitates rapid phonological learning. *Psychological Science, 19*(5), 515–523. https://doi.org/10.1111/j.1467-9280.2008.02117.x

Goldstein, M. H., & Schwade, J. A. (2010). From birds to words: Perception of structure in social interactions guides vocal development and language learning. In *The oxford handbook of developmental and comparative neuroscience* (pp. 708–729). Oxford, UK: Oxford University Press.

Goldstein, M. H., Schwade, J. A., & Bornstein, M. H. (2009). The value of vocalizing: Five-month-old infants associate their own noncry vocalizations with responses from caregivers. *Child Development, 80*(3), 636–644. https://doi.org/10.1111/j.1467-8624.2009.01287.x

Goldstein, M. H., Schwade, J., Briesch, J., & Syal, S. (2010). Learning while babbling: Prelinguistic object-directed vocalizations indicate a readiness to learn. *Infancy.* https://doi.org/10.1111/j.1532-7078.2009.00020.x

Gómez, J. C. (2007). Pointing behaviors in apes and human infants: A balanced interpretation. *Child Development, 78*(3), 729–734. https://doi.org/10.1111/j.1467-8624.2007.01027.x

Gómez, J. C., Sarria, E., & Tamarit, J. (1993). The comparative study of early communication and theories of mind: Ontogeny, phylogeny, and pathology. In S. Baron-Cohen, H. Tager-Flusberg, & D. Cohen (Eds.), *Understanding other minds: Perspectives from autism* (pp. 397–426). New York, NY: Oxford University Press.

Gottfried, A. E., Fleming, J. S., & Gottfried, A. W. (1998). Role of cognitively stimulating home environment in children's academic intrinsic motivation: A longitudinal study. *Child Development, 69*(5), 1448–1460. Retrieved from http://cat.inist.fr/?aModele=afficheN&cpsidt=1591790

Gottlieb, J., Oudeyer, P.-Y., Lopes, M., & Baranes, A. (2013). Information-seeking, curiosity, and attention: Computational and neural mechanisms. *Trends in Cognitive Sciences, 17*(11), 585–593. https://doi.org/10.1016/j.tics.2013.09.001

Goupil, L., & Kouider, S. (2016). Behavioral and neural indices of metacognitive sensitivity in pre-verbal infants. *Current Biology, 26*(22), 3038–3045. https://doi.org/10.1016/j.cub.2016.09.004

Goupil, L., Romand-monnier, M., & Kouider, S. (2016). Infants ask for help when they know they don't know. *Proceedings of the National Academy of Sciences of the United States of America,* 2016. https://doi.org/10.1073/pnas.1515129113

Gros-Louis, J., West, M. J., & King, A. P. (2014). Maternal responsiveness and the development of directed vocalizing in social interactions. *Infancy, 19*(4), 385–408. https://doi.org/10.1111/infa.12054

Gruber, M. J., Gelman, B. D., & Ranganath, C. (2014). States of curiosity modulate hippocampus-dependent learning via the dopaminergic circuit. *Neuron, 84*(2), 486–496. https://doi.org/10.1016/j.neuron.2014.08.060

Gruber, M. J., Watrous, A. J., Ekstrom, A. D., Ranganath, C., & Otten, L. J. (2013). Expected reward modulates encoding-related theta activity before an event. *NeuroImage, 64*, 68–74. https://doi.org/10.1016/j.neuroimage.2012.07.064

Guderian, S., Schott, B. H., Richardson-Klavehn, A., & Düzel, E. (2009). Medial temporal theta state before an event predicts episodic encoding success in humans. *Proceedings of the National Academy of Sciences of the United States of America, 106*(13), 5365–5370. Retrieved from http://www.pubmedcentral.nih.gov/articlerender.fcgi?artid=2663999&tool=pmcentrez&rendertype=abstract

Hampton, R. R. (2009). Multiple demonstrations of metacognition in nonhumans: Converging evidence or multiple mechanisms? *Comparative Cognition and Behavior Reviews, 1*(4), 17–28.

Harris, P. (2002). Checking our sources: The origins of trust in testimony. *Studies in History and Philosophy of Science Part A, 33*(2), 315–333. https://doi.org/10.1016/S0039-3681(02)00007-9

Hidi, S., & Harackiewicz, J. M. (2000). Motivating the academically unmotivated: A critical issue for the 21st century. *Review of Educational Research, 70*(2), 151–179. https://doi.org/10.3102/00346543070002151

Hidi, S., & Renninger, K. A. (2006). The four-phase model of interest development. *Educational Psychologist, 41*(2), 111–127. https://doi.org/10.1207/s15326985ep4102_4

Hoff, E. (2003). The specificity of environmental influence: Socioeconomic status affects early vocabulary development via maternal speech. *Child Development, 74*(5), 1368–1378. https://doi.org/10.1111/1467-8624.00612

Houston-Price, C., & Nakai, S. (2004). Distinguishing novelty and familiarity effects in infant preference procedures. *Infant and Child Development, 348*(September), 341–348. https://doi.org/10.1002/icd.364

Huttenlocher, J., Haight, W., Bryk, A., Seltzer, M., & Lyons, T. (1991). Early vocabulary growth: Relation to language input and gender. *Developmental Psychology, 27*(2), 236–248. https://doi.org/10.1037/0012-1649.27.2.236

Jaswal, V. K., & Neely, L. a. (2006). Adults don't always know best: Preschoolers use past reliability over age when learning new words. *Psychological Science, 17*(9), 757–758. https://doi.org/10.1111/j.1467-9280.2006.01778.x

Jepma, M., Verdonschot, R. G., van Steenbergen, H., Rombouts, S. A. R. B., & Nieuwenhuis, S. (2012). Neural mechanisms underlying the induction and relief of perceptual curiosity. *Frontiers in Behavioral Neuroscience, 6*(February), 5. https://doi.org/10.3389/fnbeh.2012.00005

Kang, M. J., Hsu, M., Krajbich, I. M., Loewenstein, G., McClure, S. M., Wang, J. T., & Camerer, C. F. (2009). The wick in the candle of learning: Epistemic curiosity activates reward circuitry and enhances memory. *Psychological Science, 20*(8), 963–973. https://doi.org/10.1111/j.1467-9280.2009.02402.x

Kaplan, F., & Oudeyer, P.-Y. (2007). In search of the neural circuits of intrinsic motivation. *Frontiers in Neuroscience, 1*(1), 225–236. https://doi.org/10.3389/neuro.01.1.1.017.2007

Kidd, C., & Hayden, B. Y. (2015). The Psychology and Neuroscience of Curiosity. *Neuron, 88*(3), 449–460. https://doi.org/10.1016/j.neuron.2015.09.010

Kidd, C., Piantadosi, S. T., & Aslin, R. N. (2012). The Goldilocks effect: Human infants allocate attention to visual sequences that are neither too simple nor too complex. *PLoS One, 7*(5), e36399. https://doi.org/10.1371/journal.pone.0036399

Kim, G., & Kwak, K. (2011). Uncertainty matters: Impact of stimulus ambiguity on infant social referencing. *Infant and Child Development, 20*(5), 449–463. https://doi.org/10.1002/icd.708

Kimbrough, O. D., Wieman, L. A., Doyle, W. J., & Ross, C. (1976). Infant babbling and speech. *Journal of Child Language, 3*(1), 1–11.

Kimbrough, O. D., Eilers, R. E., Neal, A. R., & Cobo-Lewis, A. B. (1998). Late onset canonical babbling: A possible early marker of abnormal development. *American Journal of Mental Retardation, 103*(3), 249–263.

Kimbrough, O. D., Eilers, R. E., Neal, A. R., & Schwartz, H. K. (1999). Precursors to speech in infancy. *Journal of Communication Disorders, 32*(4), 223–245.

Kinzler, K. D., Dupoux, E., & Spelke, E. S. (2007). The native language of social cognition. *Proceedings of the National Academy of Sciences of the United States of America, 104*(30), 12577–12580. https://doi.org/10.1073/pnas.0705345104

Kishimoto, T., Shizawa, Y., Yasuda, J., Hinobayashi, T., & Minami, T. (2007). Do pointing gestures by infants provoke comments from adults? *Infant Behavior and Development, 30*(4), 562–567. https://doi.org/10.1016/j.infbeh.2007.04.001

Knutson, B., Adams, C. M., Fong, G. W., & Hommer, D. (2001). Anticipation of increasing monetary reward selectively recruits nucleus accumbens. *The Journal of Neuroscience: The Official Journal of the Society for Neuroscience, 21*(16), RC159.

Koenig, M. A., & Echols, C. H. (2003). Infants' understanding of false labeling events: The referential roles of words and the speakers who use them. *Cognition, 87*, 179–208.

Koenig, M. A., & Harris, P. L. (2007). The basis of epistemic trust: Reliable testimony or reliable sources? *Episteme: A Journal of Social Epistemology, 4*(3), 264–284. https://doi.org/10.1353/epi.0.0017

Kovács, Á. M., Tauzin, T., Téglás, E., Gergely, G., & Csibra, G. (2014). Pointing as epistemic request: 12-month-olds point to receive new information. *Infancy, 19*(6), 543–557. https://doi.org/10.1111/infa.12060

Kutsuki, A., Egami, S., Ogura, T., Nakagawa, K., Kuroki, M., & Itakura, S. (2007). Developmental changes of referential looks in 7- and 9-month-olds: A transition from dyadic to proto-referential looks. *Psychologia, 50*(4), 319–329. https://doi.org/10.2117/psysoc.2007.319

Leibham, M., Alexander, J., Johnson, K., Neitzel, C., & Reishenrie, F. (2005). Parenting behaviors associated with the maintenance of preschoolers' interests: A prospective longitudinal study. *Journal of Applied Developmental Psychology, 26*(4), 397–414. https://doi.org/10.1016/j.appdev.2005.05.001

Liszkowski, U., Carpenter, M., Henning, A., Striano, T., & Tomasello, M. (2004). Twelve-month-olds point to share attention and interest. *Developmental Science, 7*(3), 297–307.

Liszkowski, U., Carpenter, M., Striano, T., & Tomasello, M. (2006). 12- and 18-Month-olds point to provide information for others. *Journal of Cognition and Development, 7*(2), 173–187. https://doi.org/10.1207/s15327647jcd0702

Liszkowski, U., Carpenter, M., & Tomasello, M. (2007). Reference and attitude in infant pointing. *Journal of Child Language, 34*(1), 1–20. https://doi.org/10.1017/S0305000906007689

Litman, J. (2005). Curiosity and the pleasures of learning: Wanting and liking new information. *Cognition & Emotion, 19*(6), 793–814. https://doi.org/10.1080/02699930541000101

Litman, J. a. (2008). Interest and deprivation factors of epistemic curiosity. *Personality and Individual Differences, 44*(7), 1585–1595. https://doi.org/10.1016/j.paid.2008.01.014

Litman, J. A., & Silvia, P. J. (2006). The latent structure of trait curiosity: Evidence for interest and deprivation curiosity dimensions. *Journal of Personality Assessment, 86*(3), 318–328. https://doi.org/10.1207/s15327752jpa8603_07

Locke, J. L., & Pearson, D. M. (1990). Linguistic significance of babbling: Evidence from a tracheostomized infant. *Journal of Child Language, 17*(1), 1–16.

Lowenstein, G. (1994). The psychology of curiosity: A review and reinterpretation. Psychological Bulletin 116, 75–98.

Lucca, K., & Wilbourn, M. P. (2016). Communicating to Learn: Infants' Pointing Gestures Result in Optimal Learning. *Child Development.* http://doi.org/10.1111/cdev.12707

Masataka, N. (2003). *The onset of language.* Cambridge, MA: University Press.

McCune, L. (2008). *How children learn to learn language.* Oxford, UK: Oxford University Press.

McGillion, M. L., Herbert, J. S., Pine, J., Vihman, M. M., DePaolis, R., Keren-Portnoy, T., & Matthews, D. E. (2012). What paves the way to conventional language? The predictive value of babble, pointing and SES. *Child Development, 15*(6), 817–829. https://doi.org/10.1111/ j.1467-7687.2012.01181.x

Mitchell, M. (1993). Situational interest: Its multifaceted structure in the secondary school mathematics classroom. *Journal of Educational Psychology, 3*, 424. https://doi.org/10.1017/ CBO9781107415324.004

Mölle, M., Marshall, L., Fehm, H. L., & Born, J. (2002). EEG theta synchronization conjoined with alpha desynchronization indicate intentional encoding. *European Journal of Neuroscience, 15*(5), 923–928. https://doi.org/10.1046/j.1460-9568.2002.01921.x

Moulin-Frier, C., Nguyen, S. M., & Oudeyer, P.-Y. (2013). Self-organization of early vocal development in infants and machines: The role of intrinsic motivation. *Frontiers in Psychology, 4*(1006), 1006. https://doi.org/10.3389/fpsyg.2013.01006

Nguyen, S. M., Ivaldi, S., Lyubova, N., Droniou, A., Gerardeaux-Viret, D., Filliat, D., … Oudeyer, P. Y. (2013). Learning to recognize objects through curiosity-driven manipulation with the iCub humanoid robot. In *Development and Learning and Epigenetic Robotics (ICDL), 2013 IEEE Third Joint International Conference on* (pp. 1–8). https://doi.org/10.1109/DevLrn. 2013.6652525

Oudeyer, P.-Y., & Smith, L. B. (2006). How evolution may work through curiosity-driven developmental process. *Topics in Cognitive Science.* https://doi.org/10.1017/CBO9781107415324.004

Over, H., & Carpenter, M. (2012). Putting the social into social learning: Explaining both selectivity and fidelity in children's copying behavior. *Journal of Comparative Psychology, 126*(2), 182–192. https://doi.org/10.1037/a0024555

Petitto, L. A. (1988). "Language" in the pre-linguistic child. In F. Kessel (Ed.), *Development of language and language researchers: Essays in honor of Roger Brown* (pp. 187–221). Hillsdale, NJ: Lawrence Erlbaum.

Piaget, J. (1952). *The origins of intelligence in children.* New York, NY: International University Press.

Rowe, M. L., & Goldin-meadow, S. (2009). *Differences in early gesture explain* (Vol. February, pp. 951–953).

Schachner, A., & Hannon, E. E. (2011). Infant-directed speech drives social preferences in 5-month-old infants. *Developmental Psychology, 47*(1), 19–25. https://doi.org/10.1037/a0020740

Schmitow, C., & Stenberg, G. (2013). Social referencing in 10-month-old infants. *European Journal of Developmental Psychology, 10*(5), 533–545. https://doi.org/10.1080/17405629.20 13.763473

Seehagen, S., & Herbert, J. S. (2011). Infant imitation from televised peer and adult models. *Infancy, 16*(2), 113–136. https://doi.org/10.1111/j.1532-7078.2010.00045.x

Senju, A., & Csibra, G. (2008). Gaze following in human infants depends on communicative signals. *Current Biology, 18*(9), 668–671. https://doi.org/10.1016/j.cub.2008.03.059

Shutts, K., Kinzler, K. D., McKee, C. B., & Spelke, E. S. (2009). Social information guides infants' selection of foods. *Journal of Cognitive Development, 10*(1–2), 417–428. https://doi. org/10.1055/s-0029-1237430.Imprinting

Soley, G., & Galles, N. S. (2015). Infants prefer tunes previously introduced by speakers of their native language. *Child Development, 86*(6), 1685–1692.

Southgate, V., van Maanen, C., & Csibra, G. (2007). Infant pointing: Communication to cooperate or communication to learn? *Child Development, 78*(3), 735–740. https://doi.org/10.1111/ j.1467-8624.2007.01028.x

Spielberger, C. D., & Starr, L. M. (1994). Curiosity and exploratory behaviour. In H. F. O'Neil & M. Drillings (Eds.), *Motivation: Theory and research* (pp. 221–243). Hillsdale, NJ: Erlbaum.

Stahl, A. E., & Feigenson, L. (2015). Observing the unexpected enhances infants' learning and exploration. *Science, 348*(6230), 91–94.

Stenberg, G. (2009). Selectivity in infant social referencing. *Infancy, 14*(4), 457–473. https://doi. org/10.1080/15250000902994115

Stoel-Gammon, C. (1992). Prelinguistic vocal development: Measurement and predictions. In C. A. Ferguson, L. Menn, & C. Stoel-Gammon (Eds.), *Phonological Development* (pp. 439–456). Timonium, MD: York Press.

Tamis-LeMonda, C. S., & Bornstein, M. H. (2002). Maternal responsiveness and early language acquisition. *Advances in Child Development and Behavior, 29*, 90–129.

Tamis-LeMonda, C. S., Bornstein, M. H., & Baumwell, L. (2001). Maternal responsiveness and children's achievement of language milestones. *Child Development, 72*(3), 748–767. https://doi.org/10.1111/1467-8624.00313

Tomasello, M., Carpenter, M., & Liszkowski, U. (2007). A new look at infant pointing. *Child Development, 78*(3), 705–722. https://doi.org/10.1111/j.1467-8624.2007.01025.x

Tucker-Drob, E. M., & Harden, K. P. (2013). Learning motivation mediates gene-by-socioeconomic status interaction on mathematics achievemnt in early childhood. *Learning and Individual Differences, 22*(1), 37–45. https://doi.org/10.1016/j.lindif.2011.11.015.Learning

Tummeltshammer, K. S., Wu, R., Sobel, D. M., & Kirkham, N. Z. (2014). Infants track the reliability of potential informants. *Psychological Science*, (July). https://doi.org/10.1177/0956797614540178

Vaish, A., Demir, Ö. E., & Baldwin, D. (2011). Thirteen- and 18-month-old infants recognize when they need referential information. *Social Development, 20*(3), 431–449. https://doi.org/10.1111/j.1467-9507.2010.00601.x

von Stumm, S., Hell, B., & Chamorro-Premuzic, T. (2011). The hungry mind: Intellectual curiosity is the third pillar of academic performance. *Perspectives on Psychological Science, 6*(6), 574–588. https://doi.org/10.1177/1745691611421204

Walden, T., Kim, G., McCoy, C., & Karrass, J. (2007). Do you believe in magic? Infants' social looking during violations of expectations. *Developmental Science, 10*(5), 654–663. https://doi.org/10.1111/j.1467-7687.2007.00607.x

Zarbatany, L., & Lamb, M. E. (1985). Social referencing as a function of information source: Mothers versus strangers. *Infant Behavior and Development, 8*(November), 25–33. https://doi.org/10.1016/S0163-6383(85)80014-X

Zmyj, N., Buttelmann, D., Carpenter, M., & Daum, M. M. (2010). The reliability of a model influences 14-month-olds' imitation. *Journal of Experimental Child Psychology, 106*(4), 208–220. https://doi.org/10.1016/j.jecp.2010.03.002

Chapter 3
Taking Center Stage: Infants' Active Role in Language Leaning

Catherine S. Tamis-LeMonda, Yana Kuchirko, and Daniel D. Suh

Abstract In this chapter, we highlight the ways that infants actively shape their social experiences around language—through their everyday behaviors and developmental advances. We review the perceptual, social, and cognitive capacities that infants bring to the task of learning language. We then show that infant real-time exploratory, play, communicative, and locomotor behaviors are impetuses for social interactions. As infants act on their worlds, they elicit temporally contingent, lexically rich, developmentally attuned, multimodal inputs from parents. Indeed, much of the speech that parents direct to infants is driven by what infants are doing in the moment. Finally, we examine how developmental changes in infants' language, play, and motor skills expand infants' opportunities for learning language. As infants progress in abilities such as talking and walking, they engage with the objects and people of their environments in new ways, thereby eliciting novel language inputs from parents and other caregivers.

Introduction

Infants produce a rich variety of behaviors over the course of a day, often to the exhaustion of their parents. They bang spoons and cups on tables; mouth, explore, and play with toys; hold out objects to share; wander from room to room; squeal in delight; and climb stools, couches, and chairs. Infants are intensely involved with the people, spaces, and objects of their environments, and along the way, learn a lot about what they can do and how the world works.

Whether infants' unbridled activity reflects intrinsic motivation, natural curiosity, or something else, it has serendipitous payoffs. As infants interact with objects and people, they generate rich perceptual and social feedback that paves the way for learning language. Infants hear the word "spoon" as they see and feel their spoon

C. S. Tamis-LeMonda (✉) · Y. Kuchirko · D. D. Suh
Steinhardt School of Culture, Education, and Human Development, New York University,
New York, NY, USA
e-mail: catherine.tamis-lemonda@nyu.edu

© Springer International Publishing AG, part of Springer Nature 2018
M. M. Saylor, P. A. Ganea (eds.), *Active Learning from Infancy to Childhood*,
https://doi.org/10.1007/978-3-319-77182-3_3

bang. They are warned "NO!!!" as they teeter on the brink of a changing table. They elicit imitations and verbal expansions in response to their babbles. And they are encouraged to "turn the page" as their fingers grasp the corner of a book. With age, infants develop new skills that further transform their social experiences and language environments. As infants' vocabularies expand, parents introduce new words (Masur, 1997); as sentences grow in complexity, so does parents' infant-directed speech (Snow, 1972); as infants transition to crawling and then walking, parents intensify prohibitions, imperatives and predicates (Campos, Kermoian, & Zumbahlen, 1992; Karasik, Tamis-LeMonda, & Adolph, 2014); and as infants advance in symbolic play, parents encourage increasingly advanced forms of play (Damast, Tamis-LeMonda, & Bornstein, 1996; Tamis-LeMonda & Bornstein, 1991).

Here we highlight the ways that infants orchestrate, unwittingly but fortuitously, their social experiences around language—through everyday behaviors and developmental achievements. Parents are vigilant and eager participants in infants' language-learning journey, and much of their child-directed speech is driven by what infants are doing in the moment. We first review the foundational perceptual, social, and cognitive capacities infants bring to the task of learning language. We then show that infant exploration and play, communication, and locomotion are impetuses for social interactions: Infants elicit temporally contingent, lexically rich, developmentally attuned, multimodal inputs from parents. Finally, we examine how developmental changes allow infants to engage their environments in new ways, and expand opportunities for learning language.

Our focus builds on theoretical writings of the "active infant" (Bell, 1979), transactional processes in social interactions (Sameroff, 2009), and dynamic systems theories of learning (Thelen & Smith, 1998), which have rarely been applied to infant language learning. And, most socio-cultural studies of language learning focus on the input parents provide, and overlook infants' role in eliciting that input. Thus, we flip the lens, so to speak, by considering infant behaviors in the moment and changing skills across development as primary catalysts for learning language.

Foundational Language Skills

Infants are equipped to learn language from birth (and even before). They extract phonological, semantic and grammatical regularities from language inputs, and are quick to detect temporal contingencies in word-environment connections, skills vital to language development.

Statistical Learning

Newborn infants prefer speech to other non-speech sounds (Vouloumanos & Werker, 2004) and can discriminate among the many consonants and vowels of the world's languages (Streeter, 1976; Werker, Gilbert, Humphrey, & Tees, 1981). With experience and age, infants' discrimination of familiar phonemes sharpens, but they gradually lose the ability to discriminate contrasts in non-native languages (Bosch & Sebastián-Gallés, 2003; Kuhl, Williams, Lacerda, Stevens, & Lindblom, 1992; Werker & Tees, 1984).

Infants also exploit statistical learning cues to discover which phonemes in an auditory stream belong together—the foundation to learning words. Infants treat phonemes or syllables that frequently co-occur as a single unit—such as when an infant recognizes that "bot" and "tle" form the word "bottle." Eight-month-old infants extracted statistical regularities in the co-occurrence of syllable pairs from auditory streams that contained no cues to word boundaries (Saffran, Aslin, & Newport, 1996), and were able to use those cues to segment "words" in artificial and natural languages (Pelucchi, Hay, & Saffran, 2009). Moreover, infants develop sensitivity to phonological stress patterns, for instance learning that English typically emphasizes the first syllables of words (*ta*-ble; *cray*-on; *doc*-tor) (Jusczyk, Friederici, Wessels, Svenkerud, & Jusczyk, 1993; Jusczyk, Houston, & Newsome, 1999). Infants' impressive capacities to extract statistical regularities allows them to figure out which phoneme combinations are possible in their language (Saffran & Thiessen, 2003): Seven-month-old infants learning two languages used statistical information in prosodic contours to segment noun phrases from continuous speech (Gervain & Werker, 2013; Saffran & Thiessen, 2003).

Statistical learning also helps infants identify the environmental referents of words. Infants track likelihoods of co-occurrence across streams of events (words and referents), for example, by recognizing that the likelihood of hearing the word "truck" in the presence of a truck is greater than hearing the word airplane, car, and so forth. Twelve- and 14-month-old infants were presented with pictures of different objects and novel words across trials, which created ambiguity around which words referred to which objects. However, some word-object pairs were more likely to co-occur across trials than others. Infants looked reliably longer to word-object pairs that occurred together with high likelihood than to those that did not co-occur, indicating that they used cross-modality statistical information to decipher word meanings (Smith & Yu, 2008).

Contingency Detection

Contingency detection refers to infants' basic capacity to detect and learn from the feedback generated by their actions (Rochat, 2014; Rochat & Rochat, 2009). Two-month-olds increased sucking when auditory input was contingent on sucking (Rochat & Striano, 1999) and showed heightened attention to music produced in response to pulling an arm string than music played randomly (Lewis, Alessandri, & Sullivan, 1990). During social interactions, infants become distressed when their actions fail to evoke a caregiver response, as illustrated in the classic "still-face paradigm" (e.g., Bigelow & Rochat, 2006; Cohn & Tronick, 1987; Goldstein, Schwade, & Bornstein, 2009; Moore & Calkins, 2004). Infants also perceive contingent regularities in others' behavior, for example, recognizing that adult's reaches for objects consistently result in contact with the desired objects (Baldwin, Baird, Saylor, & Clark, 2001; Feldman, 2003), or that adults reliably look toward objects of interest.

Contingency detection is foundational to language learning. Infants must be able to detect the tight temporal alignment among words, objects and events during everyday activities if they are to make sense of the speech directed to them. As an infant sees, touches, smells, and tastes an orange, simultaneously with hearing "orange," the word takes on rich meaning because of accompanying multimodal cues. Infants' keen sensitivity to the contingency of social interactions helps explain why word learning is facilitated by responsive language (Tamis-LeMonda, Kuchirko, & Song, 2014).

Summary

Statistical learning and contingency detection are basic learning mechanisms crucial to acquiring language. Infants exploit these capacities during everyday social interactions to discover how sounds combine to form words and how words map to objects and events in the environment. We next investigate how infants' exploratory, communicative, and motor actions function to elicit timely, meaningful, and lexically rich language inputs from parents. In turn, the perceptual and social feedback generated by these behaviors are seeds to learning words.

Real-Time Behaviors

Infants can only learn words to which they are exposed. A full appreciation of the language-learning process begins with infants' active role in social interactions—the moment-to-moment infant behaviors that induce social input from adults. Infant vocalizations, gestures, object exploration, and play generate rich perceptual and social feedback that fuels learning.

Vocalizations and Gestures

Infants' vocalizations elicit rich language and physical feedback from parents. Already by four weeks of age, infants produce a variety of sounds, and their caregivers respond with language immediately following infant vocalizations (Hsu & Fogel, 2003; Keller, Lohaus, Völker, Cappenberg, & Chasiotis, 1999). Parents pause after their own vocalizations to allow infants to vocalize as part of a conversational chain (Jasnow & Feldstein, 1986). Mothers are much more likely to talk following infant vocalizations than talk when infants are silent (Tamis-LeMonda, Kuchirko, & Tafuro, 2013).

The quality of infant vocalizations also matters, with consonant-vowel sounds, for instance, being more likely to elicit caregiver responses than vowel-only sounds (Gros-Louis, West, Goldstein, & King, 2006; Hsu & Fogel, 2003; Markova & Legerstee, 2006; Papoušek, 2007). To illustrate, associations between infants' preverbal vocalizations and maternal verbal responses were examined during unstructured play (Gros-Louis et al., 2006). Over 70% of infants' preverbal vocalizations were followed by mothers' contingent responses. Infant vocalizations that sounded like vowels or consonant-vowel clusters led to different social responses. Specifically, infants' vowel-like vocalizations induced social play in mothers, whereas infants' more developmentally advanced consonant-vowel vocalizations led to more maternal imitations and conversational replies (e.g., "Is that what it is?"). Consonant-vowel vocalizations were seemingly interpreted as "pseudo-words" by mothers, and were thus effective catalysts to social conversations.

Before using conventional words, infants also communicate their interests and intentions with gestures: they point to objects and people, and move their hands and bodies to represent specific objects and events (e.g., flapping arms to refer to a bird). Infants' gestures elicit gestural inputs from mothers (LeBarton, Goldin-Meadow, & Raudenbush, 2015). Gestures of 14-month-old infants elicited referential language from mothers (Tamis-LeMonda et al., 2013), and 16-month-old infants' gestures related to maternal gestures, which then related to children's vocabulary size (Iverson, Capirci, Longobardi, & Caselli, 1999).

Infants also actively participate in give-and-take, reciprocal exchanges with parents, by adapting the temporal flow of their own vocalizations and gestures to match that of their mothers. Infants vocalized and gestured within 3 s following mothers' language and gestures, and improved in their temporal attunement across the second year. And, infants who were more contingently responsive to their mothers' actions had mothers who were reciprocally more responsive to their infants, underscoring how infants' communications shape and are shaped by their social experiences (Kuchirko et al., 2017).

Object Manipulation and Play

Once infants develop hand-eye coordination and grasping abilities, they spend a substantial portion of their waking hours playing with objects in their environments. Eleven- and 13-month-old infants spent half their awake time touching, manipulating, and carrying objects during everyday routines at home (Karasik, Tamis-LeMonda, & Adolph, 2011). Infants transported objects from room to room, and frequently attempted to share those objects with mother, by holding objects up as they played on the floor or by carrying objects over to mother. During play with beads and string and sharing of books, infants touched objects about 80% of the time, providing ample opportunities for their mothers to offer relevant language inputs (Tamis-LeMonda et al., 2013). Infants' engagements with objects are salient to mothers, who respond promptly (within 2 or 3 s) by talking about the objects of infants' interests and ongoing activities.

Infant object play paves the way for exposure to precisely the type of maternal speech that supports vocabulary growth (Goldstein & Schwade, 2010; Tamis-LeMonda et al., 2014). Mothers respond to infants' object play with didactic language that refers to objects, activities, or events in the environment. They describe, label, or ask about the unique qualities of the referent or event ("What color is the spoon?" "The rabbit's hopping"). To illustrate, mothers and their 14-month-old infants were observed sharing wordless books and beads with a string. Mothers' and infants' exploration of objects (simultaneous looking and touching of objects) and mother language were coded. Infants' object play and exploration led to high rates of maternal responsiveness relative to infants being off-task (Tamis-LeMonda et al., 2013). Furthermore, mothers' verbal responses to infants' object actions were rich in content: Mothers were more likely to use didactic/referential language of high lexical diversity (language that described objects and events with nouns, verbs, adjectives, and adverbs) than regulatory language (language that directed infants' actions or attention with many pronouns) following infant communication. Notably, didactic language is associated with infants' vocabulary size, rate of vocabulary growth, and communicative diversity in early language development (e.g., Hart & Risley, 1995; Hoff, 2003, 2006; Huttenlocher, Haight, Bryk, Seltzer, & Lyons, 1991; Tamis-LeMonda, Baumwell, & Cristofaro, 2012).

Infants' object play and exploration (just as vocalizations and gestures) likewise prompt embodied inputs from mothers. Embodied inputs refer to the multimodal coordination of language with physical cues, as when a parent simultaneously looks to, and touches or points to an object while labeling it (Tamis-LeMonda et al., 2014; Tamis-LeMonda et al., 2013). For example, a mother might respond to infant object play by asking the infant, "What is that?" or "What color is that?" or "Look! It's a cup." Such embodied inputs support infants' language learning because speech that is accompanied by gestures and touch helps infants identify the topic of talk and thus decipher the meanings of utterances (e.g., Matatyaho & Gogate, 2008; Rowe & Goldin-Meadow, 2009; Tamis-LeMonda et al., 2012).

Summary

Infants actively participate in their learning experiences through vocalizations, gestures, exploration and play with objects, and so forth. These mundane, moment-to-moment behaviors create abundant opportunities for parents to respond with verbal and physical inputs that promote language learning. The next section investigates how developmental changes in infants influence their language experiences.

Developmental Changes

The advent of new skills opens up a world of opportunities for infant learning and social interactions (Adolph & Tamis-LeMonda, 2014; Iverson, 2010). Infant developmental achievements—ranging from play to language skills to locomotion—elicit new responses and language inputs from caregivers (Bornstein, 2013). Here we consider how developmental changes across the first two years instigate new language experiences for infants. We show that changing skills of infants lead to adjustments by parents in the content and complexity of their language, what parents respond to, and how they respond. In turn, these changes in parental behaviors instigate further language gains in toddlers.

Developments in Play and Language

Infants display rapid advances in play and communicative skills from the first year of life through the end of the second year. These developmental gains result in new social experiences that broaden the infants' world of language.

From Exploration to Symbolic Play As infants advance in their play, mothers reduce their responses to certain types of infant play behaviors and increase responses to others. When infants were 9 months of age, mothers responded frequently to their babies' simple object exploration (such as when an infant manipulated and fingered a toy), a form of play that was common at this age. When infants were longitudinally followed at 13 and 20 months, they engaged in more sophisticated forms of object play, such as symbolic play (e.g., feeding a doll a bottle). As infants grew in their symbolic play, mothers tuned their responses to this advanced form of play and decreased responding to simple exploration. The shift to symbolic play, therefore, leads to new language experiences. Maternal language during symbolic play is more dense, more diverse, replete with questions, and contains unique forms of reciprocal interaction language (such as mental state terms on the part of parents) to negotiate symbolic transformations ("Let's pretend we're cooking breakfast. What yummy eggs!") (Fekonja, Umek, & Kranjc, 2005; McCune-Nicolich, 1981; Pellegrini, 2009; Quinn, 2016), thereby offering children opportunities to learn new words (Adamson, Bakeman, Deckner, & Nelson, 2014; Hirsh-Pasek et al., 2015a; Hirsh-Pasek et al., 2015b).

Developmental Changes in Gestures Infant developmental change in the use of gestures prompts changes in mothers' gestures. Mothers followed age-related changes in infant gesturing with changes in their own gestures during interactions with infants 1–3 years of age (Rodrigo et al., 2006). Infant–mother correspondence was strongest for deictic gestures (notably points), which increased between infant ages of 12–24 months, and then remained stable from 24 to 36 months. As noted by the authors, mothers matched their means of communicating to that of their infants, even though mothers had a full repertoire of possibilities at hand. With younger infants, mothers use relatively primitive communicative forms, and as children progress in their communicative repertoires mothers abandon or reduce those forms of communication (Rodrigo et al., 2006). As one example of these social-interaction shifts, as infants moved from frequent use of gestures to primarily using words to communicate between 14 and 24 months, mothers increased their referential responses to infant vocalizations but decreased their responses to infant gestures (Tamis-LeMonda et al., 2013).

Growing a Vocabulary Over the course of the second year, infant vocabulary growth is rapid and impressive, and mothers are attuned to the new words that infants know. Mothers are more likely to respond to novel words spoken by their 2-year-olds than to words that infants have spoken for some time (Masur, 1997). Additionally, as infants grow their vocabularies, they are better able to answer their mothers' questions. Mothers appear to be aware of their infants' changing skills, as seen, for example, in their shift from basic descriptions to increased use of questions with growing infant vocabulary. In a longitudinal study, mothers responded with *simple labels and descriptions* to the vocalizations of their 1-year-olds, but increased their responsive *questions* to their 2-year-olds who were more skilled at language (Bornstein, Tamis-LeMonda, Hahn, & Haynes, 2008). Parental "wh" questions become increasingly important for language development in children's 2nd and 3rd years of life, when children become active conversational partners.

From Concrete to Decontextualized Talk When mothers talk with infants, they almost always focus on the here-and-now, referring to objects and people that are immediately perceptible (e.g., Snow et al., 1976). The words that adults use when addressing infants tend to be concrete (Phillips, 1973), phonologically simple (Ferguson, 1964), and contain many simple labels and descriptors (Tamis-LeMonda et al., 2012), which help novice word learners figure out the topic of conversations. As children advance in their language and cognitive skills, mothers shift from referring to objects and events in the here-and-now to decontextualized forms of language—abstract language that is removed from the immediate context (Rowe, 2013).

From Simple Words to Grammatical Complexity As toddlers grow in their syntactic skills, mothers use increasingly complex grammatical structures. Child-directed speech, particularly to infants and toddlers, contains shorter and simpler sentences, as reflected in mothers mean length of utterance (MLU), fewer subordinate clauses (Longhurst & Stepanich, 1975; Phillips, 1973), and a higher redundancy as reflected in type-token ratios (Phillips, 1973). Fathers also match the complexity of their grammar to the language skills of their infants. Mothers and fathers used fewer words, less grammatically complex language, and less diverse language with less linguistically competent infants than did parents of more linguistically advanced infants (Tamis-LeMonda et al., 2012). Of course, it could be argued that associations between parent and infant grammatical complexity (and other measures of language for that matter) are explained by genetic variance shared between children and parents. However, adoption studies (Stams, Juffer, & van IJzendoorn, 2002), laboratory manipulations (Goldstein, King, & West, 2003), and interventions that target parenting (e.g., Mendelsohn et al., 2005; Mendelsohn et al., 2007) indicate that associations between parent language and infant language are not solely attributable to heredity.

Developments in Motor Skills

Infants develop rapidly in their motor skills, progressing from simple reflexes to walking across the first two years. Learning to sit independently, crawl, and walk broadens infants' opportunities to engage with objects and people. In turn, changes to infants' interactions with their environments promote development in other domains, notably language (Libertus & Violi, 2016; Walle & Campos, 2014).

Sitting and Manual Skills A variety of significant changes accompany infants' abilities to sit without support and manually explore objects. Sitting is accompanied by changes in the characteristics of vocalizations, perhaps due to a reconfigured vocal tract, expanded lung capacity, and forward tongue position in the oral cavity (Iverson, 2010). Consequently, infant consonant-vowel vocalizations increase, which (as reviewed) are met with increases in mothers' conversational responses (Gros-Louis et al., 2006), thereby promoting language development (Iverson, 2010).

Sitting additionally creates new opportunities for infants to manually explore their environments (Rochat & Goubet, 1995). Around 6–7 months of age, infants can sit without support and reach and play with objects without falling over (Bertenthal & Von Hofsten, 1998). The freeing of the hands for object play and exertion of control over balance allows infants to engage with objects and people in new ways. Infants can hold objects up to caregivers to share, show, and even request help without toppling over (as when a baby bids for help at opening a box). These communicative acts are referred to as protoimperatives and protodeclaratives (Bates, Camaioni, & Volterra, 1976; Slobin & Tomasello, 2005), and are highly salient social bids for attention or assistance (Karasik et al., 2011). Parents are keenly attentive to the manual actions and social bids of their infants, making the sitting, hands-free, exploring infant one who is likely to spark lots of talk about the objects they are touching.

Locomotor Skills The onset of locomotion provides infants with opportunities to access places that had been out of reach when they were merely sitters. Infants can now retrieve distal objects and solicit attention from people who are in the other room (Iverson, 2010). Parents of locomoting infants (compared to pre-locomotor infants of matched ages) reported that infants increased their interactive play, back-and-forth checking with caregivers, displays of affection, and attention to distal events in the environment (Campos et al., 1992), behaviors that relate to the quantity and quality of language parents direct to infants.

Infants' mastery of upright locomotion (specifically, walking) further expands opportunities for social interactions. Upright posture increases the infant's visual field (Kretch, Franchak, & Adolph, 2014), and thus provides a perceptual advantage compared to crawling by allowing infants to continuously monitor changes to the environment as they move (Kretch et al., 2014). The serendipitous benefits of walking are conducive to following adult attention cues, which itself is foundational to language learning, because infants must identify the referents of parent talk (Iverson, 2010). Indeed, walking is accompanied by greater attention to mothers who are talking about objects or events in the environment (Franchak, Kretch, Soska, & Adolph, 2011), the type of informative, referential speech that promotes language learning. Experience with walking relates to initiation of joint engagement with parent (pointing, bringing objects over; gaze following and pointing) and receptive and productive language (Walle, 2016). Walking infants are more likely than crawling infants (again, matched for age) to produce vocalizations and gestures to direct parent's attention to objects (Clearfield, 2011; Clearfield, Osborne, & Mullen, 2008; Karasik et al., 2011).

Walking also allows infants to carry objects to share with others, and to cover more ground at a faster pace than was possible with crawling (Adolph & Tamis-LeMonda, 2014). Walking infants are more likely to access objects located farther away than are crawling infants (Clearfield, 2011; Karasik et al., 2011), and there is a surge in object sharing in walking infants at-risk for autism and those who are typically developing (Srinivasan & Bhat, 2016). Compared to crawlers, who predominantly shared objects with their mothers from stationary positions, walking infants were more likely to share objects with their mothers by walking over to them (Karasik et al., 2011). Differences in the social bids of crawlers (from stationary positions while sitting) and walkers (as moving about) generated different responses in mothers. Specifically, mothers responded to "stationary bids" with noun phrases (e.g., "Book!") but to "moving bids" with predicate phrases (e.g., "Want to read?") (Karasik et al., 2014). Thus, walking not only allows infants to follow adult gaze and actions, but also facilitates shared object interactions, which evoke new language forms that promote learning (Iverson, 2010; Walle, 2016).

Summary

Developments in language and motor skills drastically alter how infants engage with people and objects. As infants progress in play sophistication, grow their vocabularies, and combine words into simple sentences, parents change in the content and complexity of their infant-directed speech. As infants learn to sit, crawl, and walk, their new motor skills allow them to explore near and distant objects and places and carry objects over to other people. The behavioral changes associated with motor development prompt new language forms and functions from parents.

Future Directions

All too often, developmental scientists pay lip service to the active role infants play in learning language. Most research on the social context of language learning quantifies parents' language inputs to infants, with little attention to *when* and *why* parents choose to talk to their babies. Parents and other caregivers are keenly sensitive to what infants are interested in and what they can do. Consequently, the language adults direct to infants is highly dependent on infants' ongoing behaviors and skills. To truly capture the real-time dance between infants and caregivers requires moving beyond "frequencies" of behaviors to understanding the temporal structure of everyday language interactions. An understanding of language learning requires close attention to how, for example, an infant's simple point of a finger can elicit a parent's rich description about the pictures on the page of a book, or how the transition to walking results in new forms of language exchanges. There are invaluable payoffs to time-intensive behavioral coding, in which behaviors of infants and caregivers are "time locked" to one another to understand the cascading effects that infant learning and development have on social experiences. This micro-genetic approach offers a depth of understanding that is otherwise not possible by merely "counting" the speech acts or words a parent directs to the infant. Detailed behavioral coding reveals the temporal structure of interactions—the essence of human communication.

Conclusions

Infants take center stage in learning language. Here, we described three key ways that infants contribute to their own development. First, infants enter the world of language armed with basic learning mechanisms that are foundational to learning words, including capacities to detect social contingencies and statistical regularities. Infants extract statistical regularities in language inputs, which allow them to discern meaningful phonemes; cull words from continuous auditory streams; and connect words to referents in the world. Infants are also able to detect temporal connections among the actions they produce, the perceptual and sensory inputs they experience, and the words they hear.

Second, infants reap serendipitous benefits from the language inputs they elicit through their everyday behaviors. Infant touches, looks, vocalizations, gestures, and object play are catalysts for parents' infant-directed speech and actions. Parents respond to these infant behaviors with rich, multimodal cues to word meaning, which help infants connect words to their referents in the environment. Infants can exploit the richness of socially embedded, multimodal language experiences to discern the meaning of words—that "ball" and "throw" refer to the round bouncy thing they just threw to the ground; that "soap," "splash," and "water" accompany the objects and actions of bathtime; that "juice" and "cheerios" are the staples of breakfast, and so forth.

Lastly, developments in infant language and motor skill expand opportunities for infant learning and are highly salient to parents. Parents respond to infants' developmental achievements by raising the bar of social interactions: They ask more questions, increase their decontextualized talk, and produce more grammatically complex constructions with child age and skill. As infants sit, crawl, and walk, they interact with people and objects in new ways, and parents adjust their language in response to those advances. In short, infants journey through an ever-changing world of communication that is made possible by the quite basic yet highly remarkable developments of everyday behavior.

Acknowledgements Catherine S. Tamis-LeMonda is at NYU's Center for Research on Culture, Development and Education at the Steinhardt School of Culture, Education, and Human Development. We thank the children and parents who have participated in our studies over the years and helped us discover the ways that children learn through the rich play and language interactions they share with parents. We acknowledge the support from the LEGO Foundation, which continues to advance our research on the science of everyday play. Correspondences can be sent to catherine.tamis-lemonda@nyu.edu.

References

Adamson, L. B., Bakeman, R., Deckner, D. F., & Nelson, P. B. (2014). From interactions to conversations: The development of joint engagement during early childhood. *Child Development, 85*(3), 941–955.

Adolph, K. E., & Tamis-LeMonda, C. S. (2014). The costs and benefits of development: The transition from crawling to walking. *Child Development Perspectives, 8*(4), 187–192.

Baldwin, D. A., Baird, J. A., Saylor, M. M., & Clark, M. A. (2001). Infants parse dynamic action. *Child development, 72*(3), 708–717.

Bates, E., Camaioni, L., & Volterra, V. (1976). Sensorimotor performatives. In: E. Bates (Ed.), Language and context: The acquisition of pragmatics. New York: Academic Press.

Bell, R. Q. (1979). Parent, child, and reciprocal influences. *American Psychologist, 34*(10), 821.

Bertenthal, B., & Von Hofsten, C. (1998). Eye, head and trunk control: The foundation for manual development. *Neuroscience & Biobehavioral Reviews, 22*(4), 515–520.

Bigelow, A. E., & Rochat, P. (2006). Two-month-old infants' sensitivity to social contingency in mother–infant and stranger–infant interaction. *Infancy, 9*(3), 313–325.

Bornstein, M. H. (2013). Mother–infant attunement. In: Legerstee M, Haley DW, Bornstein MH, (eds), *The infant mind: Origins of the social brain* (pp 248–265). New York: The Guildford Press.

Bornstein, M. H., Tamis-LeMonda, C. S., Hahn, C.-S., & Haynes, O. M. (2008). Maternal responsiveness to young children at three ages: Longitudinal analysis of a multidimensional, modular, and specific parenting construct. *Developmental Psychology, 44*(3), 867.

Bosch, L., & Sebastián-Gallés, N. (2003). Simultaneous bilingualism and the perception of a language-specific vowel contrast in the first year of life. *Language & Speech, 46*(2/3), 217–243.

Campos, J. J., Kermoian, R., & Zumbahlen, M. R. (1992). Socioemotional transformations in the family system following infant crawling onset. *New Directions for Child and Adolescent Development, 1992*(55), 25–40.

Clearfield, M. W. (2011). Learning to walk changes infants' social interactions. *Infant Behavior and Development, 34*(1), 15–25.

Clearfield, M. W., Osborne, C. N., & Mullen, M. (2008). Learning by looking: Infants' social looking behavior across the transition from crawling to walking. *Journal of Experimental Child Psychology, 100*(4), 297–307.

Cohn, J. F., & Tronick, E. Z. (1987). Mother–infant face-to-face interaction: The sequence of dyadic states at 3, 6, and 9 months. *Developmental Psychology, 23*(1), 68.

Damast, A. M., Tamis-LeMonda, C. S., & Bornstein, M. H. (1996). Mother-child play: Sequential interactions and the relation between maternal beliefs and behaviors. *Child Development, 67*(4), 1752–1766.

Fekonja, U., Umek, L. M., & Kranjc, S. (2005). Free play and other daily preschool activities as a context for child's language development. *Studia Psychologica, 47*(2), 103.

Feldman, R. (2003). Infant–mother and infant–father synchrony: The coregulation of positive arousal. *Infant Mental Health Journal, 24*(1), 1–23.

Ferguson, C. A. (1964). Baby talk in six languages. *American Anthropologist, 66*(6_PART2), 103–114.

Franchak, J. M., Kretch, K. S., Soska, K. C., & Adolph, K. E. (2011). Head-mounted eye tracking: A new method to describe infant looking. *Child Development, 82*(6), 1738–1750.

Gervain, J., & Werker, J. F. (2013). Learning non-adjacent regularities at age 0; 7. *Journal of Child Language, 40*(04), 860–872.

Goldstein, M. H., King, A. P., & West, M. J. (2003). Social interaction shapes babbling: Testing parallels between birdsong and speech. *Proceedings of the National Academy of Sciences, 100*(13), 8030–8035.

Goldstein, M. H. & Schwade, J. (2010). From birds to words: Perception of structure in social interactions guides vocal development and language learning. In: M. S. Blum- berg, J. H. Freeman & S. R. Robinson, (eds), *The Oxford handbook of developmental behavioral neuroscience* (pp. 708–29). Oxford University Press.

Goldstein, M. H., Schwade, J. A., & Bornstein, M. H. (2009). The value of vocalizing: Five-month-old infants associate their own noncry vocalizations with responses from caregivers. *Child Development, 80*(3), 636–644.

Gros-Louis, J., West, M. J., Goldstein, M. H., & King, A. P. (2006). Mothers provide differential feedback to infants' prelinguistic sounds. *International Journal of Behavioral Development, 30*(6), 509–516.

Hart, B., & Risley, T. R. (1995). *Meaningful differences in the everyday experience of young American children.* Baltimore, MD: Paul H Brookes Publishing.

Hirsh-Pasek, K., Adamson, L. B., Bakeman, R., Owen, M. T., Golinkoff, R. M., Pace, A., . . . Suma, K. (2015a). The contribution of early communication quality to low-income children's language success. Psychological Science, 0956797615581493.

Hirsh-Pasek, K., Adamson, L. B., Bakeman, R., Owen, M. T., Golinkoff, R. M., Pace, A., . . . Suma, K. (2015b). The contribution of early communication quality to low-income children's language success. Psychological Science, 26(7), 1071–1083. doi:https://doi.org/10.1177/0956797615581493

Hoff, E. (2003). The specificity of environmental influence: Socioeconomic status affects early vocabulary development via maternal speech. *Child Development, 74*(5), 1368–1378.

Hoff, E. (2006). How social contexts support and shape language development. *Developmental Review, 26*(1), 55–88.

Hsu, H. C., & Fogel, A. (2003). Social regulatory effects of infant nondistress vocalization on maternal behavior. *Developmental Psychology, 39*(6), 976.

Huttenlocher, J., Haight, W., Bryk, A., Seltzer, M., & Lyons, T. (1991). Early vocabulary growth: Relation to language input and gender. *Developmental Psychology, 27*(2), 236.

Iverson, J. M. (2010). Developing language in a developing body: The relationship between motor development and language development. *Journal of Child Language, 37*(02), 229–261.

Iverson, J. M., Capirci, O., Longobardi, E., & Caselli, M. C. (1999). Gesturing in mother-child interactions. *Cognitive Development, 14*(1), 57–75.

Jasnow, M., & Feldstein, S. (1986). Adult-like temporal characteristics of mother-infant vocal interactions. *Child Development, 57*, 754–761.

Jusczyk, P. W., Friederici, A. D., Wessels, J. M., Svenkerud, V. Y., & Jusczyk, A. M. (1993). Infants' sensitivity to the sound patterns of native language words. *Journal of Memory and Language, 32*(3), 402.

Jusczyk, P. W., Houston, D. M., & Newsome, M. (1999). The beginnings of word segmentation in English-learning infants. *Cognitive Psychology, 39*(3), 159–207.

Karasik, L. B., Tamis-LeMonda, C. S., & Adolph, K. E. (2011). Transition from crawling to walking and infants' actions with objects and people. *Child Development, 82*(4), 1199–1209.

Karasik, L. B., Tamis-LeMonda, C. S., & Adolph, K. E. (2014). Crawling and walking infants elicit different verbal responses from mothers. *Developmental Science, 17*(3), 388–395.

Keller, H., Lohaus, A., Völker, S., Cappenberg, M., & Chasiotis, A. (1999). Temporal contingency as an independent component of parenting behavior. *Child Development, 70*(2), 474–485.

Kretch, K. S., Franchak, J. M., & Adolph, K. E. (2014). Crawling and walking infants see the world differently. *Child Development, 85*(4), 1503–1518.

Kuchirko, Y., Tafuro, L., & Tamis LeMonda, C. S. (2017). Becoming a Communicative Partner: Infant Contingent Responsiveness to Maternal Language and Gestures. Infancy.

Kuhl, P. K., Williams, K. A., Lacerda, F., Stevens, K. N., & Lindblom, B. (1992). Linguistic experience alters phonetic perception in infants by 6 months of age. *Science, 255*(5044), 606–608.

LeBarton, E. S., Goldin-Meadow, S., & Raudenbush, S. (2015). Experimentally induced increases in early gesture lead to increases in spoken vocabulary. *Journal of Cognition and Development, 16*(2), 199–220.

Lewis, M., Alessandri, S. M., & Sullivan, M. W. (1990). Violation of expectancy, loss of control, and anger expressions in young infants. *Developmental Psychology, 26*(5), 745.

Libertus, K., & Violi, D. A. (2016). Sit to talk: Relation between motor skills and language development in infancy. *Frontiers in Psychology, 7*(475). https://doi.org/10.3389/fpsyg.2016.00475

Longhurst, T. M., & Stepanich, L. (1975). Mother's speech addressed to one-, two-, and three-year-old normal children. *Child Study Journal, 5*, 3–11.

Markova, G., & Legerstee, M. (2006). Contingency, imitation, and affect sharing: Foundations of infants' social awareness. *Developmental Psychology, 42*(1), 132.

Masur, E. F. (1997). Maternal labelling of novel and familiar objects: Implications for children's development of lexical constraints. *Journal of Child Language, 24*(2), 427–439.

Matatyaho, D. J., & Gogate, L. J. (2008). Type of maternal object motion during synchronous naming predicts preverbal infants' learning of word–object relations. *Infancy, 13*(2), 172–184.

McCune-Nicolich, L. (1981). Toward symbolic functioning: Structure of early pretend games and potential parallels with language. *Child Development, 52*, 785–797.

Mendelsohn, A. L., Dreyer, B. P., Flynn, V., Tomopoulos, S., Rovira, I., Tineo, W., . . . Nixon, A. F. (2005). Use of videotaped interactions during pediatric well-child care to promote child development: A randomized, controlled trial. Journal of Developmental and Behavioral Pediatrics: JDBP, 26(1), 34.

Mendelsohn, A. L., Valdez, P. T., Flynn, V., Foley, G. M., Berkule, S. B., Tomopoulos, S., . . . Dreyer, B. P. (2007). Use of videotaped interactions during pediatric well-child care: Impact at 33 months on parenting and on child development. Journal of Developmental and Behavioral Pediatrics: JDBP, 28(3), 206.

Moore, G. A., & Calkins, S. D. (2004). Infants' vagal regulation in the still-face paradigm is related to dyadic coordination of mother-infant interaction. *Developmental Psychology, 40*(6), 1068.

Papoušek, M. (2007). Communication in early infancy: An arena of intersubjective learning. *Infant Behavior and Development, 30*(2), 258–266.

Pellegrini, A. D. (2009). *The role of play in human development*. USA: Oxford University Press.

Pelucchi, B., Hay, J. F., & Saffran, J. R. (2009). Learning in reverse: Eight-month-old infants track backward transitional probabilities. *Cognition, 113*(2), 244–247.

Phillips, J. R. (1973). Syntax and vocabulary of mothers' speech to young children: Age and sex comparisons. *Child Development, 44*, 182–185.

Quinn, S. J. (2016). Learning to play and playing to learn: The role of symbolic play in language acquisition.

Rochat, P. (2014). *Early social cognition: Understanding others in the first months of life*. Mahwah, New Jersey: Psychology Press.

Rochat, P., & Goubet, N. (1995). Development of sitting and reaching in 5-to 6-month-old infants. *Infant Behavior and Development, 18*(1), 53–68.

Rochat, P., & Rochat, P. (2009). *The infant's world*. London, UK: Harvard University Press.

Rochat, P., & Striano, T. (1999). Emerging self-exploration by 2-month-old infants. *Developmental Science, 2*(2), 206.

Rodrigo, M. J., González, A., Ato, M., Rodríguez, G., Vega, M. D., & Muñetón, M. (2006). Co-development of child-mother gestures over the second and the third years. *Infant and Child Development, 15*(1), 1–17.

Rowe, M. L. (2013). *Decontextualized language input and preschoolers' vocabulary development*. Paper presented at the Seminars in Speech and Language.

Rowe, M. L., & Goldin-Meadow, S. (2009). Early gesture selectively predicts later language learning. *Developmental Science, 12*(1), 182–187.

Saffran, J. R., Aslin, R. N., & Newport, E. L. (1996). Statistical learning by 8-month-old infants. *Science, 274*(5294), 1926–1928.

Saffran, J. R., & Thiessen, E. D. (2003). Pattern induction by infant language learners. *Developmental Psychology, 39*(3), 484.

Sameroff, A. (2009). *The transactional model*. Washington, DC: American Psychological Association.

Slobin, D. I., & Tomasello, M. (2005). Thirty years of research on language, cognition, and development: The legacy of Elizabeth bates. *Language Learning and Development, 1*(2), 139–149.

Smith, L., & Yu, C. (2008). Infants rapidly learn word-referent mappings via cross-situational statistics. *Cognition, 106*(3), 1558–1568.

Snow, C. E. (1972). Mothers' speech to children learning language. *Child Development, 43*, 549–565.

Snow, C. E., Arlman-Rupp, A., Hassing, Y., Jobse, J., Joosten, J., & Vorster, J. (1976). Mothers' speech in three social classes. *Journal of Psycholinguistic Research, 5*(1), 1–20.

Srinivasan, S. M., & Bhat, A. N. (2016). Differences in object sharing between infants at risk for autism and typically developing infants from 9 to 15 months of age. *Infant Behavior and Development, 42*, 128–141.

Stams, G. J. M., Juffer, F., & van IJzendoorn, M. H. (2002). Maternal sensitivity, infant attachment, and temperament in early childhood predict adjustment in middle childhood: The case of adopted children and their biologically unrelated parents. *Developmental Psychology, 38*(5), 806.

Streeter, L. A. (1976). Language perception of 2-month-old infants shows effects of both innate mechanisms and experience. *Nature, 259*(5538), 39–41.

Tamis-LeMonda, C. S., Baumwell, L., & Cristofaro, T. (2012). Parent–child conversations during play. *First Language, 32*(4), 413–438.

Tamis-LeMonda, C. S., & Bornstein, M. H. (1991). Individual variation, correspondence, stability, and change in mother and toddler play. *Infant Behavior and Development, 14*(2), 143–162.

Tamis-LeMonda, C. S., Kuchirko, Y., & Song, L. (2014). Why is infant language learning facilitated by parental responsiveness? *Current Directions in Psychological Science, 23*(2), 121–126.

Tamis-LeMonda, C. S., Kuchirko, Y., & Tafuro, L. (2013). From action to interaction: Infant object exploration and mothers' contingent responsiveness. *IEEE Transactions on Autonomous Mental Development, 5*(3), 202–209.

Thelen, E., & Smith, L. (1998). Dynamic systems theories. In: R. M. Lerner (Ed.), *Handbook of child psychology: Vol. 1. Theoretical models of human development* (5th ed., pp. 563–634). New York: Wiley.

Vouloumanos, A., & Werker, J. F. (2004). Tuned to the signal: The privileged status of speech for young infants. *Developmental Science, 7*(3), 270–276.

Walle, E. A. (2016). Infant social development across the transition from crawling to walking. *Frontiers in Psychology, 7*, 960.

Walle, E. A., & Campos, J. J. (2014). Infant language development is related to the acquisition of walking. *Developmental Psychology, 50*(2), 336.

Werker, J. F., Gilbert, J. H. V., Humphrey, K., & Tees, R. C. (1981). Developmental aspects of cross-language speech perception. *Child Development, 52*, 349–355.

Werker, J. F., & Tees, R. C. (1984). Cross-language speech perception: Evidence for perceptual reorganization during the first year of life. *Infant Behavior and Development, 7*(1), 49–63.

Part II
Cognitive and Linguistic Skills that Enable Active Learning

Chapter 4
Curiosity, Exploration, and Children's Understanding of Learning

David M. Sobel and Susan M. Letourneau

Abstract Children's curiosity often manifests in their exploration—actions that are intended to reveal novel information. In this chapter, we argue that in order to understand how exploration can guide children's learning, they must first develop an understanding of what learning is and when it occurs in others, as well as a more metacognitive understanding of how their own learning takes place. This knowledge allows children to recognize when they do not know particular pieces of information and strategically generate actions that can close those knowledge gaps. We present evidence that children's understanding of learning and their ability to reflect on their own learning both develop during the early elementary school years, and synthesize these findings with previous research on exploratory behavior.

Introduction

Contemporary research in cognitive development posits that children are active learners. Piaget (1952) argued that assimilation and accommodation were the result of processes in which children sought out novel data and experiences for the purposes of learning. Nativist theorists disagreed with Piaget about the age at which children begin to learn in this manner, but they did not object to the notion itself. For example, Spelke, Breinlinger, Macomber, and Jacobson (1992) described infants as possessing "active representations," which suggests "…young infants are capable of reasoning. They can represent states of the world they cannot perceive. By operating on these representations, infants come to know about states of the world they never perceive" (p. 606). Neither view claimed that children were necessarily aware that their actions would result in learning, only that they had a potential drive to explain

D. M. Sobel (✉)
Department of Cognitive, Linguistic, and Psychological Sciences, Brown University,
Providence, RI, USA
e-mail: david_sobel_1@brown.edu

S. M. Letourneau
New York Hall of Science, Queens, NY, USA

© Springer International Publishing AG, part of Springer Nature 2018
M. M. Saylor, P. A. Ganea (eds.), *Active Learning from Infancy to Childhood*,
https://doi.org/10.1007/978-3-319-77182-3_4

their environment (Brewer, Chinn, & Samarapungavan, 1998; Gopnik, 1998). One way of conceptualizing this drive is to say that children are inherently curious; they engage in explanation-seeking behaviors by exploring the world or requesting information from others (e.g., Berlyne, 1960; Burke, 1958; Lowenstein, 1994).

For example, children ask many questions (Chouinard, 2007), and in particular, they ask questions to elicit causal information from caregivers or peers (e.g., Callanan & Oakes, 1992). If they are unsatisfied with the answers they receive, they follow up to ask for more relevant information (e.g., Frazier, Gelman, & Wellman, 2009; see also Sperber & Wilson, 1986). By the time children are 3 years old, they prefer non-circular over circular explanations (Mercier, Bernard, & Clément, 2014) and rely more on informants who generate such explanations (e.g., Corriveau & Kurkul, 2014), although there is a developmental trajectory in the extent to which children prefer non-circular explanations (Baum, Danovitch, & Keil, 2008).[1]

Similarly, children's curiosity is reflected in their desire to explore when faced with uncertain situations—that is, when they recognize a gap in their knowledge about causal structures they encounter. For example, when given ambiguous evidence about how a novel object works, children explore it for longer periods of time (e.g., Schulz & Bonawitz, 2007) or explore it systematically in order to confirm a particular causal structure (e.g., Cook, Goodman, & Schulz, 2011). In this way, children's exploration may be seen as a hypothesis-testing mechanism that supports learning. Further, preschoolers learn more about causal environments through their own self-generated actions than by observing others' actions (e.g., Gopnik et al., 2004; Kushnir & Gopnik, 2005; Schulz, Gopnik, & Glymour, 2007). This is true even when the results of these actions are identical; generating actions oneself supports a different interpretation of data than when those same data are observed.

These findings, and many other investigations, suggest that exploration and explanation are fundamentally related to curiosity or the drive to understand (see e.g., Busch, Willard and Legare (this volume); Sobel & Legare, 2014, for reviews). In this chapter, we argue that in order for children to be active and intentional in using their exploration of the world to guide their own learning, they must develop two capacities: First, they must understand factors that determine when learning would or would not occur, including when and how one's actions might lead to learning. Second, they must develop an understanding of their own learning and how it takes place. Together, these abilities might allow children both to recognize gaps in their knowledge and use exploration strategically to gather pieces of information that can close those gaps. We present two lines of work that address these ideas. Finally, we will speculate on some relations between this metacognitive development and children's curiosity.

---

[1] There is a question, however, about what kinds of explanations adults treat as non-circular. For example, adults tend to prefer reductive, but nonsensical explanations over mechanistic ones that stay in the same domain of knowledge (e.g., Fernandez-Duque, Evans, Christian & Hodges, 2015; Rhodes, Rodriguez & Shah, 2014; Weisberg, Keil, Goodstein, Rawson, & Gray, 2008; Weisberg, Taylor & Hopkins, 2015; see Hopkins, Weisberg & Taylor, 2016, for a review).

Children's Understanding of How Learning Occurs

Children first use words like "learn" and "teach" in everyday conversation during the preschool years (Bartsch, Horvath, & Estes, 2003). This suggests that they have some understanding of how to use these words in communication, and what these concepts potentially mean. However, their understanding of the mental states that are required for learning to take place seems to develop later, during the early elementary school years. For example, preschoolers judge whether learning takes place based on whether an individual wants to learn something, regardless of that individual's other mental states, such as attention to necessary information (Sobel, Li, & Corriveau, 2007). Sobel et al. (2007) also examined children's conversational usage of words like "learn" and "teach" and showed that references to learning processes increase between ages 3–5. These findings all suggest that children's understanding of how one learns develops during and after the preschool years.

We (Lai, Letourneau, and Sobel, unpublished) followed up on this study by simplifying the procedure. Specifically, we presented children with two child characters being taught a song by a teacher. One character wanted to learn the song, but did not hear it. The other character did not want to learn, but did hear the song (a more extreme situation than simple indifference to learning). We asked children to choose which character would learn the song. In these circumstances, even 4-year-olds recognized the importance of perceptual access in learning—that is, even 4-year-olds reliably chose the character who didn't want to learn, but was exposed to information over a character who wanted to learn, but was not exposed to the information. This suggests that preschoolers are not simply swayed by a character's desires, but have some understanding that other mental states are involved in learning.

However, preschoolers' understanding of learning is still developing after the preschool years. In a follow-up study, we predicted that two additional factors would affect preschoolers' judgments about how learning occurred. The first was the nature of the knowledge being acquired. Facts with deterministic truth-values are either known or not at a given point in time; learning in this context is the acquisition of knowledge from a state of ignorance. Skills, in contrast, are more scalar. One gets better at a certain task with practice, but performance may vary and be subject to chance; learning in this context is the process of improving, but the knowledge is rarely deterministic. We wanted to examine whether children understood this distinction.

The second factor we considered was the volitional nature of action. Do children treat actions that cause learning as relevant to the learning process even if those actions are not intentional? Here again, facts and skills may be treated differently. Even if factual information is learned by accident, it is still learned. In contrast, accidental actions that result in a successful attempt at demonstrating a skill might not be treated as evidence for learning in the same way.

To test these ideas, we told 4- to 7-year-olds stories about a character who either wanted to learn a skill (how to throw a basketball through a hoop) or a fact (the location of a teddy bear). The character then engaged in an action either with the intention to learn (i.e., intentionally aimed at the basketball hoop or looked in a closet) or not (i.e., accidentally threw the ball in the air or opened the closet accidentally). That action resulted in a successful outcome or not (i.e., the ball landed in the basket or not; the bear was in the closet or not). Children were asked whether the character learned the skill (how to throw the ball into the basket) or the fact (where the bear was). Critically, children at all ages used the outcome as the basis for their judgment (i.e., if the ball landed in the basket, children were likely to say the character had learned how to throw the ball into the basket, and if the bear was in the closet, children were likely to say that the character had learned where the bear was). In the fact condition, this is unsurprising, as the intention is irrelevant—characters who find the bear have learned where it is regardless of how they find it. In the skill condition, however, the intention is relevant—happy accidents do not necessarily indicate learning, yet even 6- and 7-year-olds thought that they did.

Learning and Action

Curiosity often leads to actions which in turn can result in learning. Acting on the world is a critical mechanism for learning in early childhood, and there is evidence that children are more systematic in their exploration when it has the potential to reveal new information. As discussed above, children are more influenced by causal evidence they generate themselves compared with evidence generated by others.[2] These effects are most pronounced when children's actions reveal novel information as opposed to information they already know (Legare, 2012; Sobel & Sommerville, 2010). Children not only learn from their exploration of the environment, they also engage in more exploration when they observe ambiguous data or data that suggests the presence of hidden causal mechanisms (e.g., Baldwin, Markman, & Melartin, 1993; Cook et al., 2011; Gweon & Schulz, 2011; Schulz & Bonawitz, 2007; Stahl & Feigenson, 2015). More action, however, does not necessarily mean more *systematic* action, nor does it reflect a better understanding of how acting on the world leads to learning.

Because actions are so important for learning, children might also struggle to understand the relation between learning and action. Sobel and Letourneau (2017) asked whether 3- to 5-year-olds have an explicit understanding of how actions can lead to subsequent learning. Across a series of experiments, they read preschoolers stories in which characters learned about novel toys. In one set of stories (action stories), the character learned how the toy worked by acting on it. In the other set of stories (instruction stories), the character was told how the toy worked by a familiar adult. Children were asked how each character learned how the toy worked. Their open-ended responses were coded as being about the character's actions or the direct instruction that they received (among other possibilities).

---

[2] A finding also observed in adults (e.g., Coenen, Rehder, & Gureckis, 2015; Rottman & Keil, 2012; Sobel & Kushnir, 2006; Steyvers, Tenenbaum, Wagenmakers, & Blum, 2003).

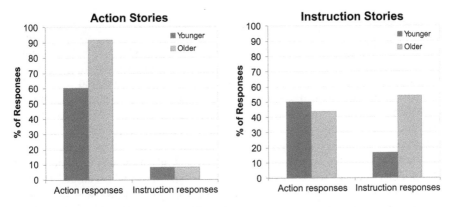

Fig. 4.1 Percentage of explanations children generated for how characters learned in terms of action and direction instruction, based on story type (taken from Experiment 2 of Sobel & Letourneau, 2017)

Figure 4.1 shows the percentage of responses that were coded as action and instruction for both story types, with age groups divided using a median split of the sample. Younger preschoolers overestimated the role of action and discounted the role of instruction in learning. They often stated that characters learned through actions in the action stories, when this was the appropriate response, but also responded similarly in the instruction stories, when this was not how the characters in the story actually learned. In these stories, a knowledgeable adult told the child what actions would make the toy work, but the characters themselves never actually touched the toy. Older preschoolers, on the other hand, were more likely to cite the appropriate source of information (the character's actions in the action stories, and the adult in the instruction stories). This suggests not only that actions may be especially salient in younger preschoolers' perceptions of how learning occurs, but also that young children may have difficulty recognizing when actions do *not* result in learning.

Children's Developing Metacognition and Their Understanding of Learning

In both of the previous sections, we have suggested that children may initially struggle to understand particular aspects of learning, but come to understand it during or slightly after the preschool years. The general argument we wish to make is that children's understanding of how actions lead to learning parallels the development of other aspects of metacognition. Consider first children's developing false belief capacities. Understanding that others' beliefs can be false might allow children to recognize that statements about knowledge can also be false. Sobel (2015) tested this by introducing 3- and 4-year-olds to characters who were being taught a skill (how to solve a set of puzzles) by a teacher. The teacher worked with the character for a little while, and then the character made a claim about their learning. Some characters said they learned how to do the puzzles; others did not. The teacher then asked all of the child characters to demonstrate their knowledge. Using a 2 × 2 design, the stories varied in the character's claims about learning and whether the character actually demonstrated the knowledge (i.e., solved the puzzles). Children were then asked whether each character actually learned how to do the puzzles. In addition to these stories, children were given a standard unexpected contents false belief test.

When the character's claims and demonstrative ability were in sync, children had no difficulty judging whether the character learned; those who claimed to have learned and could do the puzzles were judged to have learned, and those who claimed not to have learned and could not do the puzzles were judged not to have learned. When claims about learning disagreed with demonstrative ability, perfor-mance was not as clear. Older preschoolers tended to use demonstrative ability more than the younger preschoolers, but the more important factor was children's false belief knowledge. Performance on the unexpected contents task was correlated with children's use of the character's demonstrative ability when making judgments about learning. Those who passed this task (controlling for age) seemed more likely to recognize that a claim about learning could be false, and weighed it less heavily than demonstrative ability. Children who did not succeed on the false belief measure seemed to weigh the claim and the demonstrative ability equally, which resulted in their chance-level performance.

These data suggest that children's developing false belief knowledge may allow them to understand whether another's claim about learning is true or false. But chil-dren's understanding about learning and knowledge develops beyond their success on the false belief task. For example, when taught new pieces of knowledge, pre-schoolers (who succeed on false belief measures) often claim that they knew it all along (Esbensen, Taylor, & Stoess, 1997; Taylor, Esbensen, & Bennett, 1994). Preschoolers also seem to believe mental states are fixed—that thoughts do not lead to other thoughts (or mental states to other mental states) in a stream-of-consciousness-like way—while older elementary-school-aged children recognize the dynamic nature of thinking (see, e.g., Eisbach, 2004; Flavell, Green, Flavell, Harris, & Astington, 1995; Johnson & Wellman, 1982; Lagattuta & Wellman, 2001).

The broader point that we want to make is that the development of children's understanding of learning (and particularly their metacognitive reflection on their own learning) potentially parallels the development of this broader awareness of mental states. Young preschoolers have little appreciation of when others learn or why learning takes place. Their developing understanding of false belief provides them with some knowledge (e.g., that others' claims about learning can be false, and therefore should be less important for judging whether someone has learned). But more generally, children's understanding of learning goes beyond their under-standing of belief to include the knowledge that mental states are related to one another and that certain mental states and actions might lead to learning, while others are insufficient.[3] In the next section, we explore children's understanding of their own learning in more depth.

Children's Reflections on Their Own Learning

The majority of the studies reviewed above examine children's understanding of learning in a third-person context; children are asked to judge whether others will learn or have learned. Few studies have considered children's ability to articulate what they know about their own learning. Typically, those studies have focused on children's source memory. For example, Tang and Bartsch (2012), see also Tang, Bartsch, & Nunez, 2007) found that preschoolers could track some information about the source of their knowledge. They showed children information either through visual demonstration or direct instruction. One week later, these 4- to 5-year-olds could state whether they were shown or told the information, although they could not report that this was done a week prior.

Bemis, Leichtman, and Pillemer (2011) asked 4- to 9-year-olds questions they were likely to be able to answer. Children were then asked to describe how they had learned that piece of information. Even the youngest children in their sample could generate details about how they learned the information, although there was signifi-cant age-related change (i.e., older children could generate more details). Bemis, Leichtman, and Pillemer (2013) followed up on this finding by teaching 4- and 5-year-olds novel facts and then examining whether those children could articulate how they had learned that knowledge. Even the youngest children were able to state how they had learned the new facts.

This awareness of one's own knowledge relates to children's reasoning in the face of uncertainty. For example, while even toddlers are sophisticated at making causal inferences about known causes (see, e.g., Gopnik & Wellman, 2012, for a review), only 6-year-olds are capable of making diagnostic inferences under uncer-tainty (Erb & Sobel, 2014). Beck et al. (2006) suggested that 6-year-olds could prepare for multiple possible outcomes, while 4-year-olds treated the world in a more deterministic way (see also Bullock et al., 1982). Children's metamemory judgments follow a similar developmental trajectory. Five-year-olds' confidence

---

[3] A parallel can be drawn to children's understanding of pretending. At early ages, children engage in pretend play (e.g., Piaget, 1962) and understand others' pretense (e.g., Harris & Kavanaugh, 1993; Lillard & Witherington, 2004). While the sophistication of children's pretense does undergo development during the preschool years (e.g., Overton & Jackson, 1973), it is not until well after the preschool years that children begin to appreciate the metacognitive nature of pretending. For instance, understanding that pretenders must know about what they are pretending to be (Lillard, 1993), intend their actions as pretense (Lillard, 1998), or even be aware they are pretending (Sobel, 2004) all develops between the ages of 4–7 (see Lillard, 2001; Sobel, 2009, for reviews). What these data suggest is that children's engagement in a behavior (i.e., pretending, learning) is not necessarily indicative of their metacognitive understanding of how they are engaging in that behav-ior, which potentially has a more prolonged developmental trajectory.

judgments are better predictive of their accuracy on memories tests than 3-year-olds' (Hembacher & Ghetti, 2014). Moreover, children's ability to monitor their own judgments of learning based on the amount of time they studied material develops between ages 5–7 (Destan et al., 2014). These data all suggest that during and after the preschool years, children might still be developing a concept of what learning is. More important, how they understand that concept might relate to their understanding of their own learning and their perceptions of themselves as learners.

These studies led Sobel and Letourneau (2015) to investigate two facets of children's understanding of learning. We first examined how children defined learning. There is a long literature in conceptual development relating children's *intensions* (their definitions of categories) to their *extensions* (their judgments about whether particular items are members of a category). These studies often show that between the ages of 4–10, children's conceptual representation of categories goes from being based more on superficial, perceptual, or nonessential features of objects (e.g., taxis are yellow) to ones that are more central to their meaning (e.g., taxis give people rides for money) (Anglin, 1977; Keil, 1989; Keil & Batterman, 1984). We hypothesized that children might shift from concrete to more abstract, process-based understandings of learning between ages 4–10, in line with this work. But we also thought that children's definitions of learning would reveal something about the way in which they internalized the process of learning itself.

As such, the second facet we considered was how children's definitions of learning related to their ability to give examples of things they had learned before and their descriptions of how they had learned in those instances. Previous studies have demonstrated that preschoolers' intensions and extensions often show a great deal of coherence (Caplan & Barr, 1989; see also Gentner, 2003; Maguire, Hirsh-Pasek, Golinkoff, & Brandone, 2008). Therefore, asking children to describe learning in the abstract and in the context of specific examples might reveal not only their understanding of what learning means in general, but also what they do and do not consider to be examples of learning. We hypothesized that children who defined learning as an active process might also be better able to describe their own learning processes and might have different ideas about what constitutes learning.

We conducted a structured interview with 4- to 10-year-olds. Children were first asked to give a definition of learning via an open-ended question: "What do you think 'learning' means?" Children's answers were coded as identity responses (in which children simply defined learning as learning), or as being about *content* or *process*. Content responses involved defining learning based on subjects or topics (e.g., "like reading and math"). Process responses involved defining learning as related to either a source (e.g., "when your teacher tells you something") or a strategy (e.g., "when you practice again and again until you know it") that would result in knowledge change. Figure 4.2 shows the distribution of responses to this question. Children's responses showed a clear developmental shift toward a process-based understanding of learning: Only 42% of the 4- and 5-year-olds interviewed generated process responses. This was significantly less than the 6- and 7-year-olds

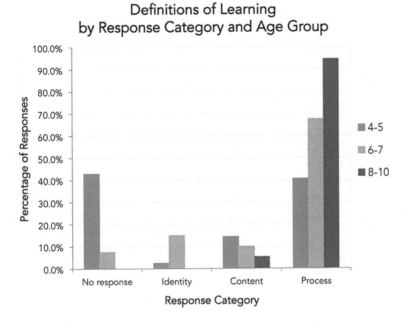

Fig. 4.2 Percentage of children in three age groups who generated each type of response when asked to define learning (taken from Sobel & Letourneau, 2015)

(66%), who in turn generated this kind of definition significantly less than the 8- to 10-year-olds (95% of the time).

After this open-ended question, children were asked to generate examples of what they had learned (e.g., "Can you think of something that you have learned?"), how they learned in each example (e.g., "How did you learn that?"), and whether they could think of other ways of learning (i.e., "How else could you learn?").[4] Children's definitions of learning related to the ways in which they reflected on both the content and the process of their own learning (what and how they described learning in the context of their own lives). If children generated a process-based definition of learning, they were more likely to give an example of learning a skill (e.g., "how to tie my shoes") or a fact (e.g., "ants have six legs"). Also, children who generated a process-based definition of learning were more likely to describe a source or a strategy through which they acquired knowledge in their examples. Both of these correlations held independent of age. Finally, children whose definitions of learning were coded as being process-based were more likely to generate multiple different strategies for learning.

These data suggest that children's understanding of learning parallels the development of their judgments about others' learning, described above. Children's

---

[4] These questions were then repeated several times over a 5-min interview, so that children could generate several different examples. The results presented here represent how children responded over the entire interview, not for any one example.

likelihood of defining learning as a process of knowledge change increased between ages 4–10, as did their ability to generate different examples of their own learning and their descriptions of how they learned information in the past. Critically, even though there was significant development in both aspects of children's responses, it was their definitions of learning, and not their age, that predicted how children were able to reflect on their own learning. Some 4-year-olds conceptualized learning as a process, and those children seemed to have better metacognitive access to details about their own learning.

We suggest that children who think of learning as an active process, and who have an explicit understanding of the strategies they can use to learn, may also be able to use exploration more intentionally to shape their own learning. This possibility has far-reaching implications for educational practices that emphasize exploration and discovery because it suggests that by supporting children in reflecting on how they learn, educators may help children become more strategic in using their actions to generate evidence that might answer their questions about the world, which in turn may support children's perceptions of themselves as active and capable learners.

Curiosity and the Development of a Concept of Learning

We want to acknowledge two important points regarding the role of children's understanding of learning and its relation to their drive to explore the world and seek out explanations. We have speculated that one facet of curiosity is children's tendency to engage in novel actions when faced with a knowledge gap—when presented with uncertain or ambiguous information. Indeed, most of the work on exploration and pedagogy shows that children will explore longer in certain conditions—for example, when given particular types of pedagogical information (e.g., Bonawitz et al., 2011; Gweon, Pelton, Konopka, & Schulz, 2014; Shneidman, Gweon, Schulz, & Woodward, 2016).

Nevertheless, this work does not necessarily show that young children are using their exploration to answer specific questions or fill a particular gap in their knowledge. Berlyne (1960) articulated a distinction between *specific exploration* and *diverse exploration* (p. 80). Specific exploration involves "[setting] out to find…a solution to an intellectual problem." Diverse exploration, in contrast, involves engaging in actions that generate new experiences. An increase in children's exploration in response to ambiguous data is not necessarily evidence of specific exploration—it is unclear whether the child is attempting to resolve the ambiguity or just wants more information. In contrast, an increase in systematic exploration is a clearer example of specific exploration.

For example, Cook et al. (2011) found that 4- to 5-year-olds explored more systematically when presented with ambiguous data. In this study, children were presented with a causal system and evidence that suggested it was stochastic or deterministic. When that system was clearly stochastic, children generated more actions that revealed conditional probability information to disambiguate a piece of causal data (i.e., when shown that a compound cause A and B was efficacious together, children systematically tested A and B individually). This behavior was rarely observed when the initial evidence suggested that the causal system acted in a deterministic manner.

But other studies suggest that such systematic exploration changes with age (Butler & Markman, 2012; Legare, 2012). For instance, Legare (2012) presented 2- to 6-year-olds with data that were inconsistent with their existing knowledge of a novel causal system, asked them to try to explain those data, and then allowed them to explore to gather more information about that situation. She found that in general, children who generated more causal-functional explanations tended to explore more judiciously to reduce knowledge gaps. She also documented that the extent to which children gather relevant information through their exploration seems to differ with age: 31% of the 2-year-olds in this study generated an action that provided them with relevant information, while up to 56% of the 6-year-olds did so.[5]

In our lab, Wister (2014) performed a replication of the Cook et al. (2011) procedure[6] with a group of younger children. She did not replicate the main finding of Cook et al. (2011) and instead showed similar patterns of exploratory behavior when children were introduced to a stochastic vs. deterministic system. However, she did show that systematic exploration in the stochastic condition (as described by Cook et al.) was related to age, with older preschoolers more likely to engage in the kinds of systematic behavior described by Cook et al. than younger preschoolers.

Based on this work, what might be developing between the ages of 4–6 is an understanding of the role of one's own actions in learning. Children's diverse exploration— cases of seeking out novel information when there is more to discover (as in Schulz & Bonawitz, 2007) or when observations are inconsistent with existing knowledge (as in Stahl & Feigenson, 2015) might reflect children's understanding that their actions can reveal information about objects in general. Such capacities might be present early in development. In contrast, children's specific exploration, their systematic and intentional use of action to gather information that fills a specific knowledge gap, might have a more prolonged developmental trajectory, consistent with several findings that younger preschoolers show less robust patterns of exploration.

An interesting question is how children's developing exploratory capacities and motivations interacts with their explanatory capacities and behaviors. There is certainly evidence that children learn causal knowledge through both exploration and their own and others' explanations (for review, see Busch, Willard and Legare, this volume; Danovich and Mills (this volume); Legare, Sobel, & Callanan, 2017). We suspect that children's learning is influenced by the interactions between explanations

---

[5] Critically, Legare (2012) reports that there is not a significant interaction between age group and explanation type (p. 181). However, this might have been because the other three explanation types did not show this pattern and age was treated categorically as opposed to continuously.

[6] The similarity of our testing session to Cook et al (2011) was validated by Claire Cook, who observed us collect data (Personal Communication, May 29, 2013), and Laura Schulz who viewed videos of the procedure (Personal Communication, August 26, 2013).

(both those generated by children themselves and those heard from others), children's exploration, and children's understanding of how actions relate to learning. That is, the way a 3-year-old learns from the interaction of exploration and explanation is potentially different from the way a 5-year-old does so because (among other reasons), 3-year-olds have a less sophisticated understanding of how learning occurs. Such a hypothesis is potentially related to how Danovich and Mills (this volume) discuss work by Walker, Bonawitz, and Lombrozo (2017) and their "windows of opportunity" for learning. Understanding how one's own actions can affect learning might be part of the background knowledge necessary for explanations to facilitate learning.

Finally, a point we also wish to emphasize is that most of the studies discussed in this chapter involved children recruited from a WEIRD population (Henrich, Heine, & Norenzayan, 2010). Different cultures may have different beliefs about the role of exploration and curiosity in learning, especially as it compares to instruction, modeling, observation, and other ways of learning. Children's learning is not simply the constructivist act of the child acting alone to process information, but rather enmeshed in the cultural practices and social norms of the community (e.g., Gauvain & Perez, 2015; Rogoff, 2003; Vygotsky, 1962). In stating that children's understanding of learning is critical to their individual exploration and curiosity, we do not wish to discount the social and cultural processes that shape how children learn from and with others (see Legare et al., 2017, for a review).

Some studies have begun to consider cultural differences in children's ideas about learning, although few have examined children's understanding of learning in social or cultural contexts. As an example, Li (2004) introduced Chinese and American kindergarteners to child characters who were engaged in school work in their home when they hear the sounds of other children playing outside. She asked children to complete the story in an open-ended fashion. More Chinese children articulated what she called the conflict between learning and play—that play was something that occurred after learning was completed. More Chinese children, however, articulated reasons why play might be beneficial for learning, and said that although play was more enjoyable, there were also positive reasons to engage in learning. This suggests that Chinese children might have a different appreciation of what learning is than do children in the US (see also Li, 2012).

Given the evidence of cross-cultural differences between the US and China in children's developing theory of mind and metacognitive capacities (e.g., Sabbagh, Xu, Carlson, Moses, & Lee, 2006; Tardif & Wellman, 2000; Wellman, Fang, Liu, Zhu, & Liu, 2006; Wellman, Fang, & Peterson, 2011), we would suggest that children in these two cultures might also show different developmental trajectories in their understanding of learning. An open question is whether this affects their curiosity or exploration, their ability to reflect on their own learning (as seen in Sobel & Letourneau, 2015), or their attitudes about themselves as learners.

These are open questions for future investigation, but it is worth pointing out that even within a single culture, sociocultural factors might influence children's understanding of learning in numerous ways. Parents show a great deal of variance in their beliefs about their children's learning—for example, how they believe children learn through play in informal settings (see e.g., Gaskins, Haight, & Lancy, 2007; Letourneau et al., 2017). Studies of parent–child interactions have documented wide variations in how parents offer explanations to their children (e.g., Crowley et al., 2001) and how they foster children's exploration (e.g., Crowley et al., 2001; Fung & Callanan, 2013; Van Schijndel et al., 2010). Another open question is how these different interaction styles affect children's developing metacognitive awareness, their understanding of how they learn, and their persistence in exploring to resolve challenges and uncertainties that they encounter.

Conclusion

We began this chapter by stating the obvious: young children are remarkably curious. Children possess powerful learning mechanisms that allow them to process information rapidly and engage in conceptual change about increasingly abstract topics (e.g., Bloom, 2000; Carey, 2009; Gopnik et al., 2004). What we have argued here is that children also develop (and need to have) a more metacognitive awareness of how their own learning happens. While children actively learn about their environment from the youngest ages (e.g., Haith, 1993; Kirkham, Slemmer, & Johnson, 2002), their understanding of the process of learning has a more prolonged developmental trajectory.

Understanding this developmental trajectory might be important for educational practices that advocate for child-directed exploration as an avenue for learning. These practices might be informed and refined by considering how children themselves understand these concepts, and by recognizing that children and families from different cultures may comprehend them differently, a point made clearly by researchers who have examined parental ethnotheories of play and learning (e.g., Gaskins et al., 2007; Parmar, Harkness, & Super, 2004; Roopnarine, 2011). By understanding how children think about the process of learning, educators might not only support children's exploration and play, but also help children begin to see their actions as tools for shaping their own learning. Interventions to promote playful learning might therefore be most effective when they allow children to reflect on the actions and cognitive processes that allow learning to take place.

Acknowledgements The authors were supported by NSF (1223777 and 1420548 to DMS) when this research was conducted and during the writing of this chapter.

References

Anglin, J. M. (1977). *Word, object, and conceptual development*. New York, NY: Norton.
Baldwin, D. A., Markman, E. M., & Melartin, R. L. (1993). Infants' ability to draw inferences about nonobvious object properties: Evidence from exploratory play. *Child Development, 64*(3), 711–728.

Bartsch, K., Horvath, K., & Estes, D. (2003). Young children's talk about learning events. *Cognitive Development, 18*(2), 177–193.

Baum, L. A., Danovitch, J. H., & Keil, F. C. (2008). Children's sensitivity to circular explanations. *Journal of Experimental Child Psychology, 100*(2), 146–155.

Beck, S. R., Robinson, E. J., Carroll, D. J., & Apperly, I. A. (2006). Children's thinking about counterfactuals and future hypotheticals as possibilities. *Child Development, 77*(2), 413–426.

Bemis, R. H., Leichtman, M. D., & Pillemer, D. B. (2011). 'I Remember When I Learned That!': Developmental and gender differences in children's memories of learning episodes. *Infant and Child Development, 20*(4), 387–399.

Bemis, R. H., Leichtman, M. D., & Pillemer, D. B. (2013). I remember when you taught me that! Preschool children's memories of realistic learning episodes. *Infant and Child Development, 22*(6), 603–621.

Berlyne, D. E. (1960). *Conflict, arousal, and curiosity*. New York, NY: McGraw-Hill.

Bloom, P. (2000). *How children learn the meanings of words*. Cambridge, MA: MIT Press.

Bonawitz, E., Shafto, P., Gweon, H., Goodman, N. D., Spelke, E., & Schulz, L. (2011). The double-edged sword of pedagogy: Instruction limits spontaneous exploration and discovery. *Cognition, 120*(3), 322–330. https://doi.org/10.1016/j.cognition.2010.10.001

Brewer, W. F., Chinn, C. A., & Samarapungavan, A. (1998). Explanation in scientists and children. *Minds and Machines, 8*(1), 119–136.

Burke, E. (1958). *A philosophical enquiry into the origin of our ideas of the sublime and beautiful*. London, England: Routledge & Kegan Paul. (Original work published 1757).

Bullock, M., Gelman, R., & Baillargeon, R. (1982). The development of causal reasoning. In W. Friedman (Ed.), *The developmental psychology of time* (pp. 209–254). New York: Academic Press.

Butler, L. P., & Markman, E. M. (2012). Preschoolers use intentional and pedagogical cues to guide inductive inferences and exploration. *Child Development, 83*(4), 1416–1428.

Callanan, M. A., & Oakes, L. M. (1992). Preschoolers' questions and parents' explanations: Causal thinking in everyday activity. *Cognitive Development, 7*, 213–233.

Caplan, L. J., & Barr, R. A. (1989). On the relationship between category intensions and extensions in children. *Journal of Experimental Child Psychology, 47*(3), 413–429.

Carey, S. (2009). *The origin of concepts*. New York, NY: Oxford University Press.

Chouinard, M. M. (2007). Children's questions: A mechanism for cognitive development. *Monographs of the Society for Research in Child Development, 72*(1), 7.

Coenen, A., Rehder, B., & Gureckis, T. M. (2015). Strategies to intervene on causal systems are adaptively selected. *Cognitive Psychology, 79*, 102–133.

Cook, C., Goodman, N. D., & Schulz, L. E. (2011). Where science starts: Spontaneous experiments in preschoolers' exploratory play. *Cognition, 120*(3), 341–349. https://doi.org/10.1016/j.cognition.2011.03.003

Corriveau, K. H., & Kurkul, K. E. (2014). "Why does rain fall?": Children prefer to learn from an informant who uses noncircular explanations. *Child Development, 85*(5), 1827–1835.

Crowley, K., Callanan, M. A., Jipson, J. L., Galco, J., Topping, K., & Shrager, J. (2001). Shared scientific thinking in everyday parent-child activity. *Science Education, 85*(6), 712–732.

Destan, N., Hembacher, E., Ghetti, S., & Roebers, C. M. (2014). Early metacognitive abilities: The interplay of monitoring and control processes in 5-to 7-year-old children. *Journal of Experimental Child Psychology, 126*, 213–228.

Eisbach, A. O. (2004). Children's developing awareness of diversity in people's trains of thought. *Child Development, 75*(6), 1694–1707.

Erb, C. D., & Sobel, D. M. (2014). The development of diagnostic reasoning about uncertain events between ages 4–7. *PloS one, 9*(3), e92285.

Esbensen, B. M., Taylor, M., & Stoess, C. (1997). Children's behavioral understanding of knowledge acquisition. *Cognitive Development, 12*(1), 53–84. https://doi.org/10.1016/S0885-2014(97)90030-7

Fernandez-Duque, D., Evans, J., Christian, C., & Hodges, S. D. (2015). Superfluous neuroscience information makes explanations of psychological phenomena more appealing. *Journal of Cognitive Neuroscience, 27*(5), 913–925.

Flavell, J. H., Green, F. L., Flavell, E. R., Harris, P. L., & Astington, J. W. (1995). Young children's knowledge about thinking. *Monographs of the Society for Research in Child Development, 60*(1), 1–113.

Frazier, B. N., Gelman, S. A., & Wellman, H. M. (2009). Preschoolers' search for explanatory information within adult-child conversation. *Child Development, 80*, 1592–1611. https://doi.org/10.1111/j.1467-8624.2009.01356.x

Fung, G., & Callanan, M. (2013). *Pedagogy versus exploration: Parent–child interactions in a museum setting.* Poster presented at biennial meetings of Society for Research in Child Development, Seattle, WA.

Gaskins, S., Haight, W., & Lancy, D. F. (2007). The cultural construction of play. In A. Goncu & S. Gaskins (Eds.), *Play and development: Evolutionary, sociocultural, and functional perspectives* (pp. 179–202). New York, NY: Taylor & Francis.

Gauvain, M., & Perez, S. (2015). Cognitive development and culture. *Handbook of Child Psychology and Developmental Science., 2*(20), 1–43.

Gentner, D. (2003). *Language in mind: Advances in the study of language and thought.* Cambridge, MA: MIT Press.

Gopnik, A. (1998). Explanation as orgasm. *Minds and Machines, 8*(1), 101–118.

Gopnik, A., Glymour, C., Sobel, D. M., Schulz, L. E., Kushnir, T., & Danks, D. (2004). A theory of causal learning in children: Causal maps and Bayes nets. *Psychological Review, 111*(1), 3–32. https://doi.org/10.1037/0033-295X.111.1.3

Gopnik, A., & Wellman, H. M. (2012). Reconstructing constructivism: Causal models, Bayesian learning mechanisms, and the theory theory. *Psychological bulletin, 138*(6), 1085–1108.

Gweon, H., Pelton, H., Konopka, J. A., & Schulz, L. E. (2014). Sins of omission: Children selectively explore when teachers are under-informative. *Cognition, 132*(3), 335–341. https://doi.org/10.1016/j.cognition.2014.04.013

Gweon, H., & Schulz, L. E. (2011). 16-month-olds rationally infer causes of failed actions. *Science, 332*, 1524. https://doi.org/10.1126/science.1204493

Haith, M. M. (1993). Future-oriented processes in infancy: The case of visual expectations. In C. Granrud (Ed.), *Visual perception and cognition in infancy* (pp. 235–264). Hillsdale, NJ: Erlbaum.

Harris, P. L., & Kavanaugh, R. D. (1993). Young children's understanding of pretense. *Monographs of the Society for Research in Child Development, 58*(1), 1–107.

Hembacher, E., & Ghetti, S. (2014). Don't look at my answer: Subjective uncertainty underlies preschoolers' exclusion of their least accurate memories. *Psychological Science, 25*(9), 1768–1776.

Henrich, J., Heine, S. J., & Norenzayan, A. (2010). Beyond WEIRD: Towards a broad-based behavioral science. *Behavioral and Brain Sciences, 33*(2-3), 111–135.

Hopkins, E. J., Weisberg, D. S., & Taylor, J. C. (2016). The seductive allure is a reductive allure: People prefer scientific explanations that contain logically irrelevant reductive information. *Cognition, 155*, 67–76.

Johnson, C., & Wellman, H. (1982). Children's developing conceptions of the mind and brain. *Child Development, 53*(1), 222–234. https://doi.org/10.2307/1129656

Keil, F. C. (1989). *Concepts, kinds, and cognitive development.* Cambridge, MA: MIT Press.

Keil, F. C., & Batterman, N. (1984). A characteristic-to-defining shift in the development of word meaning. *Journal of Verbal Learning and Verbal Behavior, 23*(2), 221–236.

Kirkham, N. Z., Slemmer, J. A., & Johnson, S. P. (2002). Visual statistical learning in infancy: Evidence for a domain general learning mechanism. *Cognition, 83*(2), B35–B42.

Kushnir, T., & Gopnik, A. (2005). Young children infer causal strength from probabilities and interventions. *Psychological Science, 16*(9), 678–683. https://doi.org/10.1111/j.1467-9280.2005.01595.x

Lagattuta, K. H., & Wellman, H. M. (2001). Thinking about the past: Early knowledge about links between prior experience, thinking, and emotion. *Child Development, 72*(1), 82–102.

Legare, C. H. (2012). Exploring explanation: Explaining inconsistent evidence informs exploratory, hypothesis-testing behavior in young children. *Child Development, 83*(1), 173–185. https://doi.org/10.1111/j.1467-8624.2011.01691.x

Legare, C. H., Sobel, D. M., & Callanan, M. (2017). Causal learning is collaborative: Examining explanation and exploration in a social context. *Psychonomic Bulletin & Review, 24*(5), 1548–1554.

Letourneau, S. M., Meisner, R., Neuwirth, J. L., & Sobel, D. M. (2017). What do caregivers notice and value about how children learn through play in a children's museum? *Journal of Museum Education, 42*(1), 87–98.

Li, J. (2004). Learning as a task or a virtue: US and Chinese preschoolers explain learning. *Developmental Psychology, 40*(4), 595–605.

Li, J. (2012). *Cultural foundations of learning: East and West*. New York, NY: Cambridge University Press.

Lillard, A. S. (1993). Pretend play skills and the child's theory of mind. *Child Development, 64*(2), 348–371.

Lillard, A. S. (1998). Playing with a theory of mind. In O. N. Saracho & B. Spodek (Eds.), *Multiple perspectives on play in early childhood education* (pp. 11–33). Albany, NY: State University of New York Press.

Lillard, A. S. (2001). Pretend play as twin earth: A social-cognitive analysis. *Developmental Review, 21*(4), 495–531. https://doi.org/10.1006/drev.2001.0532

Lillard, A. S., & Witherington, D. S. (2004). Mothers' behavioral modifications during pretense snacks and their possible signal value for toddlers. *Developmental Psychology, 40*, 95–113.

Lowenstein, G. (1994). The psychology of curiosity: A review and reinterpretation. *Psychological Bulletin, 16*(1), 75–98.

Maguire, M. J., Hirsh-Pasek, K., Golinkoff, R. M., & Brandone, A. C. (2008). Focusing on the relation: Fewer exemplars facilitate children's initial verb learning and extension. *Developmental Science, 11*(4), 628–634.

Mercier, H., Bernard, S., & Clément, F. (2014). Early sensitivity to arguments: How preschoolers weight circular arguments. *Journal of Experimental Child Psychology, 125*, 102–109.

Overton, W. F., & Jackson, J. P. (1973). The representation of imagined objects in action sequences: A developmental study. *Child Development, 44*(2), 309–314.

Parmar, P., Harkness, S., & Super, C. (2004). Asian and euro-American parents' ethnotheories of play and learning: Effects on preschool children's home routines and school behaviour. *International Journal of Behavioral Development, 28*(2), 97–104. https://doi.org/10.1080/01650250344000307

Piaget, J. (1952). *Origins of Intelligence in Children*. New York: International University Press.

Piaget, J. (1962). *Play, dreams and imitation*. Abingdon, England: Routledge.

Rhodes, R. E., Rodriguez, F., & Shah, P. (2014). Explaining the alluring influence of neuroscience information on scientific reasoning. *Journal of Experimental Psychology: Learning, Memory, and Cognition, 40*(5), 1432.

Rogoff, B. (2003). *The cultural nature of human development*. New York, NY: Oxford University Press.

Roopnarine, J. L. (2011). Cultural variations in beliefs about play, parent–child play, and children's play: Meaning for childhood development. In A. Pellegrini (Ed.), *Oxford handbook of the development of play* (pp. 19–37). New York, NY: Oxford University Press.

Rottman, B. M., & Keil, F. C. (2012). Causal structure learning over time: Observations and interventions. *Cognitive Psychology, 64*(1), 93–125.

Sabbagh, M. A., Xu, F., Carlson, S. M., Moses, L. J., & Lee, K. (2006). The development of executive functioning and theory of mind: A comparison of Chinese and US preschoolers. *Psychological Science, 17*(1), 74–81.

Schulz, L. E., & Bonawitz, E. B. (2007). Serious fun: Preschoolers engage in more exploratory play when evidence is confounded. *Developmental Psychology, 43*(4), 1045–1050. https://doi.org/10.1037/0012-1649.43.4.1045

Schulz, L. E., Gopnik, A., & Glymour, C. (2007). Preschool children learn about causal structure from conditional interventions. *Developmental Science, 10*(3), 322–332.

Shneidman, L., Gweon, H., Schulz, L. E., & Woodward, A. L. (2016). Learning from others and spontaneous exploration: A cross-cultural investigation. *Child Development, 87*(3), 723–735.

Sobel, D. M. (2004). Children's causal inferences from indirect evidence: Backwards blocking and Bayesian reasoning in preschoolers. *Cognitive Science, 28*(3), 303–333. https://doi.org/10.1016/j.cogsci.2003.11.001

Sobel, D. M. (2009). Enabling conditions and children's understanding of pretense. *Cognition, 113*, 177–188.

Sobel, D. M. (2015). Can you do it? How preschoolers judge whether others have learned. *Journal of Cognition and Development, 16*(3), 492–508.

Sobel, D. M., & Kushnir, T. (2006). The importance of decision making in causal learning from interventions. *Memory & Cognition, 34*, 411–419.

Sobel, D. M., & Legare, C. H. (2014). Causal learning in children. *Wiley Interdisciplinary Reviews: Cognitive Science, 5*(4), 413–427.

Sobel, D. M., & Letourneau, S. M. (2015). Children's developing understanding of what and how they learn. *Journal of Experimental Child Psychology, 132*, 221–229. https://doi.org/10.1016/j.jecp.2015.01.004

Sobel, D. M., & Letourneau, S. M. (in press). Preschoolers' understanding of how others learn through action and instruction. *Child Development.* https://doi.org/10.1111/cdev.12773

Sobel, D. M., Li, J., & Corriveau, K. H. (2007). "They danced around in my head and I learned them": Children's developing conceptions of learning. *Journal of Cognition and Development, 8*(3), 345–369. https://doi.org/10.1080/15248370701446806

Sobel, D. M., & Sommerville, J. A. (2010). The importance of discovery in children's causal learning from interventions. *Frontiers in Psychology, 1*, 1–7. https://doi.org/10.3389/fpsyg.2010.00176

Spelke, E. S., Breinlinger, K., Macomber, J., & Jacobson, K. (1992). Origins of knowledge. *Psychological Review, 99*(4), 605.

Sperber, D., & Wilson, D. (1986). *Relevance: Communication and cognition.* Oxford, England: Blackwell.

Stahl, A. E., & Feigenson, L. (2015). Observing the unexpected enhances infants' learning and exploration. *Science, 348*(6230), 91–94. https://doi.org/10.1126/science.aaa3799

Steyvers, M., Tenenbaum, J. B., Wagenmakers, E. J., & Blum, B. (2003). Inferring causal networks from observations and interventions. *Cognitive Science, 27*, 453–489.

Tang, C. M., & Bartsch, K. (2012). Young children's recognition of how and when knowledge was acquired. *Journal of Cognition and Development, 13*(3), 372–394. https://doi.org/10.1080/15248372.2011.577759

Tang, C. M., Bartsch, K., & Nunez, N. (2007). Young children's reports of when learning occurred. *Journal of Experimental Child Psychology, 97*(2), 149–164. https://doi.org/10.1016/j.jecp.2007.01.003

Tardif, T., & Wellman, H. M. (2000). Acquisition of mental state language in mandarin-and Cantonese-speaking children. *Developmental Psychology, 36*(1), 25–43.

Taylor, M., Esbensen, B. M., & Bennett, R. T. (1994). Children's understanding of knowledge acquisition: The tendency for children to report that they have always known what they have just learned. *Child Development, 65*(6), 1581–1604. https://doi.org/10.2307/1131282

Van Schijndel, T. J., Franse, R. K., & Raijmakers, M. E. (2010). The Exploratory Behavior Scale: Assessing young visitors' hands-on behavior in science museums. *Science Education, 94*(5), 794–809.

Vygotsky, L. S. (1962). *Thought and language.* Cambridge, MA: MIT Press.

Walker, C., Bonawitz, E., & Lombrozo, T. (2017). Effects of explaining on children's preference for simpler hypotheses. *Psychonomic Bulletin & Review, 24*(5), 1538–1547.

Weisberg, D. S., Keil, F. C., Goodstein, J., Rawson, E., & Gray, J. R. (2008). The seductive allure of neuroscience explanations. *Journal of Cognitive Neuroscience, 20*(3), 470–477.

Weisberg, D. S., Taylor, J. C., & Hopkins, E. J. (2015). Deconstructing the seductive allure of neuroscience explanations. *Judgment and Decision making, 10*(5), 429.

Wellman, H. M., Fang, F., Liu, D., Zhu, L., & Liu, G. (2006). Scaling of theory-of-mind understandings in Chinese children. *Psychological Science, 17*(12), 1075–1081.

Wellman, H. M., Fang, F., & Peterson, C. C. (2011). Sequential progressions in a theory-of-mind scale: Longitudinal perspectives. *Child Development, 82*(3), 780–792.

Wister, A. (2014). *Exploring exploration: How evidence affects 4- and 5-year-old children's exploratory play* (Undergraduate Honors Thesis). Brown University.

Chapter 5
The Process of Active Word Learning

Sofia Jimenez, Yuyue Sun, and Megan M. Saylor

Abstract Language learning is largely a robust process that seems to progress automatically in typically developing children. In the preschool years, some children may also make active, self-directed attempts at learning words that they are curious about. This may involve asking questions about unknown words that they encounter. We propose that asking information-seeking questions about word meanings requires preschoolers to monitor uncertainty, be aware of their lexical ignorance, and be motivated by curiosity. We provide some preliminary data that suggest questions about word meaning emerge during the preschool period, but children are not equally inclined to ask such questions. We also provide evidence that awareness of gaps in one's lexicon may benefit word learning and that children with larger vocabularies were more likely to ask about unknown words than those with smaller vocabularies.

Introduction

Preschoolers adroitly make use of most types of information to learn names for things. In experimental tasks, they have been shown to learn words in both ostensive and non-ostensive contexts, when being directly spoken to and when listening in on others' conversations, incidentally and with rich verbal support, with the help of constraints and heuristics, conceptual information, associations between names and objects, and social pragmatic supports (Bloom P., 2000; Hollich, Hirsh-Pasek, & Golinkoff, 2000; Shneidman & Woodward, 2016; Tare & Gelman, 2010; Waxman & Gelman, 2010). Clearly, preschoolers use multiple, redundant sources of information to learn names for things (Saylor, Baldwin, & Sabbagh, 2004).

With rare exceptions, the lion's share of research on preschoolers' word learning involves an informant providing information to a more or less passive child partici-

S. Jimenez (✉) · Y. Sun · M. M. Saylor
Department of Psychology and Human Development, Vanderbilt University,
Nashville, TN, USA
e-mail: sofia.r.jimenez@vanderbilt.edu

© Springer International Publishing AG, part of Springer Nature 2018   75
M. M. Saylor, P. A. Ganea (eds.), *Active Learning from Infancy to Childhood*,
https://doi.org/10.1007/978-3-319-77182-3_5

pant. The researcher tightly controls the provision of information. This makes a great deal of sense—if the focus of a study is to determine whether children use a particular type of word learning cue, restricting the flow of the information so that it is equated across participants is a necessary design feature. However, one unintended consequence of this is that an additional mechanism that supports word learning during the preschool period may have been obscured. In particular, previous work has failed to account for preschoolers' explicit bids for information about words they do not know. As a result, it is unknown whether preschoolers engage in self-directed attempts to gather information about words or word meanings, whether conversations about word meaning benefit vocabulary growth, and when (or if) children become curious about word meanings.

In contrast, there is clear evidence that typically developing infants and toddlers actively solicit name information from their communicative partners. One way they accomplish this is with nonverbal behaviors—such as looking, pointing, and reaching. Seminal research in the area suggests that parents who respond to infants' nonverbal attention bids by providing labels (i.e., follow-in labeling) have children with larger receptive vocabularies (Tomasello & Farrar, 1986). Infants benefit from input that is tailored to their developmental needs, both in terms of the quality and content of the input (e.g., Golinkoff, Can, Soderstrom, & Hirsh-Pasek, 2015) and the timing of names relative to their focus of attention (Cartmill et al., 2013; Trueswell, Lin, Armstrong, & Cartmill, 2016). In addition, parental sensitivity to young infants' play and language behaviors predict earlier attainment of language milestones in infancy (e.g., Tamis-LeMonda, Kuchirko, & Song, 2014; Tamis-LeMonda & Bornstein, 2001). All together, this work clarifies that parents who tailor the content of their speech and nonverbal behaviors to their infants' interests have babies with more robust language skills.

In what follows, we take seriously the possibility that children's active bids for information about language continue past the infancy period and suggest that children ask questions about words and the meanings of words to gather information about their language. We begin with a discussion of what children need to understand to ask questions about word meanings and provide some data that suggest questions about word meaning emerge during the preschool period, but that children are not all equally inclined to ask such questions. We also provide evidence suggesting that awareness of lexical gaps and questions about words may benefit vocabulary growth.

What Do Children Need to Understand to Ask a Question About a Word Meaning?

To ask a question about a word meaning, at minimum, children must recognize that they (a) do not know a word and (b) know how to seek the information. However, it is possible to be aware of a gap in one's knowledge and to have the skills for retrieving the information, while at the same time having no desire to fill the gap. One possibility is that variability in children's tendency to seek information about word meanings may also be related to the degree to which children are curious about or motivated to acquire information about words. Some children may be more curious about words than others, the types of words that individual children are interested in may also vary, and the contexts in which children are curious about word meaning may also vary. Our proposal is that children who know what they do not know, who have skills for seeking the missing information, and who are also interested in doing so will be the most likely to seek information about unknown word meanings. Research on preschoolers' metacognitive monitoring, question asking, and curiosity suggest that the three component processes involved in seeking information about words are available during the preschool period.

Knowing What They Don't Know

Although early studies on metacognitive ability suggested that preschoolers could not make reliable judgments about their learning (e.g., Brown, 1978; Flavell, 1979; Flavell, Friedrichs, & Hoyt, 1970), more recent studies have shown that preschoolers make judgments about what they do and do not know. For example, preschoolers can make implicit judgments about whether they would be able to remember a recently learned bit of information (Balcomb & Gerken, 2008) and are more likely to have high confidence in their responses in object naming tasks when they give accurate responses on subsequent recall tests (Lyons & Ghetti, 2011). These and similar findings have been taken as an indication that preschoolers can sense when they are uncertain in what they know. Their uncertainty monitoring is related to control processes. In particular, preschoolers use judgments about whether they know something to decide whether to seek help on memory tasks (Coughlin, Hembacher, Lyons, & Ghetti, 2014; Lyons & Ghetti, 2013). Children's ability to make accurate judgments about their uncertainty increases with age. Three-year-old children do not always show clear evidence of uncertainty monitoring (Hembacher & Ghetti, 2014) and are sometimes overconfident in what they know (e.g., Lipowski, Merriman, & Dunlosky, 2012). Together, these results clarify that preschoolers have an emerging set of skills for monitoring their knowledge and may also use these intuitions to guide their information-seeking behaviors.

Metacognitive monitoring skills have also been revealed in studies of preschoolers' judgments of lexical ignorance. In particular, 4-year-old children reliably predict whether words are known versus unknown (e.g., "Do you know what a hat/zav is?") and whether they will be able to name familiar and novel objects (e.g., when shown pictures and asked, "Do you know what the name for this is?" Lipowski & Merriman, 2011; Merriman & Lipko, 2008). Similar to uncertainty monitoring, across the preschool period, children become better able to recognize when a word is unknown and when they do not know the name of an object. In particular, three-year-olds tend to overestimate their knowledge of unknown words and novel objects (Merriman & Marazita, 2004).

Both uncertainty monitoring (Ghetti, Hembacher, & Coughlin, 2013; Lyons & Ghetti, 2011) and awareness of lexical ignorance (Lipowski et al., 2012) may contribute to the likelihood of preschoolers asking questions about unknown words. The precise relation between these two metacognitive skills is unclear at present. Lyons and Ghetti (2011) suggested that the familiarity judgments that support lexical awareness emerge prior to children's ability to make more nuanced judgments about the quality or certainty of their knowledge. However, there has not yet been a direct test of this possibility and on the whole the existing evidence suggests that both uncertainty monitoring and lexical awareness share a similar trajectory in development with both skills becoming more robust across the preschool period. It seems likely that the skills may share similar underlying constraints, such as memory representations that enable on-line comparisons of what is known and unknown. Nevertheless, both metacognitive skills may support children's information seeking in the context of word knowledge.

One question is whether there is evidence that metacognitive judgments, such as awareness of lexical ignorance, are related to inferences about word meaning. One piece of evidence comes from work by Merriman and colleagues: children who make accurate judgments about a word or object being unknown justify extending novel names to novel objects with their desire to avoid overlapping labels. For example, preschoolers who answered "no" when asked "Do you know what a *zav* is?" asserted that a novel (e.g., garlic press) versus a familiar object (e.g., a cup) was a "dax" because the familiar object already had a name (Marazita & Merriman, 2004; Merriman & Schuster, 1991). One question is whether a similar relation between recognition of lexical ignorance and word learning holds when children are tested in more naturalistic learning contexts.

In recent unpublished work conducted with an undergraduate student, Jordan Crawford, we have investigated the relation between metacognitive judgments and word learning during a shared reading activity. We measured awareness of lexical ignorance, general language ability (using the TELD-3, Hresko, Reid, and Hammill, 1999), and the ability to learn novel words during a book-reading task in 3- to 4-year-old ($N = 154$) children. For the test of awareness of lexical ignorance, children were asked to identify unknown words in pairs of novel and familiar words (e.g., "Which is the *new* word? The word that you *don't* know. Dax or Sock?"). In the novel word identification task, children were read a description of a novel creature (e.g., grimp as in, "The grimp is orange, lives in a tree, and has a droopy nose.") and were then asked to identify the novel creature on a subsequent comprehension test. Scores on the test of awareness of lexical ignorance were positively correlated with both novel word identification (r (152) = 0.30, $p < 0.001$) and scores on the TELD-3 (r (147) = 0.34, $p < 0.001$). These findings provide suggestive evidence that the metacognitive judgment that a word is unknown may not only be related to general language skill, but also to word-learning potential.

Wanting to Know About a Word

For children to go from recognizing that a word is unknown to obtaining a definition for the word, they have to be motivated to ask a question about its meaning. That is, in addition to the metacognitive skills described above, children's tendency to ask questions about novel words may be affected by how curious they are about words in general. Like adults, children may vary in how interested they are in words and word meanings; that is, some children may be more likely to be "word-nerds" than others. These word-interested children may be more prone to make spontaneous queries about what words mean. At present there are no available measures for testing preschoolers' interest in vocabulary (independent of their vocabulary size, which may be related to interest in words, but is likely also heavily input driven). We view interest in words as an ancillary skill; that is, children will, of course, learn words regardless of whether they find themselves pondering the meaning of unknown words, because they have access to many robust, more automatic processes to support word learning. What we are proposing is that interest in words in general or interest in particular types of words may give some children a boost. This previously untested factor might predict variability in the size and scope of children's vocabulary.

Others have suggested that children propel their word learning with their unique interests and moment-to-moment affective states. One notable example is Lois Bloom who proposed that the interests and intentions of children, rather than the language skills of adults, provided the impetus for language development (e.g., Bloom L., 1998, 2000; Bloom, Margulis, Tinker, & Fujita, 1996; Bloom, Tinker, & Kofsky Scholnick, 2001). This view of children's label acquisition put children's motivation and affective states during conversation in center stage and represented an exception to input driven and constraint based explanations of word learning (Bloom L., 2000). Bloom L. (2000) argued forcefully that word-learning researchers were ignoring children and their everyday behaviors "at the peril of the theories that … explain those behaviors," (Bloom L., 2000, p. 165). The crux of her argument was that "children do not just wait around for other people to construct the word-learning scenario for them…they create the word-learning process themselves. The words they learn are the words they want to learn, the words they need to learn" (Bloom L., 2000, p. 165). She proposed that the inferences children made about word meaning were guided, in part, by a social pragmatic constraint, the principle of relevance, which held that children's mental states—their beliefs, desires, and intentions—motivated them to determine what others' speech was most likely about. Unfortunately, without a clear framework for understanding what factors predicted individual children's interests and therefore what they would want to learn about the social pragmatic constraint did not gain traction among language researchers.

One construct that may be useful for developing a measure of children's interest in words is curiosity. Research on curiosity as a driving force in guiding children's learning was quite in fashion in the middle of the twentieth century. From the mid-

1950s to the late 1970s many studies investigated how children's minds and features of their learning environment stimulated exploration and discovery (e.g., Berlyne, 1954, 1960, 1966; Cantor & Cantor, 1964; Charlesworth, 1964; Greene, 1964; Mittman & Terrell, 1964; Smock & Holt, 1962). Daniel Berlyne (1924–1976), in particular, provided an influential framework for understanding the roots of exploratory behavior in humans (and other animals). Central to the discussion here is that Berlyne defined curiosity as, "the condition of discomfort, due to the inadequacy of information, that motivates specific exploration" (Berlyne, 1966, p. 26). Curiosity, according to Berlyne (1954, 1966) was aroused, in part, by percepts or ideas that are novel, irregular, and incongruous. He also alluded to the notion of an information-seeking sweet spot—"optimum dosages" of novelty and complexity at which information seeking is most likely to occur (Berlyne, 1966, p. 32). The idea that curiosity creates an unpleasant sensation that we seek to reduce is echoed in more contemporary views of the drive that underlies our tendency to seek out information when it is lacking or available evidence is incongruous (e.g., Litman, 2005; Loewenstein, 1994).

More recent investigations of children's interest in visual stimuli and self-guided exploration have supported many of Berlyne's proposals about curiosity. Infants seem more inclined to direct attention to visual stimuli that have just the right amount of complexity—they selectively attend to patterns that are neither too simple nor too complex (e.g., Kidd, Piantadosi, & Aslin, 2012). In other related work, Bonawitz and colleagues have shown that preschoolers were more likely to explore an object that violated their beliefs about balance relationships (Bonawitz, van Schijndel, Friel, & Schulz, 2012; Bonawitz, Bass, and Lapidow, Chap. 11). This finding suggests that a mismatch between what one believes and available evidence encourages self-guided exploration. There may be a way to create an optimal level of uncertainty so that children become curious about the meaning of a novel word. For example, presenting a novel word in a familiar context may motivate a child to try to reduce their uncertainty, but in a complex or unfamiliar context a child might be content with not understanding the novel word.

A popular contemporary theory of curiosity is Loewenstein's (1994) information gap theory (for more extensive discussions, see Jirout & Klahr, 2012; Kidd & Hayden, 2015). Loewenstein (1994) proposed that gaps between what one knows and what one would like to know engender a sense of deprivation that learners are motivated to reduce. Loewenstein (1994) argued that when an information gap in a particular knowledge network is made salient, curiosity is induced. The size of the information gap predicts how curious an individual will be about something. Under this view, larger gaps between what one knows and what one could know lead to low levels of curiosity while smaller gaps lead to high levels of curiosity. Large information-gaps do not engender curiosity because there is too much information to assimilate into what one knows. For example, a 4-year-old who hears the word "quantum" in the context of an adult conversation (about physics, presumably) may not have the same level of interest in finding out what the word means as a child who hears a parent discussing "fetlocks" in the context of a discussion of a well-known farm animal (a horse). That is, if a child hears a novel word in a context that is far removed from what they know about they may be less curious about its meaning than if the word is presented in a context that is relevant to an area of interest. Children might determine whether a new word is relevant to an area of interest through the surrounding discourse. That is, new words that are offered in the context of known words may be more likely to engender curiosity than new words offered in the context of novel information. Additionally, in a familiar context, children may not only be more interested in learning a novel word, but they might also experience stronger feelings of deprivation.

Litman and Jimerson (2004) built on Loewenstein's information gap theory by proposing that curiosity had two dimensions that motivate exploration: deprivation and interest. The deprivation dimension is associated with feeling like there is crucial missing information and an aversive feeling of uncertainty, whereas the interest dimension is driven by the enjoyment of obtaining new information. Children who are curious about the meaning of a word could be motivated by the desire to reduce feelings of deprivation or by the pleasurable feeling that results from learning something new. For example, they might need to know the meaning of the word to understand their speaking partner or to solve a problem (deprivation-type), or they may have heard an unknown word while reading about their favorite animal (e.g., horses) and feel pleasure or satisfaction when they learn new horse-related words (interest-type). Deprivation-type curiosity is a more compelling motivator of information seeking and is easier to manipulate in an experimental context because it is not as subject to individual differences as interest-type curiosity (Jirout & Klahr, 2012). It is difficult to predict what information individual children will find interesting or pleasurable. It may be possible to use the words that children already know to predict which words individual children will be most interested in learning about.

Curiosity can be conceptualized as both a trait—some children are more curious than others, and as a state—some situations elicit more curiosity (Berlyne, 1954, 1960; Day, 1971; Jirout & Klahr, 2012). Children with higher trait levels of curiosity are more likely to explore and ask questions (Jirout, 2011). State level curiosity is dependent on the situation and could be influenced by interest in a particular topic (e.g., dinosaurs) or prior knowledge and experience with the topic. For example, mystery novels and click-bait articles are specially formulated to induce state curiosity as readers are given just enough information to be motivated to keep reading but not enough to be able to predict the resolution. Unfortunately, there are few robust measures of either state or trait level curiosity for preschool-aged children (but see Jirout & Klahr, 2011 for a promising measure). If we can determine the characteristics of and contexts in which children are curious about the meanings of words, we may be able to use this information to boost children's self-driven word learning. Lois Bloom highlighted the usefulness of focusing on children's interests and mental states to understand their motivation for word learning. This child-centered approach may be supplemented by using the construct of curiosity to predict which words children may be more curious about. Applying the information-gap theory to word learning could involve designing contexts in which the optimal level of uncertainty leads to exploratory information seeking about word meaning.

Information-Seeking Skills

Once children recognize that they do not know a word and have the inclination to do something about it they still need to seek out the information about the unknown word. One way to do this is to ask questions of knowledgeable adults. Research on information seeking in the toddler and preschool period has revealed that from early in development, children are proficient question askers (e.g., Chouinard, Harris, & Maratsos, 2007; Harris, 2012; Harris, Ronfard, & Bartz, 2016). In one study, it was estimated that children between the ages of 1 and 5 asked an average of 107 questions an hour (Chouinard et al., 2007). Children not only ask many questions, but they do so with the expectation that a particular answer will be received. For example, when 2- to 4-year-olds seek information about causes (Frazier, Gelman, & Wellman, 2009) or functional information about objects (Kemler Nelson, Egan, & Holt, 2004) they repeat or rephrase their questions if their speech partner does not provide a satisfactory response. Slightly older children also seem to understand when to ask questions versus when to seek information another way. In one study, for example, 4- to 6-year-olds were more likely to use questions to seek information about invisible object properties like preferences than visible object properties like hair color (Fitneva, Lam, & Dunfield, 2013).

At the same time, there are limits on preschoolers' question-asking ability. For one, both children's ability to identify the most knowledgeable or accurate informants and to ask useful questions increases across the preschool period (e.g., Mills, Legare, Bills, & Mejias, 2010; Mills, Legare, Grant, & Landrum, 2011). It is also not clear that children's rate of question asking generalizes across learning contexts. In particular, in contrast to the high rate of question asking revealed in corpus and diary studies (e.g., Chouinard et al., 2007; Frazier et al., 2009; Harris et al., 2016) spontaneously generating questions in experimental contexts sometimes presents challenges for preschoolers. For example, in Mills et al. (2011) 21 of 48 of the children tested were excluded from the analyses for failure to independently ask questions. Other studies included explicit modelling of question-answer conversations for children (Frazier et al., 2009; Kemler Nelson et al., 2004) or the researcher provided the questions for children (Fitneva et al., 2013). Spontaneous question asking may be more limited in experimental contexts because there are contextual constraints on children's spontaneous information seeking (familiar settings with well-known adults may elicit more unprompted questions) or because there are individual differences in the abilities that support the behavior. Another possibility is that children tend to ask questions after they have had some time to wonder about what they want to know. That is, the immediacy of the experimental contexts may not support spontaneous question asking because children have not had sufficient time to become interested or curious in asking about something.

Most previous studies on preschoolers' questions have focused on their attempts to elicit causal explanations of natural phenomena (e.g., Callanan & Oakes, 1992; Chouinard et al., 2007; Frazier et al., 2009) or information about functional properties of objects (e.g., Kemler Nelson et al., 2004). These types of explanatory questions may require deeper understanding of concepts because asking "how" and "why" questions requires that children have some base of knowledge in the domain (e.g., Bloom, Merkin, & Wootten, 1982; Callanan & Oakes, 1992). Such questions may offer a window on children's reasoning about concepts and also clarify how the input children elicit may serve to grow their concepts, making them an important focus of research.

Questions about names for things have been described as a more straightforward query in which children are seeking facts. The idea being that children need a foundation of some basic information about a concept, including, for example, the names of category members, before they can ask deeper questions about unseen, causal processes (e.g., Chouinard et al., 2007). It also seems likely that in addition to label information, it would be useful for children to seek information about the definitions of unknown words, especially when the referents are not easily depicted. As one example, a child of our acquaintance recently asked what the word "grudge," meant. Grudges are not typically things that can be easily depicted. To understand the meaning of the word "grudge," and how such feelings affect social interactions, children either need to infer the meaning from context or ask a question to determine what the word means. Because word-learning questions have been classified as fact-finding questions in previous work there is little information about the quality of these kinds of questions.

In the most comprehensive study of children's question asking to date, Chouinard et al. (2007) reported a descriptive analysis of children's questions using the CHILDES database (Study 1) and a diary study of children between the ages of 1 and 5 years (Study 2). Children across both studies tended to ask more fact-based questions than explanatory questions (though the percentage of explanatory questions increased slightly with age). The most frequent types of questions included questions about labels (described as "the name for an object, or to what a name applies"), activities of people and things, and locations of things. The proportion of questions that were classified as being about labels decreased with age, but still accounted for 12 (Study 1) to 24 (Study 2) percent of the questions children asked as they approached their fifth birthday (i.e., in the 4;6–4;11 age bracket).

The label questions category in Chouinard et al. (2007) included both questions about labels (e.g., "What's that?") and questions about "to what a name applies" (e.g., "What's a jack-o-lantern?"). Because parents' responses to specific question types were not reported (given the scope of the Chouinard et al. monograph, this is not surprising) it is unclear whether children were seeking definitions (what the word means or a description of the referent) or more straightforward referent identification (pointing or indicating a visually available referent) with their queries about what a name applied to. Regardless, these data do suggest that children's label relevant questions are common during the preschool period.

To gain a better understanding of children's questions about word meanings, we used the CHILDES database (MacWhinney & Snow, 1985) to extract questions about word meaning from 6 corpora: Adam, Abe, Ross, Naomi, Sarah, and Laura using the following sentence frames: "What is X? What's X? What does X mean? What's that called? What's X called? What it mean? What it means?" One clear

Table 5.1 Six children included in analysis from CHILDES database

Child	Corpus	Questions	Age range	Definition questions	Label questions	Questions answered	Questions repeated
Abe	Kuczaj	325	3;0–5;0	65	231	223	64
Adam	Brown	3212	2;3–5;2	29	366	275	111
Naomi	Sachs	919	1;2–4;9	5	229	155	77
Sarah	Brown	837	2;3–5;1	1	66	59	6
Ross	MacWhinney	1356	1;4–7;5	21	38	47	7
Laura	Braunwald	481	1;2–7;0	2	34	29	6

result is that there was striking variability in children's tendency to ask questions about word meanings (see Table 5.1). We focused, in particular, on questions about definitions, rather than on questions about labels (because this information is already available in previous work). Below we offer a descriptive analysis of questions asked.

Since Abe, Adam, and Ross were the children who primarily asked questions about word meaning, we focused our analysis on their questions. We coded instances in which Abe, Adam, and Ross asked about a label and then asked for the meaning of a word in the same exchange. The words that children wanted to know the meaning of were recorded and we determined if their use was abstract from the context. Finally, we recorded parents' response to children's questions about word meaning.

Questions aimed at obtaining labels were more common than those eliciting definitions, but in rare instances (accounting for 5% of word meaning questions), they occurred together in the same exchange. In the example below, Abe seeks information about a toothpick using a repeated question strategy:

> Abe (2;10): What you got in your mouth? Huh?
> Father: It's a toothpick.
> Abe: A toothpinc?
> Mother: Toothpick, can you say toothpick?
> Abe: No, I don't know how to say a toothpick. Why that's a toothpick?
> Father: It's just something that's good to chew on for a minute or two.

Abe continued to ask questions until his father provided additional information about the toothpick. In this example, his first questions suggest he was requesting a label for an unknown object. After receiving the label information, he continued to ask questions about the object until his father provided functional information about the toothpick. Adam also used this repeated question technique:

> Adam (4;4): What's dis?
> Ursula: That's not a letter. That's a sign for dividing.
> Adam: What dividing means?
> Ursula: When you have lots of things and you share them with your brother you're dividing them.

However, when children asked about the meaning of the word they usually did not ask for a label beforehand. This suggests that most of the words that children asked about were words that they heard someone say before; either in the immediate conversation context or at some other time-point. Children asked about words that were directed at them, but they also occasionally asked about words that were overheard. For example, Abe asked about a word that he heard when his mother and father were speaking:

> Mother: They had an incubator.
> Father: Oh.
> Abe(4;6): (Ex)cept what is a incubator? Mother, what is a incubator?
> Mother: it's a warm container to keep eggs in.

The words that the children asked about also changed with age. In particular, they started to ask proportionally more questions about abstract words as they got older. Of the words they asked about, the percent that were in reference to abstract versus concrete entities changed dramatically: from 5% at age 2, to 26% at age 3, to 48% at age 4, to 80% at age 5 (see Table 5.2).

In our sample of questions about labels and definitions, parents answered their children's questions about words at a high rate (72% of the time). Here is one humorous example of definition being offered to Abe:

> Abe(4;2): What did Mike get?
> Father: Tenure.
> Abe: What does tenure mean?
> Father: It means he got a good job

Sometimes they deflected the question back to their child:

> Mother: It's so peculiar.
> Adam(5;2): Peculiar! It's so peculiar?
> Mother: Yes.
> Adam: What is peculiar? I don't know what peculiar is.
> Mother: You don't? What d(o) you think it is?

Other times children made attempts to answer their own question:

> Mother: In my knowledge I don't know.
> Ross(5;0): What does knowledge mean? It means... it means ...
> Father: What does knowledge mean Ross?
> Ross: I don't know.
> Father: You were about to tell us. Don't stop now.
> Ross: Not in my mind.
> Father: Not in your mind? In your mind. Knowledge means whether it's in your mind. If it's not in your mind. Then it's not in your knowledge.

Questions aimed at obtaining labels were more common than those eliciting definitions, but in rare instances, they occurred together in the same exchange. Children asked about a variety of words. They asked about proportionally more abstract words as they grew older. Overall, parents were very responsive to their child's questions, but when children did not receive adequate responses they often repeated their question until they did. When parents did not respond to their child's questions they sometimes prompted the child to try and answer their own question, possibly encouraging even deeper thinking about word meaning. One remaining question is what factors predict children's tendency to ask questions about word meanings.

Table 5.2 A list of the words that were asked about by Abe, Adam, and Ross by age

Age	2;0–2;6	2;6–3;0	3;0–3;6	3;6–4;0	4;0–4;6	4;6–5;0	>5
Abe		Bayberry Carve Dressing Huge taco Mary Pickle Al(restaurant) Square taco Toothpick	Bladder **Boring** **Infected** Joker Recess Rubber band Tornado	Burial grounds Calvary Cauliflower Cub scouts Engineer **Exhausted** Golf Goosebumps Growth spurt **Hardly** Holiday Home Moth Oiled pastels **Order (command)** **Order (purchase)** Testicles **Something being "on"**	Barbecue Bologna Flood Minute hand Rice **Tenure** Trash	Butchwax **Do** **Field trip** **Form** Gouge Incubator **Invisible** Muscles **Shit**	
Adam	Porcupine Shower	Basketball Block for animal performing Football Salad dressing	Dairy	Arrow Brace Dotted line Gears dragon flies Lizard Molar Othello Skinned	Creepy Willy **Divide** Yoyo	**Brave** **Expression** **Marvelous** **Peace time**	Café **Peculiar**

Ross	Exercise	Both	Pensive		Misunderstand	Knowledge
	Washington	Gray			Avalanche	Ark
						Final
						As
						Monopolize
						Thirsty
						Sex
						Gesundheit (health)

Bolded words are abstract

Unpublished work from our lab conducted with Rebecca Jacobson, a former undergraduate, explored the factors that influence preschool children's questions about novel words in the context of a storybook. Forty-eight 3-to 5-year-olds were read two books by their parent or a researcher that included the mention of a novel word on every page (the referent was a *modem* in one book and a *basin* in another). The premise of the stories was that a child received an object and then took it to different places (e.g., "First, he took his *modem* to the park. Then, he took the *modem* to school."). Importantly, the novel item was mentioned, but not depicted in an illustration, so asking what the word meant was the only way for children to learn what the word meant. The words were chosen based on a questionnaire (given to parents of other, same age children) that asked parents to select words that they knew the meanings of, but that their children did not. Our measure was whether children asked about the novel word in the book (e.g., by saying "What's a basin?").

For one group of children their parent read one book and a researcher read another and for another group of children their parent read both books. Parents were asked to read the book as they would normally and both parents and the researcher answered any questions children asked. Children varied in language background (i.e., they were either monolingual or bilingual) and in vocabulary size as measured by the Peabody Picture Vocabulary Test 4 (PPVT-4).

We found that a little over one-third (37.5%) of children asked about the novel words. Fourteen children asked in one story and four children asked in both stories. The person reading the book did not seem to affect children's question asking: 11 children asked in the parent-researcher condition and 7 children asked in the parent-only condition. In the parent-researcher condition, children were not more likely to ask a parent (8 children) versus a researcher (5 children, note that these numbers include 2 children who asked both the parent and the researcher). The number of questions asked across the two conditions did not differ (t (46) = 1.19, p = 0.24). Eleven bilingual children asked about the novel word and 7 monolingual children asked about the meaning of the novel word; language background was not related to requesting information about novel words (X^2 (1, N = 48) = 2.01, p = 0.16). A logistic regression also revealed that age did not influence question asking (β = 0.03, z = 0.79, p = 0.38).

In contrast, vocabulary size did seem to matter. Children's standard scores on the PPVT were significantly related to asking behavior (β = 0.11, z = 9.1, p = 0.003). The odds ratio was 1.118 with a 95% confidence interval of [1.04, 0.1.20]—meaning that for every point increase of the standard PPVT score, children were 11.8% more likely to ask about the meaning of a novel word. The average standard PPVT score of those who asked about the meanings of words was 121.33 (SD = 10.46, range = 110–140), which was significantly higher than the average standard score of those who did not ask, 106.67 (SD = 13.32, range = 76–130), independent samples t(46) = 3.99, p < 0.001.

Because the study was correlational it is not clear why children with larger vocabularies asked more questions about word meanings. It could be that children have larger vocabulary sizes because they ask more questions. Alternatively, children with larger vocabulary sizes might have been more equipped to ask about the words that they did not know because of more robust metacognitive skills. That is, they may also be better at recognizing their lexical ignorance. This proposal gains support from previous studies that have found that metalinguistic abilities are positively correlated with vocabulary size in preschoolers (Doherty & Perner, 1998; Smith & Tager-Flusberg, 1982). It may be that as children's vocabulary grows, their ability to reason about language and meaning becomes more concrete, which enables active word learning techniques like questions about definitions.

Another possibility is that children with larger vocabularies are more curious about words that they do not know. According to the information-gap theory of curiosity, small information gaps elicit more curiosity. Preschoolers with larger vocabularies may be more likely to ask for word meanings because the gap between the words they know and the unknown words used in the study is smaller than in preschoolers with smaller vocabularies. The information-gap theory would predict that preschoolers that judge the novel words to be far outside their lexicon would not be as curious about the word meaning and would be less likely to ask a question.

We were surprised that the reader did not influence children's question asking. We expected that children would ask more questions from a reader with whom they are more familiar with. Children were equally likely to ask questions about word meaning of the parent and the researcher. One factor that might have influenced this was their expectation of receiving an answer to their questions. While researchers consistently provided an age-appropriate definition of the novel word when asked by the children (i.e., "A basin is a place to put water."), parents were instructed to read the story how they normally would. As a result, they did not always respond when their children asked questions. Thus, it is possible that the experimenter's willingness to provide definitions leads to children's increased motivation to ask questions from an unfamiliar reader. Children asked their parents about the meanings of unfamiliar words 18 times (one question was a repeat). Of these instances, just over one-third (7 of 18) received a definition in response, 6 received a response that was not a definition ("What do you think?" or "I don't see it") and in 5 cases parents simply did not respond. The types of definitions offered varied: One parent provided just a synonym definition ("It's like a bowl or a sink."), three parents provided functional definitions ("A modem is used with computers."), and two provided a combination of the two definition types ("A basin is something you can put water into. It's kind of like a bowl.") There was also one instance in which a parent provided a partial definition of the word—providing a detail about the object but no direct definition ("It's on the side of the computer at home.").

One interesting possibility is that the relatively low rates of question asking when parents read the book could have been the result of children's prior experiences having questions about word meaning answered. If children had prior experiences in which they did not receive satisfying definitions when they asked what a word meant, they might have been less likely to ask. Of course, we do not know if the parents who did not define words in this study also did not define words regularly at home. A study that carefully manipulates the quality and frequency of responses to questions about word meanings to examine the impact on children's question asking would be an important next step especially since we already know that children are more likely to ask questions at home than they are in other settings, like school (Tizard & Hughes, 1984).

Conclusion

Preschool children can be active participants in word learning. Children who know what they do not know, who have skills for seeking the missing information, and who are also interested in doing so will be the most likely to seek information about unknown word meanings. Preliminary data supports the view that children ask questions about word meaning and that their knowledge of gaps in their lexicon may be related to word learning potential. Just as children have varying levels of curiosity, they also differ in their tendency to ask questions about word meaning. Children who spontaneously ask for the meanings of words have larger vocabulary sizes than children who do not, suggesting there are benefits incurred when children have the skills for seeking word learning information. Preschoolers' questions about word meaning may facilitate vocabulary growth, especially in domains that they are very curious about.

Acknowledgements This chapter was partially supported by the National Science Foundation—Graduate Research Fellowship awarded to the first author (1445197).

References

Balcomb, F. K., & Gerken, L. (2008). Three-year-old children can access their own memory to guide responses on a visual matching task. *Developmental Science, 11*(5), 750–760. https://doi.org/10.1111/j.1467-7687.2008.00725.x

Berlyne, D. (1954). A theory of human curiosity. *British Journal of Psychology*. Retrieved from http://onlinelibrary.wiley.com/doi/10.1111/j.2044-8295.1954.tb01243.x/full

Berlyne, D. (1960). *Conflict, arousal, and curiosity.* Retrieved from http://psycnet.apa.org/psycinfo/2006-09643-000

Berlyne, D. (1966). Curiosity and exploration. *Science*. Retrieved from http://science.sciencemag.org/content/153/3731/25.short

Bloom, L. (1998). *Language acquisition in its developmental context.* Retrieved from http://psycnet.apa.org/psycinfo/2005-01927-006

Bloom, L. (2000). The intentionality model of word learning: How to learn a word any word. In R. M. Golinkoff, K. Hirsh-pasek, L. Bloom, L. B. Smith, A. L. Woodward, N. Akhtar, M. Tomasello, & G. Hollich (Eds.), *Becoming a word learner: A debate on lexical acquisition* (pp. 1–21). Oxford, England: Oxford University Press. https://doi.org/10.1093/acprof:oso/9780195130324.003.002

Bloom, P. (2000). *How children learn the meanings of words.* Retrieved from http://psycnet.apa.org/psycinfo/2000-07540-000

Bloom, L., Margulis, C., Tinker, E., & Fujita, N. (1996). Early conversations and word learning : Contributions from child and adult. *Child Development, 67*(6), 3154–3175.

Bloom, L., Merkin, S., & Wootten, J. (1982). "Wh" -questions : Linguistic factors that contribute to the sequence of acquisition. *Child Development, 53*(4), 1084–1092.

Bloom, L., Tinker, E., & Kofsky Scholnick, E. (2001). The intentionality model and language acquisition: Engagement, effort, and the essential tension in development. *Monographs of the Society for Research in Child Development, 66*, 104–119.

Bonawitz, E. B., van Schijndel, T. J. P., Friel, D., & Schulz, L. (2012). Children balance theories and evidence in exploration, explanation, and learning. *Cognitive Psychology, 64*(4), 215–234. https://doi.org/10.1016/j.cogpsych.2011.12.002

Brown, A. (1978). Knowing when, where and, how to remember: A problem of metacognition. *Advances in Instructional Psychology*. Retrieved from http://ci.nii.ac.jp/naid/10012502747/

Callanan, M. A., & Oakes, L. M. (1992). Preschoolers' questions and parents' explanations: Causal thinking in everyday activity. *Cognitive Development, 7*(2), 213–233. https://doi.org/10.1016/0885-2014(92)90012-G

Cantor, J., & Cantor, G. (1964). Children's observing behavior as related to amount and recency of stimulus familiarization. *Journal of Experimental Child Psychology*. Retrieved from http://www.sciencedirect.com/science/article/pii/0022096564900396

Cartmill, E. A., Armstrong, B. F., Gleitman, L. R., Goldin-Meadow, S., Medina, T. N., & Trueswell, J. C. (2013). Quality of early parent input predicts child vocabulary 3 years later. *Proceedings of the National Academy of Sciences of the United States of America, 110*(28), 11278–11283. https://doi.org/10.1073/pnas.1309518110

Charlesworth, W. (1964). Instigation and maintenance of curiosity behavior as a function of surprise versus novel and familiar stimuli. *Child Development*. Retrieved from http://www.jstor.org/stable/1126863

Chouinard, M. M., Harris, P. L., & Maratsos, M. P. (2007). Children's questions: A mechanism for cognitive development. *Monographs of the Society for Research in Child Development, 50*(1), 1–129. Retrieved from http://discovery.ucl.ac.uk/134227/

Coughlin, C., Hembacher, E., Lyons, K. E., & Ghetti, S. (2014). Introspection on uncertainty and judicious help-seeking during the preschool years. *Developmental Science, 18*(6), 957–971. https://doi.org/10.1111/desc.12271

Day, H. (1971). *Intrinsic motivation: A new direction in education*. Retrieved from https://eric.ed.gov/?id=ED067324

Doherty, M., & Perner, J. (1998). Metalinguistic awareness and theory of mind: Just two words for the same thing? *Cognitive Development, 13*(3), 279–305. https://doi.org/10.1016/S0885-2014(98)90012-0

Fitneva, S. A., Lam, N. H. L., & Dunfield, K. A. (2013). The development of children's information gathering: To look or to ask? *Developmental Psychology, 49*(3), 533–542. https://doi.org/10.1037/a0031326

Flavell, J. H. (1979). Metacognition and cognitive monitoring: A new area of cognitive–developmental inquiry. *American Psychologist, 34*(10), 906–911. https://doi.org/10.1037/0003-066x.34.10.906

Flavell, J. H., Friedrichs, A. G., & Hoyt, J. D. (1970). Developmental changes in memorization processes. *Cognitive Psychology, 1*(4), 324–340. https://doi.org/10.1016/0010-0285(70)90019-8

Frazier, B. N., Gelman, S. A., & Wellman, H. M. (2009). Preschoolers' search for explanatory information within adult–child conversation. *Child Development, 80*(6), 1592–1611.

Ghetti, S., Hembacher, E., & Coughlin, C. A. (2013). Feeling uncertain and acting on it during the preschool years: A metacognitive approach. *Child Development Perspectives, 7*(3), 160–165. https://doi.org/10.1111/cdep.12035

Golinkoff, R. M., Can, D. D., Soderstrom, M., & Hirsh-Pasek, K. (2015). (Baby)Talk to me: The social context of infant directed speech and its effects on early language acquisition. *Current Directions in Psychological Science, 24*(5), 339–344. https://doi.org/10.1177/0963721415595345

Greene, F. (1964). Effect of novelty on choices made by preschool children in a simple discrimination task. *Child Development*. Retrieved from http://www.jstor.org/stable/1126871

Harris, P. (2012). *Trusting what you're told: How children learn from others*. Retrieved from https://books.google.com/books?hl=en&lr=&id=pD8aUdt6bFEC&oi=fnd&pg=PP6&dq=harris+2012+information+seeking&ots=Z5SgvAXlxL&sig=53zdbOa-QNBxsaVK9DCUnhyBWSs

Harris, P. L., Ronfard, S., & Bartz, D. (2016). Young children's developing conception of knowledge and ignorance: Work in progress. *European Journal of Developmental Psychology, 5629*, 1–12. https://doi.org/10.1080/17405629.2016.1190267

Hembacher, E., & Ghetti, S. (2014). Don't look at my answer: Subjective uncertainty underlies preschoolers' exclusion of their least accurate memories. *Psychological Science, 25*(9), 1768–1776. https://doi.org/10.1177/0956797614542273

Hresko, W., Reid, D., & Hamill, D. (1999). Test of Early Language Development-3 (TELD-3). Austin, TX: PRO-ED.

Hollich, G., Hirsh-Pasek, K., & Golinkoff, R. M. (2000). Breaking the languate barrier: An emergentist coalition model for the origins of word learning. *Monographs of the Society for Research in Child Development, 66*, 104–119.

Jirout, J., & Klahr, D. (2011). *Children's questions asking and curiosity: A training study. Conference abstract template.*

Jirout, J., & Klahr, D. (2012). Children's scientific curiosity: In search of an operational definition of an elusive concept. *Developmental Review, 32*(2), 125–160. https://doi.org/10.1016/j.dr.2012.04.002

Jirout, J. J. (2011). *Curiosity and the development of question generation skills.* In *Papers from the 2011 AAAI* (pp. 27–30).

Kemler Nelson, D. G., Egan, L. C., & Holt, M. B. (2004). When children ask, "what is it?" what do they want to know about artifacts? *Psychological Science, 15*(6), 384–389. https://doi.org/10.1111/j.0956-7976.2004.00689.x

Kidd, C., & Hayden, B. Y. (2015). The psychology and neuroscience of curiosity. *Neuron, 88*(3), 449–460. https://doi.org/10.1016/j.neuron.2015.09.010

Kidd, C., Piantadosi, S., & Aslin, R. (2012). The Goldilocks effect: Human infants allocate attention to visual sequences that are neither too simple nor too complex. *PloS One.* Retrieved from http://journals.plos.org/plosone/article?id=10.1371/journal.pone.0036399

Lipowski, S. L., & Merriman, W. E. (2011). Knowledge judgments and object memory processes in early childhood: Support for the dual criterion account of object nameability judgment. *Journal of Cognition and Development, 12*(4), 481–501. https://doi.org/10.1080/15248372.2010.544694

Lipowski, S. L., Merriman, W. E., & Dunlosky, J. (2012). Preschoolers can make highly accurate judgments of learning. *Developmental Psychology, 49*(8), 1505–1516. https://doi.org/10.1037/a0030614

Litman, J. (2005). Curiosity and the pleasures of learning: Wanting and liking new information. *Cognition & Emotion.* Retrieved from http://www.tandfonline.com/doi/abs/10.1080/02699930541000101

Litman, J., & Jimerson, T. (2004). The measurement of curiosity as a feeling of deprivation. *Journal of Personality Assessment.* Retrieved from http://www.tandfonline.com/doi/abs/10.1207/s15327752jpa8202_3

Loewenstein, G. (1994). Psychology of curiosity: A review and reinterpretation. *Psychological Bulletin, 116*(1), 75–98.

Lyons, K. E., & Ghetti, S. (2011). The development of uncertainty monitoring in early childhood. *Child Development, 82*(6), 1778–1787. https://doi.org/10.1111/j.1467-8624.2011.01649.x

Lyons, K. E., & Ghetti, S. (2013). I don't want to pick! Introspection on uncertainty supports early strategic behavior. *Child Development, 84*(2), 726–736. https://doi.org/10.1111/cdev.12004

MacWhinney, B., & Snow, C. (1985). The child language data exchange system. *Journal of Child Language.* Retrieved from https://www.cambridge.org/core/journals/journal-of-child-language/article/child-language-data-exchange-system/914F419D804ECA0C726F0C08E7E3C094

Marazita, J. M., & Merriman, W. E. (2004). Young children's judgment of whether they know names for objects: The metalinguistic ability it reflects and the processes it involves. *Journal of Memory and Language, 51*(3), 458–472. https://doi.org/10.1016/j.jml.2004.06.008

Merriman, W. E., & Lipko, A. R. (2008). A dual criterion account of the development of linguistic judgment in early childhood. *Journal of Memory and Language, 58*, 1012–1031. https://doi.org/10.1016/j.jml.2007.10.003

Merriman, W. E., & Marazita, J. M. (2004). Young children's awareness of their own lexical ignorance: Relations to word mapping, memory processes, and beliefs about change detection. In *Thinking and Seeing: Visual metacognition in adults and children* (pp. 57–74).

Merriman, W. E., & Schuster, J. M. (1991). Young children's disambiguation of object name reference. *Child Development, 62*(6), 1288–1301.

Mills, C. M., Legare, C. H., Bills, M., & Mejias, C. (2010). Preschoolers use questions as a tool to acquire knowledge from different sources. *Journal of Cognition and Development, 11*, 533–560. https://doi.org/10.1080/15248372.2010.516419

Mills, C. M., Legare, C. H., Grant, M. G., & Landrum, A. R. (2011). Determining who to question, what to ask, and how much information to ask for: The development of inquiry in young children. *Journal of Experimental Child Psychology, 110*(4), 539–560. https://doi.org/10.1016/j.jecp.2011.06.003

Mittman, L., & Terrell, G. (1964). An experimental study of curiosity in children. *Child Development*. Retrieved from http://www.jstor.org/stable/1126510

Saylor, M., Baldwin, D., & Sabbagh, M. (2004). Converging on word meaning. *Weaving a Lexicon*.

Shneidman, L., & Woodward, A. L. (2016). Are child-directed interactions the cradle of social learning? *Psychological Bulletin, 142*(1), 1–17. https://doi.org/10.1037/bul0000023

Smith, C. L., & Tager-Flusberg, H. (1982). Metalinguistic awareness and language development. *Journal of Experimental Child Psychology, 34*, 449–468. https://doi.org/10.1016/0022-0965(82)90071-6

Smock, C., & Holt, B. (1962). Children's reactions to novelty: An experimental study of 'Curiosity Motivation'. *Child Development*. Retrieved from http://www.jstor.org/stable/1126663

Tamis-LeMonda, C., & Bornstein, M. (2001). Maternal responsiveness and children's achievement of language milestones. *Child*. Retrieved from http://onlinelibrary.wiley.com/doi/10.1111/1467-8624.00313/full

Tamis-LeMonda, C. S., Kuchirko, Y., & Song, L. (2014). Why is infant language learning facilitated by parental responsiveness? *Current Directions in Psychological Science, 23*(2), 121–126. https://doi.org/10.1177/0963721414522813

Tare, M., & Gelman, S. A. (2010). Determining that a label is kind-referring: Factors that influence children's and adults' novel word extensions. *Journal of Child Language, 37*(5), 1007–1026. https://doi.org/10.1017/S0305000909990134

Tizard, B., & Hughes, M. (1984). *Young children learning*. Cambridge, MA: Harvard University Press.

Tomasello, M., & Farrar, M. J. (1986). Joint attention and early language. *Child Development, 57*(6), 1454–1463. https://doi.org/10.2307/1130423

Trueswell, J., Lin, Y., Armstrong, B., & Cartmill, E. (2016). Perceiving referential intent: Dynamics of reference in natural parent–child interactions. *Cognition*. Retrieved from http://www.sciencedirect.com/science/article/pii/S0010027715301013

Waxman, S., & Gelman, S. (2010). Different kinds of concepts and different kinds of words: What words do for human cognition. *The Making of Human Concepts*. Retrieved from https://books.google.com/books?hl=en&lr=&id=GDijCnSs57gC&oi=fnd&pg=PA99&ots=W1hUu4_b3f&sig=XU0N0LJN5Fbjes-7RzD-_6n5zEA

Chapter 6
Understanding When and How Explanation Promotes Exploration

Judith H. Danovitch and Candice M. Mills

Abstract Receiving and generating explanations is fundamental to children's acquisition of scientific concepts. Explanations not only support conceptual change, but they can also promote further exploration and learning. For explanations to lead to exploration, children must first recognize when the explanations that they encounter are faulty or unsatisfactory. Recognizing gaps in explanatory knowledge is a powerful motivator for children's interest in seeking out additional information to fill those gaps. However, not all children react to explanations in the same way. The likelihood of engaging in exploration may reflect individual differences in children's background knowledge and their willingness to incorporate new information into their existing beliefs. Children's responses to explanations may also be influenced by their prior experiences at home, and in their society. Understanding when and how explanations lead to exploration has important implications for education, particularly in the sciences.

Introduction

Simple observation is insufficient to meet children's learning needs or to satisfy their curiosity. To gather information about the world, children begin asking questions at a very early age (Chouinard, 2007). Although asking questions may sometimes serve as a form of amusement or a means of initiating a social interaction, children appear to be genuinely motivated to obtain answers (e.g., Frazier, Gelman, &

J. H. Danovitch (✉)
Department of Psychological and Brain Sciences, University of Louisville,
Louisville, KY, USA
e-mail: j.danovitch@louisville.edu

C. M. Mills
School of Behavioral and Brain Sciences, The University of Texas at Dallas,
Richardson, TX, USA

© Springer International Publishing AG, part of Springer Nature 2018
M. M. Saylor, P. A. Ganea (eds.), *Active Learning from Infancy to Childhood*,
https://doi.org/10.1007/978-3-319-77182-3_6

Wellman, 2009). In fact, asking effective questions is critical for children's problem-solving success (Mills, Legare, Grant, & Landrum, 2011). Some questions, such as those beginning with "who," "what," "when," or "where," result in the production of bounded facts. These types of questions can often be effectively answered with a single word or phrase indicating what something is called, where it is located, etc. Other types of questions, such as those beginning with "why" or "how," require more complex causal explanations to be answered satisfactorily. Effective explanations provide an insight into how the world works, but sometimes explanations serve an additional purpose: motivating children to learn more through exploration.

Legare (2014) proposes that explanation and exploration work in tandem, such that being prompted to explain provokes reflection on what one knows or does not know, which prompts exploration. Exploration can then lead to a revised explanation. Legare's work focuses on evidence that when children are learning about simple physical mechanisms (e.g., which kinds of objects activate a machine), their attempts to explain these mechanisms can motivate exploration in the form of hypothesis testing. Extending this argument, we propose that, in the process of learning scientific concepts, there is likely to be a relationship between explanation and exploration. In short, we posit that children use explanations to identify what they do not know, and then engage in exploration to address those gaps in their knowledge. Indeed, Lombrozo and her colleagues (Williams & Lombrozo, 2013; Lombrozo & Vasilyeva, 2017) have argued that explanations lead to learning not just due to increased attention or engagement with the material at hand, but due to the way they increase our motivation to learn. Having a question of interest helpfully explained leads to a sense of satisfaction, while an unhelpful explanation may leave us wanting; thus, we may continue to seek out information until we acquire explanations that lead to a sense of satisfaction (see also Gopnik, 1998, 2000). In many cases, this is an iterative process where children repeatedly ask questions, receive explanations, and follow up with further questions. Yet, the parameters of this process—how often it occurs, how closely spaced the questions are over time, etc.—may vary widely depending on the situation or topic.

In this chapter, we describe how receiving, evaluating, and generating explanations contributes not only to the development of conceptual knowledge, but also to children's interest in exploring and learning more about the world. Explanations that are accurate and at an appropriate level of depth facilitate learning (Wilson & Keil, 1998). However, when a strong explanation is not provided or is not available, we propose that a weak explanation prompts children's interest in learning if the following criteria are met: (a) the listener recognizes that there is more to be learned, either because the explanation is faulty or because it lacks a satisfactory level of accuracy or depth, (b) the listener's primary response to observing a knowledge gap is to feel driven to learn more, and (c) the listener is open to new information and is in a social environment that supports further learning. Below, we describe evidence supporting the role of each of these criteria in creating a pathway from explanation to exploration.

Recognizing Faulty Explanations

Explanations go beyond simply answering specific questions; they provide information that can prompt the recipient to form or to alter their understanding of how some aspect of the world works (Keil, 2006; Wellman, 2011). Much of the existing research on explanations has focused on the roles they play in developing an understanding of scientific concepts. For instance, explanations can provide insight that constrains causal inferences (see Lombrozo, 2006). Thus, learning that the sun is the center of the solar system precludes the consideration of geocentric theories as explanations for the movement of the stars in the sky. Explanations can also provide information that can be used for generalization to new exemplars. For example, an explanation that the heart keeps humans alive by conveying nutrients to the body can form the basis for understanding that the heart serves a similar function in other animals (Gutheil, Vera, & Keil, 1998). Indeed, explanations facilitate conceptual understanding even in situations where information is readily available. For instance, children may observe a phenomenon directly (e.g., balls fall down when you drop them) but still require a teacher's explanation to understand causation in a way that allows them to apply the same causal principles to other situations (e.g., predicting that other objects will fall at the same rate due to gravity, despite differing weights). Thus, explanations can potentially elevate a response from merely an answer to a catalyst for conceptual change. However, explanations vary in their quality, and sometimes a statement can sound like an explanation without providing any new information. Keil (2006) has delineated three basic criteria by which explanations are judged: relevance, coherence, and circularity. Here, we review how children come to discern if an explanation does not meet one or more of these criteria.

In its most basic form, meeting the first criterion of relevance means that an explanation provides direct information in response to the question or topic being explained. One way of measuring whether children are sensitive to an explanation's relevance is to examine whether children respond differently to responses that provide information that addresses a "how" or "why" question—even if that information is simple—than responses that do not. To understand this issue, Frazier et al. (2009) examined how preschool-aged children react to two categories of responses to children's questions: non-explanations and explanations. Non-explanations are statements that acknowledge a child's question but do not provide information that answers it. For instance, after seeing a picture of a turtle in a bird's nest, a child might ask, "Why is that turtle in that nest?" Non-explanations could include repetition of the question (e.g., "Yes, there is a turtle in that bird's nest."), descriptions that relate to the question (e.g., "That turtle is green."), personal opinions (e.g., "I don't like turtles."), or references to normative information (e.g., "Turtles aren't usually in nests."). In contrast, explanations provide some kind of causal response, even if that response is basic (e.g., "I think the turtle crawled in there by mistake."). Research examining parent–child conversations in naturalistic settings as well as children's behavior in laboratory settings has found that when preschool-aged children receive non-explanatory answers to their questions, they often repeat the original question, suggesting that they realize their question has not been answered (Frazier et al., 2009; Kurkul & Corriveau, 2017). Conversely, when children receive an explanation, they are more likely to agree or to ask a follow-up question. Thus, children's responses suggest that they are searching for explanations that are not just statements about the topic at hand (e.g., turtles), but that also provide some piece of information that is relevant to their question.

Returning to Keil's (2006) criteria for judging explanations, to meet the second criterion of coherence, an explanation cannot suffer from logical or structural problems that result in the explanation providing little to no new causal information. In early work by Osherson and Markman (1975), children under age 8 had difficulty recognizing that contradictory statements such as "the chip in my hand is white and it is not white" are necessarily false. However, more recent work suggests that children's ability to evaluate coherence may depend on the context in which the statements are presented. Children as young as 4 recognize that an informant who makes logically inconsistent statements does not "make sense" as much as an informant who makes logically consistent statements, yet children have difficulty evaluating the same statements when they are presented as coming from books rather than people (Doebel, Rowell, & Koenig, 2016). Likewise, when statements are presented individually, the ability to recognize whether explanations lack coherence appears to emerge more slowly. For instance, by age 6, children recognize when explanations produced by an individual suffer from logical inconsistencies (e.g., stating that a box is empty and contains an object at the same time; Ruffman, 1999; Morris & Hasson, 2010). That said, even 12-year-olds still show some difficulty recognizing logically inconsistent information when it is embedded within an essay, suggesting that context and task demands still influence children's ability to evaluate explanation coherence in the later elementary school years (Markman, 1979).

As for Keil's (2006) criterion of circularity, research examining evaluations of circular explanations, or explanations that repeat the information in the original question without providing any meaningful new information, has shown that even young children can detect circularity in some circumstances. When evaluating two individuals' explanations for familiar concepts (e.g., why it rains) or statements of a person's knowledge about a specific event (e.g., the location of a lost dog), preschoolers show some sensitivity to circular versus noncircular explanations (Corriveau & Kurkul, 2014; Mercier, Bernard, & Clément, 2014). In addition, by age 5, children indicate that individuals who provide noncircular explanations for less familiar biological and physical phenomena (e.g., how sleeping pills work) are more knowledgeable than individuals who provide circular ones, even if the lengths of the explanations are the same (Baum, Danovitch, & Keil, 2008). However, it is important to note that these studies all involve scenarios that pit circular explanations directly against noncircular ones. This design may make it easier for children to compare and recognize the circular explanations. A recent study from our labs (Mills, Danovitch, Rowles, & Campbell, 2017) compared children's ability to recognize the weakness of circular explanations when those explanations were presented in direct contrast to a noncircular explanation for the same question, or in isolation. We found that even though children were capable of identifying circular explanations as inferior to noncircular ones by age 5, they did not consistently evaluate single circular explanations as weak until age 7 or later. Thus, for both coherence and circularity, how well children recognize faulty explanations appears to be contingent on how the explanation is presented.

Determining if an Explanation Is Satisfactory

In many ways, the aforementioned research focuses on whether the explanation itself is worthy of further evaluation. A child must reflect on the response to a "how" or "why" question to judge if the answer is relevant, does not contradict itself (i.e., is coherent), and provides some kind of new information (i.e., is not circular). But the research does not examine how children respond to the actual content of the explanation, such as whether the explanation fits with what the child already knows and whether the level of detail is sufficient. We propose that once an explanation is determined to meet Keil's (2006) criteria, evaluation of the explanation shifts to focusing on satisfaction with the explanation.

One aspect of satisfaction relates to accuracy: does the explanation seem to fit with one's knowledge about the world? Preschool-aged children can use their existing knowledge to detect when a statement is blatantly false (e.g., Koenig, Clément, & Harris, 2004) and, by age 5, children recognize that bizarre or nonsensical explanations (e.g., an explanation that an animal keeps cool by buying ice at the store) are not effective (Mills et al., 2017). So at times, children can certainly recognize inaccurate explanations. Of course, there are sometimes issues in detecting inaccuracy, which we will return to later.

Another aspect of satisfaction relates to depth: does the explanation provide an appropriate amount of information? Notably, the parameters determining when children do or do not show satisfaction with an explanation (i.e., they stop asking follow-up questions) have only recently begun to be explored. When considering whether an explanation is satisfactory, it is important to keep in mind that scientific explanations typically have an iterative structure, such that there are always greater levels of detail to be explored (e.g., Keil, 2006). For example, a reasonable response to the question of how a bee makes honey is that the bee gathers nectar from flowers, takes the nectar back to the hive, and produces honey from it. This answer may be entirely accurate, yet it omits certain details about the causal mechanisms, such as how the bee carries the nectar to the hive or what processes transform the nectar into honey. Moreover, even if these details were included, there are still further levels of causal information that could be provided (e.g., how do the enzymes in the bee's honey stomach alter the chemical structure of the nectar). This characteristic of scientific explanations raises the question of whether there is an optimum level of depth where the explanation is satisfying, but not excessive.

A recent study by Frazier, Gelman, and Wellman (2016) examined whether there is a length and level of detail that characterizes the explanations children and adults find most satisfactory. In this study, preschool-aged children were presented with unusual or unexpected situations (e.g., a person pouring ketchup on ice cream) and provided with a non-explanation or an explanation. The explanations were either short with minimal causal information (e.g., "It was a mistake"), of moderate length with an intermediate level of information ("It was a mistake because she thought it was chocolate"), or long with elaborate causal information ("It was a mistake because she thought it was chocolate, because the ketchup and chocolate bottles look similar.") Both children and adults found all three types of explanations more satisfactory than non-explanations, and they were more satisfied with the moderate length explanation than the short one. However, the inclusion of additional causal information in the long explanation did not increase participants' satisfaction beyond the moderate length explanation. Frazier and her colleagues also found that children were also most likely to accurately recall the first causal statement in the explanation (e.g., "because she thought it was chocolate"). This suggests that children's level of satisfaction with an explanation and their retention of the information are linked, and that more detail does not correspond to increased satisfaction beyond a certain point. Similarly, this finding suggests that there may be a "sweet spot" for explanation depth. Wilson and Keil (1998) propose that it is often adaptive for adults to have relatively shallow explanatory knowledge about scientific mechanisms: there are too many scientific concepts for one person to know everything in great detail, and in many cases, a skeletal understanding is enough to satisfy everyday needs. Frazier et al.'s findings suggest that children are sensitive to the amount of detail that is optimal in terms of their understanding and memory. We propose that this sensitivity to depth is an important factor in determining when children seek out additional information as well.

The research discussed thus far involves how children evaluate explanations and, in particular, recognize when they are weak or lack detail. It suggests that by the preschool years, children are capable of recognizing explanations that violate the basic criteria of relevance, coherence, and circularity, and that they prefer explanations of moderate depth. That said, children's ability to evaluate explanations continues to improve over the elementary school years, particularly in instances when explanations are presented in isolation (which is frequently the case in real life situations). Although little work has examined the mechanisms that underlie children's developing ability to evaluate explanations, Doebel et al. (2016) provide some evidence that recognizing logical inconsistencies is linked to children's executive function and working memory skills. Doebel et al.'s results also include a statistical trend pointing toward a relation between verbal knowledge and recognizing logical inconsistency (see also Ruffman, 1999). Mills et al. (2017) find a similar trend for a relation between verbal intelligence and recognizing circularity. Further research is needed to examine these relations and to better understand the role that executive function, language, and other cognitive skills may play in the development of explanation evaluation abilities.

Recognizing Gaps in Self-Explanations

Thus far, we have demonstrated that children are able to recognize structural weaknesses in the explanations they receive or when the explanations they receive are not satisfactory. In many cases, however, explanations are not received from others but rather they are generated based on one's existing knowledge. Both explanations generated oneself (i.e., "self-explanations") and explanations provided by others (i.e., "other-explanations") have been shown to support children's learning. For example, Crowley and Siegler (1999) found that, when learning strategies for playing a game, explanations facilitated children's ability to generalize what they had learned regardless of whether the explanation was generated by the experimenter or by the child. Generating explanations has also been shown to improve the acquisition of procedural and conceptual knowledge. For example, eighth graders who were prompted to self-explain newly learned information about how the circulatory system works were better able to integrate new information with existing knowledge and to form accurate mental models than children who studied the information for more time (Chi, de Leeuw, Chiu, & LaVancher, 1994).

Self-explanations appear to have benefits for young children's learning as well. In one set of studies, 3- to 6-year-old children were asked to explain, observe, or verbally describe how a machine worked (Legare & Lombrozo, 2014). Children who provided explanations outperformed those who did not in terms of their conceptual understanding of the machine and their ability to generalize their understanding to new exemplars. Moreover, there is evidence that even when children's self-explanations are incorrect, they can still be helpful. For example, preschool children who were prompted to explain why contact with a block did or did not trigger a device to play music later made richer inductive inferences than children who were asked to simply report whether the block had triggered the music, regardless of whether the children's explanations were accurate (Walker, Lombrozo, Legare, & Gopnik, 2014). Likewise, five-year-olds who were randomly assigned to explain a gardening problem were more likely to make sophisticated judgments about the cause of the problem than children who were prompted to report the problem but not to explain it, and this was true even when the children's explanations were incorrect (Walker, Bonawitz, & Lombrozo, 2017). However, in this study, generating an explanation had no effect on the performance of children younger or older than 5. Based on these findings, Walker and her colleagues propose that there may be developmentally driven "windows of opportunity" where explaining is a particularly effective scaffold for learning. The timing and duration of these windows may be based on a number of factors, including a child's background knowledge and cognitive skills.

Building on these findings, we suggest that to understand how self-explanations relate to subsequent learning, it is also necessary to consider how children come to recognize that their self-explanations are faulty, lack depth or have gaps. Recognizing weaknesses in one's own explanatory knowledge and abilities is challenging for both children and adults. Indeed, children and adults tend to overestimate how well they can provide causal explanations of familiar mechanisms. Rozenblit and Keil (2002) describe this experience as the *illusion of explanatory depth*. For example, when asked to rate how well they can explain how a toaster works, adults tend to rate themselves fairly highly. Children also rate themselves highly, with younger children being even more optimistic than older children and adults about the depth and accuracy of their knowledge (Mills & Keil, 2004). Importantly, though, when children and adults are subsequently prompted to actually explain how a toaster works, providing an explanation (which often has glaring gaps or inconsistencies) leads them to drop in their ratings of the quality of their knowledge, as the explanation causes them to realize the shortcomings of their knowledge and become aware of their over-confidence.

Although there is evidence that children's self-evaluations become more realistic as they grow older, there is also variability among individuals. One factor that appears to influence how accurately children and adults evaluate their own explanations is how much they already know about the topic. There is a substantial literature demonstrating that adults who know less about a topic are also less likely to be aware of their ignorance (i.e., the Dunning-Kruger effect; see Dunning, 2011), and there is recent evidence that by ages 6 and 7, children also show an inverse relation between knowledge and self-evaluation (Danovitch, Fisher, Schroder, Hambrick, & Moser, 2017). That said, formal education does not necessarily lead to accurate assessment of one's own knowledge. For instance, adults who have studied a topic for their college major (e.g., a biology major studying the Krebs cycle) may overestimate their knowledge on the topic years after they have taken a class, appearing to forget that just because they knew something once does not mean that they will always know it (Fisher & Keil, 2015).

Taken together, these findings suggest that recognizing the gaps in their own understanding is more difficult for children than recognizing gaps in the explanations provided by others. Related to this idea, Mercier (2016) has proposed an "argumentative theory of reasoning" that focuses on the central idea that the main function of reasoning is to convince others of ideas. According to this theory, there is an asymmetry in reasoning: we are far better at evaluating arguments provided by others and recognizing in what ways they are wrong than at producing strong arguments ourselves. Thus, when children generate an explanation by themselves and have to evaluate it on their own (i.e., without feedback from others), it may be more difficult for children to acknowledge the limitations of their understanding than if they hear the same explanation from another person.

Nevertheless, the evidence to date suggests that even young children can, under some circumstances, accurately evaluate the quality of the explanations they hear from others as well those they generate themselves. Although children and adults show a clear preference for having some explanation over none at all, they are often satisfied with very skeletal explanations. This raises an important question: Under what circumstances *do* children seek out additional information after receiving an explanation?

When Do Explanations Prompt Exploration?

We approach the question of when and why explanations lead to exploration by examining under what circumstances children demonstrate a desire to acquire more information after receiving or generating an explanation. Frazier et al. (2009) demonstrated that preschoolers respond differently to non-explanations than explanations, in that children will continue to ask questions to receive relevant information when they receive irrelevant explanations, but they are more likely to seek out additional information when they receive relevant explanations. Thus, children's exploratory behaviors seem to be influenced by the type of explanation they have received.

As noted earlier, good explanations support learning (Wilson & Keil, 1998) and can spark conversations and provoke follow-up questions (e.g., Crowley & Callanan, 1998; Callanan & Jipson, 2001). However, providing good explanations can be challenging. Adults do not always know the answers to children's questions and cannot necessarily obtain them. Although we are not suggesting that adults should deliberately provide children with weak explanations, we propose that weak explanations can still hold benefits for learning by provoking exploration.

To better understand the consequences of receiving weak explanations on exploration, recent studies from our labs have investigated the relation between recognizing that one has received a weak explanation and showing interest in acquiring more information. In an initial study (Mills et al., 2017), 6-, 8-, and 10-year-olds were presented with questions about the behaviors of eight unfamiliar animals (e.g., Why does the echidna curl up into a ball?). For each question, a circular and noncircular explanation were prepared. Circular explanations were explanations that reiterated the information in the original question without adding any meaningful new information or providing a plausible causal mechanism (e.g., The echidna curls up into a ball because its body makes that shape when it rolls up), whereas noncircular explanations were causal explanations that provided some meaningful new information (e.g., The echidna curls up into a ball because that shields its soft belly from harm). After rating the quality of the circular and noncircular explanations, children were given the opportunity to take home information cards for each of the animals they encountered during the study. Children were offered the opportunity to take as many or as few cards home with them as they desired, and we treated their decision to do so as a signal of their intention to further explore the relevant animal.

There was a significant negative correlation between the average ratings that each of the 8- and 10-year-old children assigned to the circular explanations, and the number of animal cards each child chose to take home at the end of the study. This suggests that children who recognize that they have received a weak explanation show greater interest in acquiring more information. A second study using a new set of questions and an expanded set of animal cards replicated the link between recognizing circular explanations as weak and showing greater interest in learning among children ages 5–10. There is also some evidence that children are more likely to request additional information for explanations they themselves think are weak over ones they think are strong, even if their judgments do not necessarily match the judgments of others (Sands, Mills, Rowles, & Campbell, 2017). Taken together, these findings suggest that encountering weak explanations can motivate children to want to learn more about a scientific topic, but perhaps *only* if children are aware that the explanation they encountered was weak. Further research is needed to better understand whether interest in learning is tied to explicit awareness of weak explanations, or whether an implicit sense that an explanation is weak or faulty is sufficient.

If recognizing weaknesses in other-explanations promotes exploration, then one might posit that recognizing weaknesses in self-generated explanations should also lead to increased exploration. A recent study from our labs (Williams, Danovitch, & Mills, 2015) addressed this possibility. In this study, children ages 5–10 rated how well they could answer explanatory questions about device functions (e.g., how does a toaster work?) and animal behaviors (e.g., how does a bee make honey?). Then children were asked to give an explanation for half of the items, and re-rated their understanding of those items. After generating each post-explanation rating, children rated their interest in learning more about the device or animal using a separate scale.

Unlike research with other-explanations, we found a significant *positive* correlation between how children rated their knowledge after providing a self-explanation and their interest in learning more. In other words, children who showed some awareness of the shortcomings of their understanding (i.e., gave themselves lower ratings on average) were *less* likely to report interest in additional learning. This finding suggests the possibility that self-explanation may actually diminish exploration, at least under some circumstances. There may be a different pathway from explanation to exploration when children evaluate their own explanatory knowledge than when they evaluate explanations generated by other people. Recognizing explanation gaps may prompt elementary school-aged children to be less interested in learning more about that topic, perhaps due to feeling embarrassed or self-conscious in front of another person. That said, this line of research is still early in development, and further studies are needed to understand how the act of explaining relates to interest in learning.

Personal Influences on Explanation and Exploration

So far, we have discussed how children evaluate explanations, and how recognizing that there are gaps in the explanations that they have received may prompt exploration. Yet the pathway from explanation to exploration can vary, in part because of individual differences that may influence whether a particular child is likely to engage in exploration.

One factor that may influence whether explanation leads to exploration is the child's prior level of interest and familiarity with the topic at hand. By preschool, children express different levels of interest in science-related topics and may experience varying levels of family support for those interests (Alexander, Johnson, & Kelley, 2012). Moreover, there is evidence that familiarity with a topic influences children's explanation preferences. For instance, children ages 5–7 are more selective and adult-like in their preferences when choosing between biological explanations at varying levels of generality, but they do not distinguish between physics explanations in the same manner (Johnston, Sheskin, Johnson, & Keil, 2017). This may be because children are more familiar with the domain of biology, and therefore have a more clear sense of what types of new information are likely to be most useful. We propose that explanation quality, familiarity, and interest interact to determine whether children find an explanation satisfactory as well as whether they subsequently want to learn more. In other words, recognizing that there is a weakness or gap in the explanations one has received may be necessary but not sufficient to prompt exploration. If children are not familiar enough with the domain to know that there is a gap, or if they are simply not interested in the domain, then they are unlikely to invest energy in learning more. Their interest in learning more may also be linked to their understanding of the learning process itself (see Sobel and Letourneau, in Press).

Willingness to revise one's existing beliefs may also predict whether explanations lead to further learning and exploration. At times, children show remarkable resistance to new information (Woolley & Ghossainy, 2013), and this resistance appears to be rooted in their existing beliefs. As Shtulman (2017) has argued, both children and adults are prone to being so certain that their initial theories about the world are correct that they resist accepting new explanations. For example, in discussing the behaviors that the brain controls, fifth-grade students often believe that the brain controls voluntary functions (e.g., thinking) but not involuntary ones (e.g., balance). In one study, despite having received a science lesson at school that discussed both the voluntary and involuntary functions of the brain, children still maintained their initial belief that the brain only controls voluntary functions (Johnson & Wellman, 1982). It appeared that their pre-existing inaccurate explanations were held so strongly that the new explanations did not lead to any adjustment in their beliefs; that said, the research did not measure whether children noticed that the science lesson suggested something different nor if hearing such explanations made them curious to find out the right answer. In other cases, children *do* respond positively to new explanations, incorporating them into their explanatory framework. For instance, building on the previous study involving children's understanding of brain functions, a curriculum intervention was crafted to help children understand how the brain is involved in sensory activities, and this intervention was successful in helping children update their understanding of the brain based on this new explanatory information (Marshall & Comalli, 2012).

Understanding under what circumstances children—and adults—accept and build from new information about science and when they reject it has been of increasing interest to psychologists as of late (e.g., Bloom & Weisberg, 2007; Shtulman, 2017), and there are many open questions. One possible avenue for investigation relates to the idea that the extent to which children are likely to seek out additional information to fill in gaps in their own explanatory understanding may depend on how strongly they feel their explanation is right at its core. As noted above, children vary in their background knowledge and willingness to revise their beliefs. We posit that another important part of learning from explanations relates to how strongly children cling to their current explanatory framework for a topic or mechanism, i.e., how resistant they may be to consider that their initial explanatory knowledge is missing something.

One reason that adults sometimes resist learning from explanations relates to motivated reasoning (Kunda, 1990). Indeed, adults have been found to view explanations about climate change and vaccines through the filter of their prior beliefs (e.g., Kahan, Braman, Cohen, Gastil, & Slovac, 2010; Landrum, Lull, Akin, Hasell, & Jamieson, 2017). In other words, for scientific topics that are somehow tied to identity, people often cling to the explanatory frameworks associated with that identity. And adults often use those explanatory frameworks to talk with children about those scientific topics (e.g., evolution). We believe that when explanatory knowledge is associated with some kind of identity system, it may be more challenging for children to respond positively to evidence that their knowledge may be incorrect or have gaps. That said, there is hope. In some cases, people's initial explanatory understanding of a concept like climate change is very thin and connected to what their social group believes, and providing them with solid, simple mechanistic explanations can lead to greater acceptance of something that is initially controversial (Ranney & Clark, 2016). It is likely that for strongly held initial explanatory frameworks, striking the right balance in sharing information (e.g., the way the mechanistic explanation is worded, how it is shared) is critically important for encouraging learning.

Thus far, we have discussed how differences in the ability to evaluate explanations and investment in existing beliefs may influence the likelihood of further exploration, but even in situations where children receive the same explanation, and have the same background knowledge and interest and the same core beliefs, there may be individual differences in how much children want to know. Like adults, children may show individual differences in how much they are interested in moving beyond their current explanatory frameworks (i.e., how much they are interested in engaging in deep learning; see Fernbach, Sloman, Louis, & Shube, 2013; their need for cognition, Cacioppo, Petty, Feinstein, & Jarvis, 1996). Individual differences in personality and temperament may also contribute to variability in children's interest in learning (see Rothbart & Jones, 1998 for a review). There is even recent evidence that individual differences in children's willingness to seek out information can be tied to neurophysiological differences in sensitivity to errors (Danovitch et al., 2017). A crucial aspect of future research will be to investigate how individual differences contribute to the development of different approaches towards deep thinking.

Social Influences on Explanation and Exploration

We have discussed internal sources of individual differences in explanation evaluation and preferences, such as differences in how satisfied children are with explanations and how likely it is that children will seek out additional information. These individual differences may be a function of variability in background knowledge, interest, or cognitive skills, but they are also likely to be influenced by social factors. In particular, we propose that whether or not explanation leads to exploration is determined by children's sense of whether they are capable of receiving useful information from the people around them and in their learning environment.

Preschool-aged children understand that different people know different things (e.g., Lutz & Keil, 2002; Koenig et al., 2004), and that some sources of information are better than others (see Harris, 2012 for a review). That said, in their everyday lives, children also encounter different levels of responsiveness from their caregivers, which might in time influence both how children evaluate explanations and how likely they are to pursue information to fill weaknesses in explanations. For instance, there is evidence that the quality of parent–child communication at age 2 predicts children's engagement in shared experiences at age 3 (Hirsh-Pasek et al., 2015). Furthermore, the ways in which parents discuss evidence and reasoning are related to the ways in which their 4- to 8-year-old children discuss and evaluate evidence (Luce, Callanan, & Smilovic, 2013). Based on these findings, one might imagine that as children age and begin to produce a barrage of "why" and "how" questions, the quality of caregiver responses influences how children think about asking questions and evaluating explanations, and consequently the frequency with which they engage in exploration.

Some of the variability in the responses children receive appears to be linked to sociological factors, such as socioeconomic status. Early research suggested that middle-class British children were more likely to ask "why" questions than working-class children, and that their mothers were more likely to answer these questions and provide adequate explanations when doing so (Tizard & Hughes, 1984/2002). Similarly, analyses of conversations between American 4-year-olds and their caregivers reveal that children from mid-SES communities tend to ask more questions overall and receive a larger proportion of satisfactory responses to their questions than children from low-SES communities (Kurkul & Corriveau, 2017). Although the source of these socioeconomic differences in explanation-giving is still unclear, these differences highlight that the ways in which caregivers respond to questions influences children's subsequent exploration. Together with evidence that the quality and frequency of parent-generated explanations varies based on other factors (e.g., gender, Crowley, Callanan, Tenenbaum, & Allen, 2001), this work suggests that to understand children's information seeking and exploration, it is critical to take into account the frequency and quality of explanations they have received in the past.

Beyond this, though, we think it is important to note that explanation *quality* does not necessarily correspond to explanation *accuracy*. It may be more important for parents to encourage and model engagement in the process of inquiry than to strive to give accurate answers every time. One could imagine that a child who was discouraged from asking questions and regularly received weak or dismissive responses to questions might, over time, become less likely to engage in exploration to obtain the answers to their questions. Eventually, if the child receives enough weak or unsatisfactory explanations, they may even start paying less attention to the explanations that they receive, further diminishing their ability to evaluate explanations and making it less likely they will seek out additional information.

Finally, children's experiences with explanation and exploration both in and out of the home are likely to be influenced by culture. There have been a relatively small number of cross-cultural investigations of children's explanation seeking and evaluation, but the studies that exist suggest that there may be interesting similarities and differences between the ways in which children in Western and non-Western cultures encounter and assess explanations. Gauvain, Munroe, and Beebe (2013) have reported that children in non-Western cultures have lower rates of asking explanation seeking "why" questions than children in Western cultures, and that in non-Western cultures, asking questions may not be treated as critical for developing conceptual understanding or reasoning abilities. This raises the question of whether cultural differences in rates of question generation correspond to skill at evaluating explanations. Recent findings that Guatemalan Maya (Castelain, Bernard, der Henst, & Mercier, 2015) and Japanese (Mercier, Sudo, Castelain, Bernard, & Matsui, 2017) children show similar ways of reasoning about strong and weak arguments as Western children of the same age suggest that there may be common mechanisms underlying the development of explanation evaluation skills. Likewise, there is evidence that Yucatec Maya children engage in similar levels of exploration as American children, despite major cultural differences in the amount of direct instruction they receive and the ways in which they learn from adults (Shneidman, Gweon, Schulz, & Woodward, 2016). Consequently, it would be informative to see whether similar pathways from explanation to exploration are evident across cultures and to investigate how cultural norms may influence these pathways.

Conclusions

In this chapter, we have reviewed evidence that children are capable of evaluating explanations and recognizing when they provide insufficient information, and that, at least in some circumstances, recognizing weaknesses or gaps in explanations prompts children to seek out additional information. We also discussed potential sources of developmental and individual differences in seeking additional information, ranging from background knowledge and interest to environmental and cultural factors. Although research on the link between explanation and exploration is still relatively limited, the findings to date do suggest some implications for promoting children's engagement in scientific inquiry and exploration.

Because many children lose interest in studying science and pursuing scientific careers by the time they enter high school (despite believing that science is important; Bennett & Hogarth, 2009), promoting children's interest in scientific inquiry and exploration in early and middle childhood could be an effective means of maintaining science interest and achievement later on. There is evidence that parents who promote curiosity in their children, through activities such as encouraging questions and taking trips to science museums, have children who show higher intrinsic motivation to study science. Moreover, these children show higher levels of subsequent science achievement in high school (Gottfried et al., 2016). It is promising that recent educational standards (i.e., National Research Council, 2013) emphasize the value of scientific inquiry and include activities that support children's ability to generate and evaluate scientific explanations.

We propose that caregivers can also support the development of children's interest in science through day-to-day activities, and we offer four suggestions for doing so. First, caregivers should let children know that it is okay to ask questions, and that they support their exploration of unknown questions. Second, when children ask "how" or "why" questions, caregivers should strive to respond with explanations that provide a causal mechanism (using words like "because" is a good sign). Third, caregivers should model recognizing gaps in explanations—including their own. For example, a parent might say "I know that bees take nectar from flowers to their hive, but I am not sure what they do with it when they get there. My answer is missing a step." Finally, parents can support children's efforts to seek out explanations from different types of sources, including other people, books, and the World Wide Web, and discuss how to judge the quality of the explanations that those sources provide. Fundamentally, promoting inquiry and exploration does not require knowing the answer to every question children ask, but instead it may mean giving children the tools to recognize when the answer they have received is not satisfactory and the means to go about seeking the information they desire.

Acknowledgements This work was supported by National Science Foundation grant DRL-1551862 awarded to Judith Danovitch and grant DRL-1551795 awarded to Candice Mills. Special thanks to Asheley Landrum and Nicholaus Noles for feedback on ideas discussed in this chapter.

References

Alexander, J. M., Johnson, K. E., & Kelley, K. (2012). Longitudinal analysis of the relations between opportunities to learn about science and the development of interests related to science. *Science Education, 96*, 763–786. https://doi.org/10.1002/sce.21018

Baum, L. A., Danovitch, J. H., & Keil, F. C. (2008). Children's sensitivity to circular explanations. *Journal of Experimental Child Psychology, 100*, 146–155. https://doi.org/10.1016/j.jecp.2007.10.007

Bennett, J., & Hogarth, S. (2009). Would you want to talk to a scientist at a party? High school students' attitudes to school science and to science. *International Journal of Science Education, 31*, 1975–1998. https://doi.org/10.1080/09500690802425581

Bloom, P., & Weisberg, D. S. (2007). Childhood origins of adult resistance to science. *Science, 316*, 996–997. https://doi.org/10.1126/science.1133398

Cacioppo, J. T., Petty, R. E., Feinstein, J. A., & Jarvis, W. B. G. (1996). Dispositional differences in cognitive motivation: The life and times of individuals varying in need for cognition. *Psychological Bulletin, 119*, 197–253. https://doi.org/10.1037/0033-2909.119.2.197

Callanan, M. A., & Jipson, J. (2001). Explanatory conversations and young children's developing scientific literacy. In K. Crowley, C. D. Schunn, & T. Okada (Eds.), *Designing for science: Implications from everyday, classroom, and professional science* (pp. 21–49). Mahwah, NJ: Erlbaum.

Castelain, T., Bernard, S., der Henst, V., & Mercier, H. (2015). The influence of power and reason on young Maya children's endorsement of testimony. *Developmental Science, 19*, 957–966. https://doi.org/10.1111/desc.12336

Chi, M. T. H., de Leeuw, N., Chiu, M., & LaVancher, C. (1994). Eliciting self-explanations improves understanding. *Cognitive Science, 18*, 439–477. https://doi.org/10.1207/s15516709cog1803_3

Chouinard, M. M. (2007). Children's questions: A mechanism for cognitive development. *Monographs of the Society for Research in Child Development, 72*, 1–126. https://doi.org/10.1111/j.1540-5834.2007.00413.x

Corriveau, K. H., & Kurkul, K. (2014). "Why does rain fall?": Children prefer to learn from an informant who uses noncircular explanations. *Child Development, 85*, 1827–1835. https://doi.org/10.1111/cdev.12240

Crowley, K., & Callanan, M. (1998). Describing and supporting collaborative scientific thinking in parent-child interactions. *Journal of Museum Education, 23*(1), 12–17. https://doi.org/10.1080/10598650.1998.11510365

Crowley, K., Callanan, M. A., Tenenbaum, H. R., & Allen, E. (2001). Parents explain more often to boys than to girls during shared scientific thinking. *Psychological Science, 12*, 258–261. https://doi.org/10.1111/1467-9280.00347

Crowley, K., & Siegler, R. S. (1999). Explanation and generalization in young children's strategy learning. *Child Development, 70*, 304–316. https://doi.org/10.1111/1467-8624.00023

Danovitch, J. H., Fisher, M., Schroder, H., Hambrick, D. Z., & Moser, J. (2017). Intelligence and neurophysiological markers of error monitoring relate to children's intellectual humility. *Child Development*. https://doi.org/10.1111/cdev.12960. [Epub ahead of print].

Doebel, S., Rowell, S. F., & Koenig, M. A. (2016). Young children detect and avoid logically inconsistent sources: The importance of communicative context and executive function. *Child Development, 87*, 1956–1970. https://doi.org/10.1111/cdev.12563

Dunning, D. (2011). The Dunning-Kruger effect: On being ignorant of one's own ignorance. *Advances in Experimental Social Psychology, 44*, 247–296.

Fernbach, P. M., Sloman, S. A., Louis, R. S., & Shube, J. N. (2013). Explanation fiends and foes: How mechanistic detail determines understanding and preference. *Journal of Consumer Research, 39*, 1115–1131. https://doi.org/10.1086/667782

Fisher, M., & Keil, F. C. (2015). The curse of expertise: When more knowledge leads to miscalibrated explanatory insight. *Cognitive Science, 40*, 1–19. https://doi.org/10.1111/cogs.12280

Frazier, B. N., Gelman, S. A., & Wellman, H. M. (2009). Preschoolers' search for explanatory information within adult-child conversation. *Child Development, 80*, 1592–1611. https://doi.org/10.1111/j.1467-8624.2009.01356.x

Frazier, B. N., Gelman, S. A., & Wellman, H. M. (2016). Young children prefer and remember satisfying explanations. *Journal of Cognition and Development, 17*, 718–736. https://doi.org/10.1080/15248372.2015.1098649

Gauvain, M., Munroe, R. L., & Beebe, H. (2013). Children's questions in cross-cultural perspective: A four-culture study. *Journal of Cross-Cultural Psychology, 44*, 1148–1165. https://doi.org/10.1177/0022022113485430

Gopnik, A. (1998). Explanation as orgasm. *Minds and Machines, 8*, 101–118. https://doi.org/10.1023/A:1008290415597

Gopnik, A. (2000). Explanation as orgasm and the drive for causal knowledge: The function, evolution, and phenomenology of the theory formation system. In F. Keil & R. A. Wilson (Eds.), *Explanation and cognition* (pp. 299–323). Cambridge, MA: MIT Press.

Gottfried, A. E., Preston, K. S. J., Gottfried, A. W., Oliver, P. H., Delany, D. E., & Ibrahim, S. M. (2016). Pathways from parental stimulation of children's curiosity to high school science course accomplishments and science career interest and skill. *International Journal of Science Education, 38*, 1972–1995. https://doi.org/10.1080/09500693.2016.1220690

Gutheil, G., Vera, A., & Keil, F. C. (1998). Do houseflies think? Patterns of induction and biological beliefs in development. *Cognition, 66*, 33–49. https://doi.org/10.1016/S0010-0277(97)00049-8

Harris, P. L. (2012). *Trusting what you're told: How children learn from others*. Cambridge, MA: Harvard University Press.

Hirsh-Pasek, K., Adamson, L. B., Bakeman, R., Owen, M. T., Golinkoff, R. M., Pace, A., … Suma, K. (2015). The contribution of early communication quality to low-income children's language success. *Psychological Science, 26*, 1071–1083. https://doi.org/10.1177/0956797615581493

Johnson, C. N., & Wellman, H. M. (1982). Children's developing conceptions of the mind and brain. *Child Development, 53*, 222–234. https://doi.org/10.2307/1129656

Johnston, A. M., Sheskin, M., Johnson, S. G., & Keil, F. C. (2017). Preferences for explanation generality develop early in biology but not physics. *Child Development*. https://doi.org/10.1111/cdev.12804. [Epub ahead of print].

Kahan, D. M., Braman, D., Cohen, G. C., Gastil, J., & Slovac, P. (2010). Who fears the HPV vaccine, who doesn't, and why? An experimental study of the mechanisms of cultural cognition. *Law and Human Behavior, 34*, 501–516. https://doi.org/10.1007/s10979-009-9201-0

Keil, F. C. (2006). Explanation and understanding. *Annual Review of Psychology, 57*, 227–254. https://doi.org/10.1146/annurev.psych.57.102904.190100

Koenig, M. A., Clément, F., & Harris, P. L. (2004). Trust in testimony: Children's use of true and false statements. *Psychological Science, 15*, 694–698. https://doi.org/10.1111/j.0956-7976.2004.00742.x

Kunda, Z. (1990). The case for motivated reasoning. *Psychological Bulletin, 108*, 480. https://doi.org/10.1037/0033-2909.108.3.480

Kurkul, K. E., & Corriveau, K. H. (2017). Question, explanation, follow-up: A mechanism for learning from others? *Child Development*. Advance online publication. https://doi.org/10.1111/cdev.12726

Landrum, A. R., Lull, R. B., Akin, H., Hasell, A., & Jamieson, K. H. (2017). Processing the papal encyclical through perceptual filters: Pope Francis, identity-protective cognition, and climate change concern. *Cognition, 166*, 1–12. https://doi.org/10.1016/j.cognition.2017.05.015

Legare, C. H. (2014). The contributions of explanation and exploration to children's scientific reasoning. *Child Development Perspectives, 8*, 101–106. https://doi.org/10.1111/cdep.12070

Legare, C. H., & Lombrozo, T. (2014). Selective effects of explanation on learning during early childhood. *Journal of Experimental Child Psychology, 126*, 198–212. https://doi.org/10.1016/j.jecp.2014.03.001

Lombrozo, T. (2006). The structure and function of explanations. *Trends in Cognitive Sciences, 10*, 464–470. https://doi.org/10.1016/j.tics.2006.08.004

Lombrozo, T., & Vasilyeva, N. (2017). Causal explanation. In M. Waldmann (Ed.), *The oxford handbook of causal reasoning* (pp. 415–432). Oxford, England: Oxford University Press.

Luce, M. R., Callanan, M. A., & Smilovic, S. (2013). Links between parents' epistemological stance and children's evidence talk. *Developmental Psychology, 49*, 454–461. https://doi.org/10.1037/a0031249

Lutz, D. J., & Keil, F. C. (2002). Early understanding of the division of cognitive labor. *Child Development, 73*, 1073–1084. https://doi.org/10.1111/1467-8624.00458

Markman, E. M. (1979). Realizing that you don't understand: Elementary school children's awareness of inconsistencies. *Child Development, 50*, 643–655. https://doi.org/10.2307/1128929

Marshall, P. J., & Comalli, C. E. (2012). Young children's changing conceptualizations of brain function: Implications for teaching neuroscience in early elementary settings. *Early Education & Development, 23*, 4–23. https://doi.org/10.1080/10409289.2011.616134

Mercier, H. (2016). The argumentative theory: Predictions and empirical evidence. *Trends in Cognitive Sciences, 20*, 689–700. https://doi.org/10.1016/j.tics.2016.07.001

Mercier, H., Bernard, S., & Clément, F. (2014). Early sensitivity to arguments: How preschoolers weight circular arguments. *Journal of Experimental Child Psychology, 125*, 102–109. https://doi.org/10.1016/j.jecp.2013.11.011

Mercier, H., Sudo, M., Castelain, T., Bernard, S., & Matsui, T. (2017). Japanese preschoolers' evaluation of circular and non-circular arguments. *European Journal of Developmental Psychology*. Advance online publication. https://doi.org/10.1080/17405629.2017.1308250

Mills, C. M., Danovitch, J. H., Rowles, S. P., & Campbell, I. L. (2017). Children's success at detecting circular explanations and their interest in future learning. *Psychonomic Bulletin & Review*. Advance online publication. https://doi.org/10.3758/s13423-016-1195-2

Mills, C. M., & Keil, F. C. (2004). Knowing the limits of one's understanding: The development of an awareness of an illusion of explanatory depth. *Journal of Experimental Child Psychology, 87*, 1–32. https://doi.org/10.1016/j.jecp.2003.09.003

Mills, C. M., Legare, C. H., Grant, M. G., & Landrum, A. R. (2011). Determining who to question, what to ask, and how much information to ask for: The development of inquiry in young children. *Journal of Experimental Child Psychology, 110*, 539–560. https://doi.org/10.1016/j.jecp.2011.06.003

Morris, B. J., & Hasson, U. (2010). Multiple sources of competence underlying the comprehension of inconsistencies: A developmental investigation. *Journal of Experimental Psychology: Learning, Memory, and Cognition, 36*, 277–287. https://doi.org/10.1037/a0017519

National Research Council. (2013). *Next generation science standards*. Washington, DC: National Academies Press.

Osherson, D. N., & Markman, E. (1975). Language and the ability to evaluate contradictions and tautologies. *Cognition, 3*, 213–226. https://doi.org/10.1016/0010-0277(74)90009-2

Ranney, M. A., & Clark, D. (2016). Climate change conceptual change: Scientific information can transform attitudes. *Topics in Cognitive Science, 8*, 49–75. https://doi.org/10.1111/tops.12187

Rothbart, M. K., & Jones, L. B. (1998). Temperament, self-regulation, and education. *School Psychology Review, 27*(4), 479–491.

Rozenblit, L., & Keil, F. (2002). The misunderstood limits of folk science: An illusion of explanatory depth. *Cognitive Science, 26*, 521–562.

Ruffman, T. (1999). Children's understanding of logical inconsistency. *Child Development, 70*, 872–886. https://doi.org/10.1111/1467-8624.00063

Sands, K. R., Mills, C. M., Rowles, S. P., & Campbell, I. L. (2017). *"Click for more info": Children's engagement in information seeking to close information gaps*. Poster presented at the April 2017 meeting of the Society for Research in Child Development, Austin, TX.

Shneidman, L., Gweon, H., Schulz, L. E., & Woodward, A. L. (2016). Learning from others and spontaneous exploration: A cross-cultural investigation. *Child Development, 87*, 723–735. https://doi.org/10.1111/cdev.12502

Shtulman, A. (2017). *Scienceblind: Why our intuitive theories about the world are so often wrong*. New York, NY: Basic Books.

Sobel, D. M. & Letourneau S. M. (in press). Curiosity, Exploration, and Children's Understanding of Learning, in the book Active Learning from Infancy to Childhood Chapter to appear in Saylor, M. M. & Ganea, P. (Eds). *Active Learning from Infancy to Childhood: Social Motivation, Cognition, and Linguistic Mechanisms*. Springer International. New York, NY.

Tizard, B., & Hughes, M. (1984). *Young children learning: Talking and thinking at home and at school*. Cambridge, MA: Harvard University Press.

Walker, C., Bonawitz, E., & Lombrozo, T. (2017). Effects of explaining on children's preference for simpler hypotheses. *Psychonomic Bulletin & Review*. Advanced online publication. https://doi.org/10.3758/s13423-016-1144-0

Walker, C. M., Lombrozo, T., Legare, C. H., & Gopnik, A. (2014). Explaining prompts children to privilege inductively rich properties. *Cognition, 133*, 343–357. https://doi.org/10.1016/j.cognition.2014.07.008

Wellman, H. M. (2011). Reinvigorating explanations for the study of early cognitive development. *Child Development Perspectives, 5*, 33–38. https://doi.org/10.1111/j.1750-8606.2010.00154.x

Williams, A., Danovitch, J. H., & Mills, C. M. (2015). *How assessing one's own explanatory knowledge influences children's interest in learning*. Poster presented at the October 2015 meeting of the Cognitive Development Society, Columbus, OH.

Williams, J. J., & Lombrozo, T. (2013). Explanation and prior knowledge interact to guide learning. *Cognitive Psychology, 66*, 55–84. https://doi.org/10.1016/j.cogpsych.2012.09.002

Wilson, R. A., & Keil, F. (1998). The shadows and shallows of explanation. *Minds and Machines, 8*, 137–159. https://doi.org/10.1023/A:1008259020140

Woolley, J. D., & Ghossainy, M. (2013). Revisiting the fantasy–reality distinction: Children as naïve skeptics. *Child Development, 84*, 1496–1510. https://doi.org/10.1111/cdev.12081

Chapter 7
Explanation Scaffolds Causal Learning and Problem Solving in Childhood

Justin T. A. Busch, Aiyana K. Willard, and Cristine H. Legare

Abstract Explanation provides a window into what children know and scaffolds causal learning. Here we review research on the contributions of explanation to causal knowledge acquisition and problem solving. We discuss evidence that generating explanations enhances children's understanding of causal mechanisms and increases their persistence and skill in applying new knowledge to novel contexts. In this way, explanation operates as a tool for learning and is particularly effective in the context of explaining inconsistent or ambiguous information. Explanation also enhances problem solving by allowing children to articulate their knowledge, a process which makes gaps in their current knowledge salient. The process of generating and requesting explanations facilitates the transmission of information and often occurs during interactions with others. We discuss the social context of explanation and the implications for belief revision and for building new knowledge. Explanation works in tandem with discovery-oriented behaviors like question asking and exploration to drive causal learning and improve problem solving.

Introduction

Explanation is at the center of the scientific enterprise. Explanations describe what is known or has been discovered about an event or outcome and serve to guide future exploration as more information becomes available. Thus, explanations are also hypotheses. Scientists can formulate an explanation for a phenomenon and through experimentation find evidence for or against their hypothesis. In this way, the process of science highlights how explanation can play an integral role in the way we acquire, organize, and interpret new knowledge. Generating explanations

J. T. A. Busch · C. H. Legare (✉)
Department of Psychology, The University of Texas at Austin, Austin, TX, USA
e-mail: legare@austin.utexas.edu

A. K. Willard
Brunel University London, Uxbridge, UK

School of Anthropology and Museum Ethnography, University of Oxford, Oxford, UK

© Springer International Publishing AG, part of Springer Nature 2018
M. M. Saylor, P. A. Ganea (eds.), *Active Learning from Infancy to Childhood*,
https://doi.org/10.1007/978-3-319-77182-3_7

113

constrains future exploration, which in turn generates new information relevant to current and future explanation.

Explanation is core to the scientific process, yet explanation generation is not the exclusive domain of scientists. Children and lay adults are active explanation generators (Gopnik, 2000; Hickling & Wellman, 2001; Hilton, 1988; Keil, 2006; Keil & Wilson, 2000; Wellman, Hickling, & Schult, 1997), from the mundane (e.g., why is my Wi-Fi not working?) to the existential (e.g., how did life come to exist?). In this chapter, we define explanation broadly as any attempt to understand a causal relationship through identifying relevant functional or mechanistic information (Legare, Gelman, & Wellman, 2010; Lombrozo, 2006). Similar to the way an explanation or hypothesis in science guides future studies, explanation in childhood plays an important role in scaffolding the learning process (Legare, 2012). As such, the development of causal explanation has been an important topic in psychology since Piaget (1929) and explanation presents an important avenue to understanding cognitive development (Frazier, Gelman, & Wellman, 2016).

A substantial and influential body of research has documented that children's explanations provide insight into the development of causal knowledge and conceptual understanding (Callanan & Oakes, 1992; Frazier, Gelman, & Wellman, 2009; Hickling & Wellman, 2001; Hoyos & Gentner, 2017; Keil, 2006; Keil & Wilson, 2000; McEldoon, Durkin, & Rittle-Johnson, 2012). New research supports the proposal that explanation also plays an important role in scaffolding the learning process (Bonawitz, Fischer, & Schulz, 2012; Brewer, Chinn, & Samarapungavan, 1998; Legare, 2012; Lombrozo, 2006; Wilkenfeld & Lombrozo, 2015) and may be developmentally privileged (Legare, Wellman, & Gelman, 2009). In problem-solving tasks, generating explanations has been shown to improve performance between pre- and post-test (Fawcett & Garton, 2005).

We seek to answer two questions about children's explanations in this chapter. First, how might explanation enhance causal learning? Second, how does explanation facilitate active engagement in problem solving? If explanation serves to scaffold children's conceptual development (Bonawitz et al., 2012; Brewer et al., 1998; Legare, 2012; Lombrozo, 2006), then children's explanations should be more common in contexts that are ripe for learning and should aid in problem solving. To gain traction on these outstanding questions, it is necessary to review the literature on explanation from different angles. This chapter begins with a review of the research on how causal learning may be promoted through the process of explanation generation. Understanding what type of knowledge is promoted through explanation and what type of knowledge is not can provide insight into the mechanism that makes explanation a powerful tool for learning. We then move on to discuss what motivates children to generate explanations in the first place. The contexts in which children generate explanations provide further insight into the mechanism underlying how explanation promotes learning. Finally, we discuss how children revise explanations in response to new evidence and use explanations in problem solving. If explanation is used to increase knowledge, then we should predict that children would revise explanations to reflect new information and that explanations should also aid children in solving problems.

To answer these questions, we discuss how explanation functions in both non-social and social contexts. Much of the previous research on the topic of explanations examines self-explanation, or how children generate explanations for a phenomenon for themselves rather than explanations for the purpose of communicating ideas with others. Humans are a social species and causal learning rarely takes place in isolation (Rogoff, 2003; Vygotsky, 1962). Since so much of human reasoning takes place in social contexts, the adaptive function of reasoning may be to construct an argument or explanation in the service of persuading others and to critically evaluate their arguments and explanations in turn (Mercier & Sperber, 2011). Therefore, explanation likely did not evolve for self-explanation but as a mechanism to enhance knowledge acquisition within a social group (Mercier & Sperber, 2017). Examining explanations in the context of social interaction may provide further insight into how explanation functions as a learning mechanism and for collaborative problem solving. Indeed, research has shown that argumentation and discussion with peers improves adults' reasoning on logic tasks across cultures (Mercier, Deguchi, Van der Henst, & Yama, 2016). Furthermore, individuals who receive valid arguments against their answers on intellective tasks are more likely to change their answers and adults as well as 10-year-olds are more likely to solve intellective tasks while in groups (Trouche, Sander, & Mercier, 2014). In this chapter we seek to bring together research on explanation, how it enhances causal learning, facilitates problem solving, and operates in social and non-social contexts.

Explanation and Causal Learning

Developmental research has shown that explanations and requests for explanations are widespread in even very young children (Frazier et al., 2009; Keil, 2006; Keil & Wilson, 2000). Research examining the everyday conversations of preschool aged children and their caregivers has demonstrated that explanations increase in frequency with age but are common even at 2- to 3-years-old (Callanan & Oakes, 1992; Crowley, Callanan, Tenenbaum, & Allen, 2001). Furthermore, explanations typically serve an epistemic function by providing an interpretation for a current or past event, and do not serve an exclusively social-regulatory function (Hickling & Wellman, 2001). As such, the process of generating explanations is critical for constructing knowledge (Amsterlaw & Wellman, 2006; Cimpian & Petro, 2014; Rittle-Johnson, Saylor, & Swygert, 2008). Given the proliferation of explanatory activity through childhood and its importance in knowledge acquisition, how does explanation function in the service of causal learning?

Explanation enhances knowledge acquisition by prompting children to speculate about internal unobserved mechanisms and causal functions (Legare et al., 2010; Legare & Lombrozo, 2014). Similarly, explanation can aid in the generalization of knowledge about causal mechanism to new, perceptually similar objects (Walker, Lombrozo, Legare, & Gopnik, 2014). This suggests that the act of generating a self-explanation may direct children's learning towards understanding the broad causal mechanism underlying a phenomenon and away from perceptual features specific to that given instantiation of the phenomenon. For example, Legare and Lombrozo (2014) conducted two studies with 3- to 6-year-old children to tease apart the unique effects of explanation from the effects of simple verbalization or attention. Children were presented with a system of gears, which included a handle that could be rotated to operate a fan at the opposite side of a gear system. Some children were asked to explain the gear toy while others were told to observe or describe the toy. They found that the effect of explanation was selective; generating a self-explanation promoted the learning of the causal mechanism underlying gears across all ages. Self-explanation also increased children's ability to generalize their knowledge of gears to a novel gear toy. In contrast, generating explanations did not enhance children's learning for the perceptual features of the gear toy. However, in this study children were asked to generate an explanation for an experimenter in a lab and there was no conversational interaction between the child and the experimenter. When children generate explanations in the context of a conversational interaction with another person, is the effect of those explanations on learning any different or more robust?

Willard, Busch, Sobel, Callanan, and Legare (2016) have extended this line of research into the social domain by examining children's causal learning about gears while engaged with a parent. Parents can guide their children to understand the mechanism of a novel set of objects either through offering explanations to their children or by encouraging their children to generate their own explanations. Both of these behaviors are pedagogical tools. Offering children a mechanism explanation has been previously found to reduce the number of alternative uses of a toy children find during future exploration (Bonawitz et al., 2011). This allows for rapid learning about objects in one's environment through social learning and in doing so reduces the need for individual learning through more hands-on experience (Kline, 2015). Recent research examines how children learn in a social interaction in which the caretaker is prompted by the experimenter to encourage their child to explain at a museum's gear exhibit (Willard et al., 2016). The data show that when parents are prompted to request explanations from their children while at the exhibit, their children generate more explanatory talk and spend more time spinning the gears.

After interacting at the gear exhibit, children were presented with a preconstructed gear machine for several follow-up tasks. One of these tasks asked children to recall from memory the color of one of the gears and another asked them to identify the proper size and shape of a missing gear. Results showed that the more time children spent troubleshooting gears at the exhibit, the better they performed on these follow-up tasks. Children were then presented with a new, novel set of gears and asked to build their own machine. Preliminary results suggest that parents who asked more questions of their child in an attempt to elicit explanations also spent less time fixing locked or unconnected gears for their children. Children of the parents who asked more questions to elicit explanation persisted for longer at the task of building their own gear machine with a novel set of gear stimuli. A potential explanation for this finding is that children who are encouraged through questioning to generate explanations may be less likely to give up when they face a challenging task on their own. This research helps us understand the type of knowledge children gain through explanation, but how does explanation affect the way children generalize this knowledge into different contexts in the future?

From previous research it is clear that explanation, both self-explanation and explanations children generate for someone else, focuses children's learning on causal mechanism. Explanation may also promote causal learning when children move to generalize their knowledge into new contexts by constraining their hypotheses to those that will be most productive for learning (Walker, Lombrozo, Williams, Rafferty, & Gopnik, 2017). In an experiment with 5-year-olds Walker et al. (2017) showed that children who were prompted to explain were more likely to favor a hypothesis that accounted for a greater number of their observations during training than children in a control condition. In a second experiment they showed that children who were prompted to explain were more likely to favor a hypothesis consistent with their prior beliefs than children in a control condition. Through a third experiment the researchers ruled out the possibility that explanation simply increases attention to the task. This work suggests that explanation prompts children to favor hypotheses that are broad in scope and account for the greatest proportion of evidence. Generating explanations that accurately represent the evidence and are broad in scope is useful for children because it allows them to learn something that can be applied to a novel context and, in a way, know something true about the world based on their past experiences. The idea that children can generate true explanations to improve their epistemic standing is consistent with "inference to the best explanation" (Wilkenfeld & Lombrozo, 2015). Wilkenfeld and Lombrozo (2015) also propose however, that an explanation need not be accurate to improve epistemic standing. The simple act of generating an explanation might in fact improve epistemic standing as well.

The research on how children learn through explanation suggests that the effects of explanation are selective. Explanation seems to focus children's learning towards unobserved causal mechanism and constrains children's hypotheses to those that account for the greatest proportion of evidence. Parents and caregivers can also prompt explanation from their children. Children whose parents attempt to elicit explanations generate more explanatory talk, show greater persistence in generalizing new causal knowledge to a novel, analogous context, and show better understanding of causal mechanism. Taken together these findings provide support for "explanation to the best inference" (Wilkenfeld & Lombrozo, 2015), or the idea that just by generating explanations, whether they are accurate or not, children acquire causal knowledge. Explanations are functional in causal learning because they seem to focus children's attention onto causal mechanism and guide future exploration. If it is true that children learn by explaining, then it is important to understand what motivates children to generate explanations in the first place.

If explanation generation can be used as a tool to improve epistemic standing, then we predict that children will be highly motivated to investigate irregular or discordant information (Legare et al., 2010). Information that conflicts with a child's prior understanding of a phenomenon may be especially fruitful for explanation because the discordant information is a cue that there is more to learn about that topic. The inherent motivation to explain inconsistent information could facilitate children's learning by focusing their attention onto events that challenge their current causal knowledge and bring about amended causal reasoning by increasing awareness of uncertainty and the potential for alternative explanations for the same information (Legare, 2014). Indeed, the proposal that inconsistent, problematic, or surprising outcomes play an important role in reasoning appears across multiple literatures—philosophy of science (Hempel, 1965), social psychology (Hilton, 1995), educational research (Chi, Bassok, Lewis, Reimann, & Glaser, 1989), and infancy research (Baillargeon, 2002). For example, in a series of studies with preschool children, Legare and colleagues examined the kinds of events that prompt explanation and how explanatory biases provide insight into the function of explaining (Legare, 2012; Legare et al., 2010; Legare & Gelman, 2014). The results of these studies indicate that outcomes inconsistent with prior knowledge are especially powerful triggers for children's explanations and that the explanations children provide for inconsistent outcomes refer to unobserved causal mechanisms and internal causal properties, overriding perceptual biases. This suggests that explanation provides children with the opportunity to articulate new hypotheses for events that, at first, disconfirm their current state of knowledge (Legare, 2014; Walker, Williams, Lombrozo, & Gopnik, 2012). Although these studies did not directly measure learning, the data they present are consistent with the proposal that children's explanations play an active role in the learning process and provide an empirical basis for investigating the mechanisms by which children's explanations function in the service of discovery.

But how might the process of explaining inconsistent information promote learning? One possibility is that explaining encourages learners to formulate and entertain hypotheses they would not have spontaneously considered otherwise. Generating hypotheses in the service of explanation may influence the kinds of hypotheses formulated, as well as their impact on cognition (Bonawitz et al., 2012; Bonawitz, van Schijndel, et al., 2012; Legare & Lombrozo, 2014; Walker et al., 2012; Walker et al., 2014). In particular, both children and adults have strong intuitions about what makes something a good explanation (Bonawitz & Lombrozo, 2012; Frazier et al., 2009; Lombrozo, 2007) and explanation may promote the production of hypotheses that are judged as informative. When children generate explanations for inconsistent information there are often multiple potential true explanations. Thus, inconsistency is inherently ambiguous. For example, when faced with information that appears inconsistent with prior knowledge (e.g., a person chooses not to select their favorite food), children are faced with multiple potential explanations (e.g., person's preference could have changed, something about the particular favorite item that was undesirable, the person is on a diet, etc.). Thus, the ambiguity and uncertainty of inconsistency may motivate the bias to produce new explanations for inconsistent outcomes (Foster & Keane, 2015; Lipton, 2004).

The research on what motivates children's explanations is in line with the proposal that the act of generating an explanation can improve epistemic standing. Discordant information acts as a cue to children that their current understanding may be inaccurate and prompts them to generate an explanation. Because inconsistency is inherently ambiguous, children may be forced to grapple with possibilities and hypotheses that they may not have considered. In this way, explanations serve to enhance epistemic standing by requiring children to consider multiple potential alternatives to reach the best conclusion. Implicit within the finding that inconsistent information motivates children to consider alternative explanations is the assumption that children can revise their beliefs when they encounter new information, but what empirical evidence exists to support this assumption?

Explanation and Problem Solving

If it is the case that the act of generating explanations can improve epistemic standing, then we should expect that children should flexibly adapt their explanations and that the activity of generating explanations should aid children in problem solving, even when the explanations they generate may not be true. The capacity to actively revise existing explanations when faced with new information is an essential component of knowledge acquisition (Gopnik & Schulz, 2007) and research shows that children do readily revise their beliefs when presented with new evidence. Data from two studies by Legare, Schult, Impola, and Souza (2016) demonstrate that 3- to 6-year-olds flexibly accommodate different kinds of information when revising their explanations. Specifically, they examined how children incorporate inconsistent information into their explanations by showing children video evidence of two actors, one of whom behaves consistently with their stated preference and one of whom behaves inconsistently with their stated preference. This study converges with previous research showing that children have a strong bias to explain inconsistency over consistency (Legare et al., 2010). Importantly, these studies also show that children are able to flexibly revise their explanation across domains when they receive new evidence. The data reveal that children who observe multiple pieces of consistent evidence will maintain their original explanation. For children who observe inconsistent evidence however, they will revise their initial explanation, even across domains of reasoning, first appealing to a psychological explanation and then revising to a biological explanation (Legare et al., 2016). In these studies children were provided evidence by the experimenter, but to learn about the world outside the lab and to solve problems, children must also recognize when the evidence they have is incomplete. What is known about children's capacity to recognize when the information they have is incomplete and do children actively seek to gather information to solve problems?

Research suggests that not only do children revise their explanations when they are provided new evidence by an experimenter in a lab study, they also engage in broad exploration to gather more information in contexts where information is limited. Children are adept at using questions to satisfy their curiosity and accumulate additional evidence (Chouinard, 2007; Courage, 1989; Legare, Mills, Souza, Plummer, & Yasskin, 2013) and they are sensitive to the quality and completeness of the information they receive (Gweon, Pelton, Konopka, & Schulz, 2014). For example, research by Legare et al. (2013) found that the number of constraint-seeking questions, or questions that were appropriately worded to obtain the necessary information, predicted children's accuracy on a problem-solving task. Children also ask relevant questions and adapt the types of questions they ask to increase their efficiency in acquiring new evidence (Legare et al., 2013; Ruggeri & Lombrozo, 2015), a skill that improves over the course of development (Chouinard, 2007; Mills, Legare, Bills, & Mejias, 2010). In response to their causal questions, young children are dissatisfied with non-explanatory responses, prefer to question informants who provide noncircular explanations, and will selectively direct their questions to a knowledgeable informant, which improves their ability to successfully complete a problem-solving task (Corriveau & Kurkul, 2014; Frazier et al., 2009; Mills, Legare, Grant, & Landrum, 2011). This suggests that children not only have the ability to revise their explanations when they encounter new evidence, but they actively seek diagnostic evidence from a knowledgeable informant.

In much the same way that children's explanations are prompted by inconsistent or ambiguous information, their engagement in information seeking behaviors is also prompted by inconsistency or ambiguity. Recent research by Busch and Legare (2016) examines how 6- to 10-year-old children evaluate different types of inconclusive evidence in comparison to conclusive evidence. Using a preference paradigm where an actor selects between three different types of food, researchers were able to carefully control the evidence children saw, thereby creating three distinct types of inconclusive evidence, consistent, inconsistent, and ambiguous. Children in the three inconclusive evidence conditions were assessed on their decision to seek additional information and their accuracy in solving the task. Their performance was compared to the performance of children who received conclusive evidence. The data showed that the ability to use evidence to solve problems presents a significant cognitive challenge for young children. Across these four conditions, researchers investigated how the type of information children had influenced their decision to engage in information seeking. Across age groups, results showed that inconclusive ambiguous evidence was more likely to motivate children to seek information than conclusive evidence, whereas inconclusive consistent evidence was not. This comports with previous research demonstrating that ambiguous evidence is more likely to motivate exploration than unambiguous evidence (Cook, Goodman, & Schulz, 2011).

Ambiguous evidence may cue children to uncertainty and prompt further information seeking. This research also found that inconclusive inconsistent evidence was more likely to motivate requests for more information than conclusive evidence, but only for older children. This is consistent with previous research demonstrating that inconsistent evidence motivates both exploration and explanation in early childhood (Legare, 2014; Legare et al., 2010; Stahl & Feigenson, 2015). The type of evidence children observe when engaged in problem solving individually affects their motivation to generate explanations and seek out additional information. It remains an open question however, how children's explanations and information seeking behavior in response to evidence operate when they are engaged in a collaborative problem-solving task.

Recent research utilizing a collaborative problem-solving task promises to provide insight into how self-explanation might differ from social explanations. In one study, Busch, Eck, Mercier, and Legare (2016) examined how 6- to 10-year-old children engaged in a problem-solving task with a partner. To accurately complete this problem-solving task using transitive inference, children needed two pieces of information. Dyads were told that the goal of the task was to use video evidence to figure out an actor's favorite food between goldfish crackers, animal crackers, and broccoli. Importantly, each child in the dyad only received one of the two pieces of required information. As a result, both children in the dyad were required to generate an explanation for their partner about the evidence they had observed in order to draw an accurate conclusion. The research questions were twofold, (1) how detailed of explanations do children generate for their partner, and in turn how does this affect the dyad's ability to solve the problem collaboratively, and (2) does working collaboratively enhance children's overall accuracy in solving the task over children working individually? Dyad's interactions were coded according to the strength and completeness of the explanation they provided to their partner. The data show a significant positive relationship between those dyads where children generated complete explanations and accuracy on the task (Busch et al., 2016). To understand the effect of peer interaction on problem solving, researchers compared the performance of children who completed the task with a partner to children who completed the same transitive inference task individually. In both the individual and the peer case, children were prompted to provide an explanation of the evidence they observed. Preliminary findings from this work suggest that dyads generating incomplete explanations for their peer, performed significantly less accurately on the task than did children working alone. However, the effect of generating an explanation with a peer appears to be the opposite for dyads generating complete explanations. These dyads performed significantly better than children completing the task individually regardless of age. This work suggests that there are indeed important differences in the way explanation functions in the service of problem solving when used individually and when used with others.

Research from the field of education also provides evidence for the benefits of generating an explanation with a peer, above and beyond the benefits of self-explanation. In one study, 6- to 7-year-old children were asked to complete a card-sorting task alone or with a same-sex peer. Children who completed the task with a partner had a higher number of accurate sorts than children who completed the task alone. Furthermore, low performing children who completed the task with a partner showed significant improvement from pre- to post-test, but only when they and their partner were in the explanation condition and not when they were in the "no-talk" condition (Fawcett & Garton, 2005). Other research shows that children who engage in transactive talk with a peer while working on a scientific reasoning task obtain more complex understanding of the problem more quickly than children who generate self-explanations for the same task (Teasley, 1997). Furthermore, classroom strategies that pair 7th-graders together and have them compare and contrast solutions to a mathematics problems lead to greater gains in procedural knowledge and comparable gains in conceptual knowledge when compared to children who simply reflect on one solution at a time (Rittle-Johnson & Star, 2007).

The research on how explanation facilitates problem solving shows that children flexibly revise their explanations to accommodate new information. Biases to generate explanations for inconsistency or ambiguity mean that children's explanations are most commonly generated in contexts where there is something new to learn. Similarly, children's exploration, question asking, and information seeking are also prompted by inconsistency and ambiguity, allowing them to deftly accumulate additional information with which to revise their initial explanations. This process of explanation generation, discovery-oriented behavior, and explanation revision guides children's early developing capacity for problem solving.

Conclusion

Causal explanation is pervasive across development (Wellman, 2011) and a vast body of research shows that explanation plays an integral role in children's causal learning and problem solving. The process of generating explanations provides children an avenue to consider evidence, formulate hypotheses, and then revise those hypotheses to integrate new evidence as it comes to light. Throughout this chapter we have focused on two core questions, (1) how does explanation promote causal learning and (2) how does explanation facilitate problem solving? This research suggests that when children generate explanations, their acquisition of knowledge regarding the underlying causal mechanism for an event or phenomenon is enhanced while their memory for idiosyncratic perceptual features specific to that instance of the event is not (Legare & Lombrozo, 2014). Furthermore, in social interaction with a caregiver, children whose parents prompted them to explain a gear machine persisted longer in building their own gear machine (Willard et al., 2016). When applying their newly acquired causal knowledge to novel contexts, children who are prompted to explain are more likely to explore hypotheses that do the best job of accounting for the information they have received (Walker et al., 2017). Thus, it is clear that explanations promote learning and therefore we expect that children's explanation generation would be most common in situations where children have the opportunity to learn something new.

In line with the proposal that explanation should be more common when children have something new to learn, inconsistency and ambiguity with prior knowledge motivate more explanations than outcomes that are consistent with prior knowledge (Baillargeon, 2002; Chi et al., 1989; Legare et al., 2010). The bias to explain inconsistency or ambiguity prompts children to consider hypotheses and explanations they might not otherwise have considered (Bonawitz et al., 2012; Foster & Keane, 2015). This research suggests that inconsistent or ambiguous information confronts children with the possibility that their understanding of a phenomenon is incomplete or inaccurate, which then prompts them to generate an explanation. Whether the explanation is accurate or not, it provides a useful framework for children to incorporate new information and provides direction for future exploration. In this way children are "explaining for the best inference" in the sense that an explanation might not be true, but it functions to constrain children's ongoing discovery-oriented behaviors to useful dimensions thereby facilitating learning (Wilkenfeld & Lombrozo, 2015).

The second core question addressed in this chapter is how explanation operates in the service of problem solving. An important component of solving any problem is being able to recognize when our knowledge is incomplete. Research suggests that the process of generating explanations might facilitate problem solving because it prompts children to articulate what they know, and thereby makes salient, gaps in their knowledge. The same type of contexts that motivate explanation, namely inconsistency and ambiguity, also motivate children to engage in selective exploration (Schulz, 2012), ask questions (Chouinard, 2007), and seek out additional information before drawing conclusions (Busch & Legare, 2016). Explanation aids children in problem solving by guiding the gathering of additional, pertinent information.

The future for research on explanation requires that psychologists examine this topic in social contexts, in informal learning environments, and across diverse cultural backgrounds. New research presented in this chapter has only begun to scratch the surface on how explanation affects learning and problem solving in social interaction. The vast majority of children's time is spent in social interaction, with peers, caretakers, and teachers in formal and informal learning environments (Rogoff, 2003). How does explanation with a peer affect children's learning and problem solving? Is the spontaneous generation of social-explanations more common than self-explanations? If peers with a wide discrepancy in skill and knowledge collaborate on a task, how does that affect learning outcomes compared to a dyad where both partners are of similar skill? Ongoing work suggests that generating explanations in collaborative problem-solving tasks might allow more skilled children to accelerate the learning of a lesser skilled partner (Busch et al., 2016). Museums and science centers often implicitly assume that children come away having learned something from the exhibits (Legare, Sobel, & Callanan, 2017). But to what extent do informal learning environments motivate spontaneous explanation generation and thereby causal learning? Future research on explanation in these environments could answer this question and also provide useful insight into how informal learning environments might seed explanation. Finally, it is important that explanation is examined across diverse cultures. Wide cultural variation exists in parental theories about learning and the extent to which parents believe that children should learn through direct pedagogy (Lancy, 2008). Children from different backgrounds may differ in their experience with generating explanations in direct response to prompting from teachers or parents. Examining explanation and learning across cultures promises to provide insight into continuity and variation in cognitive development (Legare, 2017; Legare & Harris, 2016).

Explanation has been a core topic of study since Piaget and much more research remains to be done to obtain an encompassing view of children's causal knowledge acquisition and problem solving. However, an expanding literature supports the proposal that explanation plays an integral role in the development of these capacities. From early childhood, children are sensitive to cues that their current state of knowledge is incomplete, such as inconsistency and ambiguity. Inconsistency and ambiguity motivate explanation, and explanation in turn guides exploration, question asking, and information seeking and children engage in these activities whether they are alone, with a peer, or with a caretaker. Ultimately, explanation and discovery-oriented behaviors, such as information seeking, work in tandem to drive causal learning and facilitate problem solving.

References

Amsterlaw, J., & Wellman, H. M. (2006). Theories of mind in transition: A microgenetic study of the development of false belief understanding. *Journal of Cognition and Development, 7*(2), 139–172.

Baillargeon, R. (2002). The acquisition of physical knowledge in infancy: A summary in eight lessons. In U. Goswami (Ed.), *Blackwell handbook of childhood cognitive development* (pp. 47–83). Oxford, England: Blackwell.

Bonawitz, E. B., Fischer, A., & Schulz, L. E. (2012). Teaching the Bayesian child: Three-and-a-half-year-olds' reasoning about ambiguous evidence. *Journal of Cognition and Development, 13*(2), 266–280.

Bonawitz, E. B., & Lombrozo, T. (2012). Occam's Rattle: Children's use of simplicity and probability to constrain inference. *Developmental Psychology, 48*, 1156–1164.

Bonawitz, E. B., Shafto, P., Gweon, H., Goodman, N. D., Spelke, E., & Schulz, L. (2011). The double-edged sword of pedagogy: Instruction limits spontaneous exploration and discovery. *Cognition, 120*, 322–330.

Bonawitz, E. B., van Schijndel, T., Friel, D., & Schulz, L. (2012). Balancing theories and evidence in children's exploration, explanations, and learning. *Cognitive Psychology, 64*(4), 215–234.

Brewer, W. F., Chinn, C. A., & Samarapungavan, A. (1998). Explanation in scientists and children. *Minds and Machines, 8*(1), 119–136.

Busch, J. T. A., Eck, E. A., Mercier, H., & Legare, C. H. (2016). *Argumentation and the development of deductive reasoning abilities in childhood.* Poster presented at the Annual Meeting of the Society for Philosophy and Psychology, Austin, TX.

Busch, J.T.A., & Legare, C.H. (2016). The development of reasoning about evidence. Paper presented at the International Conference on Thinking, Providence, RI.

Callanan, M. A., & Oakes, L. A. (1992). Preschoolers' questions and parents' explanations: Causal thinking in everyday activities. *Cognitive Development, 7*, 213–233.

Chi, M. T. H., Bassok, M., Lewis, M. W., Reimann, P., & Glaser, R. (1989). Self-explanations: How students study and use examples in learning to solve problems. *Cognitive Science, 13*, 145–182.

Chouinard, N. M. (2007). Children's questions: A mechanism for cognitive development. *Monographs for the Society of Child Development, 72*(1), 1–13.

Cimpian, A., & Petro, G. (2014). Building theory-based concepts: Four-year-olds preferentially seek explanations for features of kinds. *Cognition, 131*(2), 300–310.

Cook, C., Goodman, N. D., & Schulz, L. E. (2011). Where science starts: Spontaneous experiments in preschoolers' exploratory play. *Cognition, 120*(3), 341–349.

Corriveau, K. H., & Kurkul, K. E. (2014). Why does rain fall? Children prefer to learn from an informant who uses noncircular explanations. *Child Development, 85*(5), 1827–1835.

Courage, M. L. (1989). Children's inquiry strategies in referential communication and in the game of Twenty Questions. *Child Development, 60*, 877–886.

Crowley, K., Callanan, M. A., Tenenbaum, H. R., & Allen, E. (2001). Parents explain more often to boys than to girls during shared scientific thinking. *Psychological Science, 12*, 258–261.

Fawcett, L. M., & Garton, A. F. (2005). The effect of peer collaboration on children's problem-solving ability. *Educational Psychology, 75*(2), 157–169.

Foster, M. I., & Keane, M. T. (2015). Why some surprises are more surprising than others: Surprise as a metacognitive sense of explanatory difficulty. *Cognitive Psychology, 81*, 74–116.

Frazier, B. N., Gelman, S. A., & Wellman, H. M. (2009). Preschoolers' search for explanatory information within adult-child conversation. *Child Development, 80*, 1592–1611.

Frazier, B. N., Gelman, S. A., & Wellman, H. M. (2016). Young children prefer and remember satisfying explanations. *Journal of Cognition and Development, 17*(5), 718–736.

Gopnik, A. (2000). Explanation as orgasm and the drive for causal understanding: The evolution, function and phenomenology of the theory-formation system. In F. Keil & R. Wilson (Eds.), *Cognition and explanation* (pp. 299–323). Cambridge, MA: MIT Press.

Gopnik, A., & Schulz, L. E. (2007). *Causal learning: Psychology, philosophy, and computation.* New York, NY: Oxford University Press.

Gweon, H., Pelton, H., Konopka, J. A., & Schulz, L. E. (2014). Sins of omission: Children selectively explore when teachers are under-informed. *Cognition, 132*(3), 335–341.

Hempel, C. G. (1965). *Aspects of scientific explanation and other essays in the philosophy of science.* New York, NY: The Free Press.

Hickling, A. K., & Wellman, H. M. (2001). The emergence of children's causal explanations and theories: Evidence from everyday conversation. *Developmental Psychology, 37*(5), 668–663.

Hilton, D. J. (1988). Logic and causal attribution. In D. J. Hilton (Ed.), *Contemporary science and natural explanation: Commonsense conceptions of causality* (pp. 33–65). Brighton, England: Harvester Press.

Hilton, D. J. (1995). The social context of reasoning: Conversational inference and rational judgment. *Psychological Bulletin, 118*, 248–271.

Hoyos, C., & Gentner, D. (2017). Generating explanations via analogical comparison. *Psychonomic Bulletin Review, 24*(5), 1364–1374.

Keil, F. C. (2006). Explanation and understanding. *Annual Review of Psychology, 57*, 227–254.

Keil, F. C., & Wilson, R. A. (2000). *Explanation and cognition.* Cambridge, MA: MIT Press.

Kline, M. A. (2015). How to learn about teaching: An evolutionary framework for the study of teaching behavior in humans and other animals. *Behavioral and Brain Science, 38*, 1–17.

Lancy, D. F. (2008). *The anthropology of childhood: Cherubs, chattel, changelings.* New York, NY: Cambridge University Press.

Legare, C. H. (2012). Exploring explanation: Explaining inconsistent information guides hypothesis-testing behavior in young children. *Child Development, 83*, 173–185.

Legare, C. H. (2014). The contributions of explanation and exploration to children's scientific reasoning. *Child Development Perspectives, 8*, 101–106.

Legare, C. H. (2017). Cumulative cultural learning: Diversity and development. *Proceedings of the National Academy of Sciences, 114*(30), 7877–7883.

Legare, C. H., & Gelman, S. A. (2014). Examining explanatory biases in young children's biological reasoning. *Journal of Cognition and Development, 15*(2), 287–303.

Legare, C. H., Gelman, S. A., & Wellman, H. M. (2010). Inconsistency with prior knowledge triggers children's causal explanatory reasoning. *Child Development, 81*(3), 929–944.

Legare, C. H., & Harris, P. L. (2016). The ontogeny of cultural learning. *Child Development, 87*(3), 633–642.

Legare, C. H., & Lombrozo, T. (2014). Selective effects of explanation on learning during early childhood. *Journal of Experimental Child Psychology, 126*, 198–212.

Legare, C. H., Mills, C. M., Souza, A. L., Plummer, L. E., & Yasskin, R. (2013). The use of questions as problem-solving strategies during early childhood. *Journal of Experimental Child Psychology, 114*, 63–76.

Legare, C. H., Schult, C., Impola, M., & Souza, A. L. (2016). Young children revise explanations in response to new evidence. *Cognitive Development, 39*, 45–56.

Legare, C. H., Sobel, D. M., & Callanan, M. (2017). Causal learning is collaborative: Examining explanation and exploration in social contexts. *Psychonomic Bulletin & Review, 24*(5), 1548–1554.

Legare, C. H., Wellman, H. M., & Gelman, S. A. (2009). Evidence for an explanation advantage in naïve biological reasoning. *Cognitive Psychology, 58*, 177–194.

Lipton, P. (2004). *Inference to the best explanation.* New York, NY: Routledge.

Lombrozo, T. (2006). The structure and function of explanations. *Trends in Cognitive Sciences, 10*(10), 464–470.

Lombrozo, T. (2007). Simplicity and probability in causal explanation. *Cognitive Psychology, 55*, 232–257.

McEldoon, K. L., Durkin, K. L., & Rittle-Johnson, B. (2012). Is self-explanation worth the time? A comparison to additional practice. *British Journal of Educational Psychology, 83*(4), 615–632.

Mercier, H., Deguchi, M., Van der Henst, J.-B., & Yama, H. (2016). The benefits of argumentation are cross-culturally robust: The case of Japan. *Thinking and Reasoning, 22*(1), 1–15.

Mercier, H., & Sperber, D. (2011). Why do humans reason? Arguments for an argumentative theory. *Behavioral and Brain Sciences, 34*, 57–111.

Mercier, H., & Sperber, D. (2017). *The enigma of reason.* Cambridge, MA: Harvard University Press.

Mills, C. M., Legare, C. H., Bills, M., & Mejias, C. (2010). Preschoolers use questions as a tool to acquire knowledge from different sources. *Journal of Cognition and Development, 11*(4), 533–560.

Mills, C. M., Legare, C. H., Grant, M. G., & Landrum, A. R. (2011). Determining who to question, what to ask, and how much information to ask for: The development of inquiry in young children. *Journal of Experimental Child Psychology, 110*, 539–560.

Piaget, J. (1929). *The child's conception of the world.* London, England: Routledge & K. Paul.

Rittle-Johnson, B., Saylor, M., & Swygert, K. E. (2008). Learning from explaining: Does it matter if mom is listening? *Journal of Experimental Child Psychology, 100*, 215–224.

Rittle-Johnson, B., & Star, J. R. (2007). Does comparing solutions methods facilitate conceptual and procedural knowledge? An experimental study on learning to solve equations. *Journal of Educational Psychology, 99*(3), 561–574.

Rogoff, B. (2003). *The cultural nature of human development.* New York, NY: Oxford University Press.

Ruggeri, A., & Lombrozo, T. (2015). Children adapt their questions to achieve efficient search. *Cognition, 143*, 203–216.

Schulz, L. (2012). The origins of inquiry: Inductive inference and exploration in early childhood. *Trends in Cognitive Science, 16*(7), 382–389.

Stahl, A. E., & Feigenson, L. (2015). Observing the unexpected enhances infants' learning and exploration. *Science, 348*(6230), 91–94.

Teasley, S. D. (1997). Talking about reasoning: How important is the peer in peer collaboration? In L. B. Resnick, R. Saljo, C. Pontecorvo, & B. Burge (Eds.), *Discourse, tools, and reasoning: Essays on situated cognition.* New York, NY: Springer.

Trouche, E., Sander, E., & Mercier, H. (2014). Arguments, more than confidence, explain the good performance of reasoning in groups. *Journal of Experimental Psychology: General, 143*(5), 1958–1971.

Vygotsky, L. S. (1962). *Thought and language.* Cambridge, MA: MIT Press.

Walker, C. M., Lombrozo, T., Legare, C. H., & Gopnik, A. (2014). Explaining prompts children to privilege inductively rich properties. *Cognition, 133*, 343–357.

Walker, C. M., Lombrozo, T., Williams, J. J., Rafferty, A. N., & Gopnik, A. (2017). Explaining constrains causal learning in childhood. *Child Development, 88*(1), 229–246.

Walker, C. M., Williams, J. J., Lombrozo, T., & Gopnik, A. (2012). Explaining influences children's reliance on evidence and prior knowledge in causal induction. In N. Miyake, D. Peebles, & R. P. Cooper (Eds.), *Proceedings of the 34th annual conference of the Cognitive Science Society* (pp. 1114–1119). Austin, TX.

Wellman, H. M. (2011). Reinvigorating explanations for the study of early cognitive development. *Child Development Perspectives, 5*(1), 33–38.

Wellman, H. M., Hickling, A. K., & Schult, C. A. (1997). Young children's psychological, physical, and biological explanations. *New Directions for Child Development, 75*, 7–25.

Wilkenfeld, D. A., & Lombrozo, T. (2015). Inference to the best explanation (IBE) versus explaining for the best inference (EBI). *Science and Education, 24*(9-10), 1059–1077.

Willard, A. K., Busch, J. T. A., Sobel, D. M., Callanan, M. A., & Legare C. H. (2016). *The impact of parent and children's explanation and exploration on children's causal learning.* Poster presented at the Annual Meeting of the Society for Philosophy and Psychology, Austin, TX.

Part III
Epistemic Trust: Selectivity in Children's Learning

Chapter 8
Insights into Children's Testimonial Reasoning

Katherine E. Ridge, Annelise Pesch, Sarah Suárez, and Melissa A. Koenig

Abstract Human testimony is a rich source of knowledge about the world, enabling us to acquire information about things both near and distant, available and unavailable, known and unknown. It also provides us with an opportunity to investigate children's reasoning about the human informants who testify. In this chapter, we discuss the testimonial reasoning that supports children's knowledge acquisition. We discuss both the evidential reasons (e.g., epistemic reliability) that children have to believe what they are told and the distinct interpersonal reasons (e.g., direct address) that children have to trust others. We suggest that children engage in a flexible reasoning process that recruits children's understanding of intentional agency, one that empowers them to monitor epistemic and moral transgressions, but also to forgive excusable errors. We offer insight into new avenues for future research, with an interest in better specifying the reasoning that children apply to testimony, and the implications this has for understanding individual and cultural differences in testimonial learning.

Introduction

Children—like adults—gain vast amounts of knowledge from others' testimony (for reviews, see Gelman, 2009; Harris, Koenig, Corriveau, & Jaswal, 2017; Koenig & Sabbagh, 2013). Given the power of testimony to extend our knowledge beyond personal first-hand experiences (Quine & Ullian, 1970), recent research has uncovered insights into how children manage certain inherent risks of communication, while discerning what to believe and whom to trust. There are different ways to characterize the epistemological problem that testimony presents, and doing full justice to the problem is beyond the scope of this chapter (see Gelfert, 2014; Goldberg, 2008; Lackey, 2008; McMyler, 2011). For our purposes here, it is enough to say that understanding the epistemological problem that testimony presents runs

K. E. Ridge · A. Pesch · S. Suárez · M. A. Koenig (✉)
Institute of Child Development, University of Minnesota, Minneapolis, MN, USA
e-mail: ridg0053@umn.edu; mkoenig@umn.edu

© Springer International Publishing AG, part of Springer Nature 2018
M. M. Saylor, P. A. Ganea (eds.), *Active Learning from Infancy to Childhood*,
https://doi.org/10.1007/978-3-319-77182-3_8

deeper than appreciating the risks posed by the occasionally incompetent or decep-
tive speaker. To appreciate the basic epistemic situation that testimony presents, it is
important to recognize that listeners encounter an opportunity for a judgment or
decision *whenever a speaker offers up their claim as a reason to believe it*. Even
when speakers do their very best as thoughtful believers and sincere testifiers, it falls
on the listener to make some kind of judgment.

In this chapter, we draw on recent research to characterize important elements of
the reasoning process that underlies children's testimonial learning decisions. In
essence, we argue that when children evaluate speakers, they do so in ways that are
characteristic of children's reasoning about intentional action more generally. We
will suggest that key aspects of children's intentional reasoning about speakers-as-
testifiers emerge quite early: Infants' sensitivity to informant reliability involves
monitoring the relation between an individual agent and her intentional actions
(e.g., Poulin-Dubois & Chow, 2009; Tummeltshammer, Wu, Sobel, & Kirkham,
2014), with an interest in the conditions that explain a speaker's anomalous actions
or statements (Henderson, Graham, & Schell, 2015; Koenig & Echols, 2003).
Children's decisions are often flexibly supported by evidence of a speaker's compe-
tencies as they relate to the specific claims being made (i.e., limits in perceptual
access) (Kondrad & Jaswal, 2012; Nurmsoo & Robinson, 2009; Reyes-Jáquez &
Echols, 2013). Children make epistemic inferences about speakers that are not
overly broad or sweeping, but that are in line with specific forms of knowledge put
on display (Brosseau-Liard & Birch, 2011; Koenig & Jaswal, 2011). Children spontaneously monitor a speaker's errors, disfluencies, bad arguments, and inconsistent
statements (e.g., Corriveau & Kurkul, 2014; Doebel, Rowell, & Koenig, 2016), and
sometimes give priority to epistemic considerations when put into conflict with
other social preferences they might have (Castelain, Bernard, Van der Henst, &
Mercier, 2016; Corriveau, Kim, Song, & Harris, 2013; Reyes-Jáquez & Echols,
2013). Taken together, one central component of children's reasoning about reliability is that it draws upon a general causal framework that aims to discern whether
speakers speak freely and intentionally from knowledge.

To make this case, we focus on three types of evidence gained from research on
children's testimonial learning: reliability assessments, knowledge attributions, and
error forgiveness. Sources can be assessed in terms of how reliably their actions—
including speech acts—relate to the world. Accuracy, fidelity, and consistency are all
different forms that relations between agents and the environment can take. Infants'
ability to distinguish variable from less-variable patterns of action will correspond
to more intentional over less intentional actions. Second, children's learning decisions suggest that they do not attribute knowledge to speakers uniformly broadly but
in ways that are circumscribed, and tailored to the specific knowledge that their
testimony reveals. Third, in work on error and ignorance, children commonly show
an interest in the situational constraints on knowledge, constraints that place limits
on what someone can claim to know or can be faulted for not knowing.

Reliability Assessments

As mentioned above, infants and young children assess an informant's reliability (Birch, Vauthier, & Bloom, 2008; Clément, Koenig, & Harris, 2004; Koenig, Clément, & Harris, 2004; for reviews, see Harris & Lane, 2014; Poulin-Dubois & Brosseau-Liard, 2016). Twelve-month-olds preferred to seek and use information from an adult who demonstrated expertise (e.g., correctly labeling parts of a toy while correctly assembling it) over an adult who incompetently interacted with the same objects (e.g., offered no labels while failing to assemble the toy; Stenberg, 2013). By 16–18 months of age, infants recognize, show surprise, and reject false claims from adults (Koenig & Echols, 2003; Pea, 1982), actively seek information from more accurate sources (Begus & Southgate, 2012), and endorse new information from accurate over inaccurate speakers (Brooker & Poulin-Dubois, 2013). By age 3, they evaluate speakers who competently label familiar objects as "knowing more," (Clément et al., 2004; Koenig et al., 2004; Koenig & Harris, 2005; Pasquini, Corriveau, Koenig, & Harris, 2007), retain reliability information for a source over time (Corriveau & Harris, 2009), and by age 7, children (and adults) avoid learning from a speaker who demonstrates just one instance of semantic inaccuracy (Fitneva & Dunfield, 2010).

Research from outside of the labeling domain indicates that children's ability to infer a source's reliability is quite general, and extends to a wide-ranging set of behaviors. For instance, 14-month-olds selectively imitated the instrumental actions of a model who used familiar objects in a competent manner (e.g., placed a shoe on his foot) but not a model who had incompetently used such objects (e.g., placed a shoe on his hand, Zmyj, Buttelmann, Carpenter, & Daud, 2010). By 14 months, infants also infer reliability from the congruence of an adult's affective display with positive or negative events in the environment. Chow, Poulin-Dubois, and Lewis (2008) found that 14-month-olds preferentially followed the gaze of an adult shown to be a "reliable looker" based on her expression of happiness when opening a box of toys. In contrast, they were less likely to follow the gaze of "unreliable looker," who displayed happiness in response to opening empty boxes. Further evidence of sensitivity to the correspondence between an agent's looking behavior (marked by "Wow, look!") and the location of a target object was demonstrated in 8-month-old infants (Tummeltshammer et al., 2014). When presented with a (100%) reliable face and less reliable one (25%) in relation to four animated locations, infants distinguished them at test by making predictive gazes that systematically followed the direction of the reliable face to a new location more than the unreliable face. Interestingly, when the same set of predictive relations held between a non-human arrow and an object's location, children learned the correspondences but did not generalize them to new locations. Thus, it seems that infants have a general capacity to learn the statistical regularities between human faces and arrows as they relate to object locations, but the familiarity of the entity being tracked affects their generalization abilities.

Knowledge Attributions

When making epistemic evaluations about a speaker, child listeners can evaluate testimony in terms of the extent to which evidence—of various forms—corroborates the claims being made by a speaker. Testimony provides a form of evidence about the world and child listeners are right to treat it this way when appropriate (for discussion, see Koenig & McMyler in press). In developmental research that treats testimony as evidence, the main object of investigation is children's "epistemic trust"—or their ability to estimate the knowledge, competence, or reliability of a source based on the evidence they have (Coady, 1992; Harris et al., 2017; Sperber et al., 2010; Sobel & Kushnir, 2013). By appealing to evidence about speakers and their claims, children further their own goals of acquiring true beliefs and avoiding false ones. On the evidential model, to the extent that testimony requires a probabilistic weighing of evidence, stronger evidence or support for a claim (e.g., direct, perceptually-obvious support) should warrant stronger confidence in that claim.

Young children place some premium on evidence that corroborates a speaker's statements. When a speaker who referred to features of a particular animal evident in a photograph (e.g., brown scales) was contrasted with a speaker who referred to the animal's non-evident features (e.g., diet), 3- to 4-year-old children attributed more knowledge to the more verifiable speaker and preferred to learn from her (Study 1, Koenig et al., 2015). Older children, and adults, however, preferred speakers who made non-obvious claims that went beyond their current perceptual experience (Koenig et al., 2015; Ridge et al., 2016). It may be that young children place a premium on claims that receive clear, indisputable support, and so credit knowledge to a speaker whose statements reference direct evidence available to them. In contrast, 6-year-olds are more flexible in their treatment of verifiability: they rely on their own perceptual access when learning about the visible properties of unfamiliar animals, but defer to an expert when learning about invisible properties (Fitneva, Lam, & Dunfield, 2013). Therefore, children may depend less on perceptually obvious support with age and shift to a greater willingness to accept testimony that is not immediately corroborated by evidence, but still flexibly call upon their own perception or knowledge when appropriate.

In a related manner, children not only consider the question of whether a speaker's claims are supported by perceptual evidence; they also consider *how* they came to make a claim. Indeed, what may be more indicative of a speaker's knowledgeability is not whether their specific utterances are true and evident but more generally, whether they have sufficient grounds to make a given claim. "their capacities to find out truths for themselves and their ability to organize and exploit them" (Ryle, 1949, p. 28). Children as young as 3 years of age distinguish between adequate and inadequate justifications for empirical claims: speakers who cite their own perceptual access, reliable testimony, and inference are judged by children as providing better support than speakers who cite their own desires, guesses, and pretending states of mind (Koenig, 2012). Children also judged speakers who offered good justifications for their claims (e.g., that books are in a backpack because backpacks generally carry books) as having the "best" way of thinking and preferred to learn from these speakers over those who offer weak support for factual claims (e.g., claiming a lunch is in the backpack based on a guess).

Children learn new information judged to be relevant to a given speaker's expertise, but often not beyond (Jaswal, 2006; Koenig & Jaswal, 2011; Sobel & Corriveau, 2010; Stephens & Koenig, 2015). For example, Kushnir, Vredenburgh, and Schneider (2013) found that preschoolers sought labels for novel objects from a previously competent labeler but asked someone who had demonstrated mechanical expertise to fix malfunctioning toys, suggesting that they modify their information-seeking behaviors based on others' relevant expertise (see also, Brooker & Poulin-Dubois, 2013; Danovitch & Keil, 2004; Lutz & Keil, 2002). Children's willingness to learn from someone is often bound or limited to the specific form of knowledge that a speaker displayed in their prior language use or behavior. Such circumscribed learning patterns suggest that their learning decisions are not simply a matter of crediting more or less knowledge to a speaker, but are informed by how or why the speaker's knowledge was acquired.

Error Forgiveness

In work on accuracy, children typically watch a speaker name objects inaccurately without being provided with an explanation for that speaker's errors (e.g., Koenig & Harris, 2005; Koenig & Woodward, 2010). Research that provides such explanations by way of limitations in access or limited knowledge of English converge in showing that children do not treat mistaken speech acts uniformly—but rather, seek to determine whether errors were produced freely and intentionally by the speaker. Critical evidence stems from children's forgiveness or excusal of certain mistakes and their condemnation or blame of others. For example, children forgive errors that result from a speaker's lack of relevant perceptual access, and accept information from previously inaccurate speakers whose perceptual access was restored (Nurmsoo & Robinson, 2009; Reyes-Jáquez & Echols, 2013). Not unlike work in rational imitation, such research suggests that children's decisions to learn from a speaker depends upon their assessment of the speaker's reasons for making an anomalous statement (see also, Einav & Robinson, 2010; Kondrad & Jaswal, 2012).

An interest in whether a speaker's statements are consistent with her perceptual access is evident in infancy. In Koenig and Echols (2003), when both speakers were looking directly at familiar objects, 16-month-olds actively corrected and looked longer at speakers who incorrectly labeled the objects than one who correctly labels them. Conversely, when both speakers were turned away from the objects, infants looked marginally longer at a speaker who offered correct labels over one who offered incorrect labels. Slightly older children prefer informants who are in a better position to know, or have better access to relevant information than children do themselves. By 22 months of age, children update their representation of an absent object based on testimony from an adult with privileged perceptual access (Ganea,

Shutts, Spelke, & DeLoache, 2007) and by 3 years of age, abandon their initial beliefs in favor of a contradicting claim if that speaker is better perceptually informed than themselves (Ma & Ganea, 2010; Robinson & Whitcombe, 2003).

Children's forgiveness of errors indicates that children's testimonial reasoning is sensitive to the epistemic grounds that speakers have. By examining speakers' anomalous or false statements in a range of contexts, researchers have revealed a pattern that suggests that children base their decisions to accept or reject a claim on their assessment of whether the speaker's claims were made intentionally and knowledgably, or whether they were constrained by limits of the situation. Such reasoning bears similarity to work on rational imitation, which demonstrates infants' assessments of situational constraints in their interpretation of anomalous, unusual, or failed actions of an agent. Gergely, Bekkering, and Király (2002) found that after observing an adult freely activate a light box by deliberately touching it with her forehead, most 14-month-olds also first attempted to turn on the light using their forehead. Replicating results from Meltzoff's (1988) seminal study, infants engaged in the model's unfamiliar and less efficient strategy despite the availability of more natural or direct means (i.e., their hands). Gergely and colleagues suggest that, given no obvious situational explanation for this anomalous action, infants inferred that the head action offered some unseen advantage in operating the light, and there-fore, adopted that action when given the opportunity. In fact, when another group of 14-month-olds observed an adult use her forehead when her hands were occupied by holding a blanket around herself, most infants instead used their hands to turn on the light. Presumably, in the blanket case, they inferred that the model used her forehead to operate the light-box not because it was her intention to use her head, but because her hands were unavailable in this case. In other words, 14-month-old infants took into account the situational limits on the actor's action and imitated not what agents actually did do, but made an inference about what an unconstrained agent would have done. Similarly, when children evaluate speakers who make anomalous statements, they consider various situational explanations—if avail-able—that provide compelling grounds for that speech act.

Indeed, children show a nuanced understanding of the circumstances that can lead to excusable labeling errors: By age 3, they are willing to overlook a history of inaccuracy, but only when the informant's past mistakes were explained by limits in perceptual access to relevant information bearing on the claim (e.g., stating an object's color based on touch alone; Nurmsoo & Robinson, 2009). Importantly, children's speaker evaluations indicate their understanding that a speaker's limited perceptual access is not only a legitimate, exculpatory reason for inaccuracy, but it can be temporary and remediable, as they were willing to accept information from the same speaker when her perceptual access was restored. When inaccuracy is explained by the situational constraints placed on the speaker, children seem to treat such errors as responsive to the environment, and thus transient and reparable. In contrast, if no plausible explanation for an error exists, children are more likely to treat it as a failure of the speaker and grounds to question their competence.

Children also accept claims from forthcoming speakers who openly acknowl-edge their epistemic limits and profess their ignorance but reject claims from someone with a history of inexplicable inaccuracy. When a speaker admitted ignorance to the names of familiar objects, preschoolers endorsed her later claims about a different set of objects but did not respond as charitably toward someone who inaccurately labeled familiar objects (Kushnir & Koenig, 2017). In fact, when the previously inaccurate speaker had privileged perceptual access to a hidden object, preschoolers still rejected her reports about the location of the object. However, they accepted claims of a hidden object's location from the ignorant speaker who was upfront and aware of her ignorance in the past. Ignorant speakers make no unreliable claims to know and do not make claims that conflict with reality or the child's knowledge. Indeed, children might treat certain forms of ignorance as an explanation or constraint on what someone can claim to know, whereas overt inaccuracy with no explanation invites more fundamental attributions of character—such as incompetence or malevolence.

Further evidence for children's ability to evaluate the intentionality of speakers and their claims in testimonial learning is suggested by research on error magnitude. For instance, Einav and Robinson (2010) found that 6- to 7-year-olds prefer a speaker who narrowly mislabels a butterfly as "a bee" over a speaker who grossly mislabels the butterfly "a car". Preschoolers also discriminate between serious and less serious labeling errors when given reason to avoid a speaker. Kondrad and Jaswal (2012) found that when two speakers mislabel a partially visible object (e.g., only the handle of a comb), 4- to 5-year-olds avoid those speakers whose errors seem entirely inconsistent with the partial evidence available (e.g., labeling it "a thunderstorm"). Instead, they prefer to learn from speakers whose errors were detected but in line with the available evidence (e.g., "a brush"). Thus, children overlooked a history of inaccuracy when those mistakes were explained by their access to information. Furthermore, Stephens and Koenig (2015) showed that when both speakers' access was fixed, children treated categorical, semantic errors as a more serious breach and avoided such speakers more broadly than speakers who made episodic errors about an object's variable location. It is important to note that children recognize all such mistaken statements as false. The interesting finding lies in the different inferences drawn about a speaker's reliability based on the *content and context* of their errors. When children encounter episodic or narrow errors explained by limited visual access, they appreciate that such errors are explained—folk-psychologically—by limits of the speaker's situation and in these cases, are not very informative about the competence of the speaker. Opportunities for future research include identifying various other kinds of constraints on action that explain or contextualize anomalous statements, and that spare negative attributions toward the speaker.

Taken together, such research suggests that when errors cannot be adequately explained by limits of the environment, children view these errors as more prognostic of a speaker's incompetence and future unreliability. First, such inferences offer a basic source of protection against speakers whose incompetence poses a more general threat to knowledge. Second, key aspects of this reasoning process emerge early: infants and young children are not only monitoring informants for evidence of accuracy—they show an interest in the epistemic conditions that explain a speaker's error or anomalous statement (Brosseau-Liard & Birch, 2011; Henderson et al., 2015; Koenig & Echols, 2003). Third, this reasoning process presumably develops in tandem with children's growing knowledge base, allowing them to better check a broader range of anomalous statements for violations to their pre-existing knowledge, draw more nuanced inferences from a broader class of anomalies, and generate new explanations for errors. A key component of children's testimonial learning is their ability to determine when human agents speak intentionally, and without constraint. This supports the ability to contextualize errors—to penalize, correct, or mistrust those who err in ways that beg explanation and excuse those whose errors are warranted by the situation.

When Epistemic Reliability and Socio-Moral Information Conflicts

Children's testimonial learning in exchanges involving moral agents also recruits their more general understanding of intentional action. More recent insight into children's testimonial reasoning comes from studies that put social or moral information about informants in direct conflict with epistemic considerations. For example, in a study by Lane, Wellman, and Gelman (2013), 3- and 4-year-olds attributed knowledge to an agent with positive traits even though that agent lacked relevant perceptual access to the information. In work by Corriveau et al. (2013), 3-year-olds favored a speaker with a native accent despite her history of inaccuracy, and Reyes-Jáquez and Echols (2013) showed that 5-year-olds were more willing to excuse errors from speakers who bore some similarity to the child (see also Ma & Woolley, 2013). Similarly, Landrum, Mills, and Johnston (2013) found that 3- to 5-year-olds endorsed claims offered by a benevolent speaker with irrelevant expertise over a mean speaker with relevant expertise. Such findings suggest that children sometimes weigh information about moral and social in-group members more heavily in their learning decisions than perceptual access or expertise.

Why might children sometimes favor affiliated or similar individuals even when they have proven unreliable? Reyes-Jáquez and Echols (2013) offer an intriguing explanation—one that implicates the picture of testimonial reasoning discussed above. They argue that children's social preferences or biases for familiar or similar agents might be especially pronounced when errors go unexplained and are left open to interpretation. In a single design, they presented children with agents whose errors were explained—by wearing a blindfold, as well as agents whose errors were unexplained—by wearing the same item as a scarf. Children were familiarized to similar and dissimilar puppet agents, and preferred to ask and endorse information from the more similar agent. Afterward, children witnessed two phases, one in which both agents were accurate, followed by a phase where one was accurate, and one was inaccurate. Sometimes the similar agent was inaccurate, other times the dissimilar agent was inaccurate; and depending on condition, the inaccuracy was explained by the blindfold, or unexplained by the scarf. When the errors were explained by the blindfold, children did not demonstrate their preference for the more similar agent—because their errors were excused. However, when the errors went unexplained by the scarf, children were more likely to endorse information from the more similar agent.

In much of the selective learning literature, failure to discredit the testimony from problematic sources, for either socio-moral or evidential reasons, has been conceptualized as reflecting children's "specific bias to trust" or an instance of "lack of distrust" (Vanderbilt, Liu, & Heyman, 2011). The prevailing evidential treatment of selective learning features only one interpretation of "trust," based on evidential considerations concerning the moral or epistemic reliability of a source. However, by treating testimony as a species of evidence, and children's trusting decisions as exclusively responsive to evidence of moral and epistemic varieties, we risk neglecting the other ways in which children trust others (Koenig & McMyler in press). For example, adults who get married promise to be with their spouse forever despite knowing the high statistical likelihood of divorce, and spouses often trust each other's claims and promises when evidence is scant or problematic (Marušić, 2015). This suggests that trust is not to be reduced to our predictions of others' behavior based on evidence; rather, we often proceed by placing our trust in them without having evidence, or even against the evidence that is available. When do children's interpersonal extensions of trust influence their moral or practical decisions? When do they influence their epistemic decisions to learn? Raising a distinction between practical and epistemic decisions to trust might explain why children are willing to learn from an agent despite evidence of their ill intentions, and their unwillingness to share with that agent. Certainly, there are cases in which it would make sense to learn from someone despite their interpersonal flaws, and there will be cases in which it makes sense to mistrust someone with expertise. Investigating the different ways in which we trust others can begin to help scientists understand how or why young children trust others interpersonally in some cases, and evaluate the evidence provided in others (Koenig & McMyler in press; Marušić, 2015).

Recent work has begun to examine children's judgments of multidimensional agents (i.e., agents that have conflicting epistemic and moral characteristics) in not only a set of selective learning decisions, but also in more practical or social decisions. This work offers a way to evaluate whether children's epistemic "trust," seen in their selective learning decisions, is reflected in other, more social judgments. In one study, Hetherington, Hendrickson, and Koenig (2014) familiarized preschoolers to either an antisocial in-group or prosocial out-group member. This design uniquely used two agents whom embodied conflicting traits across multiple domains. Interestingly, although the antisocial behavior of the in-group member reduced children's liking of and willingness to share with her compared to a neutral out-group member, it did not guide their decisions to learn new information from her. Similarly, when 18-month-old infants encountered an agent who incorrectly labeled a set of objects, their willingness to learn novel information from that agent was reduced but their willingness to share with her was not (Brooker & Poulin-Dubois, 2013). When niceness and expertise were contrasted in a single design, children were found to base their epistemic inferences on both expertise and niceness but their social inferences were based uniquely on niceness (Landrum, Pflaum, & Mills, 2016). Pesch and Koenig (2017) investigated how direct interpersonal violations (failed promises and failed threats) are reflected in practical decisions to delay gratification and to share with an agent, as distinct from epistemic decisions learn from that agent. When the agent's promises or threats failed, 3- and 4-year-olds waited and shared less with an agent who did not keep her promises. Despite this, children were indiscriminate in their decisions to accept her claims. Taken together, these studies suggest that epistemic and practical decisions might stem from different types of appraisals that children make about agents and offers preliminary support for a distinction in the types of trust that children extend to others.

Thus, studies that look at more complex agents and interactions between the agent and child that potentially involve more than one form of trust offer a new avenue for understanding children's testimonial learning. In the traditional selective trust paradigm, children are provided with epistemic or social evidence about two agents and their decisions to learn largely reflect a preference for more positively valenced agents. However, when agents are multidimensional, children's decisions to learn are responsive to epistemic attributes, while practical decisions (sharing, helping, waiting) are responsive to the moral goodwill signaled by the agent. In future work, it will be important to more closely examine the type of information offered to children about agents at familiarization and compare it to the agent's speech acts at test, as there may be certain speech acts—promises, acts of telling—which present interpersonal considerations for trust while other speech acts—explanations, demonstrations, and arguments—that elicit evidential appraisals (for discussion, see Koenig & McMyler in press).

Individual Differences in Epistemic Trust

Does children's testimonial reasoning vary not only over development, but across individuals? Here, we review research characterizing cultural and contextual variations in children's decisions about whether or not to excuse anomalous statements when learning from speaker testimony.

Whether any given statement counts as anomalous for a child will depend upon what else they believe. In research examining the role of children's religious belief in their testimonial learning, Corriveau and Kurkul (2014) asked 5- and 6-year-old children to make judgments about the reality status of protagonists in realistic, religious, and fantastical stories. They found that children from religious backgrounds were more likely to accept that protagonists in religious stories were real people. Thus, it appears that children's skepticism towards improbable scenarios (e.g., protagonists with superhuman powers) is informed by their formal or informal experiences with religious education, in which they are be exposed to speakers who discuss and endorse various miraculous possibilities. Along these lines, Iranian children, who are regularly exposed to religious narratives in daily life, are also prone to think of both realistic and fantastical figures in stories as real (Davoodi, Corriveau, & Harris, 2016).

In addition to religious values, recent research suggests that parents' authoritarian value influence children's decisions about whether to excuse or reject speaker errors. Reifen Tagar, Federico, Lyons, Ludeke, and Koenig (2014) found that 3- and 4-year-olds with more authoritarian parents placed a greater trust in adults who named objects accurately and showed greater vigilance against those who spoke inaccurately. Furthermore, children of parents high in authoritarianism gave greater weight to a status-based "adult = reliable" heuristic in trusting an ambiguously conventional adult. In light of the discussion above, it may be that because the inaccurate statements were unexplained by the situation, this allowed children's status-based preferences to be more clearly expressed. It is also possible that regardless of whether errors can be explained by limits of the situation or the ignorance of the agent, children from authoritarian backgrounds are especially prone to make character-like attributions to inaccurate agents. In either case, children's use of status-based or convention-based cues in testimonial learning varies as a function of parents' tendency to value deference or obedience to authority.

What other parent beliefs might explain individual differences in children's learning? Parents' epistemological values, or their beliefs about the nature and justification of knowledge, have been found to predict measures of their children's learning, including children's emphasis on evidence in discussions about science (Luce, Callanan, & Smilovic, 2013). Along these lines, parent epistemological beliefs are also predictive of children's decisions to accept or reject information from informants varying in how competently they utilized evidence to form conclusions (Suárez & Koenig, 2017). Interestingly, parents' evaluativist epistemological understanding—or the tendency to value evidence as a basis for belief—was associated with children's relative reluctance to attribute knowledge to, and endorse the conclusions of, poor reasoners. Thus, children whose parents value evidence as a justification of belief are more likely to have young children who reflect this epistemological value in their social learning decisions.

Further evidence that cultural or family values are reflected in children's testimonial learning comes from cross-cultural work on children's deference to consensus. Corriveau et al. (2013) found that deference to a group's consensus is greater among Asian-American children, who were especially deferential to group consensus in a public setting compared to Caucasian-American children. That is, children from more collectivist cultural backgrounds may rely more on group consensus in their testimonial reasoning.

Beyond cultural values, a child's spoken language may also influence their testimonial learning decisions. Lucas, Lewis, Pala, Wong, and Berridge (2013) found that Turkish preschoolers—who are exposed to language with evidential markers indicating what evidence exists for a statement—were more selective in their preferences for accurate informants relative to Chinese and English children. Thus, speaking a language that obliges speakers to state the sources of their knowledge may sensitize preschoolers to informant reliability.

In sum, it appears that cultural, family, and linguistic factors influence children's testimonial learning. Thus, a child's age is only one of the many factors that can impact the considerations he or she makes when learning from others. Children may be more or less sensitive to specific cues to reliability (or lack thereof) in accordance with cultural and family beliefs, values, and practices. Further research should clarify how contextual factors may influence children's judgments about both epistemic and interpersonal trust, as well as how enculturation interacts with cognitive developments to inform children's decisions to accept or reject testimony.

Summary

The work described in this chapter highlights important implications for how researchers conceptualize and study children's testimonial reasoning. We have outlined a growing body of literature showing that children reason about epistemic reliability with an interest in whether a given statement was produced intentionally by the agent or whether it was constrained by limits in the situation. When children receive a testimonial claim, it elicits both a check against what they know, and a form of reasoning about the speaker's epistemic conditions, credentials and their basis for knowing what they claim. In fact, as soon as infants can assess the truth of an utterance, they show an interest in assessing the grounds speakers have for their claims (Koenig & Echols, 2003; Koenig & Woodward, 2010). So in testimonial learning, as soon as children assess the meaning of a claim and can evaluate its truth value, they appear to be ready to monitor the epistemic conditions of the source who made the claims. As Gilbert Ryle (1949) was right to stress, "We are less interested in the stock of truths people acquire and retain, than in their capacities to find things out for themselves and their ability to organize and exploit them" (p. 28).

The field has continued to improve the general methodological paradigm used, shifting its focus to include more complex agents and to present more various decisions in order to comprehensively describe children's learning decisions and speaker evaluations. For example, it may be that in some cases, children attribute more knowledge to one informant but prefer to share or play or affiliate with another. The particular conditions (e.g., a speaker who is smart but mean) that elicit this type of dissociated reasoning process will likely be of special interest to researchers, but would not necessarily be captured unless studies include trials that tap into both the child's epistemic and practical judgments. In other words, study designs should account for both the epistemic and interpersonal considerations that feature in children's evaluations of others, with an eye for the range of social and cultural influences that affect their learning decisions.

References

Begus, K., & Southgate, V. (2012). Infant pointing serves an interrogative function. *Developmental Science, 15*, 611–617. https://doi.org/10.1111/j.1467-7687.2012.01160.x

Birch, S. A. J., Vauthier, S. A., & Bloom, P. (2008). Three- and 4-year-olds spontaneously use others' past performance to guide their learning. *Cognition, 107*, 1018–1034. https://doi.org/10.1016/j.cognition.2007.12.008

Brooker, I., & Poulin-Dubois, D. (2013). Is a bird an apple? The effect of speaker labeling accuracy on infants' word learning, imitation, and helping behaviors. *Infancy, 18*, 46–68. https://doi.org/10.1111/infa.12027

Brosseau-Liard, P. E., & Birch, S. A. J. (2011). Epistemic states and traits: Preschoolers appreciate the differential informativeness of situation-specific and person-specific cues to knowledge. *Child Development, 82*, 1788–1796. https://doi.org/10.1111/j.1467-8624.2011.01662.x

Castelain, T., Bernard, S., Van der Henst, J. B., & Mercier, H. (2016). The influence of power and reason on young Maya children's endorsement of testimony. *Developmental Science, 19*, 957–966. https://doi.org/10.1111/desc.12336

Chow, V., Poulin-Dubois, D., & Lewis, J. (2008). To see or not to see: Infants prefer to follow the gaze of a reliable looker. *Developmental Science, 11*, 761–770. https://doi.org/10.1111/j.1467-7687.2008.00726.x

Clément, F., Koenig, M. A., & Harris, P. (2004). The ontogenesis of trust. *Mind & Language, 19*, 360–379. https://doi.org/10.1111/j.0268-1064.2004.00263.x

Coady, C. (1992). *Testimony: A philosophical study*. Oxford, UK: Clarendon Press.

Corriveau, K. H., & Harris, P. L. (2009). Preschoolers continue to trust a more accurate informant 1 week after exposure to accuracy information. *Developmental Science, 12*, 188–193. https://doi.org/10.1111/j.1467-7687.2008.00763.x

Corriveau, K. H., Kim, E., Song, G., & Harris, P. L. (2013). Young children's deference to a majority varies by culture and judgment setting. *Journal of Cognition and Culture, 13*, 367–381. https://doi.org/10.1163/15685373-12342099

Corriveau, K. H., & Kurkul, K. E. (2014). "Why does rain fall?": Children prefer to learn from an informant who uses noncircular explanations. *Child Development, 85*, 1827–1835. https://doi.org/10.1111/cdev.12240

Danovitch, J. H., & Keil, F. (2004). Should you ask a fisherman or a biologist?: Developmental shifts in ways of clustering knowledge. *Child Development, 75*, 918–931. https://doi.org/10.1111/j.1467-8624.2004.00714.x

Davoodi, T., Corriveau, K. H., & Harris, P. L. (2016). Distinguishing between realistic and fantastical stories in Iran. *Developmental Psychology, 52*, 221–231. https://doi.org/10.1037/dev0000079

Doebel, S., Rowell, S. F., & Koenig, M. A. (2016). Young children detect and avoid logically inconsistent sources: The importance of communicative context and executive function. *Child Development, 87*, 1956–1970. https://doi.org/10.1111/cdev.12563

Einav, S., & Robinson, E. J. (2010). Children's sensitivity to error magnitude when evaluating informants. *Cognitive Development, 25*, 218–232. https://doi.org/10.1016/j.cogdev.2010.04.002

Fitneva, S. A., & Dunfield, K. A. (2010). Selective information seeking after a single encounter. *Developmental Psychology, 46*, 1380–1384. https://doi.org/10.1037/a0019818

Fitneva, S. A., Lam, N. H. L., & Dunfield, K. A. (2013). The development of children's information gathering: To look or to ask? *Developmental Psychology, 49*, 533–542. https://doi.org/10.1037/a0031326

Ganea, P. A., Shutts, K., Spelke, E., & DeLoache, J. S. (2007). Thinking of things unseen: Infants' use of language to update object representations. *Psychological Science, 18*, 734–739. https://doi.org/10.1111/j.1467-9280.2007.01968.x

Gelfert, A. (2014). *A critical introduction to testimony*. London, England: Bloomsbury.

Gelman, S. A. (2009). Learning from others: Children's construction of concepts. *Annual Review of Psychology, 60*, 115–140. https://doi.org/10.1146/annurev.psych.59.103006.093659

Gergely, G., Bekkering, H., & Király, I. (2002). Rational imitation in preverbal infants. *Nature, 415*, 755. https://doi.org/10.1038/415755a

Goldberg, S. C. (2008). Testimonial knowledge in early childhood, revisited. *Philosophy and Phenomenological Research, 76*, 1–36. https://doi.org/10.1111/j.1933-1592.2007.00113.x

Harris, P. L., Koenig, M. A., Corriveau, K. H., & Jaswal, V. K. (2017). Cognitive foundations of learning from testimony. *Annual Review of Psychology, 69*, 251–273. https://doi.org/10.1146/annurev-psych-122216-011710

Harris, P. L., & Lane, J. D. (2014). Infants understand how testimony works. *Topoi, 33*, 443–458. https://doi.org/10.1007/s11245-013-9180-0

Henderson, A. M. E., Graham, S. A., & Schell, V. (2015). 24-Month-olds' selective learning is not an all-or-none phenomenon. *PLoS One, 10*(6), e0131215. https://doi.org/10.1371/journal.pone.0131215

Hetherington, C., Hendrickson, C., & Koenig, M. (2014). Reducing an in-group bias in preschool children: The impact of moral behavior. *Developmental Science, 17*, 1042–1049. https://doi.org/10.1111/desc.12192

Jaswal, V. K. (2006). Preschoolers' favor the creator's label when reasoning about an artifact's function. *Cognition, 99*, B83–B92. https://doi.org/10.1016/j.cognition.2005.07.006

Koenig, M. A. (2012). Beyond semantic accuracy: Preschoolers evaluate a speaker's reasons. *Child Development, 83*, 1051–1063. https://doi.org/10.1111/j.1467-8624.2012.01742.x

Koenig, M. A., Clément, F., & Harris, P. L. (2004). Trust in testimony: Children's use of true and false statements. *Psychological Science, 15*, 694–698. https://doi.org/10.1111/j.0956-7976.2004.00742.x

Koenig, M. A., Cole, C. A., Meyer, M., Ridge, K. E., Kushnir, T., & Gelman, S. A. (2015). Reasoning about knowledge: Children's evaluations of generality and verifiability. *Cognitive Psychology, 83*, 22–39. https://doi.org/10.1016/j.cogpsych.2015.08.007

Koenig, M. A., & Echols, C. H. (2003). Infants' understanding of false labeling events: The referential role of words and the people who use them. *Cognition, 87*, 181–210. https://doi.org/10.1016/S0010-0277(03)00002-7

Koenig, M. A., & Harris, P. L. (2005). Preschoolers mistrust ignorant and inaccurate speakers. *Child Development, 76*, 1261–1277. https://doi.org/10.1111/j.1467-8624.2005.00849.x

Koenig, M. A., & Jaswal, V. K. (2011). Characterizing children's expectations about expertise and incompetence: Halo or pitchfork effects? *Child Development, 82*, 1634–1647. https://doi.org/10.1111/j.1467-8624.2011.01618.x

Koenig, M. A., & McMyler, B. (in press). Testimonial knowledge: Understanding the evidential, uncovering the interpersonal. In M. Fricker, P. J. Graham, D. Henderson, N. Pedersen, & J. Wyatt (Eds.), *The Routledge handbook of social epistemology*. New York, NY: Taylor & Francis.

Koenig, M. A., & Sabbagh, M. A. (2013). Selective social learning: New perspectives on learning from others. *Developmental Psychology, 49*, 399–403. https://doi.org/10.1111/10.1037/a0031619

Koenig, M. A., & Woodward, A. L. (2010). Sensitivity of 24-month-olds to the prior inaccuracy of the source: Possible mechanisms. *Developmental Psychology, 46*, 815–826. https://doi.org/10.1037/a0019664

Kondrad, R. L., & Jaswal, V. K. (2012). Explaining the errors away: Young children forgive understandable semantic mistakes. *Cognitive Development, 27*, 126–135. https://doi.org/10.1016/j.cogdev.2011.11.001

Kushnir, T., & Koenig, M. A. (2017). What I don't know won't hurt you: The relation between professed ignorance and later knowledge claims. *Developmental Psychology, 53*, 826–835. https://doi.org/10.1037/dev0000294

Kushnir, T., Vredenburgh, C., & Schneider, L. A. (2013). "Who can help me fix this toy?" The distinction between causal knowledge and word knowledge guides preschoolers' selective requests for information. *Developmental Psychology, 49*, 446–453. https://doi.org/10.1037/a0031649

Lackey, J. (2008). *Learning from words: Testimony as a source of knowledge.* Oxford, UK: Oxford University Press.

Landrum, A. R., Mills, C. M., & Johnston, A. M. (2013). When do children trust the expert? Benevolence information influences children's trust more than expertise. *Developmental Science, 16,* 622–638. https://doi.org/10.1111/desc.12059

Landrum, A. R., Pflaum, A. D., & Mills, C. M. (2016). Inducing knowledgeability from niceness: Children use social features for making epistemic inferences. *Journal of Cognition and Development, 17,* 699–717. https://doi.org/10.1080/15248372.2015.1135799

Lane, J. D., Wellman, H. M., & Gelman, S. A. (2013). Informants' traits weigh heavily in young children's trust in testimony and in their epistemic inferences. *Child Development, 84,* 1253–1268. https://doi.org/10.1111/cdev.12029

Lucas, A. J., Lewis, C., Pala, F. C., Wong, K., & Berridge, D. (2013). Social-cognitive processes in preschoolers' selective trust: Three cultures compared. *Developmental Psychology, 49,* 579–590. https://doi.org/10.1037/a0029864

Luce, M. R., Callanan, M. A., & Smilovic, S. (2013). Links between parents' epistemological stance and children's evidence talk. *Developmental Psychology, 49,* 454–461. https://doi.org/10.1037/a0031249

Lutz, D. J., & Keil, F. C. (2002). Early understanding of the division of cognitive labor. *Child Development, 73,* 1073–1084. https://doi.org/10.1111/1467-8624.00458

Ma, L., & Ganea, P. A. (2010). Dealing with conflicting information: Young children's reliance on what they see versus what they are told. *Developmental Science, 13,* 151–160. https://doi.org/10.1111/j.1467-7687.2009.00878.x

Ma, L., & Woolley, J. D. (2013). Young children's sensitivity to speaker gender when learning from others. *Journal of Cognition and Development, 14,* 100–119. https://doi.org/10.1080/15248372.2011.638687

Marušić, B. (2015). *Evidence and agency: Norms of belief for promising and resolving.* New York, NY: Oxford University Press.

McMyler, B. (2011). *Testimony, trust, and authority.* New York, NY: Oxford University Press.

Meltzoff, A. N. (1988). Infant imitation after a 1-week delay: Long-term memory for novel acts and multiple stimuli. *Developmental Psychology, 24,* 470–476. https://doi.org/10.1037/0012-1649.24.4.470

Nurmsoo, E., & Robinson, E. J. (2009). Children's trust in previously inaccurate informants who were well- or poorly-informed: When past errors can be excused. *Child Development, 80,* 23–27. https://doi.org/10.1111/j.1467-8624.2008.01243.x

Pasquini, E. S., Corriveau, K. H., Koenig, M., & Harris, P. L. (2007). Preschoolers monitor the relative accuracy of informants. *Developmental Psychology, 43,* 1216–1226. https://doi.org/10.1037/0012-1649.43.5.1216

Pea, R. (1982). Origins of verbal logic: Spontaneous denials by 2- and 3-year-olds. *Journal of Child Language, 9,* 597–626. https://doi.org/10.1017/S0305000900004931

Pesch, A., & Koenig, M. A. (2017). *Varieties of trust in children's learning and practical decisions.* Manuscript submitted for publication.

Poulin-Dubois, D., & Brosseau-Liard, P. (2016). The developmental origins of selective social learning. *Current Directions in Psychological Science, 25,* 60–64. https://doi.org/10.1177/0963721415613962

Poulin-Dubois, D., & Chow, V. (2009). The effect of a looker's past reliability on infants' reasoning about beliefs. *Developmental Psychology, 45,* 1576–1582. https://doi.org/10.1037/a0016715

Quine, W. V. O., & Ullian, J. S. (1970). *The web of belief.* New York, NY: Random House.

Reifen Tagar, M., Federico, C. M., Lyons, K. E., Ludeke, S., & Koenig, M. A. (2014). Heralding the authoritarian? Orientation toward authority in early childhood. *Psychological Science, 25,* 883–892. https://doi.org/10.1177/0956797613516470

Reyes-Jáquez, B., & Echols, C. H. (2013). Developmental differences in the relative weighing of informants' social attributes. *Developmental Psychology, 49,* 602–613. https://doi.org/10.1037/a0031674

Ridge, K. E., Koenig, M. A., Cole, C., Meyer, M., Kushnir, T., & Gelman, S. (2016). *Children's evaluations of speakers using two epistemic properties of testimony*. Paper presented at the 46th Annual Meeting of the Jean Piaget Society, Chicago, IL.

Robinson, E. J., & Whitcombe, E. (2003). Children's suggestibility in relation to their understanding about sources of knowledge. *Child Development, 74*, 48–62. https://doi.org/10.1111/1467-8624.t01-1-00520

Ryle, G. (1949). *The concept of mind*. London, England: Hutchinson.

Sobel, D. M., & Corriveau, K. H. (2010). Children individuals' expertise for word learning. *Child Development, 81*, 669–679. https://doi.org/10.1111/j.1467-8624.2009.01422.x

Sobel, D. M., & Kushnir, T. (2013). Knowledge matters: How children evaluate the reliability of testimony as a process of rational inference. *Psychological Review, 120*, 779–797. https://doi.org/10.1037/a0034191

Sperber, D., Clément, F., Heintz, C., Mascaro, O., Mercier, H., Origgi, G., & Wilson, D. (2010). Epistemic vigilance. *Mind & Language, 25*, 359–393. https://doi.org/10.1111/j.1468-0017.2010.01394.x

Stenberg, G. (2013). Do 12-month-old infants trust a competent adult? *Infancy, 18*, 873–904. https://doi.org/10.1111/infa.12011

Stephens, E. C., & Koenig, M. A. (2015). Varieties of testimony: Children's selective learning in semantic versus episodic domains. *Cognition, 137*, 182–188. https://doi.org/10.1016/j.cognition.2015.01.004

Suárez, S., & Koenig, M. A. (2017). Children's use of speaker calibration for selective trust: Developmental trends and individual differences. In E. Luchkina's (Chair), *The changing mechanism of selective trust: Evidence from 3-to- 8-year- olds*. Symposium conducted at the Society for Research in Child Development Biennial Meeting, Austin, TX.

Tummeltshammer, K. S., Wu, R., Sobel, D. M., & Kirkham, N. Z. (2014). Infants track the reliability of potential informants. *Psychological Science, 25*, 1730–1738. https://doi.org/10.1177/0956797614540178

Vanderbilt, K. E., Liu, D., & Heyman, G. D. (2011). The development of distrust. *Child Development, 82*(5), 1372–1380. https://doi.org/10.1111/j.1467-8624.2011.01629.x

Zmyj, N., Buttelmann, D., Carpenter, M., & Daud, M. M. (2010). The reliability of a model influences 14-month-olds' imitation. *Journal of Experimental Child Psychology, 106*, 208–220. https://doi.org/10.1016/j.jecp.2010.03.002

Chapter 9
Mechanisms of Selective Word Learning: Evidence and Implications

Haykaz Mangardich and Mark A. Sabbagh

Abstract Much of the current literature on selective social learning focuses on the external factors that trigger children's selectivity. In this chapter, we review behavioral, eye-tracking, and electrophysiological evidence for how children selectively learn words—what the internal processes are that enable them to block learning when they doubt the epistemic quality of the source. We propose that young children engage a semantic-blocking mechanism that allows for the initial encoding of words but disrupts the creation of lexico-semantic representations. We offer a framework that can be extended to other selective word learning contexts to investigate whether a similar semantic-gating mechanism is engaged in different contexts. Lastly, we propose several implications for the evidence we review on the standard model of word learning.

Introduction

Most of what we learn about the world in both formal and informal settings comes from social sources; teachers, mentors, parents, and peers all provide important knowledge across a variety of domains. One case in which we have to learn from others is the meanings of words. Words are arbitrarily associated with their referents and have meaning because of their consistent, intentional use by members within a socio-linguistic community (Kalish & Sabbagh, 2007). To learn the meanings for words, children need to attend to expert speakers and their possible communicative intentions when using words. Yet, learning from others is potentially perilous given that informants are themselves human agents with their own intentions and understandings of the world. Thus, when children hear a speaker refer to a picture of a cow as a "shoe" and then provide a label for a novel object, it is beneficial for children to *selectively* block learning from that speaker. Although a large body of research over the last 15 years has mapped out the extent to which various social

H. Mangardich (✉) · M. A. Sabbagh
Department of Psychology, Queen's University, Kingston, ON, Canada
e-mail: 12hm30@queensu.ca; sabbagh@queensu.ca

© Springer International Publishing AG, part of Springer Nature 2018
M. M. Saylor, P. A. Ganea (eds.), *Active Learning from Infancy to Childhood*,
https://doi.org/10.1007/978-3-319-77182-3_9

cues lead to children's selective social learning (see Koenig & Sabbagh, 2013; Mills, 2013 for recent reviews), very little is known about the mechanisms by which that selectivity manifests.

The goal of this chapter is to review the extant literature investigating the cognitive mechanisms of selective word learning. Specifically, we aim to accomplish the following: (1) consider evolutionary theories for selective social learning behavior, which provide a basis for exploring its underlying mechanisms; (2) review current behavioral evidence for how children selectively block word learning from speakers who might lack knowledge; (3) illustrate with examples from the literature how event-related potentials (ERPs) and eye-tracking techniques can be integrated with selective learning paradigms to more closely investigate mechanisms of selective word learning; and (4) discuss the implications these findings have on standard models of word learning more generally.

We begin by considering an example of an everyday experience in which children might demonstrate selective word learning. Imagine a first grader on a class field trip at a children's museum. The child is keen to learn about dinosaurs at the dinosaur exhibit. Upon seeing a Protoceratops display, the 6-year-old points to a large bone protruding from the back of the dinosaur's head extending over its neck and asks his teacher "Know what that triangle thing is? Popping from the head? Looks like the dinosaur has a shield!" The teacher, intending to provide useful information, looks at the information card in front of the display but finds no information about the name of the novel object. Undeterred, she remembers that on her previous visit a dinosaur exhibit docent called the novel object a "frill." She looks back toward the child and says "Hmm, I don't know. I think it might be called a frill."

The first thing to notice about the interaction is that the child points to the novel object to establish common ground with the teacher, and asks a question to signal his interest in learning about the novel object's label. In response, the teacher provides a label for the novel object ("frill") while expressing some uncertainty about the accuracy of her information. Crucially, the word-referent link the teacher provides can be either true or false. Thus, the child needs to weigh the available information (e.g., the teacher's gaze toward the information card along with her verbal hedges) to decide whether he should invest the cognitive effort to acquire the word-referent link she offered.

If the child judges the word-referent link to be valuable information in spite of the teacher's admitted uncertainty, perhaps because the teacher appears to have read the information card or has proven to be correct in the past in these instances, then word learning occurs through the following two steps. First, the child attends to, and categorically encodes, the labeling event (i.e., "she called that thing a frill") and then second, uses that representation of the labeling event as a basis for creating a conventional lexico-semantic representation for the novel word (i.e., "that thing is a frill"). Put in another way, successful word learning involves both encoding an episodic representation that captures the spatio-temporal co-occurrences of the spoken novel word and its referent during the labeling event (Nazzi and Bertoncini, 2003), and forming a lexico-semantic representation that captures the semantically meaningful relation between the two elements (Friedrich & Friederici, 2017). If, however, the child judges the teacher's uncertainty as a sign that the word should not be learned, then he can avoid learning by interrupting either of these two basic word learning components. Before exploring the specific mechanisms through which children can disrupt the typical word learning process, we consider explanations for why children might have evolved these mechanisms in the first place.

Why Are Children Selective Social Learners?

Evolutionary theorists posit that children's selective social learning depends on a host of cognitive mechanisms that have evolved to allow humans to effectively extract accurate and relevant information from their social environment. Given our deep reliance on communication with expert members of our culture to learn about important things in our world, it is likely that we have evolved cognitive mechanisms for epistemic vigilance to prevent the cost of acquiring inaccurate or irrelevant information (Sperber et al., 2010). According to Sperber et al. (2010), most human communication occurs intentionally as the speaker utters a message with the communicative intention to be understood and the informative intention to make the addressee think or act according to what is understood. Correspondingly, the addressee comprehends and acquires the speaker's message with the intention of acquiring accurate and relevant information. On some occasions, however, the speaker might provide false information due to ignorance or deception. If the addressee recognizes this possibility, she can engage epistemic vigilance to prevent the cost of acquiring that false information. Beyond supporting human communication, cultural evolutionary theorists posit that selective social learning evolved to support the accumulation of adaptive, cultural knowledge over successive generations. In this view, children are selective learners driven to acquire information from cultural models who are most likely to share culturally relevant information (Chudek, Brosseau-Liard, Birch, & Henrich, 2013; Heyes, 2016).

In sum, evolutionary accounts for selective social learning address the fitness consequences of the behavior and posit ultimate explanations for what motivates children to be selective. To better understand selective social learning behavior, however, we need to understand its underlying proximate mechanisms. Proximate mechanisms include both the external triggers and the internal mechanisms involved in eliciting a behavior (Scott-Phillips, Dickens, & West, 2011). Current evidence in the developmental psychology literature largely informs us of the external triggers for children's selectivity. Broadly, these external triggers can be characterized along two dimensions. The first concerns the epistemic and moral qualities of the *speaker*—children are unlikely to learn well from speakers who show signs of ignorance or meanness (Birch & Bloom, 2002; Jaswal & Neely, 2006; Koenig, Clément, & Harris, 2004; Mascaro & Sperber, 2009; Sabbagh & Baldwin, 2001). The second concerns the quality of the *content*—children are unlikely to learn from well-meaning speakers if the information they provide is likely to be irrelevant to the child (e.g., names for objects that are said to be from a faraway country) (Corriveau

& Harris, 2009; Henderson, Sabbagh, & Woodward, 2013; Sperber et al., 2010). Thus, the extant literature informs us about the proximate mechanisms of selective social learning by revealing the various external triggers that result in children's selectivity.

Comparatively less is known, however, about the internal mechanisms that render selective learning. Although we know much about why and when children do it, we know little about how. The goal of this chapter is to consider the cognitive mechanisms supporting children's selective word learning across two contexts in which the epistemic quality of the speaker is manipulated: (1) the "ignorant speaker" paradigm in which the speaker expresses explicit uncertainty about the correct meaning for a novel word and (2) the "inaccurate speaker" paradigm in which the speaker has a history of labeling familiar objects inaccurately.

Two Possible Mechanisms of Selective Word Learning: Inattention and Semantic-Blocking

On the basis of the simple cognitive model of word learning sketched out above there are at least two possibilities for how the child can avoid learning labels from ignorant or inaccurate speakers. One possibility is that the child might strategically ignore the teacher's labeling event, which would lead to a failure to encode the labeling event itself. That is, children might simply ignore ignorant speakers. A second possibility is that the child might attend to the teacher's labeling event, but then block whatever processes are necessary for the subsequent creation of the lexico-semantic representation. In other words, instead of simply ignoring ignorant speakers, children might have a "semantic-blocking" mechanism that allows them to track a given speakers' labeling behavior while also recognizing that the word-referent association is not informative and worthy of entry into the lexicon.

These two possibilities for how children might manifest selective social learning have different consequences on the kinds of linguistic representations the child might create for the new word-relation taught by the teacher (Mangardich & Sabbagh, 2017). If the child blocks learning through inattention, then we would expect to see no evidence that he encoded any representation at all for the teacher's labeling event. By not attending to the teacher's labeling event, perhaps because the teacher has been inaccurate in the past in museum settings or because another feature of the display captures the child's attention, the child can preserve the cognitive resources that could otherwise be applied to comprehend and acquire other information that is likely to be both true and relevant. In contrast, if the child blocks learning through semantic-blocking, then we would expect to see evidence that he encoded an initial representation for the teacher's labeling event, but no evidence that he encoded a conventional semantic representation. By gating the formation of conventional semantic representations yet still encoding an initial representation, the child retains a trace of the word in memory that can serve as a basis for interpreting the term "frill" the next time the teacher uses it (e.g., "last time, my teacher called the bone coming out of the dinosaur's head a frill, so she must now be referring to the bone coming out of this dinosaur's head when she says frill").

Below, we review behavioral studies that used carefully designed experimental and comprehension test procedures to test between these two possibilities by assessing the kinds of linguistic representations children create for new words trained by ignorant and inaccurate speakers. We discuss how findings from these studies provide some evidence to hint at the form that the cognitive mechanism of children's selective word learning might take.

Evidence for Semantic-Blocking

Behavioral

An important first step to characterizing the mechanisms for selective social learning is to address whether children provide evidence for having formed a semantic representation when presented with a label by an ignorant speaker. To make this first step, Sabbagh, Wdowiak, and Ottaway (2003) used a proactive interference paradigm to test the extent to which 3- and 4-year-olds represent word-referent links spoken by ignorant speakers in lexical memory. In this study, children first saw either an ignorant or knowledgeable speaker attach a novel word to one of three possible novel referents. Then, in both conditions, a second knowledgeable speaker entered the room and attached the same novel word to a different one of the three novel referents. The authors reasoned that if children in the ignorant speaker condition formed a word-referent link, then they should show proactive interference when encountering the new word-referent association from the second speaker. However, results revealed that children in the ignorant condition did not show difficulty in learning the alternative link from the second speaker, although children in the knowledgeable condition showed evidence of difficulty learning the second label, as expected. These findings suggest that children's exposure to an ignorant speaker's novel word-referent link did not affect their ability to associate the same word with an alternative referent, and thus they likely did not form a lexico-semantic representation based on the ignorant speaker's labeling event.

What remains unclear from this study is whether children blocked the formation of lexico-semantic representations for novel words trained by an ignorant speaker through inattention or semantic-blocking. As was noted above, children might have ignored the ignorant speaker and thus not encoded even their labeling events, or they might have specifically disrupted the processes that are associated with forming lexico-semantic representations based on information gleaned during labeling events. To address this question, Sabbagh and Shafman (2009) used a modified comprehension test procedure to provide a more sensitive assessment of whether children encode an initial representation for an ignorant speaker's labeling event. In this study, 3- and 4-year-olds first received novel word training by either an ignorant or knowledgeable speaker. Children then completed a test phase in which they were either asked a standard "semantic" question (e.g., "Which one of these things is a blicket?") or an "episodic" question (e.g., "Which one did *I* say is a blicket?"). Results showed that 4-year-olds (but not 3-year-olds) were more likely to respond correctly to the episodic question ($M = 1.92$ out of 2) compared to semantic comprehension questions ($M = 0.67$ out of 2). This finding suggests that children do pay attention to the speaker's labeling event to encode an initial representation for the word-referent link, however, this representation does not seem to affect children's performance on a standard comprehension test question.

Results from this study provided initial evidence that children might engage a semantic-blocking mechanism that allows them to encode an initial representation, but blocks the formation of a semantic representation. The evidence thus far, however, does not fully support a semantic-blocking mechanism because it remains unclear whether the initial representations are episodic or weakly encoded semantic representations. That is, although the retrieval cue in the episodic question ("Which one did *I* say is a blicket?") supported children's better performance on this question relative to the semantic question, these findings do not clarify whether children retrieved a weakly encoded episodic representation or a weakly encoded semantic representation. Children may simply have encoded weak semantic representations, and the episodic question with the retrieval cue was a more sensitive assay of those representations than the semantic question. Later in this chapter, we will describe some research that addresses this very question using different methodologies.

Before describing those findings, though, it is interesting to note that a similar pattern of findings from studies that use the inaccurate speaker paradigm points to the possible involvement of a semantic-blocking mechanism. Across two studies, Koenig and Woodward (2010, Study 2 and 3) investigated the representations 2-year-olds created for new words trained by a speaker who either accurately or inaccurately labeled familiar objects. In a comprehension test that immediately followed novel word training, toddlers responded systematically to both inaccurate and accurate sources, suggesting that they were not diverting attention away from the inaccurate speaker's labeling event, and encoded some sort of trace of the trained word-object association. However, when the experimenters administered the comprehension test after a 2-min delay, toddlers' responses in the inaccurate condition became unsystematic thereby suggesting that the initial representations they formed were fragile. These results are consistent with those found by Sabbagh and Shafman (2009) and suggest that children encode an initial representation for new words trained by ignorant and inaccurate speakers. This consistent pattern of findings across contexts suggests that, although the higher-level inferences supporting children's selectivity differs in the ignorant and inaccurate speaker paradigms (Kushnir & Koenig, 2017), the same internal mechanisms for selective word learning might be engaged.

In sum, the behavioral studies reviewed above show that children encode an initial representation for words trained by ignorant and inaccurate speakers. However, additional research is required to assess whether these initial word representations are episodic or semantic in nature to determine if children selectively learn words by engaging a semantic-blocking mechanism. To date, the behavioral studies on selective word learning have assessed children's word learning using explicit comprehension test questions in which children are shown objects and asked to select a spoken word's referent given two or more alternatives. Researchers can determine whether children's responses on these test questions vary systematically so as to indicate that they have encoded some kind of representation for a word. Moreover, additional detail about the strength of these representations can be gained by administering the comprehension test questions after a brief delay or with a contextual cue.

However, explicit comprehension test questions only capture the product of children's overt responses and do not tap into the dynamics of the decision-making process leading children to their response. One way researchers can capture these dynamics is by using neurophysiological techniques that offer excellent temporal resolution and can reveal the cognitive processes involved in children's word recognition. Below, we review two studies that have integrated the use of ERPs and eye-tracking techniques with the ignorant and inaccurate speaker paradigms, respectively, to investigate the cognitive mechanisms of selective word learning.

Event-Related Potentials

ERPs are the averaged electrophysiological brain activity recorded from the scalp time-locked to the presentation of a particular stimulus. ERPs are characterized by a sequence of positive and negative voltage fluctuations referred to as components, normally labeled according to their polarity and the time point post-stimulus at which they peak (e.g., a positive component that peaks at 100 ms is a "P100").

Of particular interest for the study of language processing are ERPs elicited to a target word in what is generally known as a match-mismatch paradigm. In two versions of this paradigm, participants first hear a single word (e.g., "biceps") or a sentence with a missing final word (e.g., "Before exercising Jack always stretches his ___"), and then subsequently have their ERPs recorded as they hear a target word that is either congruent/matches (e.g., "muscles") or incongruent/mismatches (e.g., "table") with the single word or sentence context. When comparing ERPs to congruent and incongruent trials in both the single word and sentence match-mismatch paradigms, two ERP components emerge that are thought to index how the target word is represented.

The first component is the N200, which is a negative-going fluctuation that peaks around 200 ms and occurs over fronto-central, central, and centro-parietal sites. The N200 component has a larger (negative) amplitude on incongruent relative to congruent trials in the match-mismatch paradigm (termed the N200 effect). The N200 effect is thought to functionally reflect the perceptual comparison of a target word with an expected word form (van Den Brink, Brown, & Hagoort, 2001). This is based on findings showing that participants demonstrate larger N200 responses when they hear a target word that has an initial sound that mismatches the initial sound of the expected word (e.g., participants hear target word "queen" when the expected word is "eyes") given the sentence context (e.g., "Phil put some drops in his ___"), compared to when they hear a target word (e.g., "icicles") that has an initial sound that matches the initial sound of the expected word (Connolly, Stewart, & Phillips, 1990; Connolly, Phillips, Stewart, & Brake, 1992; Connolly & Phillips, 1994; Hagoort & Brown, 2000; van Den Brink et al., 2001).

The second component is the N400 which occurs over central and centro-parietal sites and, like the N200, also has a larger (negative) amplitude on incongruent relative to congruent trials (termed the N400 effect). However, unlike the N200 which is sensitive to the perceptual comparison of a target word with an expected word, the N400 effect is generally thought to reflect the extent to which a target word's meaning is congruent with an established semantic context (Kutas & Federmeier, 2011). For instance, a large body of evidence shows that participants demonstrate larger N400 responses when they hear a target word that is semantically incongruent (e.g., "socks") relative to when they hear a target word that is semantically congruent (e.g., "butter") given the sentence context (e.g., "She spread her bread with ___") (Federmeier & Kutas, 1999; Kutas & Hillyard, 1980). Moreover, the N400 effect appears even when there is a perceptual overlap between the target word (e.g., "luggage") and the expected word (e.g., "luck") given the sentence context (e.g., "The gambler had a bad streak of ___"), suggesting that the effect is specific to processing the target word's semantics (Connolly & Phillips, 1994).

The evidence we have reviewed above for the functional significance of the N200 and N400 components comes from classic language studies in which adults' ERPs are recorded to familiar words in a sentence match-mismatch paradigm. More recently, researchers have used the single word match-mismatch paradigm to investigate whether young children create semantically meaningful relations for newly trained word-object mappings (Borgström, von Koss Torkildsen, & Lindgren, 2015; Friedrich & Friederici, 2008, 2011; Junge, Cutler, & Hagoort, 2012; von Koss Torkildsen et al., 2008, 2009). In these studies, young children first experience novel word training in which a novel label (e.g., "rasme") is repeatedly associated with a picture of a novel object across multiple trials. Following this computerized training, young children first see a picture of a trained novel object and then have their ERPs recorded as they either hear the object's correct label (congruent trials) or a different object's label (incongruent trials). If young children demonstrate larger N200 responses on incongruent trials when the initial sound of the novel target word does not match the initial sound of the expect word form, this implies that children have created a perceptual representation for the word-object pairing (Junge et al., 2012). Learning the semantic meaning of the new word-referent link, however, requires not just pairing together the link into an initial representation, but also an appreciation of the causal reasons for that pairing—that the word functions to communicate about the concept (novel object) it was paired with. If young children demonstrate larger N400 responses on incongruent trials when the meaning of the novel target word does not match the meaning of the expected word, this implies that children have created lexico-semantic representation for the novel word that meaningfully refers to the object it was paired with during training (Friedrich & Friederici, 2011).

In sum, ERPs elicited to trained novel words in a single word match-mismatch paradigm reveal the distinct presence of both perceptual (N200 effect) and lexico-semantic representations (N400 effect). Recall that it is unclear from the behavioral evidence whether children's initial representations for an ignorant speaker's labeling event are episodic or semantic in nature. That is, do children encode a perceptual representation or a semantic representation for a speaker's word referent-link? We recently conducted a study that integrated the single word match-mismatch paradigm with an ignorant speaker paradigm to gain insight into the kinds of word representations children create for newly trained words and to determine if children block learning through inattention or through semantic-blocking (Mangardich & Sabbagh, 2017).

In this study, 6-year-olds saw either an ignorant or knowledgeable speaker hesitantly provide a novel label for one of two possible novel toys. The ignorant speaker's hesitancy reflected ignorance of the conventional label because he stated that the toys were made by a friend (friend-made condition: e.g., "I'd really like to call one of the toys *my friend made* a Keck, but I don't know which one!"), whereas the knowledgeable speaker stated that he made the toys himself (speaker-made condition), and thus his hesitancy reflected only that he had not yet determined which one of the toys he created that he wanted to label with the novel name (e.g., "I'd really like to call one of the toys *I made* a Keck, but I don't know which one!"). After this novel word training, children in both conditions were fitted with an EEG net and had their ERPs recorded as they heard a recording of the speaker using the novel word, followed by a picture of either the object the word was paired with during training (congruent trial) or a distracter object that was also present during training (incongruent trial). We reasoned that if children block learning from ignorant speakers through inattention, then children should demonstrate neither an N200 nor N400 because they would not have encoded either a perceptual or a semantic representation for the trained word-referent links. If, however, children block learning through semantic-blocking, then children should demonstrate an N200 but no N400 because they would have encoded an initial representation but no semantic representation.

Results revealed that children trained by an ignorant speaker demonstrated ERP evidence that supported the semantic-blocking hypothesis: they demonstrated an N200 but no N400 effect. In contrast, children trained by a knowledge speaker showed both an N200 and N400 effect, suggesting that they had created both a perceptual and a semantic representation. These findings clearly indicate that children engage a semantic-blocking mechanism that enables them to create an initial representation, but block the formation of a semantic representation. Future work is needed to characterize the neurocognitive mechanisms through which this semantic-blocking mechanism is instantiated.

Eye-Tracking

Eye-tracking refers to the monitoring of participants' eye-movements to determine how they allocate their attention to objects in a visual display as they hear a spoken sentence. By examining the sequences of eye-movements time-locked to particular words in the speech stream, it is possible for researchers to monitor the rapid cognitive processes involved in understanding spoken language (Fernald, Pinto, Swingley, Weinbergy, & McRoberts, 1998). One eye-tracking technique that has been useful for investigating the time-course of children's language processing is what is known as the looking-while-listening (LWL) task. In this task, children's eye-movements are recorded as they see a pair of objects (e.g., a ball and a shoe) and hear a sentence which includes the label for the target object (e.g., "Where is the *ball*? Can you see it?"). If children understand the target word, then on trials in which they happen to be looking at the distracter object when they hear the word (a distracter-initial trial), they should shift their eye-gaze to the picture of the target object. If, however, children happen to already be looking at the target object upon hearing the target word (a target-initial trial), then their eye-gaze should remain on this object. Typically, researchers record children's visual fixations to the distracter and target objects after the onset of the spoken target word. Researchers can then plot the proportion of distracter-initial and target-initial trials in which children shift their gaze. If the proportion of trials in which gaze shifts occur is higher for distracter-initial trials compared to target-initial trials, this is an indication that children understand the spoken word (Golinkoff, Ma, Song, & Hirsh-Pasek, 2013). Although the LWL task has primarily been used to measure children's language processing of familiar words, this task can also be used to investigate children's learning of newly trained words.

A recent series of studies from Barry (2016) used the LWL eye-tracking paradigm to investigate whether young children encode initial representations for novel word-object links trained by an inaccurate speaker. In this study, 2-, 3-, and 4-year-olds first saw a familiarization video of a speaker who labeled familiar objects either accurately or inaccurately. Following this familiarization video, young children received novel word training in which they saw a video of the same speaker label one of two novel objects that appeared on the screen. Immediately after this novel word training and after a 2-minute delay, young children's eye-movements were recorded in a LWL test phase as they saw the same two novel objects that were trained together appear on the screen and heard the speaker say "Look at the [target object's label]!" Results showed that during novel word training, 2-, 3-, and 4-year-olds in the inaccurate speaker condition directed their visual attention to the target object that was being labeled significantly more than chance, suggesting that all children attended to the inaccurate speaker's labeling event. Despite this, analysis of eye-movements during test revealed that only 3- and 4-year-olds in the inaccurate speaker condition (but not 2-year-olds) spent a significantly greater proportion of time looking to the target object than chance. This pattern of findings suggests that 3- and 4-year-olds encoded an initial representation for the word-referent links trained by an inaccurate speaker, and provides some evidence to suggest that semantic-blocking may be a developmental achievement that comes online around 3- to 4-year-olds of age rather than a developmental starting point.

However, additional evidence is needed to implicate a semantic-blocking mechanism by testing whether the initial representations 3- and 4-year-olds create for novel words trained by inaccurate speakers are semantic in nature. One way in which eye-tracking research can investigate this question is by analyzing the time-course of children's visual fixations to target and distracter objects immediately after target word onset in the LWL test phase. Previous research has shown that young children and adults tend to fixate on objects that have a perceptual association with the target word (e.g., participants look towards a picture of a bus upon hearing the target word "bee") earlier than they fixate on objects that have a semantic association with the target word (e.g., a picture of a cat) (Chow, Davies, & Plunkett, 2017; Huettig & McQueen, 2007). Future research can leverage this pattern of findings to index whether young children create episodic or semantic representations for trained novel word-object links. For instance, if young children fixate on the target novel object upon hearing its label in the earlier time span in which they have been shown to fixate on perceptually related objects (approximately 330–1130 ms from Chow et al., 2017), but then stop fixating on the target object in the later time span in which they have been shown to fixate on semantically related objects (approximately 630 ms onwards), then this would indicate that the representations young children formed for the new words are episodic rather than semantic in nature.

New Directions

The main goal of our chapter has been to review evidence regarding how young children avoid learning new words from ignorant and inaccurate speakers. The early indicators are that children do not ignore ignorant or inaccurate speakers. Instead, children pay attention to the word-referent links that are offered by these speakers, but then block these links from becoming lexico-semantic representations. For the remainder of the chapter, we will turn our attention to what we think might be some broader implications for these findings, not just for the mechanisms that support selective social learning, but the mechanisms that promote the acquisition of lexico-semantic representations more generally.

Standard Model of Word Learning

Recall that our starting point for developing hypotheses about the cognitive systems that are responsible for selective social learning was the observation that children need to first encode their experience of a labeling event (e.g., "she called that thing a frill") and then use that experience as the basis for a conventional lexico-semantic representation (e.g., "that thing is a frill"). This basic observation mirrors the basis of the standard model of word learning (Davis & Gaskell, 2009; McClelland, McNaughton, & O'Reilly, 1995). On this model, the neurocognitive systems that are important for the different aspects of word learning (i.e., encoding labeling events and creating lexico-semantic representations) are separate but complimentary. The first system is the episodic memory system which stores an association between a spoken word and a referent, and the context in which they are experienced into an "episodic representation." This system is thought to depend on subcortical mechanisms within the medial temporal lobe (MTL) and hippocampus (Moscovitch, Nadel, Winocur, Gilboa, & Rosenbaum, 2006). The second system is the semantic memory system which is associated with establishing a stable lexico-semantic representation for the new word-referent link. In contrast to the first system, this system is thought to rely on neocortical mechanisms, in particular regions of association cortex, that allow for connections between some new piece of information and a wider semantic network (Binder, Desai, Graves, & Conant, 2009; Martin & Chao, 2001; Patterson, Nestor, & Rogers, 2007).

The evidence for the distinct, sequential operation of these two complementary systems comes primarily from work with adults. For instance, in one recent study, Tamminen and Gaskell (2013) trained participants a novel word for a subordinate category (e.g., "feckton is a type of cat that has stripes and is bluish-grey"). Immediately after novel word training and after a 1 day or week delay, participants completed a primed lexical decision task. They reasoned that if participants had formed a lexico-semantic representation for the new word (e.g., "feckton"), then they would show priming of semantically related words (e.g., "kitten") even though those related words were not paired with the novel word during training. Participants were tested immediately after training and after a week. Results showed that while there was not strong evidence for semantic priming immediately after training, a small but significant semantic priming effect was found when the training and test sessions were separated by a week. This suggests that lexico-semantic representations are created subsequent to the initial encoding of the labeling event, and also that they are elaborated somewhat slowly and out of explicit consciousness requiring a period of offline consolidation. These findings join several others in providing evidence that integrated lexico-semantic representations—ones that are said to interact with established words in the mental lexicon—emerge only after first encoding episodic word-referent links (e.g., Clay, Bowers, Davis, & Hanley, 2007; Davis, Di Betta, Macdonald, & Gaskell, 2009; Takashima, Bakker, Van Hell, Janzen, & McQueen, 2014, 2017; van Der Ven, Takashima, Segers, & Verhoeven, 2015).

Challenging the Standard Model of Word Learning

In sum, according to the standard model, the creation of cortical lexico-semantic representations is generally thought to be slower than the encoding of labeling events, sometimes likened to the process of "consolidation" whereby representations become increasingly stable with further use and experience (e.g., Davis & Gaskell, 2009; Dumay & Gaskell, 2007; Tamminen, Payne, Stickgold, Wamsley, & Gaskell, 2010). However, the evidence we reviewed above from Mangardich and Sabbagh (2017) is at odds with this characterization. Namely, we found that children in the knowledgeable speaker condition had created both episodic and semantic representations for trained novel words whereas children in the ignorant speaker condition had created only episodic representations. This was the case even though across both conditions, children received the same number of exposures to the novel words and were exposed to approximately the same amount of time post encoding (~15 min). This suggests that children in the knowledgeable speaker condition had created lexico-semantic representations that were qualitatively distinct from episodic representations not through repeated exposure or a period of offline consolidation as proposed by the standard model, but instead as a consequence of the social context.

What is interesting in the present context is that this standard model provides some specific hypotheses about how to characterize the mechanisms associated with selective word learning. Specifically, similar to how we framed our hypotheses from the outset, children's selective learning can involve disrupting either the faster "episodic representation" or the slower "consolidation" process which is necessary to lead to a lexico-semantic representation. The literature that we reviewed suggested that even in situations in which children show selective learning, they show evidence of having established an early episodic representation of the link between the word and referent. Thus, the standard model would suggest that the mechanisms that support selective learning must block, specifically, the consolidation processes associated with forming a stable lexico-semantic representation.

However, as described above, key features of our findings do not square with this hypothesis. Most notably, the presence of lexico-semantic representations was assessed and detected shortly after training, well before the processes of semantic consolidation are usually thought to occur (Mangardich & Sabbagh, 2017). Thus, under the appropriate circumstances, lexico-semantic representations are created very quickly after exposure to labeling events. Of course, these representations may change over time as children gain more experience and engage the processes normally associated with consolidation, but their initial creation may not be the result of slower consolidation processes. There are several important implications of this challenge to the standard model.

The first implication is that multiple memory systems simultaneously process information in labeling events, such that distinct episodic and lexico-semantic representations are created in parallel for new words rather than sequentially. While there is no doubt that the initial acquisition of new words depends on the episodic system, recent evidence suggests that at least under some conditions, the semantic system in word learning is rapidly engaged and not just the result of a later consolidation period.

In some sense, this proposal regarding the mechanisms of selective social learning is related to the broader theory of "natural pedagogy" (e.g., Csibra & Gergely, 2006, 2009). According to this theory, human infants and children have evolved adaptations to recognize speaker ostensive cues (e.g., eye-contact) as indicators that a speaker intends to communicate new and relevant information for them to acquire (Csibra & Gergely, 2006, 2009; Gergely, Egyed, & Király, 2007). This triggers in young children a fast learning system that enables them to rapidly acquire a semantic representation for an object's properties (such as its name) that is generalizable beyond the speaker's singular labeling episode (Csibra & Gergely, 2006, 2009). There are several dramatic demonstrations showing that when cues to pedagogical intent are absent, even very young children will not show evidence of imitating or otherwise learning from a model adult (e.g., Southgate, Chevallier, & Csibra, 2009). The theory of natural pedagogy provides a higher-level explanation for our own findings; namely, it is possible that the creation of a lexico-semantic representation is disrupted because the speaker's ignorance may be a clue that the speaker does not (or cannot) have valid pedagogical intentions.

An important question for our proposal and the theory of natural pedagogy concerns whether there are plausible neurocognitive mechanisms for supporting semantic encoding without the longer term processes of consolidation. It does seem that there is such evidence. For instance, findings from functional neuroimaging studies that record neural activation during the retrieval of acquired word-object associations shortly after novel word training consistently show robust activation in areas of the left-lateralized neocortical system that is thought to be important for semantic representation (Binder et al., 2009), including the angular gyrus, middle temporal gyrus, inferior and superior frontal gyri, precuneus, and posterior inferior parietal lobe (e.g., Atir-Sharon, Gilboa, Hazan, Koilis, & Manevitz, 2015; Breitenstein et al., 2005; Ferreira, Göbel, Hymers, & Ellis, 2015; Mestres-Missé, Càmara, Rodriguez-Fornells, Rotte, & Münte, 2008; Mestres-Missé, Rodriguez-Fornells, & Münte, 2010; Takashima et al., 2014, 2017). Moreover, ERP studies of word learning that use the N400 as an index of lexico-semantic representations (including our own) consistently report fast semantic learning in young children and adults shortly after novel word training (e.g., Borovsky, Kutas, & Elman, 2010; Borovsky, Elman, & Kutas, 2012; Friedrich & Friederici, 2008, 2011, 2017; Junge et al., 2012; Mangardich & Sabbagh, 2017; Perfetti, Wlotko, & Hart, 2005). Together, these findings show that the neocortical system associated with semantic learning is activated shortly after exposure to a novel word and does not require consolidation processes that unfold over a longer period (Nadel, Hupbach, Gomez, & Newman-Smith, 2012).

Given that semantic representations can be created over a very short period, the question then turns to how those processes might be gated (or "blocked") by the social context. One possibility that comes from the neuroscience literature is that word learning in children has features that are similar to "reward learning." Associations between a stimulus and a reward are typically learned quickly when the prospective likelihood of the reward and the value of the reward are high (Schultz, 2010). With this in mind, we speculate that upon detecting a speaker's communicative intention in a labeling event, the child assigns value to their following referential communication, perhaps as a result of extensive exposures to co-occurrences between eye-gaze and positive experiences, or through a natural sensitivity to pedagogical cues to acquire culturally relevant information (Senju & Johnson, 2009).

Some concrete evidence for a connection between the word learning and the neural circuitry typically associated with reward learning comes from studies with adults who show that exposure to contexts that are typically associated with social learning (e.g., triadic joint attention) results in activation of the reward network (e.g., midbrain dopaminergic system) (Schilbach et al., 2010). Activation in the ventral striatum results in dopamine release, which, through projections back to the prefrontal cortex (Dominey & Inui, 2009; Tekin & Cummings, 2002), may modulate neocortical function to initiate the rapid semantic encoding of new word-referent links in pedagogical contexts. Indeed, further evidence from neuroimaging studies shows that learning the meaning of new words presented in verbal contexts reveals co-activation and enhanced coupling of the left ventral striatum with the left inferior frontal gyrus, an area known to be involved in semantic processing (Mestres-Missé et al., 2008; Ripollés et al., 2014). Additional evidence for the neuromodulatory role of dopamine on semantic processing regions comes from studies showing that increased dopamine release during the encoding of new words results in increased activity in fronto-temporal semantic processing regions (Cohen, Rissman, Suthana, Castel, & Knowlton, 2014) and better recall of novel word-object pairings over five learning sessions and enhanced recognition after a 1-month follow-up (Shellshear et al., 2015). Collectively, these findings suggest that humans have evolved a fast learning mechanism that supports the rapid semantic encoding of novel words as "conventional knowledge" that refers to more general instruments for talking about the world within a particular socio-linguistic community.

Briefly, our findings suggest that fast word learning requires more than increased attention to the target word-object link. Some "data-driven" approaches to word learning suggest that children learn words through passive attention to word-object co-occurrences in their environment (e.g., Smith & Yu, 2008). On this model, the role of socio-pragmatic cues is to simply align attention towards specific word-object links (MacDonald, Yurovsky, & Frank, 2017) at which point the normal processes of episodic encoding and semantic consolidation can occur. Although our findings do not refute that children can learn words in this sequential way, our findings suggest a much stronger role for the social context, per se. The dissociable presence between episodic and lexico-semantic representations suggests that irrespective of whether children attend to a labeling event, more is needed to acquire a meaningful relation between a word and its referent. It might be that, in addition to learning mechanisms that acquire the cross-situational statistics, children can use evidence that a particular piece of information (such as a word) has high prospective value and use that information to rapidly establish lexico-semantic representations (Bloom, Tinker, & Scholnick, 2001).

Conclusion

In this chapter, we reviewed behavioral, eye-tracking, and electrophysiological evidence for how children selectively learn words—what the brain processes are that enable them to block learning when they doubt the epistemic quality of the source. All lines of evidence suggest that around the age of 3 years, young children block word learning by engaging a semantic-blocking mechanism that allows for the initial encoding of words but disrupts the creation of lexico-semantic representations.

We offer a framework for investigating cognitive mechanisms of selective word learning that can be extended to explore whether children block learning in other contexts in the same way. One implication the framework and its evidence has for word learning more generally is that successful word learning occurs through the parallel encoding of episodic and lexico-semantic representations. This view differs from the traditional "complimentary learning systems" model of word learning which suggests that the initial encoding occurs in the episodic-hippocampal system and that the creation of neocortical lexico-semantic representations requires a longer period of time through consolidation. In line with the theory of natural pedagogy, we speculate that children see words as high-value targets for learning and that rapid learning manifests through dopaminergic modulation of the cortical circuitry that is important for establishing lexico-semantic representations. Finally, our evidence suggests that children do not always encode lexico-semantic representations for novel words even though they attend to the speaker's labeling event, presenting a challenge to current accounts of statistical learning which suggest that children learn the meaning of novel words simply through passive attention to the social and physical data in their environments. Instead, we believe that there is evidence now to suggest that the social context plays a critical "gating" role in rapidly establishing lexico-semantic representations, and it is the modulation of this process that accounts for the phenomenon of selective social learning.

References

Atir-Sharon, T., Gilboa, A., Hazan, H., Koilis, E., & Manevitz, L. M. (2015). Decoding the formation of new semantics: MVPA investigation of rapid neocortical plasticity during associative encoding through Fast Mapping. *Neural Plasticity, 2015*, 1–17. https://doi.org/10.1155/2015/804385

Barry, R. A. (2016). *Selective word learning in toddlers: An eye tracking investigation of the mechanism* (Order No. 10165848). Available from ProQuest Dissertations & Theses Global. (1832932561). Retrieved from https://search.proquest.com/docview/1832932561?accountid=6180

Binder, J. R., Desai, R. H., Graves, W. W., & Conant, L. L. (2009). Where is the semantic system? A critical review and meta-analysis of 120 functional neuroimaging studies. *Cerebral Cortex, 19*(12), 2767–2796. https://doi.org/10.1093/cercor/bhp055

Birch, S. A. J., & Bloom, P. (2002). Preschoolers are sensitive to the speaker's knowledge when learning proper names. *Child Development, 73*, 434–444. https://doi.org/10.1111/1467-8624.00416

Bloom, L., Tinker, E., & Scholnick, E. (2001). The intentionality model of language acquisition: Engagement, effort and essential tension in development. *Monographs of the Society for Research in Child Development, 66*(4), 7–101.

Borgström, K., von Koss Torkildsen, J., & Lindgren, M. (2015). Substantial gains in word learning ability between 20 and 24 months: A longitudinal ERP study. *Brain and Language, 149*, 33–45. https://doi.org/10.1016/j.bandl.2015.07.002

Borovsky, A., Elman, J. L., & Kutas, M. (2012). Once is enough: N400 indexes semantic integration of novel word meanings from a single exposure in context. *Language Learning and Development, 8*(3), 278–302. https://doi.org/10.1080/15475441.2011.614893

Borovsky, A., Kutas, M., & Elman, J. (2010). Learning to use words: Event-related potentials index single-shot contextual word learning. *Cognition, 116*(2), 289–296. https://doi.org/10.1016/j.cognition.2010.05.004

Breitenstein, C., Jansen, A., Deppe, M., Foerster, A. F., Sommer, J., Wolbers, T., & Knecht, S. (2005). Hippocampus activity differentiates good from poor learners of a novel lexicon. *NeuroImage, 25*(3), 958–968. https://doi.org/10.1016/j.neuroimage.2004.12.019

Chow, J., Davies, A. A., & Plunkett, K. (2017). Spoken-word recognition in 2-year-olds: The tug of war between phonological and semantic activation. *Journal of Memory and Language, 93*, 104–134. https://doi.org/10.1016/j.jml.2016.08.004

Chudek, M., Brosseau-Liard, P., Birch, S., & Henrich, J. (2013). Culture-gene coevolutionary theory and children's selective social learning. In M. R. Banaji & S. A. Gelman (Eds.), *Navigating the social world: What infants, children, and other species can teach us* (pp. 181–185). New York, NY: Oxford University Press.

Clay, F., Bowers, J. S., Davis, C. J., & Hanley, D. A. (2007). Teaching adults new words: The role of practice and consolidation. *Journal of Experimental Psychology: Learning, Memory, and Cognition, 33*(5), 970–976. https://doi.org/10.1037/0278-7393.33.5.970

Cohen, M. S., Rissman, J., Suthana, N. A., Castel, A. D., & Knowlton, B. J. (2014). Value-based modulation of memory encoding involves strategic engagement of fronto-temporal semantic processing regions. *Cognitive, Affective, & Behavioral Neuroscience, 14*(2), 578–592. https://doi.org/10.3758/s13415-014-0275-x

Connolly, J. F., & Phillips, N. A. (1994). Event-related potential components reflect phonological and semantic processing of the terminal word of spoken sentences. *Journal of Cognitive Neuroscience, 6*(3), 256–266. https://doi.org/10.1162/jocn.1994.6.3.256

Connolly, J. F., Phillips, N. A., Stewart, S. H., & Brake, W. G. (1992). Event-related potential sensitivity to acoustic and semantic properties of terminal words in sentences. *Brain and Language, 43*(1), 1–18. https://doi.org/10.1016/0093-934X(92)90018-A

Connolly, J. F., Stewart, S. H., & Phillips, N. A. (1990). The effects of processing requirements on neurophysiological responses to spoken sentences. *Brain and Language, 39*(2), 302–318. https://doi.org/10.1016/0093-934X(90)90016-A

Corriveau, K., & Harris, P. L. (2009). Choosing your informant: Weighing familiarity and recent accuracy. *Developmental Science, 12*(3), 426–437. https://doi.org/10.1111/j.1467-7687.2008.00792.x

Csibra, G., & Gergely, G. (2006). Social learning and social cognition: The case for pedagogy. In Y. Munakata & M. H. Johnson (Eds.), *Processes of change in brain and cognitive development. Attention and performance XXI* (pp. 249–274). Oxford, UK: Oxford University Press.

Csibra, G., & Gergely, G. (2009). Natural pedagogy. *Trends in Cognitive Sciences, 13*, 148–153. https://doi.org/10.1016/j.tics.2009.01.005

Davis, M. H., Di Betta, A. M., Macdonald, M. J., & Gaskell, M. G. (2009). Learning and consolidation of novel spoken words. *Journal of Cognitive Neuroscience, 21*(4), 803–820. https://doi.org/10.1162/jocn.2009.21059

Davis, M. H., & Gaskell, M. G. (2009). A complementary systems account of word learning: Neural and behavioural evidence. *Philosophical Transactions of the Royal Society B: Biological Sciences, 364*(1536), 3773–3800. https://doi.org/10.1098/rstb.2009.0111

Dominey, P. F., & Inui, T. (2009). Cortico-striatal function in sentence comprehension: Insights from neurophysiology and modeling. *Cortex, 45*(8), 1012–1018. https://doi.org/10.1016/j. cortex.2009.03.007

Dumay, N., & Gaskell, M. G. (2007). Sleep-associated changes in the mental representation of spoken words. *Psychological Science, 18*(1), 35–39.

Federmeier, K. D., & Kutas, M. (1999). A rose by any other name: Long-term memory structure and sentence processing. *Journal of Memory and Language, 41*(4), 469–495. https://doi. org/10.1006/jmla.1999.2660

Fernald, A., Pinto, J. P., Swingley, D., Weinbergy, A., & McRoberts, G. W. (1998). Rapid gains in speed of verbal processing by infants in the 2nd year. *Psychological Science, 9*(3), 228–231.

Ferreira, R. A., Göbel, S. M., Hymers, M., & Ellis, A. W. (2015). The neural correlates of semantic richness: Evidence from an fMRI study of word learning. *Brain and Language, 143*, 69–80. https://doi.org/10.1016/j.bandl.2015.02.005

Friedrich, M., & Friederici, A. D. (2008). Neurophysiological correlates of online word learning in 14-month-old infants. *Neuroreport, 19*, 1757–1761. https://doi.org/10.1097/ WNR.0b013e328318f014

Friedrich, M., & Friederici, A. D. (2011). Word learning in 6-month-olds: Fast encoding–weak retention. *Journal of Cognitive Neuroscience, 23*, 3228–3240. https://doi.org/10.1162/jocn_a

Friedrich, M., & Friederici, A. D. (2017). The origins of word learning: Brain responses of 3-month-olds indicate their rapid association of objects and words. *Developmental Science*. https://doi.org/10.1111/desc.12357

Gergely, G., Egyed, K., & Király, I. (2007). On pedagogy. *Developmental Science, 10*(1), 139–146. https://doi.org/10.1111/j.1467-7687.2007.00576.x

Golinkoff, R. M., Ma, W., Song, L., & Hirsh-Pasek, K. (2013). Twenty-five years using the intermodal preferential looking paradigm to study language acquisition: What have we learned? *Perspectives on Psychological Science, 8*(3), 316–339. https://doi.org/10.1177/1745691613484936

Hagoort, P., & Brown, C. M. (2000). ERP effects of listening to speech: Semantic ERP effects. *Neuropsychologia, 38*(11), 1518–1530. https://doi.org/10.1016/S0028-3932(00)00052-X

Henderson, A. M., Sabbagh, M. A., & Woodward, A. L. (2013). Preschoolers' selective learning is guided by the principle of relevance. *Cognition, 126*(2), 246–257. https://doi.org/10.1016/j. cognition.2012.10.006

Heyes, C. (2016). Who knows? Metacognitive social learning strategies. *Trends in Cognitive Sciences, 20*(3), 204–213. https://doi.org/10.1016/j.tics.2015.12.007

Huettig, F., & McQueen, J. M. (2007). The tug of war between phonological, semantic and shape information in language-mediated visual search. *Journal of Memory and Language, 57*(4), 460–482. https://doi.org/10.1016/j.jml.2007.02.001

Jaswal, V. K., & Neely, L. A. (2006). Adults don't always know best preschoolers use past reliability over age when learning new words. *Psychological Science, 17*(9), 757–758. https://doi. org/10.1111/j.1467-9280.2006.01778.x

Junge, C., Cutler, A., & Hagoort, P. (2012). Electrophysiological evidence of early word learning. *Neuropsychologia, 50*(14), 3702–3712. https://doi.org/10.1016/j.neuropsychologia.2012. 10.012

Kalish, C. W., & Sabbagh, M. A. (2007). Conventionality and cognitive development: Learning to think the right way. *New Directions for Child and Adolescent Development, 115*(115), 1–9. https://doi.org/10.1002/cad.178

Koenig, M. A., Clément, F., & Harris, P. L. (2004). Trust in testimony: Children's use of true and false statements. *Psychological Science, 15*(10), 694–698. https://doi.org/10.1111/j.0956-7976.2004.00742.x

Koenig, M. A., & Sabbagh, M. A. (2013). Selective social learning: New perspectives on learning from others. *Developmental Psychology, 49*(3), 399–403. https://doi.org/10.1037/a0031619

Koenig, M. A., & Woodward, A. L. (2010). Sensitivity of 24-month-olds to the prior inaccuracy of the source: Possible mechanisms. *Developmental Psychology, 46*(4), 815–826. https://doi. org/10.1037/a0019664

Kushnir, T., & Koenig, M. A. (2017). What I don't know won't hurt you: The relation between professed ignorance and later knowledge claims. *Developmental Psychology, 53*(5), 826–835. https://doi.org/10.1037/dev0000294

Kutas, M., & Federmeier, K. D. (2011). Thirty years and counting: Finding meaning in the N400 component of the event related brain potential (ERP). *Annual Review of Psychology, 62*, 621–647. https://doi.org/10.1146/annurev.psych.093008.131123

Kutas, M., & Hillyard, S. A. (1980). Reading senseless sentences: Brain potentials reflect semantic incongruity. *Science, 207*(4427), 203–205.

MacDonald, K., Yurovsky, D., & Frank, M. C. (2017). Social cues modulate the representations underlying cross-situational learning. *Cognitive Psychology, 94*, 67–84. https://doi.org/10.1016/j.cogpsych.2017.02.003

Mangardich, H., & Sabbagh, M. A. (2017). Children remember words from ignorant speakers but do not attach meaning. *Developmental Science*. https://doi.org/10.1111/desc.12544

Martin, A., & Chao, L. L. (2001). Semantic memory and the brain: Structure and processes. *Current Opinion in Neurobiology, 11*(2), 194–201. https://doi.org/10.1016/S0959-4388(00)00196-3

Mascaro, O., & Sperber, D. (2009). The moral, epistemic, and mindreading components of children's vigilance towards deception. *Cognition, 112*(3), 367–380. https://doi.org/10.1016/j.cognition.2009.05.012

McClelland, J. L., McNaughton, B. L., & O'Reilly, R. C. (1995). Why there are complementary learning systems in the hippocampus and neocortex: Insights from the successes and failures of connectionist models of learning and memory. *Psychological Review, 102*(3), 419–457. https://doi.org/10.1037/0033-295X.102.3.419

Mestres-Missé, A., Càmara, E., Rodriguez-Fornells, A., Rotte, M., & Münte, T. F. (2008). Functional neuroanatomy of meaning acquisition from context. *Journal of Cognitive Neuroscience, 20*(12), 2153–2166. https://doi.org/10.1162/jocn.2008.20150

Mestres-Missé, A., Rodriguez-Fornells, A., & Münte, T. F. (2010). Neural differences in the mapping of verb and noun concepts onto novel words. *NeuroImage, 49*(3), 2826–2835. https://doi.org/10.1016/j.neuroimage.2009.10.018

Mills, C. M. (2013). Knowing when to doubt: Developing a critical stance when learning from others. *Developmental Psychology, 49*(3), 404–418. https://doi.org/10.1037/a0029500

Moscovitch, M., Nadel, L., Winocur, G., Gilboa, A., & Rosenbaum, R. S. (2006). The cognitive neuroscience of remote episodic, semantic and spatial memory. *Current Opinion in Neurobiology, 16*(2), 179–190. https://doi.org/10.1016/j.conb.2006.03.013

Nadel, L., Hupbach, A., Gomez, R., & Newman-Smith, K. (2012). Memory formation, consolidation and transformation. *Neuroscience & Biobehavioral Reviews, 36*(7), 1640–1645. https://doi.org/10.1016/j.neubiorev.2012.03.001

Nazzi, T., & Bertoncini, J. (2003). Before and after the vocabulary spurt: Two modes of word acquisition? *Developmental Science, 6*(2), 136–142. https://doi.org/10.1111/1467-7687.00263

Patterson, K., Nestor, P. J., & Rogers, T. T. (2007). Where do you know what you know? The representation of semantic knowledge in the human brain. *Nature Reviews. Neuroscience, 8*(12), 976–987. https://doi.org/10.1038/nrn2277

Perfetti, C. A., Wlotko, E. W., & Hart, L. A. (2005). Word learning and individual differences in word learning reflected in event-related potentials. *Journal of Experimental Psychology: Learning, Memory, and Cognition, 31*(6), 1281–1292. https://doi.org/10.1037/0278-7393.31.6.1281

Ripollés, P., Marco-Pallarés, J., Hielscher, U., Mestres-Missé, A., Tempelmann, C., Heinze, H. J., … Noesselt, T. (2014). The role of reward in word learning and its implications for language acquisition. *Current Biology, 24*(21), 2606–2611. https://doi.org/10.1016/j.cub.2014.09.044

Sabbagh, M. A., & Baldwin, D. A. (2001). Learning words from knowledgeable versus ignorant speakers: Links between preschoolers' theory of mind and semantic development. *Child Development, 72*(4), 1054–1070. Retrieved from http://www.jstor.org/stable/1132429

Sabbagh, M. A., & Shafman, D. (2009). How children block learning from ignorant speakers. *Cognition, 112*(3), 415–422. https://doi.org/10.1016/j.cognition.2009.06.005

Sabbagh, M. A., Wdowiak, S. D., & Ottaway, J. M. (2003). Do word learners ignore ignorant speakers? *Journal of Child Language, 30*(4), 905–924. https://doi.org/10.1017/S0305000903005828

Schilbach, L., Wilms, M., Eickhoff, S. B., Romanzetti, S., Tepest, R., Bente, G., … Vogeley, K. (2010). Minds made for sharing: Initiating joint attention recruits reward-related neuro-circuitry. *Journal of Cognitive Neuroscience, 22*(12), 2702–2715. https://doi.org/10.1162/jocn.2009.21401

Schultz, W. (2010). Dopamine signals for reward value and risk: Basic and recent data. *Behavioral and Brain Functions, 6*(1), 24. https://doi.org/10.1186/1744-9081-6-24

Scott-Phillips, T. C., Dickens, T. E., & West, S. A. (2011). Evolutionary theory and the ultimate-proximate distinction in the human behavioral sciences. *Perspectives on Psychological Science, 6*, 38–47. https://doi.org/10.1177/1745691610393528

Senju, A., & Johnson, M. H. (2009). The eye contact effect: Mechanisms and development. *Trends in Cognitive Sciences, 13*(3), 127–134. https://doi.org/10.1016/j.tics.2008.11.009

Shellshear, L., MacDonald, A. D., Mahoney, J., Finch, E., McMahon, K., Silburn, P., … Copland, D. A. (2015). Levodopa enhances explicit new-word learning in healthy adults: A preliminary study. *Human Psychopharmacology: Clinical and Experimental, 30*(5), 341–349. https://doi.org/10.1002/hup.2480

Smith, L., & Yu, C. (2008). Infants rapidly learn word-referent mappings via cross-situational statistics. *Cognition, 106*(3), 1558–1568. https://doi.org/10.1016/j.cognition.2007.06.010

Southgate, V., Chevallier, C., & Csibra, G. (2009). Sensitivity to communicative relevance tells young children what to imitate. *Developmental Science, 12*(6), 1013–1019. https://doi.org/10.1111/j.1467-7687.2009.00861.x

Sperber, D., Clément, F., Heintz, C., Mascaro, O., Mercier, H., Origgi, G., & Wilson, D. (2010). Epistemic vigilance. *Mind and Language, 25*(4), 359–393. https://doi.org/10.1111/j.1468-0017.2010.01394.x

Takashima, A., Bakker, I., Van Hell, J. G., Janzen, G., & McQueen, J. M. (2014). Richness of information about novel words influences how episodic and semantic memory networks interact during lexicalization. *NeuroImage, 84*, 265–278. https://doi.org/10.1016/j.neuroimage.2013.08.023

Takashima, A., Bakker, I., Van Hell, J. G., Janzen, G., & McQueen, J. M. (2017). Interaction between episodic and semantic memory networks in the acquisition and consolidation of novel spoken words. *Brain and Language, 167*, 44–60. https://doi.org/10.1016/j.bandl.2016.05.009

Tamminen, J., & Gaskell, M. G. (2013). Novel word integration in the mental lexicon: Evidence from unmasked and masked semantic priming. *The Quarterly Journal of Experimental Psychology, 66*(5), 1001–1025. https://doi.org/10.1080/17470218.2012.724694

Tamminen, J., Payne, J. D., Stickgold, R., Wamsley, E. J., & Gaskell, M. G. (2010). Sleep spindle activity is associated with the integration of new memories and existing knowledge. *Journal of Neuroscience, 30*(43), 14356–14360. https://doi.org/10.1523/JNEUROSCI.3028-10.2010

Tekin, S., & Cummings, J. L. (2002). Frontal–subcortical neuronal circuits and clinical neuropsychiatry: An update. *Journal of Psychosomatic Research, 53*(2), 647–654. https://doi.org/10.1016/S0022-3999(02)00428-2

van Den Brink, D., Brown, C., & Hagoort, P. (2001). Electrophysiological evidence for early contextual influences during spoken-word recognition: N200 versus N400 effects. *Journal of Cognitive Neuroscience, 13*(7), 967–985. https://doi.org/10.1162/089892901753165872

van Der Ven, F., Takashima, A., Segers, E., & Verhoeven, L. (2015). Learning word meanings: Overnight integration and study modality effects. *PLoS One, 10*(5), e0124926. https://doi.org/10.1371/journal.pone.0124926

von Koss Torkildsen, J., Hansen, H. F., Svangstu, J. M., Smith, L., Simonsen, H. G., Moen, I., & Lindgren, M. (2009). Brain dynamics of word familiarization in 20-month-olds: Effects of productive vocabulary size. *Brain and Language, 108*, 73–88. https://doi.org/10.1016/j.bandl.2008.09.005

von Koss Torkildsen, J., Svangstu, J. M., Hansen, H. F., Smith, L., Simonsen, H. G., Moen, I., & Lindgren, M. (2008). Productive vocabulary size predicts event-related potential correlates of fast mapping in 20-month-olds. *Journal of Cognitive Neuroscience, 20*, 1266–1282. https://doi.org/10.1162/jocn.2008.20087

Chapter 10
The Role of Testimony in Children's Belief in the Existence of the Unobservable

Ian L. Campbell and Kathleen H. Corriveau

Abstract In the current chapter, we focus on how children come to develop concepts about things they cannot observe for themselves. We argue that the formation of belief in the unobservable—which includes entities that are difficult or impossible to experience first-hand—arises primarily through the testimony from trusted adults. We note that the impact of testimony is similar for both natural (e.g., scientific or historical facts) and supernatural (e.g., God, Santa Claus) concepts. We suggest that children's own developing understanding of physical possibility constrains the impact of testimonial information, leading to differences in how children come to think of natural and supernatural unobservables. Finally, we present a broader perspective of testimony's role in children's concept formation, examining the known and potential impacts of the community and cultural consensus.

Introduction

When children learn about the world, they are highly reliant on the testimony they hear from others. Testimony, or verbal information provided by others, presents children with crucial frameworks for developing generalized concepts. However, the impact of testimony on children's conceptual development likely depends on the extent to which conceptual evidence is observable. When developing conceptions of observable phenomena, such as natural kinds or causal mechanisms, children can rely on evidence from first-hand experience. Under these circumstances, language from a trusted adult can complement evidence by helping the child to attend to the relevant feature, or by elaborating on the observed mechanism. For example, a child

I. L. Campbell · K. H. Corriveau (✉)
Applied Human Development, Boston University,
Boston, MA, USA
e-mail: kcorriv@bu.edu

© Springer International Publishing AG, part of Springer Nature 2018
M. M. Saylor, P. A. Ganea (eds.), *Active Learning from Infancy to Childhood*,
https://doi.org/10.1007/978-3-319-77182-3_10

learning about the concept of weight can observe several differences between a bowling ball and a flower. Testimony from a trusted adult may help to orient the child toward the relevant feature (mass) and away from irrelevant features such as color, shape, or texture. Furthermore, testimony provides the child with terminology to label and understand why some things are heavy, and some are light, and some things are heavier or lighter than others. Thus, even when learning about concepts they can experience for themselves—without the assistance of testimony—children might be left with an incomplete and/or vague conceptual understanding of the world.

Children themselves often understand the importance of listening to testimony. Under many circumstances, testimony can override competing physical evidence (e.g., Bascandziev & Harris, 2010; Corriveau & Harris, 2010; Harris, 2012; Jaswal & Markman, 2007; Lane & Harris, 2014). For example, when shown a picture of an animal who looks more cat-like than dog-like, 3-year-olds are willing to ascribe dog features—such as eating bones—to the animal if a trusted adult labels it as a dog (Jaswal & Markman, 2007). Note, however, that in many instances, children may be resistant to endorsing verbal claims that directly conflict with their perceptions. For example, a child may discount testimony from an inaccurate or ignorant informant (e.g., Koenig & Harris, 2005; Pasquini, Corriveau, Koenig, & Harris, 2007). As such, children's perceptions and testimony both contribute to their concept formation regarding observable entities and phenomena.

Testimony is even more critical for the development of a conceptual understanding of unobservable, or difficult-to-observe, phenomena and events. For example, children and adults believe in the existence of bacteria or vitamins even though these entities are, under normal circumstances, unobservable (Harris, Pasquini, Duke, Asscher, & Pons, 2006; Shtulman, 2013). Many children also believe in the existence of supernatural entities such as the Tooth Fairy, God, or the soul even though they too are, under normal circumstances, unobservable (Goldstein & Woolley, 2016; Guerrero, Enesco, & Harris, 2010; Richert & Harris, 2006, 2008; Shtulman, 2013). As these examples illustrate, belief in the unobservable includes phenomena that fall within the domains of both natural and supernatural phenomena. These examples also highlight the fact that children are likely to be guided by the testimony of other people. Ordinarily, children have no direct observational access to these phenomena and yet they are inclined to trust what they are told about their existence (Harris, 2012; Harris & Corriveau, 2011, 2014).

It is important to note that, although children do not have first-hand access to information about the unobservable, they undeniably play an active role in acquiring testimony from trusted sources through the types of questions they ask. Work on the content of children's questions highlights that children often engage in "passages of intellectual search" through a series of questions and explanations with a trusted adult, often focusing on phenomena that are inconsistent with the child's conception of how the world works (Chouinard, Harris, & Maratsos, 2007; Isaacs, 1930; Tizard & Hughes, 1984; Vosniadou, 1994). Through the child's questions, an adult's explanation, and the child's follow-up—especially if the explanation provided was not satisfactory—children actively seek out and construct theories not only of the here-and-now, but also of conceptions about the past and present (Callanan & Oakes, 1992; Kurkul & Corriveau, 2017; Canfield & Ganea, 2014).

Just as they do with testimony about observable entities, children evaluate the testimony provided by others about the unobservable *in light of* their own conceptual beliefs. Consider the case of the shape of the earth. The idea that the earth is a sphere conflicts with several presuppositions of physics: namely, that objects require support and that the ground is flat. Thus, even though children receive testimony about the shape of the earth, they do not take in such testimony indiscriminately. Rather, they go through multiple mental models of the earth before arriving at the correct adult version (Callanan, Jipson, & Soennichsen, 2002; Vosniadou & Brewer, 1992). Importantly, such an adult conception of the earth requires children to go beyond the testimony they are told to build a coherent conception of the earth as a sphere.

In the current chapter, we focus on the relation between the testimony children hear about natural and supernatural unobservables and their own developing conception of what is possible. We present evidence that testimony is the primary mechanism for children's conceptual understanding of the unobservable. We note that the impact of testimony is similar for both natural (e.g., scientific or historical facts) and supernatural (e.g., God, Santa Claus) unobservable concepts. We then turn to the impact of the child's own prior beliefs about physical possibilities in constraining their acceptance of testimony. We present a broader perspective of testimony's role in children's concept formation, examining the known and potential impacts of the community and cultural consensus. We conclude by highlighting future directions in research for these topics.

Testimony as a Mechanism for Belief in the Existence of the Unobservable

Although children can learn much about the world through their own first-hand experience, the influence of testimony on children's formation of both natural and supernatural unobservable concepts cannot be understated. In fact, multiple studies have established that children are able to understand claims from trusted adults about unobserved phenomena and often incorporate those claims into their own knowledge (Gelman, 2009; Harris, 2012; Mills, 2013; Sobel & Kushnir, 2013). Familiar examples include children's understanding of the shape of the earth, the relation between mental processes and the brain, the functioning of internal bodily organs, and the existence of the soul (Corriveau, Pasquini, & Harris, 2005; Harris & Corriveau, 2014; Harris & Koenig, 2006). That is, children's gradual appreciation that the earth is a sphere (Siegal, Butterworth, & Newcombe, 2004), that mental process is closely linked to brain processes (Johnson, 1990), that life is sustained by hidden organs such as the heart and the lungs (Slaughter, Jaakkola, & Carey, 1999; Slaughter & Lyons, 2003), and the invariance of the soul and its relation to mental processes (Richert & Harris, 2006, 2008) all critically depend on their assimilation of testimony they hear from other people about these phenomena.

In this way, children's mental picture of the natural world extends well beyond the mundane world of empirical experience even if key components of it are grounded in that experience. By focusing on children's learning from testimony, we also highlight the importance of considering the sociocultural contexts in which learning is situated (e.g., Bandura, 1977; Rogoff, 1993; Vygotsky, 1978), and thus, we anticipate potential differences in children's approach to learning about novel situations based on their cultural background.

Given that children are surprisingly selective in learning from the testimony of others (e.g., Chow, Poulin-Dubois, & Lewis, 2008; Corriveau & Harris, 2009a, 2009b, 2010; Einav & Robinson, 2011; Fitneva & Dunfield, 2010; Koenig, 2012; Koenig & Jaswal, 2011; Harris & Corriveau, 2011; Mascaro & Sperber, 2009), we can ask how far children's selective use of other's testimony leads to parallels between their thinking about natural and supernatural unobservable phenomena—granted that, in both cases, children's beliefs and understanding reach beyond first-hand, empirical experience.

In an initial investigation of this type, Harris et al. (2006) asked 5- and 6-year-old children about the existence of various unobservable entities: natural *scientific* entities, and two types of supernatural entities: supernatural entities whose existence was *endorsed* by the testimony of the community (e.g., God, Santa Claus), and supernatural *equivocal* entities whose existence was not typically endorsed through adult testimony (e.g., mermaids, ghosts). Children were first asked about whether or not the entity existed, and then were asked about their certainty of its existence. They were also asked several follow-up questions including their belief in whether or not such judgments would be met with community consensus, the visual appearance of the entity, and their justification for the existence/non-existence of the entity.

Inspection of the results indicates several notable parallels between children's belief in unobservable scientific and endorsed entities. First, when asked about ordinarily unobservable natural phenomena such as bacteria and ordinarily unobservable supernatural endorsed phenomena such as God and the Tooth Fairy, 5- and 6-year-olds were much more certain about the existence of the natural phenomena than in the existence of supernatural equivocal phenomena. They also expressed much more confidence in the existence of scientific and endorsed entities than in the existence of equivocal entities. Note, however, that their confidence in the existence of scientific and endorsed entities was not identical: they expressed more confidence in scientific entities than in endorsed entities.

Recall that children were asked several follow-up questions, which also highlight parallels in their thinking about unobservable scientific and endorsed entities. Children claimed that other people in the community shared their beliefs that both scientific and endorsed entities were likely to exist, but equivocal supernatural entities were not likely to exist. They also acknowledged that, notwithstanding their confidence, they had no firm ideas about the visual appearance of any of the various phenomena—reinforcing the assumption that children's beliefs in their existence were not based on any first-hand encounter or empirical experience. Instead, the data indicate that children based their confidence in the existence of these entities based on testimony they heard about those entities.

Nevertheless, when asked to justify their beliefs, children rarely referred directly to what they had been told by other people (despite the assumption that such testimony was, in fact, a major contributor to children's beliefs). Instead, they referred to the properties or characteristics of the phenomena, especially to their causal powers. For example, in the case of bacteria, children might refer to the way that bacteria can cause people to feel sick; in the case of God, children might refer to God's power as a creator. In summary, this investigation underlined intriguing parallels between the way that children contemplate natural, scientific phenomena as compared to supernatural phenomena that lie outside of everyday empirical experience.

Follow-up research attested to the stability of these findings. The initial investigation had been conducted in Boston, but two other subsequent investigations with separate populations where children might hear different testimony about the existence of unobservable entities yielded similar conclusions (Guerrero et al., 2010; Harris, Abarbanell, Pasquini, & Duke, 2007). The first investigation took place at a Catholic school in Spain, where children heard extensive testimony about the existence of supernatural religious entities such as God. The second investigation took place in a Mayan community of Mexico, where children heard testimony about the existence of supernatural endorsed phenomena that are different from those endorsed in the USA. Would the pattern of responses between scientific, endorsed, and equivocal entities look similar? Somewhat surprisingly, despite the existence of modest quantitative differences (e.g., children uniformly expressed unequivocal confidence in the existence of bacteria, whereas they expressed considerable but not unequivocal confidence in the existence of God), children reasoned about and justified their belief in natural scientific and supernatural endorsed phenomena in a similar fashion across all three cultural settings.

We argue that the consistency across all three cultural settings highlights the fact that the testimony that children are receiving about such entities influences their knowledge about the entity's existence. Research on children's sensitivity to adult discourse about unobservable phenomena, both explicit and implicit, is still at an early stage. However, some recent studies are encouraging and informative. Woolley, Ma, and Lopez-Mobilia (2011) asked children to watch video clips in which two adults conversed casually about unfamiliar animals (e.g., a bilby, a takin, a civet, etc.). When children heard an implicit reference to the existence of the novel animal in the video (e.g., one of the adults in the video remarked that she had seen a baby takin) 5-, 7-, and 9-year-olds were likely to judge that the animal was real rather than not real in a subsequent interview. By implication, young children do not need to be explicitly told about the existence of a creature or phenomenon that they have not seen. Rather, if its existence is presupposed in conversation, they will infer and accept its existence.

Similar results from Canfield and Ganea (2014) echo the power of implicit language when endorsing the existence of scientific and supernatural endorsed phenomena. In two studies, parent–child dyads and older sibling–child dyads were invited to discuss the existence of various unobservable phenomena—including scientific, endorsed, and equivocal items. Testimony provided by adults and older siblings differed in the type of content provided, as well as the surrounding implicit language. Discourse content for scientific and endorsed entities was similar. Adults and older siblings were more likely to provide real-world examples when talking about scientific and endorsed, as compared to equivocal entities. Despite the fact that the content was similar for scientific and endorsed entities, the surrounding language differed. Adults often used modulations of assertion—saying, for example, "I believe in God"—when talking about endorsed entities. By contrast, they rarely used such language when talking about scientific entities. Such language likely signals to the child that the community consensus around the existence of the entities likely differs.

Other research indicates that testimony paired with explicit acts also influences children belief in the existence of the unobservable. Wooley and colleagues (Boerger, Tullos, & Woolley, 2009; Woolley, Boerger, & Markman, 2004) introduced 3- to 7-year-old children to a novel fantastical being: the Candy Witch. The Candy Witch was said to come on Halloween night and leave a toy for the child in exchange for candy. After hearing testimony about the existence of the Candy Witch, half of the children overheard a phone conversation—presumably between the parent and the Candy Witch—arranging for the swap. The remaining half heard testimony about the Candy Witch's existence, but did not have the additional experience of overhearing a phone call. Children of parents who engaged in the phone call—which presupposes the existence of the novel fantastical being—were more likely to believe that the Candy Witch was real than children whose parents did not engage in such acts (Boerger et al., 2009; Woolley et al., 2004). Moreover, older children were more likely than younger children to believe in her reality status. Such an inferential strategy of using both explicit and implicit testimonial cues is likely to be effective whether children are learning about natural scientific or endorsed supernatural phenomena (see also Goldstein & Woolley, 2016; Prentice, Manosevitz, & Hubbs, 1978; Rosengren, Kalish, Hickling, & Gelman, 1994).

The Role of Physical Possibility in Constraining Belief in the Unobservable

We have highlighted the important role of adult testimony in children's belief in things they cannot see for themselves. Yet, despite continued endorsements from trusted adults about the existence of such entities, children gradually come to doubt the existence of many supernatural endorsed entities such as the Tooth Fairy and Santa Claus. We suggest that children's own developing understanding of possibility might help to discount the credibility of testimony. Research framed in terms of young children as budding scientists has shown that, in various domains, including everyday physics, biology, and psychology, they appreciate the constraints imposed by natural causal laws (Schult & Wellman, 1997; Shtulman, 2009; Shtulman & Carey, 2007; Sobel, 2004; Woolley & Cox, 2007). To take two well-studied examples: first, in the domain of biology, children come to realize that there are constraints on the life cycle: for all living creatures, death is ultimately inevitable and irreversible (Brent et al., 1996; Harris, 2011; Kenyon, 2001). Second, in the domain of psychology, children come to realize that there are constraints on knowledge such that, in the absence of relevant informational access, human beings will lack true knowledge (Lane, Wellman, & Evans, 2010; Lane, Wellman, & Evans, 2014; Perner, 1991).

In the current chapter, we focus on children's developing understanding of physical possibility to constrain their use of testimony (Johnson & Harris, 1994; Rosengren et al., 1994; Sharon & Woolley, 2004; Tullos & Woolley, 2009; Shtulman, 2009; Shtulman & Carey, 2007; Subbotsky, 1994), but it is likely that a similar weighting happens between adult testimony and children's use of biological and psychological possibility. Indeed, all of the supernatural endorsed entities have various fantastical properties that defy physical laws. A thoughtful consideration of the incongruity between the testimony provided by a trusted adult and the child's own understanding of what is physically possible may help children to discredit the veracity of such claims about the unobservable (see also Corriveau, Harris, et al., 2009 for similar discrediting in the face of physical evidence). Figure 10.1 displays how testimony may interact with a child's understanding of physical possibility during the testimonial transmission process. If adult testimony about the unobservable is consistent with physical possibility, children are likely to believe the entity exists. However, if the testimony is inconsistent with the child's own knowledge of possibility, children will likely take that into account when making decisions about whether or not to trust such testimony.

Some recent research has explored the relation between children's skepticism about the existence of supernatural endorsed entities and their understanding of physical possibility. Shtulman and Yoo (2015) invited 3- to 9-year-old children to consider whether or not Santa Claus would be able to perform various impossible activities. For example, children were asked to consider whether or not Santa could travel around the world in a single night. Children were also invited to consider the possibility of other events that violated physical laws (but did not include mention of Santa). Responses were coded as to whether or not children provided a quasi-causal mechanism to justify their response. The number of explanations about Santa's

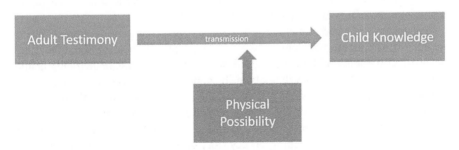

Fig. 10.1 Schematic depiction of the relation between adult testimony and physical possibility in children's belief in the unobservable

activities containing a causal mechanism was associated with scores on the physical possibility judgments, suggesting that a greater understanding of physical possibility was associated with more complex explanations to justify the existence of Santa.

Some of our own work on children's judgments of the existence of protagonists in unfamiliar narratives also highlights children's developing use of physical possibility. Corriveau, Kim, et al. (2009) presented 3- to 6-year-old children with unfamiliar stories and asked them to judge the reality status of the main character in the story. Some of the stories were quasi-historical in the sense that they offered a realistic account of events that had befallen the protagonist. Other stories included fantastical elements, such as boats with invisible sails or magical food. Whereas 3- and 4-year-olds were unable to systematically judge the reality status based on story context, 5- and 6-year-olds reliably judged characters in quasi-historical stories as real, and characters in fantastical stories as pretend. Moreover, when asked to justify their choice of reality status, 5- and 6-year-olds frequently appealed to the real-world plausibility of the quasi-historical stories, as well as noted the violations of causality in the fantastical stories. Taken together, older preschoolers appeared to use natural (quasi-historical) and supernatural (fantastical) narrative cues to infer the status of a novel protagonist (see also Woolley & Van Reet, 2006).

Why, as compared to older children did the 3- and 4-year-olds struggle to make inferences about the status of novel protagonists based on narrative cues? Although children of this age can readily differentiate between ordinary and "magic" events (Johnson & Harris, 1994), they are still developing their understanding of the difference between impossible and improbable events (Shtulman & Carey, 2007), and they may not yet recognize that physical possibility is the primary feature that differentiates unfamiliar fantastical narratives from more reality-based ones. Accordingly, in a follow-up study, we asked if alerting young children to the physical possibility or impossibility of key story events would assist them when making judgments about the reality status of story characters. We presented stories to children in three phases: in a *pretest* phase, children were presented with stories and asked to judge the reality status of the protagonist. Next, in a *training* phase, children heard the story with one additional question. Before asking children to judge the reality status of the story character, they were asked about the physical possibility of the central story event. Finally, to determine if such training influenced children's judgments in the absence of a prompt, in a *posttest* phase children heard the stories exactly as they were presented in the *pretest*.

The results indicated that children were receptive to the training prompt. When invited to consider the possibility of the story event prior to judging about the character's reality status, children were significantly more systematic in their judgments. They also were able to justify their claims by appropriately attending to the realistic elements in the quasi-historical stories and the violations of physical laws in the fantastical stories. Moreover, the changes based on the short training period also influenced their judgments in the posttest trials—even in the absence of the prompt to consider the physical possibility of key story events. Thus, even by the age of 3, young children make use of physical possibility when making judgments of novel narratives that differ in context.

Belief in Religious Narratives

Taken together, we have presented a relatively straightforward story: the testimony provided by trusted adults influences the formation of the belief in both natural and supernatural unobservable entities and events, and children's own understanding of physical possibility moderates the extent to which such beliefs will be trusted. We have shown that the influence of both testimony and physical possibility is relatively consistent across entities and events that are not typically seen as similar: scientific, quasi-historical, and supernatural endorsed. One challenge, of course, is that whereas belief in some supernatural agents—such as Santa Claus and the Tooth Fairy—appears to *decrease* with age (Blair, McKee, & Jernigan, 1980; Goldstein & Woolley, 2016; Prentice et al., 1978; Sharon & Woolley, 2004), belief in God as a supernatural agent is often sustained. Indeed, research indicates that belief in God as a supernatural agent *increases* with age (Barrett, Richert, & Driesenga, 2001; Giménez-Dasí, Guerrero, & Harris, 2005; Kelemen, 2004; Lane et al., 2010; Lane, Wellman, & Evans, 2012; Legare, Evans, Rosengren, & Harris, 2012; Rottman & Kelemen, 2012) and that adult religious beliefs often exceed those of children (Legare et al., 2012)—despite the fact that an adult understanding of physical possibility is arguably more sophisticated than that of children. Indeed, if anything, God's supernatural powers as the creator of the universe certainly exceed those of Santa Claus and the Tooth Fairy, who simply deliver and exchange packages on certain nights. If children were simply relying on physical possibility as a mechanism to doubt the testimony of others, they should be more skeptical of God's existence than that of Santa's.

Research focusing on children understanding of magic indicates that they are willing to suspend disbelief in physical impossibility following adult testimony under certain circumstances. For example, 4- to 6-year-old children were shown a "magic" box and told that it could change pictures of objects into actual objects (Subbotsky, 1985). When they were invited to attempt such transformations for themselves, they were surprised at their failure to successfully transform the pictures into objects. Similarly, when presented with a bottle of "magic water" that could "turn you and everything around you into what was two years ago," children were reluctant to drink the water (Subbotsky, 1994; see also Subbotsky, 2011 for similar reluctance in adults). Thus, these studies highlight children's willingness to believe that an ordinarily impossible event could occur—and to subsequently act on the basis of that belief—following adult testimony.

In sum, the data on children's sustained belief in God as a supernatural agent and their willingness to believe in physically impossible events brought about through magic suggests that, although children can use physical possibility to discount the veracity of testimony, under some circumstances testimony can override children's own knowledge of what could be possible. This underlines the following prediction: children who are exposed to testimony—either implicit or explicit—about the existence of God as a supernatural agent may place God in a separate category of endorsed entities than children who have not been exposed to such narratives. A second open question concerns the extent to which belief in God as a supernatural agent impacts children's belief in other aspects of physical possibility. There is some data to suggest that this might not be the case: children's understanding of supernatural agents does not transfer to their intuitions about the real world (Richert & Smith, 2011; Skolnick & Bloom, 2006). Moreover, children and adults are able to navigate flexibly between expectations and explanations based on natural causal laws and those based on their understanding of the power of endorsed divine agents (Legare et al., 2012). Thus, their exposure to testimony about the existence of God—a powerful supernatural agent with significant causal powers—might not impact their belief in other impossible entities or events.

In some recent research, we explored how exposure to testimony about religious narratives might impact the scope of children's belief in the impossible (Corriveau, Chen, & Harris, 2014). We compared four groups of 5- and 6-year-old children who varied in their school attendance and their family church attendance. One group of children had not received systematic religious testimony: they attended public school and did not attend religious services with their family. The remaining three groups of children did receive religious testimony: either via religious instruction in parochial school, attending religious services with their family, or both. As in Corriveau, Kim, Schwalen, and Harris (2009), children heard unfamiliar narratives and were asked to judge the reality status of the protagonist. Children heard three types of narratives: narratives that were quasi-historical and contained only real-world events (*naturalistic*), narratives that contained ordinarily impossible events and the causal agent was God (*religious*), and narratives that contained ordinarily impossible events and the causal agent was a different supernatural power (*fantastical*). Replicating our previous finding, when children heard *naturalistic* stories, all 4 groups of children stated that the protagonist could exist, and justified their claim by highlighted the physical possibility of the story events. Consistent with the testimony they had been exposed to, when children heard *religious* narratives, the three groups of children who had received systematic testimony about religion stated that the protagonist could exist and justified their claim usually by explicitly referring to religion. By contrast, the secular children who had not been exposed to religious narratives stated that the protagonist was likely fantastical, and highlighted the ordinarily impossible story events to justify their claim.

Would exposure to religious testimony influence children's belief in other ordinarily impossible events? The results from children's judgments of *fantastical* stories suggest that this is the case. As expected, the group of secular children with no systematic religious instruction viewed the protagonists in these stories as likely to be pretend, and justified their claim by referring to the key story events that were implausible. But the three groups of children who were exposed to religious narratives were much more likely to say that this protagonist was real. Moreover, consistent with the hypothesis that religious testimony might impact children's judgment of impossibility, children in these groups sometimes justified their responses by explicitly recalling ordinarily impossible events that occurred in religious narratives. For example, when told a story where a fairy parted the sea, children noted that God had made that event happen in the Bible.

Further reflection of the justifications by children exposed to religion invited the following hypothesis: rather than modify the scope of unobservable entities and events children viewed as possible, exposure to religious narratives could provide an extended library of narratives children might be familiar with, and such familiarity explained children's willingness to believe in the existence of the protagonist. Indeed, although a narrative about a fairy parting the sea would technically be something the child had not heard before, children might recall the biblical passages of God helping Moses by parting the Red Sea. On this hypothesis, children might be willing to suspend disbelief in the face of physical impossibility if the story context was familiar to a Biblical narrative, but would appropriately employ their understanding of the impossible in unfamiliar contexts.

To test this hypothesis, we presented a new group of religious and secular 5- and 6-year-olds with stories that did and did not include familiar causal violations (Corriveau, Chen, & Harris, 2014; Study 2). As in our previous research, even if the narrative included an unfamiliar impossible event, children who had been exposed to religious testimony were more likely than secular children to state that the protagonist could be real. Thus, exposure to religious testimony appears to impact the extent to which children use their understanding of physical possibility when considering conflicting testimony—even if such testimony does not include familiar references to religious teaching.

The Importance of Community-Based Testimony

The previous section highlights that children's relative use of testimonial evidence and physical possibility when developing conceptions about the unobservable might vary based on individual factors. We argue that when children weigh others' testimony and their own understanding of possibility, they consider the extent to which such testimony is met with community consensus. Indeed, one reason why the impact of religious testimony may be so robust in the face of violations of causal laws is because such testimony is consistent across members of the child's religious community (note also that the fact that the testimony is both oral and written may also influence children's judgments, Corriveau, Einav, et al., 2014; Einav, Robinson, & Fox, 2013).

Community or cultural consensus provides a new dimension of testimonial impact, as it can provide an *aggregation* of multiple testimonies endorsing a concept. As other researchers have noted, transmission of cultural consensus can be vital to communicating concepts that are difficult to directly observe, such as societal innovations and technological advances (Henrich, 2016; Richerson & Boyd, 2005). For example, Henrich (2016) outlines how cultural consensus enabled multiple cultures in the Americas to ensure their staple crop, manioc, was prepared for safe consumption. Manioc, or cassava, is naturally poisonous but does not immediately sicken or kill people who eat it—it takes many years for its lethal effects to manifest. Over time, cultures such as the Tukanoans managed to identify manioc as the cause of the apparently sudden illnesses in their population and dis-cover ways to detoxify the crop in a complex multi-stage process. Utilizing the power of cultural consensus, the Tukanoans and others ensured that future genera-tions were able to safely eat manioc. Without this consensus, any given individual, or even generation would be unable to prevent manioc poisoning because the effects are effectively unobservable. This is evidenced by the fact that after manioc was imported to Africa as a food crop, local people were slow to realize the poisonous nature of the plant and develop similar food processing techniques (Henrich, 2016).

Do children use community consensus to calibrate their own confidence? Recent experimental work suggests that they can do so from an early age. For example, preschool children attend to cues of assent or dissent from bystanders when making inferences about the credibility of an informant (Fusaro & Harris, 2008). Preschoolers are also sensitive to agreement amongst informants, preferring to map a novel label to a referent indicated by a 3-person majority as opposed to one indicated by a lone dissenter (Chen, Corriveau, & Harris, 2011, 2013; Corriveau, Fusaro, et al., 2009). Children use such consensus cues to make inferences about the credibility of indi-vidual members of the majority even when the consensus—or the bystanders—is no longer present. Moreover, preschoolers sometimes defer to information from a con-sensus even in the face of conflicting physical evidence (Corriveau & Harris, 2010; Corriveau, Kim, Song, & Harris, 2013; Haun & Tomasello, 2011). Thus, such con-sensus information appears to be a strong cue that further emphasizes the impor-tance of privileging the information provided by testimony. Figure 10.2 displays how community consensus may strengthen, or reinforce, the transmission of adult testimony. When the testimony from a trusted adult is consistent with the testimony from various other sources, the transmission signal might be strong enough to over-ride the child's own competing knowledge of physical possibility. This might

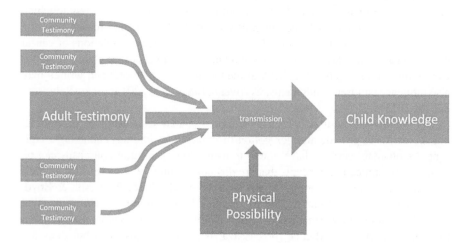

Fig. 10.2 Schematic depiction of the relation between adult testimony (as reinforced by commu-nity consensus) and physical possibility in children's belief in the unobservable

explain why consensus information is enough to override instances described above where consensus testimony is in conflict with observed physical evidence.

Recall that in the aforementioned Harris et al. (2006) study, children were asked about their confidence that a community member would also share the child's belief in the existence of unobservable entities. The results indicated that children's confidence in the existence of supernatural and natural entities mirrored the level of general endorsement they believed those entities would likely receive in their communities. Children were more confident in the existence of universally endorsed entities such as germs than highly endorsed (but not universally so) entities such as God. Additionally, they were more confident in the existence of both germs and God than of supernatural non-endorsed entities like mermaids. These data are consistent with the possibility that children derived their confidence from the community consensus that they perceived regarding the phenomena in question. As such, children likely monitor endorsement of unobserved entities and phenomena in aggregate—calibrating their own views according to what the opinions of their community.

Some recent work from Iran also highlights how consensus information might influence children's judgments of what could be possible (Davoodi, Corriveau, & Harris, 2016). Iran is considered a religious theocracy, and Iranian children are exposed to religious instruction through a formal educational curriculum and through family religious testimony and practices. Thus, children in Iran are exposed to a strong testimonial consensus about the veracity of miracles in the Quran. This allowed us to ask whether similar to the findings of the religious children growing up in Boston, children growing up in such a culture might also differ in their judgments of what could be possible. Following previous studies, we told 3- to 6-year-old children novel quasi-historical and supernatural narratives and invited them to judge the reality status of the story protagonists. Note that none of the narratives included any reference to religion, and the supernatural causal mechanism in the stories was never Allah. Nevertheless, similar to the religious children in Boston (Corriveau, Chen, et al., 2014), Iranian children noted that the protagonists in supernatural narratives might be real. Indeed, the youngest age group of children were equally likely to judge the story characters as real, regardless of the plausibility of key story events. We interpret these findings to indicate that regular exposure to narratives that include miraculous elements from a variety of sources influences children's willingness to weigh testimonial evidence much more strongly than their own understanding of physical possibility.

Conclusions

In this chapter, we have attempted to highlight the importance of testimonial information for both observable and unobservable bodies of knowledge. We have highlighted that when children learn about the unobservable, testimonial input is important for two types of information that are often viewed as separate: information about the natural world and information about the supernatural. Indeed, one of the strongest pieces of evidence for children's trust in testimony is their belief in the existence of ordinarily invisible scientific entities such as germs as well as unobservable special beings such as the Tooth Fairy, Santa Claus, and God. Yet, even when learning about unobservable concepts that can only be transmitted through testimony, children's belief in such concepts does differ subtly by domain. That is, children are more confident in the existence of natural (scientific or historical) entities and events than they are in supernatural culturally endorsed entities, such as the Tooth Fairy—and they are more confident in the existence of the Tooth Fairy than they are in supernatural unendorsed entities such as mermaids and fairies.

We have highlighted three reasons why this might be the case. First, the testimony that children hear about these three different types of entities likely differs in explicit and implicit ways. Children might become increasingly sensitive to these subtle variations in testimonial input and use such variations to make inferences about an unknown entity's credibility. Some evidence indicates that children can take advantage of explicit differences between testimonial input when categorizing entities (Woolley et al., 2011), but more research is needed to determine how variations in implicit markers such as modulations of parental assertion (Canfield & Ganea, 2014) might influence children's subsequent trust in the existence of the unobservable.

Children also make use of their own developing understanding of the possible and the impossible. We focus specifically on children's use of physical possibility, but we note that children are likely to take advantage of their knowledge of psychological and biological possibility in similar ways. When testimony is consistent with physical possibility, children are more likely to believe in the existence of the unobservable. By contrast, when testimony is inconsistent with children's own understanding of what is possible, children are less likely to be swayed by testimony when developing conceptions of the world.

One notable exception for the use of possibility as a discounting mechanism concerns children's sustained belief in religious concepts. We argue that children's sensitive antennae toward information provided by their cultural community—in addition to information provided by their parents—helps to enhance the transmission signal of testimonial information and override children's own understanding of physical possibility. Future research should explore variability in the testimony children receive in their cultural community regarding, for example, religious beliefs to more systematically explore children's relative weighting of consensus testimony and physical possibility. Of particular importance is the impact of community-based testimony that is not a unanimous consensus. For example, how would children growing up in community of religious pluralism differ in their understanding of the unobservable than children growing up in a religious theocracy? It is likely that systematic cross-cultural research is needed to thoroughly evaluate such questions.

Future research should also continue to evaluate how children and adults consider the content of testimony to develop conceptions about the world beyond what they can experience for themselves. We note that most research on the use of testimony—including research highlighted in this volume (Ridge et al., in this volume)—focuses on how children evaluate the credibility of the source of the information. Yet a continued evaluation of information content will allow children to remain vigilant to guard against testimony that should be avoided. Indeed, some research indicates that even toddlers are able to use some linguistic cues such as argument circularity to evaluate the credibility of testimonial content (Castelain, Bernard, & Mercier, 2017; Mercier, Bernard, & Clément, 2014; Mercier et al., 2014)—and may subsequently use such content to make inferences about the credibility of the source (Corriveau & Kurkul, 2014). Such an interaction between content evaluation and prior belief may be especially important for children's belief in the unobservable.

References

Bandura, A. (1977). Self-efficacy: Toward a unifying theory of behavioral change. *Psychological Review, 84*(2), 191.

Barrett, J. L., Richert, R. A., & Driesenga, A. (2001). God's beliefs versus mother's: The development of nonhuman agent concepts. *Child Development, 72*(1), 50–65.

Bascandziev, I., & Harris, P. L. (2010). The role of testimony in young children's solution of a gravity-driven invisible displacement task. *Cognitive Development, 25*(3), 233–246.

Blair, J. R., McKee, J. S., & Jernigan, L. F. (1980). Children's belief in Santa Claus, Easter Bunny and Tooth Fairy. *Psychological Reports, 46*(3), 691–694.

Boerger, E. A., Tullos, A., & Woolley, J. D. (2009). Return of the candy witch: Individual differences in acceptance and stability of belief in a novel fantastical being. *British Journal of Developmental Psychology, 27*(4), 953–970.

Brent, S. B., Speece, M. W., Lin, C., Dong, Q., & Yang, C. (1996). The development of the concept of death among Chinese and US children 3–17 years of age: From binary to "fuzzy" concepts?. *OMEGA-Journal of Death and Dying, 33*(1), 67–83.

Callanan, M. A., Jipson, J. L., & Soennichsen, M. S. (2002). Maps, globes, and videos: Parent–child conversations about representational objects. In S. G. Paris (Ed.), *Perspectives on object-centered learning in museums* (pp. 261–283). Mahwah, NJ: MIT Press.

Callanan, M. A., & Oakes, L. M. (1992). Preschoolers' questions and parents' explanations: Causal thinking in everyday activity. *Cognitive Development, 7*, 213–233.

Canfield, C. F., & Ganea, P. A. (2014). 'You could call it magic': What parents and siblings tell preschoolers about unobservable entities. *Journal of Cognition and Development, 15*(2), 269–286.

Castelain, T., Bernard, S., & Mercier, H. (2017). Evidence that two-year-old children are sensitive to information presented in arguments. *Infancy*. doi:https://doi.org/10.1111/infa.12202.

Chen, E. E., Corriveau, K. H., & Harris, P. L. (2011). A cross-cultural examination of the influence of social group membership and consensus cues in children's trust in testimony. In *The society of research on child development biennial meeting*, Montreal, Canada.

Chen, E. E., Corriveau, K. H., & Harris, P. L. (2013). Children trust a consensus composed of outgroup members—But do not retain that trust. *Child Development, 84*(1), 269–282.

Chouinard, M. M., Harris, P. L., & Maratsos, M. P. (2007). Children's questions: A mechanism for cognitive development. *Monographs of the Society for Research in Child Development, 72*(1), 1–129.

Chow, V., Poulin-Dubois, D., & Lewis, J. (2008). To see or not to see: Infants prefer to follow the gaze of a reliable looker. *Developmental Science, 11*(5), 761–770.

Corriveau, K., & Harris, P. L. (2009a). Choosing your informant: Weighing familiarity and recent accuracy. *Developmental Science, 12*(3), 426–437.

Corriveau, K., & Harris, P. L. (2009b). Preschoolers continue to trust a more accurate informant 1 week after exposure to accuracy information. *Developmental Science, 12*(1), 188–193.

Corriveau, K. H., Chen, E. E., & Harris, P. L. (2014). Judgments about fact and fiction by children from religious and nonreligious backgrounds. *Cognitive Science, 39*(2), 353–382.

Corriveau, K. H., Einav, S., Robinson, E. J., & Harris, P. L. (2014). To the letter: Early readers trust print-based over oral instructions to guide their actions. *British Journal of Developmental Psychology, 32*(3), 345–358.

Corriveau, K. H., Fusaro, M., & Harris, P. L. (2009). Going with the flow: Preschoolers prefer nondissenters as informants. *Psychological Science, 20*(3), 372–377.

Corriveau, K. H., & Harris, P. L. (2010). Preschoolers (sometimes) defer to the majority in making simple perceptual judgments. *Developmental Psychology, 46*(2), 437.

Corriveau, K. H., Harris, P. L., Meins, E., Fernyhough, C., Arnott, B., Elliott, L., & De Rosnay, M. (2009). Young children's trust in their mother's claims: Longitudinal links with attachment security in infancy. *Child Development, 80*(3), 750–761.

Corriveau, K. H., Kim, A. L., Schwalen, C. E., & Harris, P. L. (2009). Abraham Lincoln and Harry Potter: Children's differentiation between historical and fantasy characters. *Cognition, 113*(2), 213–225.

Corriveau, K. H., Kim, E., Song, G., & Harris, P. L. (2013). Young children's deference to a consensus varies by culture and judgment setting. *Journal of Cognition and Culture, 13*(3-4), 367–381.

Corriveau, K. H., & Kurkul, K. E. (2014). "Why does rain fall?": Children prefer to learn from an informant who uses noncircular explanations. *Child Development, 85*(5), 1827–1835.

Corriveau, K. H., Pasquini, E. S., & Harris, P. L. (2005). "If it's in your mind, it's in your knowledge": Children's developing anatomy of identity. *Cognitive Development, 20*(2), 321–340.

Davoodi, T., Corriveau, K. H., & Harris, P. L. (2016). Distinguishing between realistic and fantastical figures in Iran. *Developmental Psychology, 52*(2), 221.

Einav, S., & Robinson, E. J. (2011). When being right is not enough: Four-year-olds distinguish knowledgeable informants from merely accurate informants. *Psychological Science, 22*(10), 1250–1253.

Einav, S., Robinson, E. J., & Fox, A. (2013). Take it as read: Origins of trust in knowledge gained from print. *Journal of Experimental Child Psychology, 114*(2), 262–274.

Fitneva, S. A., & Dunfield, K. A. (2010). Selective information seeking after a single encounter. *Developmental Psychology, 46*(5), 1380.

Fusaro, M., & Harris, P. L. (2008). Children assess informant reliability using bystanders' nonverbal cues. *Developmental Science, 11*(5), 771–777.

Gelman, S. A. (2009). Learning from others: Children's construction of concepts. *Annual Review of Psychology, 60*, 115–140.

Giménez-Dasí, M., Guerrero, S., & Harris, P. L. (2005). Intimations of immortality and omniscience in early childhood. *European Journal of Developmental Psychology, 2*(3), 285–297.

Goldstein, T. R., & Woolley, J. (2016). Ho! Ho! Who? Parent promotion of belief in and live encounters with Santa Claus. *Cognitive Development, 39*, 113–127.

Guerrero, S., Enesco, I., & Harris, P. L. (2010). Oxygen and the soul: Children's conception of invisible entities. *Journal of Cognition and Culture, 10*(1), 123–151.

Harris, P. L. (2011). Conflicting thoughts about death. *Human Development, 54*(3), 160–168.

Harris, P. L. (2012). *Trusting what you're told: How children learn from others*. London, England: Harvard University Press.

Harris, P. L., Abarbanell, L., Pasquini, E. S., & Duke, S. (2007). Imagination and testimony in the child's construction of reality. *Intellectica, 2*, 69–84.

Harris, P. L., & Corriveau, K. H. (2011). Young children's selective trust in informants. *Philosophical Transactions of the Royal Society of London B: Biological Sciences, 366*(1567), 1179–1187.

Harris, P. L., & Corriveau, K. H. (2014). Learning from testimony about religion and science. In E. Robinson & S. Einav (Eds.), *Trust and skepticism: Children's selective learning from testimony* (pp. 28–41). Hove, England: Psychology Press.

Harris, P. L., & Koenig, M. A. (2006). Trust in testimony: How children learn about science and religion. *Child Development, 77*(3), 505–524.

Harris, P. L., Pasquini, E. S., Duke, S., Asscher, J. J., & Pons, F. (2006). Germs and angels: The role of testimony in young children's ontology. *Developmental Science, 9*(1), 76–96.

Haun, D., & Tomasello, M. (2011). Conformity to peer pressure in preschool children. *Child Development, 82*(6), 1759–1767.

Henrich, J. (2016). *The secret of our success: How culture is driving human evolution, domesticating our species, and making us smarter.* Princeton, NJ: Princeton University Press.

Isaacs, N. (1930). Children's "why" questions. In S. Isaacs (Ed.), *Intellectual growth in young children* (pp. 291–349). London, England: Routledge.

Jaswal, V. K., & Markman, E. M. (2007). Looks aren't everything: 24-month-olds' willingness to accept unexpected labels. *Journal of Cognition and Development, 8*(1), 93–111.

Johnson, C. N. (1990). If you had my brain, where would I be? Children's understanding of the brain and identity. *Child Development, 61*(4), 962–972.

Johnson, C. N., & Harris, P. L. (1994). Magic: Special but not excluded. *British Journal of Developmental Psychology, 12*(1), 35–51.

Kelemen, D. (2004). Are children "intuitive theists"? Reasoning about purpose and design in nature. *Psychological Science, 15*(5), 295–301.

Kenyon, B. L. (2001). Current research in children's conceptions of death: A critical review. *OMEGA-Journal of Death and Dying, 43*(1), 63–91.

Koenig, M. A. (2012). Beyond semantic accuracy: Preschoolers evaluate a speaker's reasons. *Child Development, 83*(3), 1051–1063.

Koenig, M. A., & Harris, P. L. (2005). Preschoolers mistrust ignorant and inaccurate speakers. *Child Development, 76*(6), 1261–1277.

Koenig, M. A., & Jaswal, V. K. (2011). Characterizing children's expectations about expertise and incompetence: Halo or pitchfork effects? *Child Development, 82*(5), 1634–1647.

Kurkul, K. E., & Corriveau, K. H. (2017). Question, explanation, follow-up: A mechanism for learning from others? *Child Development, 89*(1), 280–294.

Lane, J. D., & Harris, P. L. (2014). Confronting, representing, and believing counterintuitive concepts: Navigating the natural and the supernatural. *Perspectives on Psychological Science, 9*(2), 144–160.

Lane, J. D., Wellman, H. M., & Evans, E. M. (2010). Children's understanding of ordinary and extraordinary minds. *Child Development, 81*(5), 1475–1489.

Lane, J. D., Wellman, H. M., & Evans, E. M. (2012). Sociocultural input facilitates children's developing understanding of extraordinary minds. *Child Development, 83*(3), 1007–1021.

Lane, J. D., Wellman, H. M., & Evans, E. M. (2014). Approaching an understanding of omniscience from the preschool years to early adulthood. *Developmental Psychology, 50*(10), 2380–2392.

Legare, C. H., Evans, E. M., Rosengren, K. S., & Harris, P. L. (2012). The coexistence of natural and supernatural explanations across cultures and development. *Child Development, 83*(3), 779–793.

Mascaro, O., & Sperber, D. (2009). The moral, epistemic, and mindreading components of children's vigilance towards deception. *Cognition, 112*(3), 367–380.

Mercier, H., Bernard, S., & Clément, F. (2014). Early sensitivity to arguments: How preschoolers weight circular arguments. *Journal of Experimental Child Psychology, 125*, 102–109.

Mills, C. M. (2013). Knowing when to doubt: Developing a critical stance when learning from others. *Developmental Psychology, 49*(3), 404.

Pasquini, E. S., Corriveau, K. H., Koenig, M., & Harris, P. L. (2007). Preschoolers monitor the relative accuracy of informants. *Developmental Psychology, 43*(5), 1216.

Perner, J. (1991). *Understanding the representational mind.* Cambridge, MA: MIT Press.

Prentice, N. M., Manosevitz, M., & Hubbs, L. (1978). Imaginary figures of early childhood: Santa Claus, Easter Bunny, and the Tooth Fairy. *American Journal of Orthopsychiatry, 48*(4), 618.

Richerson, P. J., & Boyd, R. (2005). *Not by genes alone: How culture transformed human evolution.* Chicago, IL: University of Chicago Press.

Richert, R. A., & Harris, P. L. (2006). The ghost in my body: Children's developing concept of the soul. *Journal of Cognition and Culture, 6*(3), 409–427.

Richert, R. A., & Harris, P. L. (2008). Dualism revisited: Body vs. mind vs. soul. *Journal of Cognition and Culture, 8*(1), 99–115.

Richert, R. A., & Smith, E. I. (2011). Preschoolers' quarantining of fantasy stories. *Child Development, 82*(4), 1106–1119.

Rogoff, B. (1993). Children's guided participation and participatory appropriation in sociocultural activity. In R. H. Wozniak & K. W. Fischer (Eds.), *The Jean Piaget symposium series. Development in context: Acting and thinking in specific environments* (pp. 121–153). Hillsdale, NJ: Lawrence Erlbaum Associates.

Rosengren, K. S., Kalish, C. W., Hickling, A. K., & Gelman, S. A. (1994). Exploring the relation between preschool children's magical beliefs and causal thinking. *British Journal of Developmental Psychology, 12*(1), 69–82.

Rottman, J., & Kelemen, D. (2012). Is there such a thing as a Christian child? Evidence of religious beliefs in early childhood. *Science and the World's Religions, 1*, 205–238.

Schult, C. A., & Wellman, H. M. (1997). Explaining human movements and actions: Children's understanding of the limits of psychological explanation. *Cognition, 62*(3), 291–324.

Sharon, T., & Woolley, J. D. (2004). Do monsters dream? Young children's understanding of the fantasy/reality distinction. *British Journal of Developmental Psychology, 22*(2), 293–310.

Shtulman, A. (2009). The development of possibility judgment within and across domains. *Cognitive Development, 24*(3), 293–309.

Shtulman, A. (2013). Epistemic similarities between students' scientific and supernatural beliefs. *Journal of Educational Psychology, 105*(1), 199.

Shtulman, A., & Carey, S. (2007). Improbable or impossible? How children reason about the possibility of extraordinary events. *Child Development, 78*(3), 1015–1032.

Shtulman, A., & Yoo, R. I. (2015). Children's understanding of physical possibility constrains their belief in Santa Claus. *Cognitive Development, 34*, 51–62.

Siegal, M., Butterworth, G., & Newcombe, P. A. (2004). Culture and children's cosmology. *Developmental Science, 7*(3), 308–324.

Skolnick, D., & Bloom, P. (2006). What does Batman think about SpongeBob? Children's understanding of the fantasy/fantasy distinction. *Cognition, 101*(1), B9–B18.

Slaughter, V., Jaakkola, R., & Carey, S. (1999). Constructing a coherent theory: Children's biological understanding of life and death. In *Society for Research in Child Development, 1995, Indianapolis, IN, US; Portions of the chapter were presented at this meeting and at the 1997 meeting in Washington, DC.* Cambridge University Press.

Slaughter, V., & Lyons, M. (2003). Learning about life and death in early childhood. *Cognitive Psychology, 46*(1), 1–30.

Sobel, D. M., & Kushnir, T. (2013). Knowledge matters: How children evaluate the reliability of testimony as a process of rational inference. *Psychological Review, 120*(4), 779.

Sobel, D. M. (2004). Exploring the coherence of young children's explanatory abilities: Evidence from generating counterfactuals. *British Journal of Developmental Psychology, 22*(1), 37–58.

Subbotsky, E. (1994). Early rationality and magical thinking in preschoolers: Space and time. *British Journal of Developmental Psychology, 12*(1), 97–108.

Subbotsky, E. (2011). The ghost in the machine: Why and how the belief in magic survives in the rational mind. *Human Development, 54*(3), 126–143.

Subbotsky, E. V. (1985). Preschool children's perception of unusual phenomena. *Soviet Psychology, 23*, 91–114.

Tizard, B., & Hughes, M. (1984). *Children learning at home and in school.* London, England: Fontana.

Tullos, A., & Woolley, J. D. (2009). The development of children's ability to use evidence to infer reality status. *Child Development, 80*(1), 101–114.

Vosniadou, S. (1994). Universal and culture-specific properties of children's mental models of the earth. In L. A. Hirschfeld & S. A. Gelman (Eds.), *Mapping the mind: Domain specificity in cognition and culture* (pp. 412–430). New York, NY: Cambridge University Press.

Vosniadou, S., & Brewer, W. F. (1992). Mental models of the earth: A study of conceptual change in childhood. *Cognitive Psychology, 24*, 535–585.

Vygotsky, L. (1978). Interaction between learning and development. *Readings on the Development of Children, 23*(3), 34–41.

Woolley, J. D., Boerger, E. A., & Markman, A. B. (2004). A visit from the Candy Witch: Factors influencing young children's belief in a novel fantastical being. *Developmental Science, 7*(4), 456–468.

Woolley, J. D., & Cox, V. (2007). Development of beliefs about storybook reality. *Developmental Science, 10*(5), 681–693.

Woolley, J. D., Ma, L., & Lopez-Mobilia, G. (2011). Development of the use of conversational cues to assess reality status. *Journal of Cognition and Development, 12*(4), 537–555.

Woolley, J. D., & Van Reet, J. (2006). Effects of context on judgments concerning the reality status of novel entities. *Child Development, 77*(6), 1778–1793.

Part IV
Active Learning in Diverse Contexts

Chapter 11
How Conversations with Parents May Help Children Learn to Separate the Sheep from the Goats (and the Robots)

Jennifer L. Jipson, Danielle Labotka, Maureen A. Callanan, and Susan A. Gelman

Abstract We examined how children's active participation in parent–child conversations helps them organize the conceptual space of the animal domain. Three complementary research studies inform our understandings: (1) a diary study of family conversations about animals, (2) an investigation of how parent–child conversations about the properties of varied living and nonliving entities may inform children's developing understanding of animacy, and (3) an examination of parent–child conversations about animals that vary in similarity to humans. We found that parents share information that is scientifically accurate alongside information that may encourage anthropomorphic and anthropocentric reasoning about animals. This information is greeted by an active child who can sort through the give-and-take of conversation to (ultimately) construct coherent representations of the biological domain. This rich portrait of parent–child conversation contrasts with the model of the child as a mere recipient of parental wisdom.

Introduction

Young children reveal considerable interest in science-related domains (e.g., biology, physics, psychology). An extensive literature describes the content and structure of children's content knowledge in these domains and argues that children

J. L. Jipson (✉)
Department of Psychology and Child Development, California Polytechnic State University, San Luis Obispo, CA, USA
e-mail: jjipson@calpoly.edu

D. Labotka · S. A. Gelman
Department of Psychology, University of Michigan, Ann Arbor, MI, USA

M. A. Callanan
Department of Psychology, University of California, Santa Cruz, CA, USA

© Springer International Publishing AG, part of Springer Nature 2018
M. M. Saylor, P. A. Ganea (eds.), *Active Learning from Infancy to Childhood*,
https://doi.org/10.1007/978-3-319-77182-3_11

construct naive theories about the world that guide them as they make sense of their experiences (Gelman and Kalish, 2006). A complementary literature describes children's engagement in processes of scientific thinking wherein they purposefully seek knowledge, test theories against evidence, generate causal explanations, and engage in a process of modifying underlying conceptual structures to account for discrepancies (Kuhn, 2010; Legare, Gelman, & Wellman, 2010; Schulz & Bonawitz, 2007). Children's interest in science-related topics and their inquiry-based approach to learning leads many researchers and educators to enthusiastically endorse the "young child as scientist" metaphor for learning. Nonetheless, the image of young children as lone scientists is misleading (Gelman, 2009). Children's understandings are informed by their experiences in many rich social contexts (Harris, Bartz, & Rowe, 2017; Rogoff, 2014). Importantly, "informed by" does not mean "governed by"—children do not passively absorb information from others, nor do they lie in wait for others to spark their curiosity. Rather, they solicit and draw out information from knowledgeable others, help shape learning, and selectively attend to some cues and not others as they interpret new information against the background of what they already know.

Cashing out how to reconcile these two insights—children are active learners, and children are social learners—requires serious consideration of how active learning occurs in social contexts. How do children elicit information from others? What kinds of information do they seek? What kinds of information do others share? How do children use that information over development? In this chapter, we examine these active social learning processes by looking at how children's engagement with their parents helps them to organize the conceptual space of the animal domain. Below we motivate our focus on parent–child conversation, and explain our particular interest in conversations about animals (and animal-like artifacts, such as robots).

Why Focus on Parent–Child Conversation?

Parent–child conversations are powerful settings for children's everyday learning. Children from diverse backgrounds ask their parents questions about a wide range of topics (Callanan & Oakes, 1992; Callanan, Castañeda, Luce, & Martin, 2017), and parents share information that provides opportunities to construct and revise conceptual understandings (Benjamin, Haden, & Wilkerson, 2010; Callanan & Jipson, 2001; Crowley et al., 2001; Gelman, Coley, Rosengren, Hartman, & Pappas, 1998; Haden et al., 2014; Jant, Haden, Uttal, & Babcock, 2014; Tizard & Hughes, 1984). Two prior studies are particularly relevant to our focus on parent–child conversations about animals and animal-like artifacts. First, Jipson and Callanan (2003) investigated mother–child conversations about biological and nonbiological changes in size and found that mothers provided cues about domain-specific processes by using the word "grow" to refer primarily to biological events. On the rare occasion when they used "grow" to refer to nonbiological entities (e.g., a crystal), they often overtly discussed this use as atypical. Second, Rigney and Callanan (2011) found that parents used more animate pronouns (he/she) and talked more about psychological states when discussing typical animals (e.g., fish) than atypical animals (e.g., anemones) at an aquarium. Thus, parent talk contains both explicit information and implicit cues, and raises questions about how children use this information to inform their developing conceptual understandings.

Why Focus on Animal Concepts?

Animals are ubiquitous in young children's lives, in direct experience (pets, zoo visits) and in media (books, film), and young children display strong interest in animals, consistent with the notion of "biophilia" (Wilson, 1984). For example, 2-year-olds talk more about animals than toys that represent those same animals (LoBue, Bloom Pickard, Sherman, Axford, & DeLoache, 2013), and preschoolers pay more attention to live animals than stuffed animals (Nielsen & Delude, 1989). A focus on parent–child conversations about animals allows us to observe how children engage others to learn about a topic about which they are intensely interested.

There is also a clear theoretical reason for focusing on animals. Many researchers have investigated children's sensitivity to broad ontological distinctions (e.g., living/nonliving, animate/inanimate) because they have important implications for categorization, property induction, and generating predictions and explanations. Moreover, distinguishing biological from nonbiological kinds (e.g., that dogs are alive, but not cars) often rests on nonobvious properties, and thus cannot be learned wholly asocially. As Harris and Koenig (2006) point out, phenomena that are beyond the scope of everyday individual observation require social transmission, including verbal "testimony." Investigations of how parents talk about animals with young children can reveal how parents contribute to children's developing ontological understandings by discussing nonobvious properties and suggesting domain-specific causal mechanisms.

Finally, a focus on animals can inform debates about how children reason about the place of humans relative to other animals. When and why do children engage in anthropomorphism (projecting human qualities onto nonhuman entities) and anthropocentrism (treating human qualities and experiences as a baseline against which other animals are measured)? Carey (1985) famously argued that children are initially anthropocentric, with 5-year-old children treating humans as the most significant living thing, and judging other animals' biological properties based on how similar they were to humans. Only later did children in her studies reason from a more biological perspective. Children and adults have likewise demonstrated a human-centered pattern of reasoning for animals' psychological properties (Coley, 1995). Other work, however, has shown that these patterns of inference vary depending on children's cultural background and experiences with animals (Bang & Medin, 2010; Coley, 1995; Inagaki & Hatano, 2002; Medin, Waxman, Woodring, & Washinawatok, 2010; Tarlowski, 2006; Waxman & Medin, 2007). Particularly relevant here are the findings of Herrmann, Waxman, and Medin (2010), who replicated

Carey's findings with 5-year-olds, but found that 3-year-olds did not reason anthropocentrically. Herrmann et al. suggest that anthropocentrism may not be a starting point but instead may arise from exposure to anthropomorphic representations.

Anthropomorphic portrayals of animals and artifacts are plentiful in children's media. Moreover, when animals are presented as having human-like properties, children appear less likely to reason from a biological perspective about real animals (Ganea, Canfield, Simons-Ghafari, & Chou, 2014; Waxman et al., 2014).These intriguing findings motivate the need to better understand children's everyday opportunities to learn about animals. For example, how often do parents speak about animals in anthropomorphic vs. more scientific ways? And how does children's conceptual understanding relate to parents' talk?

In this chapter, we share preliminary findings from three complementary research studies: (1) a diary study of family conversations about animals, (2) an investigation of how parent–child conversations about the properties of varied living and nonliving entities may inform children's developing understanding of animacy, and (3) an examination of parent–child conversations about animals that vary in similarity to humans. These studies provide initial evidence regarding how parent–child interactions may serve as a context where children actively elicit information about animals, participate in conversations in ways that support their specific interests and conversational goals, selectively evaluate what is being discussed, and use these experiences to develop, extend, and refine their understandings of the wide array of phenomena related to the animal domain. We do not at this point have systematic evidence to support a full theory of how active learning occurs within natural conversations. Rather, our goal in this chapter is to highlight questions, hypotheses, and provocative examples, to engender future investigations.

Study 1: Everyday Family Conversations About Animals

Study 1 examined whether and how families talk about animals as they go about their daily routines. Sixty-seven families participated in a 2-week diary study that involved tracking the conversations about nature that they had with their 3- to 5-year-old children. Most parents were highly educated and European-American; however, we also included a sample of Mexican-heritage families where parents had only basic schooling (average of 9 years). We examined how often animals came up in family conversation, who initiated such talk, and what elements of the conversational context seemed to influence the interaction.

Families often focused on animals (34% of the conversations)—more than any other topic regarding nature (e.g., astronomy, weather, plants). Seventy-one percent of family conversations about animals were initiated by children. Fifty-four percent of child-initiated conversations about animals began with children's questions, and 46% began with children's statements. Children eagerly invited parents to engage with them in talk about animals, and by doing so actively created opportunities to extend what they might have learned through independent exploration and reflection. To illustrate, one parent documented an interaction with her 5-year-old son in which he asked, "What do tigers and lions eat?" and "Do you know if they eat each other or other animals?" This example, although perhaps seemingly mundane, illustrates active efforts to use conversations with a parent to satisfy their curiosity. First, this child actively organized his knowledge about tigers and lions: identifying features they have in common, assuming that they eat similar things, predicting that they are both meat-eaters, and entertaining the possibility that they are cannibals. The example also shows that the child identified a gap in his knowledge; he does not know exactly *what* kind of meat tigers and lions eat. To gain understanding, he makes an effort to learn from his mother's presumed greater knowledge. The mother reported that she told him that she did not know but would "look it up," modeling that some information is beyond the scope of parental expertise, that it is acceptable to admit gaps in one's knowledge, and that there are strategies for discovering new information from more distal sources. In just a few short conversational turns, this simple exchange reveals important ways that a child actively extends his understandings within a conversational context with his mother, and illustrates how parent–child conversations may support the development of new ways of problem-solving. An intriguing aspect of this exchange that we return to later is that the conversation took place in the car on the way to school, and there was no reported situational trigger for the child to ask those questions.

Although less well-studied than questions, children's statements also appear to be an effective strategy for eliciting information from others, with parents having the opportunity to choose whether and how to respond. A close reading of a series of diary reports from a single family illustrates the power of simple statements to launch deeper learning opportunities. In the first example, the child's observations of cows in a field on the way home from school sparked a conversation that included observations, descriptions of evidence, questions, and new vocabulary.

> While heading home, (child's name) pointed out the window and said "Cows, mama!" I asked her what they were doing. She said they were lying down and sleeping. I told her that they were likely not sleeping, that they were ruminating. She asked what that was, so I was excited to share. She thought it was "gross."

A week later, as the same family was driving home from school, the daughter again pointed out an animal as they were passing by. Once again, the mother eagerly shared scientific understandings and vocabulary.

Child: Mama Look! Horses!
Mother: What are they doing?
Child: Eating.
Mother: What are they eating?
Child: Them are eating grass.
Mother: Do they seem to enjoy it? Is it delicious?
Child: Yeah. I don't like grass. Grass isn't healthy for my body. Is grass healthy for the horse's body?
Mother: Yes, they are able to digest grass to get nutrients but people cannot. That's why we eat
    things like berries and broccoli and chicken and peanut butter.
Child: Oh, I like peanut butter and burritos.

In both examples, the mother, an expert in Agriculture Education, eagerly shares her disciplinary knowledge and interest in animals. Her daughter takes initiative in pointing out animals she notices, possibly reflecting an awareness of how to exploit her mother's expertise to create a new learning opportunity. Sensitivity to others' knowledge states was demonstrated systematically by Mills, Legare, Grant, and Landrum (2011), who found that children address questions to conversational partners who they perceive to have relevant knowledge.

Diary reports from another family demonstrate that children's statements about what they notice do not consistently elicit such deep levels of engagement from parents.

> While driving, (child's name) said, "There's bird poop on my window." I said "Oh yeah?" She continued talking about poop and I told her I didn't want to talk about it anymore.

> While browsing the plant section of a hardware store, (child's name) said "Look a white butterfly! Two of them!" and I said, "I see them. I wonder what they are doing here." She said "they want flowers" and then something about how she likes yellow butterflies better. We ended the conversation with that comment.

> While I was gardening, (child's name) said, "Look a bumble bee!" (although it really was a honey bee). And I said "Oh, it's getting nectar from that flower." She dropped the conversation there.

Over the course of multiple interactions, the child in this family gains insight into the topics that her mother is willing to discuss, perhaps learning that some topics are more productive or "worthy" than others. Additional investigations are needed to explore whether children also selectively direct their inquiry behaviors to those who are most likely to be responsive to the particular topic of interest.

Child-initiated conversations are only one way in which conversations begin. In this study, parents initiated 22% of all animal-related conversations (the remaining 7% were attributed to others, such as siblings). Parents, like children, often began conversations about animals in an authentic, spontaneous manner by describing their observations. For example, one mother pointed out a skunk on the sidewalk as they were driving by. She reported that her daughter then told her that skunks are awake at night and sleeping during the day, and that she replied with, "That's right, they are nocturnal." This was followed by a conversation involving the mother, daughter, and brother in which they began listing other nocturnal animals. After this brainstorming session, the mother asked, "Are people nocturnal?" to which the children emphatically replied, "No! People go to sleep at night!" Thus, this mother's casual mention of an observed animal opened the door to a sophisticated discussion of animal properties. Likewise, a father called his child's attention to a bug in the yard: "Do you want to see a cute bug?" The child assented and her parents then launched into a very science-focused didactic exchange including new vocabulary, features, and biological mechanisms (e.g., "It's called a praying mantis. What color is it?"; "Lots of stuff outside is brown right now so it wants to blend in"; "It's called camouflage. What color would I be if I wanted to blend in here?").

An open question is whether the approaches taken by parents have differing consequences for children's active processing and subsequent learning. The children in these examples responded to their parents' "bids", which may reinforce their parents' interest in continuing such talk. Yet the parents in these examples approached the conversations in distinct ways, with some more explicitly pedagogical than others. When children initiate conversations, parents' contributions may be guided by children's active interests and curiosity; however, when parents initiate, children may be less engaged. Parents may introduce conversational topics for a variety of reasons, such as to provide intentional teaching moments, as authentic demonstrations of interest, or to intersect with their knowledge of their children's individual interests and prior experiences. A full understanding of how children learn in informal contexts requires continued attention to moments of child inquiry, but also greater attention to the ways that children participate in and learn under different conversational circumstances. Keil (1998), for example, cautions that when adults are overly didactic and give unsolicited detailed explanations, children may experience "explanatory satiation" and become unreceptive to the information provided. Similarly, Callanan et al. (2017) found that children displayed higher levels of verbal engagement when parents related ongoing museum activities to children's previous personal experiences than when parents gave scientific explanations. Palmquist and Crowley (2007) show that when parents perceive their children to be experts on a topic, they concede their role as guide and co-investigator, resulting in lost opportunities to further extend their children's learning. More work is needed to learn how parents and children navigate their roles to co-create interactions with meaningful consequences for learning.

The settings within which conversations arise may influence how the interaction unfolds. Four of the seven diary study conversations described above took place in cars. Callanan and Oakes (1992) found that reflective moments can be a conducive setting for questions, more often than moments of active play. There are likely other situations in which families may have opportunities for reflection, such as bath time or bedtime. Research has yet to fully document the ways that routine settings intersect with dynamics of family conversations. Doing so is important, not only to yield better understandings of how daily routines support children's learning but also to generate additional research opportunities to investigate parent–child conversations. At the same time, this goal presents methodological challenges, as researchers are not always in the right place at the right time to document family conversations. Lab-based designs permit researchers to strategically observe "rare events," but do not capture everyday interactions that children initiate. They are further limited in not revealing how parents and children work through conceptually challenging issues over the course of multiple conversations (Callanan, Jipson, & Soennichsen, 2002; Crowley & Galco, 2001; Crowley & Jacobs, 2002). Finding ways to gain insight into the nature of temporally disconnected, yet conceptually related, conversations will further inform our understanding of children's active, anytime/anywhere efforts to learn.

Finally, in addition to providing opportunities for children to learn about particular animals, parent–child conversations may also help children develop their understanding of "animals" as a broader category. We observed that when families talked about animals, they frequently (59% of the time) mentioned biological properties (eating, sleeping), and occasionally talked about psychological (wanting, knowing) and sensory (seeing, hearing) properties (17% and 9%, respectively). We next turn to two more structured studies that systematically explored whether families *limit* their conversations about animate properties to animals, and whether families equivalently attribute such properties to all animals (e.g., bees vs. dogs).

Study 2: Parent–Child Talk about Animals, Artifacts, and Edge Cases

Young children make clear distinctions regarding the life status and biological properties of prototypical living (e.g., dog) and nonliving kinds (e.g., chair) (Opfer & Gelman, 2011). These understandings are often discussed as reflecting children's attention to static (e.g., having a face) and dynamic features (e.g., movement). This may characterize prototypical items, where simple cues indicate membership in a single ontological category. However, many entities have properties suggestive of membership in multiple categories. Reasoning about these entities is more challenging and children may recruit multiple sources of information to aid their efforts. Here we examine the scope and specificity of parents' speech about living and nonliving kinds, investigate the extent to which the content of parent talk aligns with children's reasoning, and consider children's role in shaping the conversational context.

We invited 36 parent–child dyads to participate in a semi-structured play session, spending 5 min engaging with each of the following items, presented individually: a rodent (degu), a sea star (commonly called a "starfish"), a toy car, a stuffed animal, and a robotic dog (for detailed analyses of conversations about the toy car, animal, and robot, see Jipson et al., 2016). These items vary in their life status and animacy cues. Coding focused on identifying parents' attribution of biological, psychological, sensory, and artifact properties to each item, and their use of animate (he/she, his/hers) vs. inanimate (it/that) pronouns.

Conversations About Clear Cases

Parents' speech about the animal and toy car clearly signaled domain boundaries. When talking about the rodent, they used animate pronouns (*M% of utterances* = 33.7%) significantly more than inanimate pronouns (M = 10%), and they mentioned animate properties—biological (M = 7.1%, e.g. "Oh you see him breathing?"), psychological (M = 6.0%, e.g. "maybe he likes to sleep in there"), sensory (M = 4.1%, e.g. "He's using his nose to smell us")—more than they did artifact properties (M = 0.9%, e.g. "Can you make him go through the tube?"). In contrast, parents mentioned artifact properties (M = 3.9%, e.g., "How do you turn it on?") for the toy car significantly more than they did biological ($M = 0.5\%$, e.g., "Why's he sick?"), psychological ($M = 0.4\%$, e.g., "Why doesn't she like that?"), or sensory properties ($M = 0.1\%$, e.g., "Do you think it's getting tired?"). In addition, they referred to the car most often as an "it" or "that" ($M = 15.3\%$) rather than a "he" or "she" ($M = 1.7\%$). In a subsequent property-projection task, children differentiated the rodent and toy car in ways that align with parents' discussion. Thus, parent talk may be an important source of information for children as they learn to differentiate living from nonliving kinds, and to identify domain-specific processes relevant to each.

The match between parent speech and children's understandings could suggest a view of children as passive recipients of the information their parents share. However, a close look at how children respond to the moments where parents' talk deviated from expected patterns reveals that children seem to take a more active critical stance. Parents' discussion of animate properties for the toy car is the most instructive. Notably, parents never introduced a biological property when discussing the toy car but occasionally talked about psychological and sensory capabilities. Children's reactions varied. One approach was to make no comment about domain violations, as when a mother responded to her child's claim that "It [the car] can shoot somebody" by asking, "Why would it *want to* shoot someone?" Her child responded matter-of-factly with reference to visible features and not desires, "Because it has shooters" (referring to headlights). Another child showed no response to her mother's warning not to "hurt" the car, and continued her rather rough physical exploration. A different response was to interpret parents' domain-blurring statements as jokes; one child laughed after her mom asked, "Do you think it's [the car is] getting *tired*?" In another example, one mother asked, "Do you think it's a *sad* or a *happy* car?" and her son replied, "It's a *bleeding* car." The child's extension to other animate properties may have been in fun, or may have been an attempt to test domain boundaries; whatever the motivation, the mother's laughter and incredulous response ("It's bleeding?") indicated that his proposal was unconventional. These domain-blurring examples, however, were the exception—parents largely differentiated between prototypical living and nonliving items in clear ways. This suggests a social learning process in which children weigh parents' deviations against what their parents more typically say and against what they already know about the items.

Conversations About Atypical Animals and Animal Toys

We also observed parent–child conversations about potentially ontologically ambiguous items: a sea star, stuffed animal toy, and robotic dog. We reasoned that talk about these "edge cases" might provoke explicit inquiry about ontology. Table 11.1 indicates how often parents mentioned each type of property and pronoun, with examples illustrating domain-specific and -blurring content.

Table 11.1 Parent talk about edge cases

	Sea star	Stuffed animal toy	Robotic dog
Biological	4.1% He *eats* plants If you cut off a leg it will *grow* a new one	4.7% What does he like to *eat*? Is that where he *poops*?	3.8% He's *peeing*! Is he *sleepin'*?
Psychological	1.8% Do you think it *likes* to climb on those rocks? Do you think he's *trying* to catch something?	2.3% What if he doesn't *like* it and he *tries* to bite you? This one might be *sad* if you wanted something else	3.2% He *knows* there's a wall there You better be careful, if he's *mad* he might bite
Sensory	0.9% Do you think they *feel* with those points too? ...if it accidentally gets *hurt*	1.4% Is he *tired*? She doesn't want you to *hurt* her toy	1.6% What happens if you cover his eyes so he can't *see*? You think he's *hungry*?
Artifact	0.1% ...or if it (an arm) *breaks* off	0.9% It's just *for* play Can *you make it* fit through the hole?	7.3% Is that how you *make* it work? What's that *button* do?
Pronouns	Animate (17%) Inanimate (10.6%)	Animate (23.5%) Inanimate (8.1%)	Animate (30.6%) Inanimate (15%)

Mean proportion of utterances are presented along with examples of parent talk about these items

Sea Star

Parents' explicit and subtle cues indicated that they consider the sea star to be a living kind. They mentioned biological, psychological, and sensory capabilities proportionally more than artifact properties, and used significantly more animate than inanimate pronouns. Yet parents provided less biological talk about the sea star than the rodent. Further, whereas parents talked about both biological and psychological properties at high rates for the rodent, they emphasized biological over psychological properties for the sea star. This pattern aligns with children's reasoning in the property projection task; children clearly identified the sea star as a biological kind on par with the rodent, yet were more likely to attribute psychological properties to the rodent than the sea star. Children's efforts to understand the sea star may have been informed by parent talk and/or their own expectations about specific features (e.g., that a face signals psychological capacities). This example illustrates that it is difficult, from observational data alone, to determine whether parent–child convergence reflects parental influences on children or instead a third factor that drives both parent and child understandings.

Taking a close look at parent–child conversations about the sea star reveals an intriguing pattern involving unfamiliar entities. In the left-hand column of the example below, the child repeatedly indicated that he did not know what kind of animal the sea star was. This self-appraisal led him to seek information in two distinct ways: by asking direct questions *and* by offering up potential labels for parent endorsement. This process is consistent with work by Harris et al. (2017), who found that young children are sensitive to what they do not know, and selectively seek information from others who may be able to provide missing information. It is important to note that offering labels in the face of uncertainty is itself a strategy for eliciting information from others, as the child's tentative labels can then be accepted or rejected by the parent. Ultimately, in this case, his mother also expressed ignorance and the conversation then turned to a topic with no conventional answer—the item's proper name. Only after the pair later reached an agreement that the item was a "starfish" did they begin to consider its status as an animal that can sleep, eat, move autonomously, and die.

Initial conversation: what is it?	Pursuant conversation: what does it do?
Parent: Is it a plant or an animal or a fish?	Child: It's *waking* up
Child: It's an animal but I don't know what it is	Child: It's moving its arms!
Parent: Is it moving on its own?	Parent: What do you think that *eats*?
Child: *I don't know what it is*	Parent: Candies?
Child: Maybe it's a squid	%com: Mom and child laugh
Parent: Huh?	Child: It's *waking* up!
Child: What kind of animal is it?	Parent: It's *moving*?
Parent: I don't know	Parent: Yes it is
Child: What name is it?	Parent: It is definitely *moving*
Parent: Mmm, I don't know	Child: It's not, it's *not dead*
Child: Maybe the name is Kathy?	
(they discuss potential proper names)	
Parent: I wonder what it is	
Child: I think it's an octopus	
Child: A little octopus	
Parent: Or a starfish	
Child: Mom!	
Parent: Hmm?	
Child: I think it's a starfish	

Greif et al. (2006) found that the first thing children ask when they come across something new (artifact or animal) is, "What is it?" Spelke (2017) pointed out that this is puzzling because a label in and of itself provides very little information about what an entity does, how it functions, or what causal mechanisms are relevant to explain its behavior. Yet, this question reflects a belief that the label reveals an item's real identity and essence (Gelman, 2003). Chouinard (2007) identified a similar pattern; children started out by asking for straightforward factual information and only once that information was obtained, moved on to probe for more conceptually meaningful information (such as explanations). Such a sequence was illustrated in another family's conversation about the sea star in which the child immediately exclaimed, "A starfish!" The mother shared the child's enthusiasm, asked her child to count the legs, and then guided him to notice that one leg was shorter than the others. She then explained that "starfish" have a unique ability to regrow new legs when one breaks. This possibility fascinated her 5-year-old child, who moved quickly through a complicated learning arc in which he was at first skeptical ("It will?"), then confirmed that the creature was in fact a starfish ("He has plants, so he's a starfish."), proposed that the outcome of a lost leg would be death ("It would die."), and then finally accepted his mother's claim that this kind of creature, in contrast to himself, could grow a new one ("It would grow a new one on right there."). Reminiscent of Tizard and Hughes's (1984) concept of "passages of intellectual search," the child's attention to, interest in, and expression of doubt regarding a surprising characteristic of the sea star served to spark an informative discussion about a core biological mechanism, growth. Indeed, in other studies, surprising events (e.g., a light-up toy that fails to light up) have been particularly powerful elicitors of children's questions (Frazier, Gelman, & Wellman, 2009, 2016) and explanations (Legare et al., 2010). Further investigation of the sequence of child inquiry is needed to see whether a pattern of moving from labeling to more complex properties bears out in a domain-general manner across conversation topics and settings.

Stuffed Animal Toy

In contrast to the items considered thus far, parent speech about the stuffed animal diverged from its actual ontological status. Parents mentioned biological and psychological capabilities at equivalent rates, and their biologically related talk was significantly higher that their mention of sensory or artifact capabilities. Parents' pronoun use supported their anthropomorphic treatment of the stuffed animal, with greater use of animate than inanimate pronouns. Thus, based on parent talk alone, children might be misled into thinking of the stuffed animal as a living kind. However, this was not at all the case; children in the property projection task rarely endorsed biological properties for the stuffed animal and only endorsed psychological or sensory properties at chance levels or below. This mismatch between parent talk and children's reasoning highlights a critical broader question about children's learning processes: how do children come to disregard parents' testimony? One possibility is that children do not perceive stuffed animals to be at all ambiguous in terms of category membership, and use this confidence to discount parents' talk as non-literal. Alternatively, parents may provide children with subtle cues to signal that their talk is playful rather than factual. Lillard and Witherington (2004) demonstrated that when engaging in pretense play, parents exhibited marked changes in demeanor and intonation. We did not code for indicators of pretense in parents' talk about this item, but view this as a fruitful question for the future. Another important cue to explore further is parents' expressions of uncertainty. In the examples about the stuffed animal in Table 11.1, parents introduced psychological properties using hedges such as "what if" and "might," which indicate uncertainty. Parental comments about biological properties, in contrast, presupposed that the item had these properties. For instance, asking "What does he like to eat?" implies that this entity eats. Parents' use of hedges, qualifications, and expressions of uncertainty have been noted in prior work. Jipson and Callanan (2003) observed that when parents used a biological causal mechanism (growth) to describe nonbiological increases in size, they often qualified this use through subtle hedges (e.g., "well, it *kinda* grows"). Henderson and Sabbagh (2010) documented a similar phenomenon in object labeling tasks, finding that parents provided subtle indicators of ignorance or uncertainty when talking about objects for which they did not know the label. In future coding, it will be important to identify whether parents' use of these sentence structures is systematic, and the extent to which children are sensitive to these subtle cues. Although experimental research shows that children are more likely to learn words from confident speakers than those who express uncertainty (Sabbagh & Baldwin, 2001), additional work is needed to more fully understand how children interpret nuances in parents' speech that might have consequences for their developing conceptual understandings.

Robotic Dog

Parent speech about the robotic dog provides a critical test of the criteria they respect when signaling domain boundaries. As a human-made artifact designed to represent an animal, it exhibits behaviors that may encourage anthropomorphism. Yet, because it is a relatively recent technology, parents may adopt a scientific perspective to help children understand this new, potentially confusing, entity. The sample utterances about the robotic dog provided in Table 11.1 show that parents shift between characterizing the robotic dog as animate, and suggesting a more inanimate status. Parents mentioned artifact properties often and significantly more than animate properties, yet they also mentioned biological and psychological properties at equal rates to one another. Parents also used significantly more animate than inanimate pronouns. In Jipson et al. (2016), parents treated the robotic dog in a less animate way than they did the rodent, but in a more animate way than the toy car. Parental speech about the robotic dog may thus leave children with more questions than answers. When responding to forced-choice questions about a robotic dog's properties, children overwhelmingly endorsed artifact properties and rejected biological properties—yet they reasoned at chance levels about psychological and sensory capabilities (see also Kahn et al., 2011; Saylor, Somanader, Levin, & Kawamura, 2010). The relation between parent talk and children's reasoning suggests that the indeterminacy of parental speech may be particularly consequential for properties that cannot be inferred from children's own observations.

In sum, parents provide rich domain-specific information that is likely to be important to children as they learn about animals and animal-like artifacts. Parents are selective in the explicit and implicit cues to animacy that they discuss. Our results uncover a contrast between parents' largely domain-specific talk about the rodent and toy car, the domain-specific yet comparatively tempered talk about the sea star, and the complex blurring of domain-related information about toy animals. This suggests that learning about the world requires an active child who is both open to information conveyed via social testimony and skeptical when that information does not cohere with existing beliefs.

Study 3: Parent–Child Conversations About Animals that Vary in Similarity to Humans

A biologically accurate understanding of animals encompasses all types, from humans to sea sponges. For example, worms are animals even though they do not share mammalian characteristics with humans. However, prior research shows that young children's reasoning about the animal domain is not uniform. Five-year-olds from urban backgrounds often attribute biological and psychological properties to humans but less so to animals that are more distant from humans (Carey, 1985; Coley, 1995). On the other hand, neither rural children nor 3-year-old urban children show such anthropocentrism (Herrmann et al., 2010; Waxman & Medin, 2007), thus indicating the importance of age and context. Here, we focus on some initial data from our study of how parent–child conversations might contribute to anthropocentrism by means of subtle or implicit cues.

We invited 3- to 6-year-olds and their parents ($N = 30$ dyads) to view a set of videos on a computer, simulating the experience of attending a zoo. This "virtual zoo" included animals varying in their similarity: humans, chimps, rhinos, beavers, owls, fish, and bees. We aimed to sample across an intuitive folk "hierarchy" based on animals' distance from humans with a five-way distinction: humans, nonhuman primates, non-primate mammals, non-mammalian vertebrates, and insects. We coded participants' conversations for their use of animate and inanimate pronouns, as well as their talk about biological (e.g., eating), psychological (e.g., thinking, emotions), and sensory (e.g., seeing) features. Here, we ask how parents and children used each type of pronoun and how they paired pronouns with properties. We also use excerpts from the data to speculate about how other aspects of talk about animals may vary depending on where the animals fall on the animacy hierarchy.

Pronouns and Properties

Our investigation of pronouns focused on how often parents and children used animate/inanimate pronouns for each animal (see Table 11.2) and in what contexts. Children demonstrated a nearly linear decrease in the proportion of animate pronouns in animals' dissimilarity to humans—with one exception (bees). This latter result is surprising, but may reflect salient anthropomorphic media portrayals of

Table 11.2 Proportion of pronouns that are animate, as a function of speaker and item type

	Parents	Children
Human	0.99	1.00
Chimp	0.97	0.95
Non-primate mammal (Rhino, Beaver)	0.94	0.84
Non-mammal vertebrate (Owl, Fish)	0.83	0.73
Insect (Bee)	0.68	0.88

bees (e.g., Bee Movie) and/or metaphorical language (e.g., busy as a bee, queen bee). In contrast, parents used animate pronouns at a fairly consistent and high rate for mammals but at lower rates for non-mammal vertebrates and lowest for the insect. This parent–child mismatch may be a result of greater anthropocentric reasoning on the part of children than adults. However, the adults' lower rates of animate pronoun use for non-mammal vertebrates and insects show they are not treating all animals as equally animate.

Given that parents showed some variation in their pronoun use for non-mammal vertebrates and insects, we investigated whether they used animate pronouns in any systematic way. The following conversations from the same family illustrate a potential pattern.

Example #1: Owl	Example #2: Chimp
Parent: You see that owl? *It's* kinda hiding, right? Child: That's what I saw. Parent: No, that is fine. *It* just blends in with the tree. *It's* like *it* is wearing camouflage Child: *It* flies? Parent: Mm hmm Child: Where is *it* going? Parent: I don't know. I think **he** is **trying** to—Oh! Look what **he** just did	Parent: Look at **his** cute face. See how **he** walks? He uses **his** arms to help **him** walk

This mother used inanimate pronouns when discussing the owl's actions, but switched to animate pronouns when mentioning a psychological process. In contrast, she used animate pronouns for the chimp across all topics. Analysis of parents' talk about non-mammal vertebrates and insects showed that parents often paired animate pronouns with animate properties (0.97 and 0.74, respectively) and did so more than they did for other types of topics (e.g., behavior; non-mammal vertebrates: 0.78; insects: 0.67). This contrasts with the consistent use of animate pronouns across topics for animals more similar to humans (see Table 11.2). Subtle variations in parents' treatment of different animals may contribute to children's anthropocentric reasoning.

Parental Responses to Children's Statements

In a conversational context, children have the opportunity to express their beliefs, which can serve (intentionally or not) to elicit parental affirmations, expansions, or corrections. We examined the content of parent–child conversations about each animal to see how parents may have responded differently to similar utterances from their children depending on the animal being discussed. Below are excerpts from one family's conversations about what two animals eat.

Example #1: Bee	Example #2: Chimp
Parent: What do you think the bee's doing?	Parent: What do they [chimps] eat?
Child: Uh eating?	Child: Trees
Parent: What's it eating?	Parent: Trees?
Child: It's honey!	Parent: I thought you were gonna say bananas
Parent: Honey?	Parent: Everyone thinks they eat bananas
	Child: Yeah and they do
	Parent: They do

When the mother asked the child about the bee, the child incorrectly stated that it was eating honey (adult bees eat pollen and nectar). The mother questioned the response ("Honey?"), but did not provide any correction or push the child on her understanding of what bees do with honey. When the child stated that chimps eat trees, the mother used the same strategy of questioning the child's response, but she pushed the child on this concept, introducing bananas into the conversation; the child eventually took up this suggestion, agreeing that chimps eat bananas. A similar pattern can be found in excerpts from a different family's conversation.

Example #1: Bee	Example #2: Owl
Parent: You can eat honey for breakfast	Parent: Remember when we were talking about owls the other day? What kind of food do they eat?
Child: The big bees eat the little bees for lunch.	Child: What kind of food? Grass! Grass! They eat grass!
(parent changes topic)	Parent: Hmm they eat grass? No
	Child: I think he is eating grass
	Parent: I think owls eat like small animals
	Child: He eats grass
	Parent: They eat grass? Hmm

In the first excerpt, the mother did not address the child's claim that big bees eat little bees for lunch, moving on to another topic instead. However, with the owl, an animal more similar to humans, the mother questioned the child's assertion that the owl was eating grass and provided information about what owls actually eat. After the child insisted for a third time that owls eat grass, the mother resorted to questioning the assertion without correcting it.

In these examples, children presented incorrect guesses, which then elicited further discussion in some contexts but not others. These illustrate the give-and-take of an active child within a conversational context: the child actively offers guesses or hypotheses about how the world works, only some of which are taken up by a parent. A parent's choices about whether to correct their child may have been influenced by the animal's similarity to humans, for example, feeling that it was more important to correct misunderstandings that hit closer to home. Alternatively, this variation may be related to parents' own content knowledge; they may be hesitant to correct their child when they are not certain of the answer themselves. Tarlowski (2006) found that children differentially relied on similarity when projecting novel properties onto animals depending on whether they were children of biologists. As such, parents' willingness and/or capability to answer questions or correct misconceptions may affect how children come to learn that animals all share basic biological properties.

Children also attempted to draw connections between animals and themselves, as illustrated in these examples from different families (see also Shatz, 1994).

Example #1: Otter	Example #2: Fish
Parent: So how is he building the dam? He's chewing the stick into the shape he needs it	Mom: And do you know what the fish use to swim?
Child: Long front teeth	Child: (*flapping arms*) Um their ummmm
Parent: He has long front teeth	Child: Their um, little thin- their little things
Child: No like this (motions to teeth with hands)	(*laughs*)
Parent: That's right, like fangs	Child: I don't know
Child: Fangs, I have fangs	Mom: Fins?
Parent: That's right, ours are over here	Child: Yeah their fins
Parent: And beavers are right up front, their longest teeth are up front	Mom: And do you know how they- they breathe?
	Child: By blowing bubbles?
	Mom: Nope
	Child: How?
	Mom: They don't breathe- They don't have a nose
	Child: Oh kay umm
	Mom: Their gills right?
	Child: Gills, yeah

This tendency to compare other animals to the self is consistent with a body of work showing that making connections between distinct entities can facilitate the discovery of deeper commonalities and thus promote novel solutions to problems (Gentner, 2010). Importantly, in such moments, children provide insight into their thought process which parents can capitalize upon to extend their children's learning. When discussing beavers, the child directly compared the beaver's teeth to her own. The mother built on the comparison to bolster the child's understanding, pointing out similarities and differences between humans' and beavers' teeth. In the second example, the child answered his mother's question about how fish swim by flapping his arms, drawing a connection to his own body. By using a physical gesture instead of a verbal response (e.g., "their arms"), he conveyed that arms correspond to fins but are not the same thing. Encountering an imperfect correlate may lead to a sense of distinction between fish and humans. Indeed, this inability to draw perfect comparisons to humans is highlighted by the mother in her follow-up in which she noted that fish do not actually breathe (at least, not in the way that humans do) and that they do not have noses. Comparisons to the self often served as a launching point for a more extended conversation about the properties of animals in relation to humans. Additional coding is needed to identify whether parents and children are systematically influenced by an animal's similarity to humans in their efforts to make connections between themselves and nonhuman animals.

Conclusions and Implications

In this chapter, we focused on examining how parent–child conversations may contribute to children's developing understanding of the boundaries of and variations within the animal domain. Our findings illustrate multiple ways that parent–child conversations have potential importance for children's learning. Our first study established that families often talked about animals as they engaged in everyday activities, and that children initiated many of these conversations, using multiple approaches to influence their direction. Our second study demonstrated the active roles of both parent and child in generating conversational contexts replete with opportunities to learn about fundamental distinctions between animate and inanimate entities. Finally, our third study showcased a newer direction where we are looking at how parent–child conversation reveals underlying assumptions about animals that vary in their similarity to humans.

One clear contribution of this work is that it establishes that typical interactions between parents and children are brimming with information relevant to conceptual learning about animals. Parents share information that is scientifically accurate alongside information that may encourage anthropomorphic and anthropocentric reasoning about animals. Despite this wealth of information, parental content alone is insufficient to understand children's learning processes; critically important is a closer look at the social context in which information is generated and interpreted. Even a cursory scan of the diary reports and transcripts suggests that it is rarely the case that parents didactically provide "mini-lessons" that teach children what they need to know, with children passively accepting and filing away new knowledge. For one thing, parents mislead as well as inform, such as talking about inanimate objects (such as robots or stuffed animal toys) as if they were alive, or treating certain animals as "more alive" than others (e.g., chimps vs. bees), or failing to directly confront or correct children's misconceptions. Why parents misinform in these ways likely has many sources—including their own knowledge gaps, as well as a desire to be entertaining and playful, to delight in the child's unique perspective on the world, and to respect the child's ideas. Regardless, this "messy input" is greeted by an active child who can sort through the give-and-take of conversation to (ultimately) construct coherent representations of the biological domain. This rich portrait of parent–child conversation contrasts with the model of the child as a mere recipient of parental wisdom. Instead, we are finding that parents and children elicit, share, and engage with information about animals using multiple strategies and sources of information.

We close this chapter with a set of observations about the various strategies that we observed children using during conversations with parents that may help inform their conceptual understandings of the animal domain. We highlight areas in which future systematic work will be particularly informative to efforts to understand children's role in advancing their own conceptual learning. As demonstrated below, there are many possible approaches that children can, and do, take in creating meaningful opportunities to learn from parents. We do not have enough data to make claims about whether there is a single "best" approach, or an ideal combination. Indeed, we do not anticipate that research will delineate such a clear outcome. Every parent–child pair has unique experiences that shape their perspectives, strategies, and behavior. As a result, children must learn to influence and navigate the dynamics of conversations within their family, to co-construct meanings that match their learning goals, motivation, and available resources. Thus, children are not only active in their use of the following approaches, but also in their decisions of when, how, and with whom to use them.

Preparing for Learning Conversations

Opportunities to learn from others can begin in children's everyday observations about the world around them. Children identify patterns in the physical world, which leads them to develop expectations, test those expectations, evaluate their understandings, and perhaps refine those understandings to fit new information (Carey, 1985). Children also begin to curate their experiences and develop emerging and sustained individual interests, preferentially engaging in certain content-related experiences over others (Hidi and Renninger, 2006). Preparation also entails paying attention to the social context. As children gain the insight that other people have thoughts and desires that differ from their own, they may begin to track the topics that their parents are interested in and know something about, pay attention to the contexts within which parents are most likely to be responsive, and discern the conversational approaches that are effective with particular people in particular settings. That is, part of being an active learner is figuring out what topics are worth discussing, and developing strategies to seek out information from those who are likely to be knowledgeable and responsive.

Initiating Learning Conversations

Children do not wait for others to deliver interesting material for their conceptual consideration, but rather elicit information from others both explicitly (e.g., via questions) and implicitly (e.g., looking quizzical, or offering an uninformed guess that parents can confirm or reject). Even before children develop strong language skills, they intentionally elicit information from others via pointing or shrugging (Tomasello, Carpenter, & Liszkowski, 2007). Scant research attention has been paid to older children's nonverbal strategies to engage others, such as exclamations of surprise, rapt attention, and gesture. There is a need for future research to move beyond a focus on verbal utterances and explore how children's nonverbal markers of interest and attention may serve to elicit parent–child conversation. There is no doubt, though, that the ability to enter into conversations provides a powerful new tool for learning from others. Much research focuses on how children use questions to engage others in conversations about topics of interest (Callanan & Oakes, 1992; Chouinard, 2007; Frazier et al., 2009). Studies of children's questions provide insight into their interests and are discussed in detail elsewhere in this volume (see Danovitch and Mills; Jimenez, Sun and Saylor; Sobel and Leourneau). Our data further support the importance of questions as a strategy for initiating conversations; about half of child-initiated diary conversations began when children asked a question. The other half, however, were comprised of spontaneous statements child made about something noticed in the environment, or a personal experience that the child wanted to share with a parent. We do not yet know whether there are any patterns in children's decisions to use questions vs. statements as a way to initiate parent–child conversations, but this would be a productive avenue for continued research.

Children's active role in contributing to learning conversations can also be seen when they are responsive to others' initiation attempts. Parents' efforts to engage their children are only as effective as children let them be. In other words, productive learning conversations must engage both active children and active parents; these are not mutually exclusive. An active parent can evoke children's curiosity, but a child has to be open to engaging with the topic and with the parent. We suggest that observational research will be important here as parents may be less likely to report unsuccessful efforts to engage children.

Maintaining and Extending Learning Conversations

Once both parents and children are jointly involved in a learning conversation, our data showed multiple ways that children play a key role in maintaining, directing, and extending the engagement. One approach that we observed and will be assessing further is that of admissions of ignorance and uncertainty. Children's appraisal of their own knowledge gaps positions them to identify when it might be worthwhile to solicit missing information from others, and their willingness to verbal acknowledge their state of ignorance (or uncertainty) serves to invite others to support their learning. Consistent with Sabbagh and Callanan (1998), when children are saying "I don't know" as a way of conversational turn-taking, there is evidence that parents respond with informative comments. Harris et al. (2017) point out that an alternative to denials of knowledge is question-asking. We additionally propose that sometimes children choose to make bold guesses, to put their hypotheses out there in order to elicit parental feedback. Although these approaches certainly differ in many ways, they are similar in providing evidence of children's efforts to use conversational contexts to pursue new knowledge.

Evaluating Information and Learning in Parent–Child Conversations

A final, and critically important, way that children actively use parent–child conversations to inform their conceptual understandings is through their selective evaluation of the ideas generated with parents. Data from our studies demonstrate that under certain conditions, children show an openness to new information provided by parents (e.g., for properties that are difficult to observe, for factual information that children think parents may know more about). In some cases children may generalize this information and extend it to new areas, as when a child hearing that cars might have emotions, went on to consider biological properties for the car. We also noted children's displays of measured skepticism when parents' comments did not align with their own understandings. Mills (2013; Busch, Willard, and Legare, this volume) provides a framework for understanding the elements that contribute to children's "knowing when to doubt." In our data, doubt is apparent when children disregard or challenge information provided by parents, which was evident in our systematic evaluation of the differences between parents' talk and children's reasoning in Studies 2 and 3. We also discussed in a more qualitative manner several examples that were suggestive of children's active disregard for information from parents.

In sum, across several studies we see parent–child conversations as a context within which children play an active role in constructing and enhancing their understanding of the animal domain. They make known their interest in animals and create opportunities to explore those interests with parents. These conversations provide opportunities for children to learn about features that are common to animals as a category, features that are specific to particular animals, and how animals differ from other kinds of entities. Thus, any accounting of the origins of children's naive theories of biology must include attention to what children learn from others, particularly parents. In engaging in conversations with parents, children reveal themselves to indeed be little scientists—but not lone scientists. They take full advantage of opportunities to recruit their parents' engagement in order to identify what they know and do not know about the world around them, and to enhance their developing understandings. Additional research is needed to examine how parents' and children's participation relates to the topics under consideration and to their cultural backgrounds. As a field, we are just beginning to understand how children learn *with* (vs. *from*) others; we are confident that work in this area will help provide a missing piece of the puzzle in efforts to understand how children come to understand the complexity of the world in which they live.

References

Bang, M., & Medin, D. (2010). Cultural processes in science education: Supporting the navigation of multiple epistemologies. *Science Education, 94*(6), 1008–1026.

Benjamin, N., Haden, C. A., & Wilkerson, E. (2010). Enhancing building, conversation, and learning through caregiver-child interactions in a children's museum. *Developmental Psychology, 46*(2), 502–515.

Callanan, M. A., Castañeda, C. L., Luce, M. R., & Martin, J. L. (2017). Family science talk in museums: Predicting children's engagement from variations in talk and activity. *Child Development, 88*(5), 1492–1504.

Callanan, M. A., & Jipson, J. L. (2001). Explanatory conversations and young children's developing scientific literacy. In K. Crowley, C. D. Schunn, & T. Okada (Eds.), *Designing for science: Implications from everyday, classroom, and professional settings*. Mahwah, NJ: Erlbaum.

Callanan, M. A., Jipson, J. L., & Soennichsen, M. S. (2002). Maps, globes, and videos: Parent-child conversations about representational objects. In S. Paris (Ed.), *Perspectives on children's object-centered learning in museums*. Mahwah, NJ: Erlbaum.

Callanan, M. A., & Oakes, L. M. (1992). Preschoolers' questions and parents' explanations: Causal thinking in everyday activity. *Cognitive Development, 7*(2), 213–233.

Carey, S. (1985). *Conceptual change in childhood*. Cambridge, MA: MIT Press.

Chouinard, M. M. (2007). Children's questions: A mechanism for cognitive development. *Monographs of the Society of Research in Child Development, 72*(1), 7–9.

Coley, J. D. (1995). Emerging differentiation of folkbiology and folkpsychology: Attributions of biological and psychological properties to living things. *Child Development, 66*(6), 1856–1874.

Crowley, K., Callanan, M. A., Jipson, J. L., Galco, J., Topping, K., & Shrager, J. (2001). Shared scientific thinking in everyday parent-child activity. *Science Education, 85*, 712–732.

Crowley, K., & Galco, J. (2001). Everyday activity and the development of scientific thinking. In K. Crowley, C. D. Schunn, & T. Okada (Eds.), *Designing for science: Implications from everyday, classroom, and professional settings* (pp. 393–413). Mahwah, NJ: Erlbaum.

Crowley, K., & Jacobs, M. (2002). Building islands of expertise in everyday family activity. In G. Leinhardt, K. Crowley, K. Knutson, G. Leinhardt, K. Crowley, & K. Knutson (Eds.), *Learning conversations in museums* (pp. 333–356). Mahwah, NJ: Erlbaum.

Frazier, B. N., Gelman, S. A., & Wellman, H. M. (2009). Preschoolers' search for explanatory information within adult-child conversation. *Child Development, 80*(6), 1592–1611.

Frazier, B. N., Gelman, S. A., & Wellman, H. M. (2016). Young children prefer and remember satisfying explanations. *Journal of Cognition and Development, 17*(5), 718–736.

Ganea, P., Canfield, C., Simons-Ghafari, K., & Chou, T. (2014). Do cavies talk? The effect of anthropomorphic picture books on children's knowledge about animals. *Frontiers in Psychology, 5*, 1–9.

Gelman, S. A. (2003). *The essential child: Origins of essentialism in everyday thought*. New York: Oxford University Press.

Gelman, S. A. (2009). Learning from others: Children's construction of concepts. *Annual Review of Psychology, 60*, 115–140.

Gelman, S. A., Coley, J. D., Rosengren, K. S., Hartman, E., & Pappas, A. (1998). Beyond labeling: The role of maternal input in the acquisition of richly structured categories. *Monographs of the Society for Research in Child Development, 63*(1), Serial No. 253.

Gelman, S. A., & Kalish, C. W. (2006). Conceptual development. In: W. Damon & R. M. Lerner (Series Eds.), & D. Kuhn & R. S. Siegler (Eds.), *Handbook of child psychology: Vol. 2 cognition, perception, and language* (6th ed., pp. 687–733). Hoboken, NJ: Wiley.

Gentner, D. (2010). Bootstrapping the mind: Analogical processes and symbol systems. *Cognitive Science, 34*, 752–775.

Greif M. L., Kemler-Nelson D. G., Keil F. C., Guitierrez F. (2006). What do children want to know about animals and artifacts? Domain-specific requests for information. *Psychological Science, 17*, 455–459.

Haden, C. A., Jant, E. A., Hoffman, P. C., Marcus, M., Geddes, J. R., & Gaskins, S. (2014). Supporting family conversations and children's STEM learning in a children's museum. *Early Childhood Research Quarterly, 29*(3), 333–344.

Harris, P. L., Bartz, D. T., & Rowe, M. L. (2017). Young children communicate their ignorance and ask questions. *Proceedings of the National Academies of Science, 114*, 7884–7891.

Harris, P. L., & Koenig, M. A. (2006). Trust in testimony: How children learn about science and religion. *Child Development, 77*(3), 505–524.

Henderson, A. E., & Sabbagh, M. A. (2010). Parents' use of conventional and unconventional labels in conversations with their preschoolers. *Journal of Child Language, 37*(4), 793–816.

Herrmann, P., Waxman, S. R., & Medin, D. L. (2010). Anthropocentrism is not the first step in children's reasoning about the natural world. *Proceedings of the National Academy of Sciences, 107*(22), 9979–9984.

Hidi, S. & Renninger, K. A. (2006). The four-phase model of interest development. *Educational Psychologist, 41(2)*, 111–127.

Inagaki, K., & Hatano, G. (2002). *Young children's naïve thinking about the biological world.* New York, NY: Psychology Press.

Jant, E. A., Haden, A., Uttal, D. H., & Babcock, E. (2014). Conversation and object manipulation influence children's learning in a museum. *Child Development, 85*(5), 2029–2045.

Jipson, J. L., & Callanan, M. A. (2003). Mother-child conversations and children's understanding of biological and nonbiological changes in size. *Child Development, 74*(2), 629–644.

Jipson, J. L., Gulgoz, S., Gelman, S. A. (2016). Parent-child conversations regarding the ontological status of a robotic dog. *Cognitive Development, 39*, 21–35.

Kahn, P.J., Reichert, A.L., Gary, H.E., Takayuki, K., Ishiguro, H., Shen, S., ..., Gill, B. (2011). The new ontological category hypothesis in human-robot interaction. In: *Proceedings of the 6th international conference on human robot interaction* (pp. 159–160).

Keil, F. C. (1998). Words, mom, and things: Language as a road map to reality. *Monographs of the Society for Research in Child Development, 63*(1), 149–157.

Kuhn, D. (2010). Teaching and learning science as argument. *Science Education, 94*(5), 810–824.

Legare, C. H., Gelman, S. A., & Wellman, H. M. (2010). Inconsistency with prior knowledge triggers children's causal explanatory reasoning. *Child Development, 81*(3), 929–944.

Lillard, A. S., & Witherington, D. C. (2004). Mothers' behavior modifications during pretense and their possible signal value for toddlers. *Developmental Psychology, 40*(1), 95–113.

LoBue, V., Bloom Pickard, M., Sherman, K., Axford, C., & DeLoache, J. S. (2013). Young children's interest in live animals. *British Journal of Developmental Psychology, 31*(1), 57–69.

Medin, D., Waxman, S., Woodring, J., & Washinawatok, K. (2010). Human-centeredness is not a universal feature of young children's reasoning: Culture and experience matter when reasoning about biological entities. *Cognitive Development, 25*, 197–207.

Mills, C. M. (2013). Knowing when to doubt: Developing a critical stance when learning from others. *Developmental Psychology, 49*(3), 404–418.

Mills, C. M., Legare, C. H., Grant, M. G., & Landrum, A. R. (2011). Determining whom to question, what to ask, and how much information to ask for: The development of inquiry in young children. *Journal of Experimental Child Psychology, 110*, 539–560.

Nielsen, J. A., & Delude, L. A. (1989). Behavior of young children in the presence of different kinds of animals. *Anthrozoös, 3*(2), 119–129.

Opfer, J. E., & Gelman, S. A. (2011). Development of the animate-inanimate distinction. In U. Goswami (Ed.), *The Wiley-Blackwell handbook of childhood cognitive development* (2nd ed., pp. 213–238). Oxford, England: Wiley-Blackwell.

Palmquist, S., & Crowley, K. (2007). From teachers to testers: How parents talk to novice and expert children in a natural history museum. *Science Education, 91*(5), 783–804.

Rigney, J. C., & Callanan, M. A. (2011). Patterns in parent–child conversations about animals at a marine science center. *Cognitive Development, 26*(2), 155–171.

Rogoff, B. (2014). Learning by Observing and Pitching In to family and community endeavors: An orientation. *Human Development, 57*(2–3), 69–81.

Sabbagh, M. A., & Baldwin, D. A. (2001). Learning words from knowledgeable versus igno-
rant speakers: Links between preschoolers' theory of mind and semantic development. *Child Development, 72*(4), 1054–1070.

Sabbagh, M. A., & Callanan, M. A. (1998). Metarepresentation in action: 3-, 4-, and 5-year-olds' developing theories of mind in parent-child conversations. *Developmental Psychology, 34*, 491–502.

Saylor, M. M., Somanader, M., Levin, D. T., & Kawamura, K. (2010). How do young children deal with hybrids of living and non-living things: The case of humanoid robots. *British Journal of Developmental Psychology, 28*(4), 835–851.

Schulz, L. E., & Bonawitz, E. B. (2007). Serious fun: Preschoolers engage in more exploratory play when evidence is confounded. *Developmental Psychology, 43*(4), 1045–1050.

Shatz, M. (1994). *A toddler's life: Becoming a person.* New York, NY: Oxford University Press.

Spelke, E. S. (2017). Core Knowledge, Language, and Number. *Language Learning and Development, 13*, 147–170.

Tarlowski, A. (2006). If it's an animal it has axons: Experience and culture in preschool children's reasoning about animates. *Cognitive Development, 21*(3), 249–265.

Tizard, B., & Hughes, M. (1984). *Young children learning.* Cambridge, MA: Harvard.

Tomasello, M., Carpenter, M., & Liszkowski, U. (2007). A new look at infant pointing. *Child Development, 78*, 705–722.

Waxman, S., & Medin, D. (2007). Experience and cultural models matter: Placing firm limits on childhood anthropocentrism. *Human Development, 50*, 23–30.

Waxman, S., Herrmann, P., Woodring, J., Medin, D. (2014). Humans (really) are animals: Picture-book reading influences 5-year-old urban children's construal of the relation between humans and non-human animals. *Frontiers in Psychology.*

Wilson, E. O. (1984). *Biophilia: The human bond with other species.* Cambridge, MA: Harvard.

Chapter 12
Choosing to Learn: Evidence Evaluation for Active Learning and Teaching in Early Childhood

Elizabeth Bonawitz, Ilona Bass, and Elizabeth Lapidow

Abstract Choosing to take certain actions has direct consequences for learning. Do children tend to choose actions that support learning? We present research suggesting that before reaching kindergarten, children demonstrate proficiency in active learning that cannot be accounted for by simple heuristics for decision-making. Instead, children's choices reveal a sophisticated ability to evaluate evidence (computing information gained by particular actions); potential evidence is compared to other possible rewards and costs associated with actions. This early emerging ability to select evidence underpins informal teaching of, and reasoning about, others. Specifically, we discuss recent empirical work demonstrating that preschool-aged children are able to evaluate potential evidence to support their own learning, another's learning, and that they can even evaluate a teacher's evidential selection for a third party's learning.

Introduction

Socrates gives us a fairly disturbing hypothetical to describe the problem of induction: Consider the underground den described in Plato's Republic (Jowett, 1941), in which humans are chained from childhood, seeing "only their own shadows, which the fire throws on the opposite wall of the cave... To them truth would be literally nothing but the shadows of the images." Socrates is explaining that we can never be sure about the truth of the world. It is an important problem to be sure, but lucky for us, we have tools to lessen (albeit not eliminate) our uncertainties. We are not restrained, passive observers from birth. Unlike Socrates' prisoners, we are equipped with the ability to choose. We can select what we want to attend to, we can pick our

E. Bonawitz (✉) · I. Bass
Psychology Department, Rutgers University, Newark, NJ, USA
e-mail: elizabeth.bonawitz@rutgers.edu

E. Lapidow
Psychology Department, University of California, San Diego, CA, USA

© Springer International Publishing AG, part of Springer Nature 2018
M. M. Saylor, P. A. Ganea (eds.), *Active Learning from Infancy to Childhood*,
https://doi.org/10.1007/978-3-319-77182-3_12

favorite people to emulate, we can decide to play with one toy or another; we can look, we can ask, and we can act. Most importantly, in action we reap the benefits of effects. We see events, we are told truths, and we observe outcomes. This gathering of evidence—that we ourselves cause—connects us to the world behind the shadows. It enriches our knowledge in ways beyond Socrates's passive learners. It is thus an important factor to insert into the Piagetian constructivist circle (Piaget, 1954): we see and are curious, *we choose to act*, we observe evidence, we revise beliefs, we see anew.

Why one initially chooses to act to learn is an important question for us constructivists. This choice, curiosity, is perhaps one of the longest studied and yet least well-understood aspects of psychology. Part of the problem in studying curiosity is that, as Berlyne (1978) suggested it defines both the need to satiate specific knowledge ("where did my daughter hide my shoes this morning?") and diversive knowledge ("reading further will keep me from feeling bored"); it includes both perceptual stimuli ("what was that sudden flash I noticed out of the corner of my eye?") and the epistemic ("how can I learn more about black holes?"). Researchers appear to contradict each other attempting to specify the drives to resolve curiosity: on the one hand we are curious because we want to resolve the unpleasurable, aversive state caused by lack of coherence (as with the Information Gap Model, Loewenstein, 1994); on the other hand, curiosity is driven by the pleasurable, satisfying experience of learning (Spielberger and Starr, 1994; or, as with "Explanation as Orgasm"; Gopnik, 2000). Its role in cognition has been argued to be fundamental to numerous factors including creativity (Csikszentmihalyi, 1996; Day & Langevin, 1969), emotional intelligence (Leonard & Harvey, 2007; Penney, 1965), and learning (Stahl & Feigenson, 2015, 2017; Jirout & Klahr, 2012). It seems a hopeless endeavor to characterize the trait, and certainly beyond what any reasonable person would undertake pre-tenure. It would be hubristic at best, and likely plain foolish to attempt to tackle such a large topic.

With this in mind, perhaps you will forgive us for instead focusing on *how* one chooses to act. The "why" and "how" of choosing to act may seem entangled, but here we will attempt to disentangle, by focusing on how children decide what, among many options, they should attend to, ask about, or intervene on. This choice is itself a multifaceted decision. It requires considering what options exist, what evidence is possible, and which, among these possibilities will be most rewarding.

Are children "active learners" in the sense that they tend to make good choices when considering the options, evidence, and rewards? Consider the complexity of the world. There are potentially infinite options to consider, each with many possible outcomes, and a plethora of costs and rewards that may play into each action. In such a world, even random actions may lead to learning, but an active learner—one who wishes to exhibit some meaningful control over her environment—*evaluates* these options. She must predict the possible outcomes of actions and consider the consequent pros and cons of each.

A learner who can perform these evaluations can choose between evidential options for themselves, whether in choosing to explore particular events over other events or in choosing to approach particular informants over other informants. But, she may also be able to choose between evidential options to teach others. Teaching requires recognizing the evidential needs of others, to get a learner from one stage of knowledge to another. Thus, the ability to select evidence to teach others may emerge as a result of the ability to select evidence to explore for one's self.

Finally, a learner who can perform these kinds of evaluations may even be able to use this evidential reasoning ability to evaluate the teaching of another. That is, she may be able to recognize the knowledge lacking in others. She might then understand what evidence is needed to support learning as well as what evidence is available to the teacher. Finally, she may reconcile all of this information to evaluate whether the teacher has performed well—given the needs of the learner and the resources of the teacher.

Here we will describe some recent studies in developmental psychology that investigate evidential reasoning abilities. These studies will support the claim that children are thoughtful, active learners and teachers. Before reaching school, young learners consider possible opportunities for evidence, and choose options that are likely to lead to learning. Preschoolers can also choose between evidential options when teaching others. And, they can even apply this ability in their evaluations of others' teaching. That these skills are so early emerging supports a story in which we are built for learning. Our evidential reasoning abilities may emerge because we are optimally designed to make informative exploratory choices to support learning and teaching.

Evidence Selection in Choosing to Explore

A simple view of choosing to learn suggests that pursuing novel or surprising events is sufficient for a theory of learning in early childhood. But, what remains lacking in this simplified view is that in any environment, myriad actions are possible for the learner. Novel and surprising events are only a draw with respect to some other alternative. Given this, any agent who acts on the world to learn must be able to weigh these many actions and evaluate their potential. There is something to be learned by almost any action, so to understand *how* one chooses to learn, we must consider that the child performs a kind of utility calculus over possible choices. Schulz and Bonawitz (2007) have shown that children will overcome a novelty preference to play more with the familiar toy if information about the family toy is confounded. Bonawitz, van Schijndel, Friel, and Schulz (2012) have found that children also forgo novelty when there are opportunities for learning from events that are surprising with respect to beliefs. Under a naïve theory of curiosity-driven learning, we would have no way to predict how children would trade off the choice of a novel toy with a familiar but confounded or surprising one. In order to predict these results, a comprehensive theory of active learning would need to take into account expectations about (1) the learning opportunities that could arise with either choice (i.e., exploring a novel versus confounded toy), (2) other potential learning utilities (e.g., whether one toy will need to be mastered later), and (3) other rewards that are connected with the choices (e.g., whether one toy is "simply" more appealing, flashy, or exciting).

A further consideration for active learning is that not all opportunities for learning are ideal. It might not be surprising to imagine a learner who shows little interest in simple events that have been mastered. But this does not mean a learner should always favor the "richer" events. Information can quickly become overwhelming; events can become too complicated to be useful to support learning. Indeed, work by Kidd, Piantadosi, and Aslin (2012) has found that, beyond factors of novelty or familiarity, children's visual attention behavior is sensitive to differences in information content. Infants preferentially look away from very simple, high probability events. However, infants also look away from very complex, low probability events that offer little or hard-to-obtain information. Instead, infants prefer events that are neither too simple nor too complex; they go for a Goldilocks sweet-spot for information gathering (Kidd et al., 2012). This finding suggests that direction of visual attention (and auditory, see Kidd, Piantadosi, & Aslin, 2014) is not just an indiscriminate response to stimuli salience or novelty, but is dependent on the probability of being able to learn from the complexity of information.

Another point to be clarified in a theory of children's active learning is how a learner decides between whether to learn (e.g., explore something new) or whether to exploit a known reward. A curiosity-driven model of choice might be predicted to always favor the novel options over known rewards, but surprisingly this does not seem to be the case for children in early childhood. For example, in one set of studies in our lab (Lapidow and Bonawitz, in review) we suggest that, despite the preference for novel and uncertain outcomes, children as young as four choose *not* to explore in contexts where there is not good reason to do so. Our task took the form of a game, in which preschoolers (age range: 48–68 months) tried to collect marbles by selecting and revealing boxes from different "sets" (see Fig. 12.1a). All the boxes in a set were identical in appearance, and every set had a different appearance and distribution of average amounts of marbles that were in each box. (Rather than actually containing different amounts of marbles, boxes had arrangements of black dots drawn inside them, which children understood corresponded to the amounts of marbles they would be given by the experimenter.) On each trial, the experimenter brought up one set of boxes and selected one box from it at random. Children were then given a choice between selecting (and thereby revealing) the contents of this unknown box or a known box, which had a different appearance from the set and was presented open to show the number of marbles inside. Thus, children were repeatedly given a choice between exploring to reveal new information, or avoiding uncertainty by selecting an already known outcome.

If children simply always favor novel over known options, then we would expect to see them choose the unknown box on the majority of task trials because it offers the opportunity for novel information. However, this choice was presented in a context where children could form no expectations about the possible outcomes of the unknown box (as they had no prior information about the contents of any of the sets). Furthermore, children had no way of applying their learning about the task to future choices so there was no utility in the information gained (the contents of

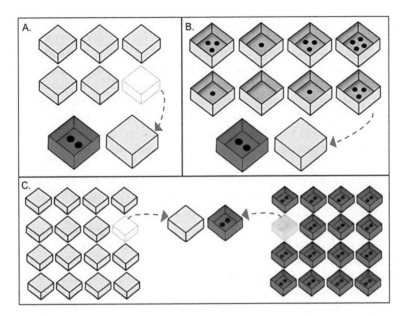

Fig. 12.1 Task designs for Studies 1, 2, and 3 in Lapidow and Bonawitz (in review). In Study 1 (**a**), on each trial, a closed box is drawn at random from one of five sets of six identical boxes. In Study 2 (**b**), the contents of all eight boxes in one of the ten sets of identical boxes are shown to participants, then the boxes are closed, mixed, and one is drawn at random from the set. In Study 3 (**c**), one set of boxes is known to contain exactly two dots in each and the other set's contents are unknown. On each trial, one box is drawn from the 'known' set and opened, and one box is drawn from the 'unknown' set and remains closed

selected, unknown boxes, were only revealed after the end of the game). Under these conditions, children showed an "ambiguity aversion" and *avoided* the novel box, preferring instead to stick with the known reward (64% of the trials; $p = 0.04$).

We conducted a second study to investigate whether children can compute expected values of rewards and use this information in their exploratory decisions. The procedure of the task was identical to the one described above, except that participants were first shown the contents of the sets of boxes. Then, a box was randomly sampled from this set (see Fig. 12.1b). Although children could not see the value of the particular box that was chosen, because they were provided with information about the overall distribution of possible outcomes, a savvy chooser could compute an expected value to this unknown box. Thus, if children's exploratory choices incorporate probabilistic expectations of this sort, we might expect children to choose the definitively known box when the expected value of the sampled box is lower, but for this pattern to flip as the expected value of the unknown box becomes larger.

To test whether children considered the expected value, we varied the distributions of rewards in each set, such that the ratio of the reward in the known box to the expected value of the reward in the unknown box included a range, 1:4, 1:2, 1:1, 2:1, and 4:1. Each ratio was tested twice, with a different set with different exact amounts inside the boxes used each time. There was a significant overall correlation between the ratio of known to unknown reward and choices to explore ($r = 0.88$, $t = 3.21$, $p < 0.05$), as well as significantly different choice behavior at the lowest and highest ratios ($p = 0.008$). Children chose to explore least often (42% of choices) when the expected value of the unknown was smaller than the value of the known amount (1:4), and they explored most often (69% of choices) when the expected value of the unknown box was higher than the value of the known amount (4:1). Thus, children appear able to compute and consider expected rewards when choosing whether to explore.

Our final question in this line of studies was whether children were more likely to explore unknown rewards, when learning about these rewards could be useful for later decision-making. That is, we provided children with a positive utility for learning about the boxes. In this study, we again presented children with the choice of revealing new information or selecting a known amount. However, in this version of the task we used two sets of boxes on each trial: a known set, for which participants are told and shown that all boxes contain the same amount; and an unknown set, for which the amounts are unknown (see Fig. 12.1c). Then, on each trial, the known and unknown options were drawn, apparently at random, from these sets. Our question pertained to understanding the conditions that might encourage children to overcome an ambiguity aversion (as demonstrated in the first study) to explore the unknown boxes.

Children were tested in one of three conditions that differed in whether the sets remained consistent across the task and in when unknown boxes would be revealed if selected. The No-Feedback condition used the same two sets of known and unknown boxes on each trial of the task, but if an unknown box was selected, it was not revealed until after the game was over. Thus, learners would not gain any information about the contents of unknown boxes until after such knowledge would be useful. In the Feedback-Switch condition, the contents of the selected unknown box would be revealed immediately (so children would receive the immediate satisfaction of learning about the contents of the selected box); however, we changed the sets of boxes (each with different possible distributions) after every trial of the task. Thus, learning the contents of a particular box (and thus something about the set from which it was drawn) would not provide any utility for future decisions because it would not provide information about the new set used in the next trial. Finally, in the Feedback-Stay condition, the rewards in selected boxes were revealed immediately and the same set of boxes was drawn from repeatedly. Thus, in this condition, children would have the opportunity to learn about the competing distribution if they selected it, which would have the benefit of future decision-making about the two sets. Therefore, children in all three conditions were given a choice between exploring by revealing an unknown outcome or obtaining a reward of a known amount, but whether exploration could lead to meaningful information gain was varied.

Results revealed sophisticated reasoning in preschoolers' explore-exploit decisions. Most children did not explore in the No-Feedback condition (40.7%)

replicating the ambiguity aversion results found in Study 1. Exploratory choices were slightly higher for children in the Feedback-Switch condition (53.7%), presumably because receiving a little bit of feedback about past decisions is intrinsically rewarding. Critically, however, children in the Feedback-Stay condition choose to explore a whopping 76.8% of the time, significantly more than children in the No-Feedback ($p < 0.001$) and Feedback-Switch ($p < 0.001$) conditions. Children chose to explore significantly more when there was a potential to gain useful information that would increase their knowledge and allow them to make more informed decisions for future exploratory choices.

Children's exploratory choices thus depend on more than simple novelty or familiarity biases. Instead, children weigh multiple factors. Their choices depend on the degree to which there is uncertainty (such as that caused by confounding or by events that are belief violating), the degree of complexity in the stimulus, whether there are known rewards and unknown risks, the expected reward value of an action, and whether the information to be gained by exploring will be useful for later decision making.

Evidence Selection in Choosing Informants

So far we have suggested that we must extend beyond a simplified account of active learning that only considers novelty or familiarity. Instead, children appear to come equipped to evaluate myriad factors when considering what to learn about. Of course, children are not left alone to explore the world without feedback from parents and peers. They are surrounded by other people who themselves may be sources of information. Thus, a child who weighs opportunities for information must also be able to consider informants; she must be able to reason about the pedagogical goals, intentions, and knowledge state of others to effectively extract information from her interactions with others.

Indeed, children are well equipped to reason about others' mental states in guiding their learning. For example, Bonawitz et al. (2011) showed children a novel toy with many interesting pieces (knobs, tubes, buttons) that might afford an interesting event (perhaps squeaking, lighting up, or making music). In one condition children were given strong pedagogical cues and told, "this is how my toy works" as the demonstrator pulled a tube out and caused the toy to squeak. In another condition children were shown the same outcome (the tube causing the toy to squeak) but the event happened accidentally. What should children infer about the number of possible additional causes in the toy? Although one event has been demonstrated, there is uncertainty pertaining to whether (and how many) remaining causal properties the toy has. In the accidental condition, children explored the toy broadly suggesting that they believed the toy was likely to have additional properties. In contrast, children in the pedagogical condition constrained their exploration to the pedagogically demonstrated function; this less variable play suggests that children believed that there was likely only one causal property (the demonstrated squeaking event). Thus, children were sensitive to whether information was presented by a knowledgeable, helpful other, with the intention to teach (as in the pedagogical condition) and used this information to shape their exploration.

Children can also use another's mental states and goals to discern whether questions are being asked for the purposes of teaching (as in "pedagogical questions"; Yu et al., 2017) or merely whether questions are being posed for the purposes of seeking information. For example, in a study much like the novel toy study described above, Yu et al. (in review) asked children about the to be discovered toy with the question "What does this button do?" Importantly, in one condition, the person asking was known to be knowledgeable about how the toy worked, but in another condition, the person asking was ignorant about the toy's functions. In both conditions, children explored the toy more variably than when the same information was presented as a direct instruction. However, children were significantly more likely to discover and correctly repeat the target, queried function in the knowledgeable condition, than in the ignorant condition. These results suggest that even when evaluating the questions of another person, children can consider the knowledge state of the questioner and use this information to guide their exploratory choices.

This socially savvy reasoning also helps to explain why children sometimes change their minds when faced with repeated questioning (e.g. Krahenbuhl et al., 2009). Bonawitz et al. (in revision; see also Gonzalez et al., 2012) have suggested that this switching behavior can be a rational inference, if the repeated questioning is taken as a cue to the correct answer. Critically, this inference depends on the knowledge of the questioner. Across several studies, Bonawitz et al. (in revision) found that when the questioner was shown to be knowledgeable about the answer on a task where children had uncertainty about the correct answer, children were likely to switch responses following a neutral prompt ("are you sure?"). However, when the questioner was known to be ignorant of the correct answer, this switching pattern was significantly reduced. These results further demonstrate the power of children's reasoning about others' intentions in guiding their decision-making. Indeed, a growing body of research has demonstrated that the inferences of even very young children depend on their assumptions about another's intentions while generating evidence (Gweon, Tenenbaum, & Schulz, 2010; Wellman, Kushnir, Xu, & Brink, 2016).

Taken together, these studies demonstrate that children are sensitive to the knowledge state of others in guiding their inferences, but they do not speak to whether children *choose among informants as possible sources of information*. That is, being guided in your exploratory choices because a knowledgeable other shapes your goals is certainly a prevalent part of childhood learning. However, it does not speak to whether children are active choosers in these processes. One possibility is that children *seek out* information differentially, depending on the assumptions about another's knowledge.

Do children create opportunities for learning by seeking out these knowledgeable and helpful informants? Conversation with knowledgeable and fully fluent adults may provide opportunities to gain information, both by directly asking questions and by eliciting feedback or correction. Ongoing research in our lab is looking at spontaneous speech in preschool children, aged 3- to 5-years-old, to see whether there are systematic differences in their queries, depending on the target of the conversation. Specifically, our hypothesis is that children may be more likely to seek out information and produce opportunities for feedback when speaking with knowledgeable adults than when speaking to other (less knowledgeable) children or when speaking aloud to themselves.

Using a clip-on microphone recorder, individual preschooler's spontaneous speech productions were recorded in 40-minute sessions during the school day. During the recording, an experimenter observed the child and recorded their visible behaviors and interactions with other individuals in the classroom. Recordings were then transcribed, pairing speech productions (including grammatical errors) of the participant with their actions and, critically, their speech partners—whether the child was speaking to an adult, another child, or themselves. This allowed us to explore whether particular kinds of speech acts by children are more likely depending on the target of their conversation.

Our preliminary analysis coding for 25 preschoolers has thus looked at whether there are differences in information seeking behaviors, depending upon speech-partner type (self, other children, adults). Our results show that children in a preschool classroom spend more time speaking to other children, which is not surprising given the high student to teacher ratios. Children also produce an equal proportion of utterances that are questions whether speaking to adults, other children, or themselves. However, we wondered whether the *types* of questions that children generate vary with respect to whom children are speaking. We coded for whether a question might elicit a learning opportunity (e.g., "How does that work?" "Can you help me?" "What is that?" "Like this?"), and compared these questions to conversational clarification questions (e.g., "What did you say?", or repeating words: "Sprinkles?") or general information seeking questions (e.g., "When is mommy coming?" "Can I play with that now?").

Our analysis revealed that the proportion of questions that were for learning content was much higher when children were talking to adults (39%) as compared to when talking to other children (9%, $p < 0.004$) or when speaking to themselves (11%, $p < 0.001$). This initial result supports the idea that children might be more likely to seek out information for learning concepts from individuals that are more likely to be knowledgeable. Thus, although past work has demonstrated that children ask abundant questions in early childhood (Callanan & Oakes, 1992; Chouinard, 2007), and that older children can use principles such as information gain to effectively choose which questions to ask (Ruggeri, Lombrozo, Griffiths, & Xu, 2016), this preliminary data provides tentative support for the claim that children also consider *who to ask* and *what to ask* discriminately.

Past research has provided evidence for the claim that children are able to reason about the knowledge state and intentions of others in guiding exploration (e.g. Bonawitz et al., 2011). However, this recent preliminary research suggests that children are not only being guided by these inferences about others, but also that they use this knowledge to decide from whom to choose to learn. Children can evaluate the potential information sources of both objects and people in their decision-making.

When exploring events, they consider the information and reward from possible choices; when querying others, they consider the information another person may provide by considering their expertise.

Evidence Selection in Teaching

We have suggested that children are active learners in the sense that they evaluate possible opportunities for acquiring evidence and then make choices that support learning. This ability to evaluate evidence and distinguish helpful from unhelpful information may be critical for young children's learning. Indeed, evidential reasoning skills emerge early in development (Bonawitz, Ullman, Gopnik, & Tenenbaum, 2012; Koerber, Sodian, Thoermer, & Nett, 2005), and even infants understand that certain evidence may be more useful to different people (Knudsen & Liszkowski, 2012; Liszkowski, Carpenter, & Tomasello, 2008).

However, just because children appear to effectively evaluate evidence in the service of their own learning, does not mean they apply this evidential reasoning in the service of teaching another. Nonetheless, children appear to be highly sensitive to the special role of evidence selection in pedagogy. For example, 6-year-olds select diverse samples to teach a novel concept to a peer, but not to learn that concept for themselves (Rhodes, Gelman, & Brickman, 2010). Further, Rhodes, Bonawitz, Shafto, Chen, and Caglar (2015) found that even preschoolers are capable of selecting evidence to communicate different pedagogical goals, even when the goal is to lead a learner to a *false* conclusion. Rhodes et al. (2015) showed 3- to 6-year-olds a novel toy that activated when any block was placed on it. They then asked children to pick two blocks to either (1) teach a naïve puppet how the toy really worked, or (2) trick her into thinking that only red blocks made it go. Children reliably selected blocks that would best communicate the pedagogical goal, regardless of whether the goal was to teach or to deceive. Even young children thus appear to be acutely aware how pedagogical sampling can constrain learners' inferences, and tailor their evidence selection to specific pedagogical goals.

Are a learner's knowledge and beliefs also used to guide young children's evidential demonstrations? In one set of studies (Bass et al., in review), we investigated this question within a group of 3- and 4-year-olds. Children were first shown a novel toy, and learned that it activated any time a red block was placed on top of it. Then, children showed two confederates (one at a time) how to use the toy. Each confederate saw just one of two red blocks (square or circle) activate the toy, after which they voiced either a false belief about the toy's causal mechanism ("I see, square/circle blocks make the toy go!"), or a true belief ("Red blocks make the toy go!"); see Fig. 12.2. After ensuring that children understood the confederates' beliefs, one of the two confederates returned to the room; both red blocks (square and circle) were placed on the toy simultaneously, the toy activated, and the confederate asked, "Huh, why did that happen?", ambiguously referencing one of the two blocks (see also Legare, Gelman, & Wellman, 2010 for a similar method). Children were asked

Fig. 12.2 Children first learned the true causal rule of the toy (red blocks make it go). Then, children showed two confederates that red blocks of different shapes activated the toy; confederates formed either false or true beliefs based on this evidence. In the test trial, children showed one of the confederates that both red blocks made the toy go, and then pointed to one block and explained why the toy activated

to point to just one of the two blocks and explain why the toy activated. If children are using the confederate's false belief to guide their evidence selection, they should point to the shape that the confederate did not see, because that evidence contradicts (and may thus rectify) the confederate's false belief. In contrast, if the confederate has a true belief, children should point at either block at chance rates, since there is no false belief to rectify.

We found that 75% of 4-year-olds in the False-Belief condition ($N = 20$) pointed to the block that the confederate had not seen (which differed significantly from chance, $p = 0.041$), while only 50% of 3-year-olds in the False-Belief condition did so ($N = 20$; $p = 1.0$). Further, only 45% of 4-year-olds in the True-Belief condition ($N = 20$) provided contradictory evidence ($p = 0.824$), significantly fewer than 4-year-olds in the False-Belief condition (χ^2, $p = 0.027$), suggesting that older preschoolers were not simply pointing to the block that the confederate did not see, but rather tailoring their evidence selection to their learner's beliefs. Therefore, while all children successfully *tracked* the confederate's beliefs, only the older preschoolers used the confederate's incorrect beliefs to guide their subsequent evidential demonstrations.

These results suggest that the development of Theory of Mind (ToM) is closely related to pedagogical evidence selection. To examine this relationship, we (Bass et al., in review) ran a second experiment asking whether preschoolers with more proficient false-belief understanding would be better at pedagogical evidence selection, and also whether training pedagogical skill might improve ToM abilities. We assessed children's ToM understanding (Wellman & Liu, 2004) on a preliminary testing day, and compared their performance on two teaching tasks. Children who failed the false-belief battery (i.e., scored 0 or 1 out of 3 points) were either trained on the two pedagogical tasks for 6 weeks beginning on the preliminary testing day (training condition; $N = 22$) or given a 6-week delay (control condition; $N = 18$), after which their false-belief understanding was reassessed. Children who passed the false-belief battery ($N = 21$) completed each pedagogical task just once on the preliminary testing day. We also assessed children's performance on a numerical conservation task as a control measure of more general cognitive development.

Both pedagogical tasks required children to select evidence to lead a naïve learner to a correct target hypothesis. In the novel word task, a novel word represented a target concept (e.g., "Dax means fork."), which children had to teach to a confederate by presenting pictures that did and did not represent the novel word, without explicitly saying what the word meant. In the causal toy task, a causal toy activated when some combination of its two mechanisms were operated, and children demonstrated to a confederate which combinations of mechanisms did and did need to be operated to make the toy go. The number of prompts children required before providing necessary and sufficient evidence was the primary measure for both tasks, with fewer prompts representing more advanced pedagogical skill.

We first asked whether false-belief understanding at pre-test predicted children's performance on the pedagogical tasks on the preliminary testing day (i.e., prior to any training). As we predicted, children who passed the false-belief battery at pre-test provided necessary and sufficient evidence with significantly fewer prompts than those who had failed the battery, $t(41) = 2.38, p = 0.022$. This effect was driven by differences in performance on the causal toy task ($t(41) = 3.17, p = 0.003$), which persisted when controlling for age ($p = 0.018$) and numerical conservation scores ($p = 0.004$), suggesting that ToM is directly related to the ability to select evidence in the service of teaching.

To evaluate the effect of training pedagogical skill on ToM understanding, we compared false-belief failers in the training condition to those in the control condition on false-belief improvement from pre- to post-test. Looking only at failers who had the most room for improvement (i.e., those who answered zero false-belief questions correctly at pre-test), we observed improved false-belief understanding for children in the training condition ($M_{improve} = 0.19$, SD $= 0.26$; $t(11) = 2.55$, $p = 0.027$), but not for children in the control condition ($M_{improve} = 0.08$; $p = 0.170$). Importantly, conservation scores did not differ for either group between pre- and post-test (p's ≥ 0.197), suggesting that the pedagogical training targeted ToM without necessarily leading to general improvement in cognitive reasoning.

Overall, we found evidence for a meaningful relationship between children's capacity to reason about others' minds and the ability to select optimal evidence to teach others. Young children are thus not only able to evaluate evidence to decide when to explore and learn for themselves (e.g., Lapidow and Bonawitz, in review); they also reason about what kinds of evidence would be useful in teaching another. Our findings also tie into prior work that has observed children's sensitivity to others' knowledge states when using their questions to guide exploratory choices (Yu et al., 2017), suggesting that reasoning about others' minds may be manifest in many distinct aspects of evidential reasoning. Children thus draw from many sources in their environments, including the minds of others, to form rich representations of the utility of evidence for learning.

Evaluating Other's Evidence Selection

Children are sensitive to the quality of evidence when learning from events and consider evidence when helping others learn. Do they also make inferences about the quality of information when reasoning about the effectiveness of potential informants? As discussed above, children implicitly use another's knowledge state to guide their actions (Bonawitz et al., 2011), and may even use this knowledge to guide the kinds of information they seek from and present to differently skilled others. Furthermore, children are sensitive to how evidence is presented by others. For example, children avoid learning from informants who provide inaccurate information (Jaswal & Neely, 2006; Koenig, Clément, & Harris, 2004; Pasquini, Corriveau, Koenig, & Harris, 2007); and, children prefer to learn from informants who have provided fully informative evidence, instead of those who have omitted relevant information (Gweon & Asaba in press; Gweon, Pelton, Konopka, & Schulz, 2014).

However, it remains an open question as to whether children can explicitly evaluate another teacher, based on the constraints the teacher faces and how they select evidence for another given these constraints. This kind of reasoning may be more complicated than reasoning about evidence for one's own exploration or even than reasoning about evidence to help teach another. To reason about a teacher's ability to select evidence for another, one must be able to suppress one's own knowledge while reasoning about the ideal evidence given the teacher and learner's beliefs. Furthermore, rather than potentially implicit responses to evidence and stimuli, evaluating another's actions requires at least some explicit representations of these factors. Nonetheless, given the importance of evidential reasoning and natural pedagogy in early childhood, it may be the case that even young children can make informed decisions about both the resources available to the teacher and the effectiveness of selected evidence for teaching another.

Recent work from our lab (Bass, Bonawitz, & Gweon, 2017) explored the nuance of children's evaluations of under-informative teachers. We familiarized preschool-aged children with a novel toy with four functions. Then, children watched videos of different teachers first exploring the toy, and then teaching some subset of what they had discovered to a naïve learner. The number of functions the teacher discovered and taught in these videos was systematically varied. After watching each video, children rated the teacher on a 20-point scale.

We found that children rated a teacher higher if they had demonstrated two of the toy's functions instead of just one ($p = 0.019$). Children were thus sensitive to the *degree* of a teacher's omission, suggesting that children have a nuanced understanding of precisely how helpful different sets of evidence are. Surprisingly, we also found that children were sensitive to the informant's epistemic state: Relative to an informant who had discovered all four functions and taught just one (thereby omitting three of the four functions she knew), children exonerated an informant who had discovered just one function and taught it, thus teaching everything she knew ($p = 0.017$). Although both of these teachers taught identical information, children were willing to pardon under-informative pedagogy when it could be explained by a teacher's limited knowledge. Therefore, while preschoolers are only just beginning to reason explicitly about others' minds (e.g., Wellman, Cross, & Watson, 2001; Wellman & Liu, 2004), they are able to integrate a teacher's mental state into their evaluation of her quality. These findings suggest that children use the quality of evidence to make highly nuanced inferences about others' efficacy as teachers, and that the ability to reason about others' knowledge may play an important role in children's evidential reasoning.

Together, the work discussed here suggests that young children are able to reason fluidly and comprehensively about the quality of evidence, both as learners evaluating the source of that evidence, and as teachers sampling evidence for others. This finding is particularly striking when considering that children must be able to withhold their own beliefs to evaluate the best evidence provided by another for a third party. However, this ability may derive from a core drive to understand the world by evaluating evidence to support exploratory decision making and learning from others.

Final Remarks

Perhaps it is shocking that after a mere 1000 days or so on the planet children are not only able to evaluate and choose between exploratory learning opportunities but also reason about the evidence required to help another learn and to apply this reasoning to evaluate the likely effectiveness of teachers. Yet, it is also difficult to see how else a learning agent that meets the high bar of human intelligence could be designed. Given the complexity of our environment and the nearly infinite opportunities for exploration, an intelligent being must have some ability to evaluate options and choose the paths with greatest opportunities. Exploratory diligence provides well-timed evidence to support learning. Whether it be an optimal intervention or an ideal inquiry, children who control their actions appear to be well served by their choices. Furthermore, we are all served by the cognitive ratcheting effect that comes from our ability to apply evidential reasoning when teaching.

The results of particularly precocious evidential reasoning described here seem to stand in conflict with another line of research: In scientific reasoning tasks children often have great difficulty designing informative interventions to learn about variables and their causes (e.g., Dunbar & Klahr, 1989; Kuhn, 1989; Kuhn, Amsel, & O'Laughlin, 1988; Kuhn & Phelps, 1982). How might we reconcile the idea that children are sophisticated drivers of their own discovery with the fact that scientific inquiry skills are so elusive? One answer is that whether children are metacognitively able to plan careful experiments does not preclude happenstance learning from your own interventions. Children indeed perform informative, deconfounding interventions during their spontaneous exploratory play after seeing both confounded (Cook, Goodman, & Schulz, 2011) and contradicting (van Schijndel, Visser, van Bers, & Raijmakers, 2015) evidence. Nonetheless, that children can apply these abilities in evidential selection for teaching, yet not necessarily apply these abilities to formal scientific practice, remains a puzzle. A valuable enterprise might utilize the implicit proclivities described here to support other skills such as explicit scientific reasoning.

Another important open question involves the role of emotion in learning. Indeed, while we have focused on the role of evidence in exploratory decision-making, the choice of when and what to explore is also driven by emotional evaluations (e.g., Valdesolo, Shtulman, & Baron, 2017). It is a great mystery why some people seem to have insatiable curiosity while others are content to remain comfortable in the known. Children, in particular, may have more conducive dispositions for constant curiosity (Gopnik, 2009), but it is not clear how these drives intersect with emotional development. Although it is likely that emotions play an important role in learning (and anyone with a toddler can tell you that children are extremely emotional beings), there are surprisingly few studies that explore how emotion in early development plays into a drive to explore and learn. If we are to fully understand the utilities driving children's exploration, emotion must be a factor to be studied.

Finally, the account of children's active learning and teaching presented here suggests that at some level children are maintaining a set of beliefs about the world, considering multiple opportunities for evidence to discern between these beliefs, and then selecting the best action based on these utilities. However, such an account may put an unrealistic demand on our young learners. Given the vast (and potentially infinite) space of possible options in the world, how could a learner consider so many possibilities? In other research, we have taken inspiration from machine learning accounts that use sampling algorithms to help solve this computational problem—only requiring the learner to entertain one or a few options at a time, but still producing behavior that on aggregate appears to match optimal predictions from probabilistic models (Denison, Bonawitz, Gopnik, & Griffiths, 2013; Bonawitz, Denison, Gopnik, & Griffiths, 2014; Bonawitz, Denison, Griffiths, & Gopnik, 2014; Bonawitz, Ullman, et al., 2012, in review). These models are an important step to describing how learners move from one belief to the next, while addressing the problem of computational intractability given by uncertainty in the world. These same approaches may help elucidate how multiple options for learning are evaluated in the mind.

Our ability to choose to act plays an important role in learning. The act of acting provides a clearer causal story of the world (Woodward, 2005), which partly solves the problem of Plato's cave. Active learning also likely supports cognitive functions, such as enhancing memory for evidence that was generated from self-directed interventions (Markant, Ruggeri, Gureckis, & Xu, 2016). We have suggested that core abilities are required to support this decision making, and these same abilities also underlie our early emerging natural pedagogical skills. To choose effectively, agents must use more than simple heuristics; they must be able to evaluate the possible rewards and costs of different actions and their outcomes. These rewards may entail information gain, so learning agents must be able to evaluate and select evidence effectively.

We have provided some support for the claim that children are learning agents. Evidential selection emerges very early in development and may even be a core component of the constructivist cycle. Children evaluate potential evidence to support their own learning; they evaluate potential evidence to support another's learning; and, perhaps most impressively, they evaluate a teacher's evidential selection for a third party's learning. While there is still much we do not understand about the roots of curiosity and action in cognitive development, the ability to choose and evaluate evidence seems a critical component. It is in choosing that we become active learners, drivers of our epistemic destinies.

Acknowledgements Thanks to Yue Yu, Yang Yang, Koeun Choi, Joseph Colantonio, Zachary Walden, Carla Macias, Megan Saylor, and Patricia Ganea for helpful feedback on an earlier draft of this chapter. The research presented in this chapter was supported in part by NSF SMA SL-CN (#1640816), NSF SES (#1627971), and the Rutgers University—Newark Chancellor's Seed Grant Program to EB.

References

Bass, I., Bonawitz, E., & Gweon, H. (2017). Didn't know, or didn't show? Preschoolers consider epistemic state and degree of omission when evaluating teachers. In G. Gunzelmann, A. Howes, T. Tenbrink, & E. Davelaar (Eds.), *Proceedings of the 39th annual conference of the cognitive science society* (pp. 105–110). Austin, TX: Cognitive Science Society.

Bass, I., Bonawitz, E., Shafto, P., Hanson, M., Ramarajan, D., Gopnik, A., & Wellman, H. (in review). Children's developing theory of mind and pedagogical evidence selection.

Berlyne, D. E. (1978). Curiosity and learning. *Motivation and Emotion, 2*(2), 97–175.

Bonawitz, E., Denison, S., Gopnik, A., & Griffiths, T. L. (2014). Win-Stay, Lose-Sample: A simple sequential algorithm for approximating Bayesian inference. *Cognitive Psychology, 74*, 35–65.

Bonawitz, E., Denison, S., Griffiths, T. L., & Gopnik, A. (2014). Probabilistic models, learning algorithms, and response variability: Sampling in cognitive development. *Trends in Cognitive Sciences, 18*(10), 497–500.

Bonawitz, E., Shafto, P., Gweon, H., Goodman, N. D., Spelke, E., & Schulz, L. (2011). The double-edged sword of pedagogy: Instruction limits spontaneous exploration and discovery. *Cognition, 120*(3), 322–330.

Bonawitz, E., Ullman, T., Gopnik, A., & Tenenbaum, J. (2012, November). Sticking to the Evidence? A computational and behavioral case study of micro-theory change in the domain of magnetism. In *2012 IEEE international conference on development and learning and epigenetic robotics (ICDL)* (pp. 1–6). IEEE.

Bonawitz, E. B., Fischer, A., & Schulz, L. (2012). Teaching 3.5-year-olds to revise their beliefs given ambiguous evidence. *Journal of Cognition and Development, 13*(2), 266–280. https://doi.org/10.1080/15248372.2011.577701

Bonawitz, E. B., Ullman, T., Bridgers, S., Gopnik, A., & Tenenbaum, J. B. (in revision). Chicken-and-egg: A computational, historical, and behavioral case study of micro-theory change in the domain of magnetism.

Bonawitz, E. B., van Schijndel, T. J., Friel, D., & Schulz, L. (2012). Children balance theories and evidence in exploration, explanation, and learning. *Cognitive Psychology, 64*(4), 215–234. https://doi.org/10.1016/j.cogpsych.2011.12.002

Callanan, M. A., & Oakes, L. M. (1992). Preschoolers' questions and parents' explanations: Causal thinking in everyday activity. *Cognitive Development, 7*, 213–233. https://doi.org/10.1016/0885-2014(92)90012-G

Chouinard, M. M. (2007). Children's questions: A mechanism for cognitive development. *Monographs of the Society for Research in Child Development, 72*, 7–9.

Cook, C., Goodman, N. D., & Schulz, L. E. (2011). Where science starts: Spontaneous experiments in preschoolers' exploratory play. *Cognition, 120*(3), 341–349.

Csikszentmihalyi, M. (1996). *Flow and the psychology of discovery and invention*. New York, NY: Harper Collins.

Day, H. I., & Langevin, R. (1969). Curiosity and intelligence: Two necessary conditions for a high level of creativity. *The Journal of Special Education, 3*(3), 263–268.

Denison, S., Bonawitz, E., Gopnik, A., & Griffiths, T. L. (2013). Rational variability in children's causal inferences: The sampling hypothesis. *Cognition, 126*(2), 285–300.

Dunbar, K., & Klahr, D. (1989). Developmental differences in scientific discovery processes. In D. Klahr & K. Kotovsky (Eds.), *The 21st Carnegie-Mellon symposium on cognition: Complex information processing: The impact of Herbert A. Simon*. Hillsdale, NJ: Lawrence Erlbaum.

Gonzalez, A., Shafto, P., Bonawtiz, E. B., & Gopnik, A. (2012). Is that your final answer? The effects of neutral queries on children's choices. In Proceedings of the Annual Meeting of the Cognitive Science Society, *34*(34).

Gopnik, A. (2000). Explanation as orgasm and the drive for causal knowledge: The function, evolution, and phenomenology of the theory formation system. In F. Keil & R. Wilson (Eds.), *Cognition and explanation* (pp. 299–323). Cambridge, MA: MIT Press.

Gopnik, A. (2009). *The philosophical baby: What children's minds tell us about truth, love and the meaning of life*. New York, NY: Random House.

Gweon, H., & Asaba, M. (2017). Order matters: Children's evaluation of under-informative teachers depends on context. *Child Development*. https://doi.org/10.1111/cdev.12825

Gweon, H., Pelton, H., Konopka, J. A., & Schulz, L. E. (2014). Sins of omission: Children selectively explore when agents fail to tell the whole truth. *Cognition, 132*(3), 335–341. https://doi.org/10.1016/j.cognition.2014.04.013

Gweon, H., Tenenbaum, J. B., & Schulz, L. E. (2010). Infants consider both the sample and the sampling process in inductive generalization. *Proceedings of the National Academy of Sciences, 107*(20), 9066–9071.

Jaswal, V. K., & Neely, L. A. (2006). Adults don't always know best preschoolers use past reliability over age when learning new words. *Psychological Science, 17*(9), 757–758. https://doi.org/10.1111/j.1467-9280.2006.01778.x

Jirout, J., & Klahr, D. (2012). Children's scientific curiosity: In search of an operational definition of an elusive concept. *Developmental Review, 32*(2), 125–160.

Jowett, B. (Ed.). (1941). *Plato's the republic*. New York, NY: The Modern Library.

Kidd, C., Piantadosi, S. T., & Aslin, R. N. (2012). The Goldilocks effect: Human infants allocate attention to visual sequences that are neither too simple nor too complex. *PLoS One, 7*(5), e36399. https://doi.org/10.1371/journal.pone.0036399

Kidd, C., Piantadosi, S. T., & Aslin, R. N. (2014). The Goldilocks effect in infant auditory attention. *Child Development, 85*(5), 1795–1804. https://doi.org/10.1111/cdev.12263

Knudsen, B., & Liszkowski, U. (2012). One-year-olds warn others about negative action outcomes. *Journal of Cognition and Development, 14*(3), 424–436. https://doi.org/10.1080/15248372.2012.689387

Koenig, M. A., Clément, F., & Harris, P. L. (2004). Trust in testimony: Children's use of true and false statements. *Psychological Science, 15*(10), 694–698. https://doi.org/10.1111/j.0956-7976.2004.00742.x

Koerber, S., Sodian, B., Thoermer, C., & Nett, U. (2005). Scientific reasoning in young children: Preschoolers' ability to evaluate covariation evidence. *Swiss Journal of Psychology, 64*(3), 141–152. https://doi.org/10.1024/1421-0185.64.3.141

Kuhn, D. (1989). Children and adults as intuitive scientists. *Psychological Review, 96*(4), 674–689.

Kuhn, D., Amsel, E., & O'Laughlin, M. (1988). *The development of scientific thinking skills.* Orlando, FL: Academic Press.

Kuhn, D., & Phelps, E. (1982). The development of problem-solving strategies. In H. Reese (Ed.), *Advances in child development and behavior* (Vol. 17, pp. 1–44). New York, NY: Academic Press.

Lapidow, E., & Bonawitz, E. (in review). Rational action: Ambiguity, expectation, and information gain influence preschooler's choices in exploration.

Legare, C. H., Gelman, S. A., & Wellman, H. M. (2010). Inconsistency with prior knowledge triggers children's causal explanatory reasoning. *Child Development, 81*(3), 929–944. https://doi.org/10.1111/j.1467-8624.2010.01443.x

Leonard, N. H., & Harvey, M. (2007). The trait of curiosity as a predictor of emotional intelligence. *Journal of Applied Social Psychology, 37*(8), 1914–1929.

Liszkowski, U., Carpenter, M., & Tomasello, M. (2008). Twelve-month-olds communicate helpfully and appropriately for knowledgeable and ignorant partners. *Cognition, 108*(3), 732–739. https://doi.org/10.1016/j.cognition.2008.06.013

Loewenstein, G. (1994). The psychology of curiosity: A review and reinterpretation. *Psychological Bulletin, 116*(1), 75.

Markant, D. B., Ruggeri, A., Gureckis, T. M., & Xu, F. (2016). Enhanced memory as a common effect of active learning. *Mind, Brain, and Education, 10*(3), 142–152.

Pasquini, E. S., Corriveau, K. H., Koenig, M., & Harris, P. L. (2007). Preschoolers monitor the relative accuracy of informants. *Developmental Psychology, 43*(5), 1216–1226. https://doi.org/10.1037/0012-1649.43.5.1216

Penney, R. K. (1965). Reactive curiosity and manifest anxiety in children. *Child Development, 36*(3), 697–702.

Piaget, J. (1954). *The construction of reality in the child.* New York, NY: Ballantine Books. https://doi.org/10.1037/11168-000

Rhodes, M., Bonawitz, E., Shafto, P., Chen, A., & Caglar, L. (2015). Controlling the message: Preschoolers' use of information to teach and deceive others. *Frontiers in Psychology, 6,* 867. https://doi.org/10.3389/fpsyg.2015.00867

Rhodes, M., Gelman, S. A., & Brickman, D. (2010). Children's attention to sample composition in learning, teaching and discovery. *Developmental Science, 13*(3), 421–429. https://doi.org/10.1111/j.1467-7687.2009.00896.x

Ruggeri, A., Lombrozo, T., Griffiths, T. L., & Xu, F. (2016). Sources of developmental change in the efficiency of information search. *Developmental Psychology, 52*(12), 2159.

Schulz, L. E., & Bonawitz, E. B. (2007). Serious fun: Preschoolers engage in more exploratory play when evidence is confounded. *Developmental Psychology, 43*(4), 1045–1050. https://doi.org/10.1037/0012-1649.43.4.1045

Spielberger, C. D., & Starr, L. M. (1994). Curiosity and exploratory behavior. Motivation: Theory and research, 221–243.

Stahl, A. E., & Feigenson, L. (2015). Observing the unexpected enhances infants' learning and exploration. *Science, 348*(6230), 91–94.

Stahl, A. E., & Feigenson, L. (2017). Expectancy violations promote learning in young children. *Cognition, 163,* 1–14.

Valdesolo, P., Shtulman, A., & Baron, A. S. (2017). Science is awe-some: The emotional antecedents of science learning. *Emotion Review, 9*(3), 215–221.

van Schijndel, T. J., Visser, I., van Bers, B. M., & Raijmakers, M. E. (2015). Preschoolers perform more informative experiments after observing theory-violating evidence. *Journal of Experimental Child Psychology, 131,* 104–119.

Wellman, H. M., Cross, D., & Watson, J. (2001). Meta-analysis of theory-of-mind development: The truth about false belief. *Child Development, 72*(3), 655–684.

Wellman, H. M., Kushnir, T., Xu, F., & Brink, K. A. (2016). Infants use statistical sampling to understand the psychological world. *Infancy, 21*(5), 668–676.

Wellman, H. M., & Liu, D. (2004). Scaling of theory-of-mind tasks. *Child Development, 75*(2), 523–541. https://doi.org/10.1111/j.1467-8624.2004.00691.x

Woodward, J. (2005). *Making things happen: A theory of causal explanation.* New York, NY: Oxford University Press.

Yu, Y., Bonawitz, E., & Shafto, P. (2017). Pedagogical Questions in Parent–Child Conversations. Child development. https://doi.org/10.1111/cdev.12850

Yu, Y., Landrum, A., Bonawitz, E., & Shafto, P. (in review) Questioning supports effective transmission of knowledge and increased exploratory learning in pre-kindergarten children.

Chapter 13
Bilingual Children: Active Language Learners as Language Brokers

Georgene L. Troseth, Jeannette Mancilla-Martinez, and Israel Flores

Abstract All children are active language learners, including those learning more than one language. Growing up bilingual offers children particular cognitive strengths and helpful patterns of interaction, along with some cognitive, perceptual, and academic challenges, particularly for children in families of low socioeconomic status. Many immigrants in the USA face language and cultural barriers in gaining access to resources. To overcome those barriers, families often engage in "language brokering," in which children act as interpreters and translators between parents and US society. Parent–child interaction during language brokering resembles "dialogic reading" prompts and questioning strategies that have been successfully used to support vocabulary development among young children. This chapter outlines bilingual children's active engagement with language in challenging cognitive and social situations, and describes promising innovations to promote bilingual language learning.

Introduction

Most children in the world grow up in environments that expose them to more than one language, yet research on early language development has largely been carried out with children who have been exposed to a single language (Akhtar & Menjivar, 2012; Konishi, Kanero, Freeman, Golinkoff, & Hirsh-Pasek, 2014). Growing up bilingual offers children particular cognitive strengths and helpful patterns of interaction, along with some cognitive, perceptual, and academic challenges, particularly for children in families of low socioeconomic status. In this chapter, we describe a set of abilities that bilingual children develop because of negotiating

G. L. Troseth (✉) · I. Flores
Department of Psychology and Human Development, Vanderbilt University,
Nashville, TN, USA
e-mail: georgene.troseth@vanderbilt.edu

J. Mancilla-Martinez
Department of Teaching and Learning, Vanderbilt University, Nashville, TN, USA

© Springer International Publishing AG, part of Springer Nature 2018
M. M. Saylor, P. A. Ganea (eds.), *Active Learning from Infancy to Childhood*,
https://doi.org/10.1007/978-3-319-77182-3_13

between two languages, including attentional control, perspective taking, and meta-linguistic skills. Additionally, the practice of "language brokering," in which bilingual children of immigrant families serve as linguistic mediators between their parents and the majority culture, may serve as a "zone of proximal development" promoting children's social and cognitive development under challenging conditions. We end by describing several uses of digital media to promote young bilingual children's language development.

One Language System, Two Languages

Bilingualism is currently thought of as two languages within a single language system (Kroll, Dussias, Bice, & Perrotti, 2015). Neural support for processing the two languages is mostly shared, and both languages are always active when bilinguals listen to or plan speech or read words in either language (Abutalebi & Green, 2007, 2008). Because of this parallel activation, the languages compete for cognitive resources, so bilinguals must acquire a way to regulate that competition. Thus, being bilingual tunes up aspects of Executive Function (EF)—self-regulatory cognitive processes that help people monitor and control their thoughts and actions (Carlson, 2005) including the ability to selectively focus attention, switch between tasks, and resolve conflicting alternatives. In contrast to children juggling two auditory languages, speech-sign bilinguals who acquired both American Sign Language and English in the first year of life do not show the EF advantage, because their two languages can be produced simultaneously without competing for production resources in the same modality (Emmorey, Luk, Pyers, & Bialystok, 2008).

Researchers have wondered if the EF advantage could be explained by differences in culture or parent education. At least one study reports culturally based advantages in EF abilities favoring Chinese over US preschoolers (Sabbagh, Xu, Carlson, Moses, & Lee, 2006). Other research provides evidence that parent socioeconomic status (SES) predicts aspects of EF (see Hackman & Farah, 2009). However, results from a large number of studies carried out in multiple labs indicate that, after controlling for culture and/or SES, children who are exposed to two languages have certain cognitive advantages over those being raised with a single language. In a meta-analysis of 63 studies that compared children across the dimension of one versus multiple languages, cognitive correlates of bilingualism included attentional control, working memory, abstract and symbolic representational skills, and metalinguistic awareness (Adesope, Lavin, Thompson, & Ungerleider, 2010). This skill set is thought to be the brain's response to the cognitive challenge of dealing with two languages. Barac and Bialystok (2011) present a helpful historical timeline of much of this research.

In one of the first studies of bilingual EF, 4- and 5-year-old bilinguals outperformed same-age monolinguals (with similar receptive vocabulary and memory span) on tasks relying on attentional control (Bialystok, 1999). Later research included tests of several aspects of EF to narrow down those functions affected by juggling two languages. Bilingual children outperformed monolinguals on tasks requiring inhibition of *attentional control to competing cues*, but not on tasks requiring inhibition of a response or withholding a practiced response (Martin-Rhee & Bialystok, 2008; also see Carlson & Meltzoff, 2008). Other research revealed that bilingual children had an advantage over monolinguals when tasks required *monitoring, switching,* and *updating* responses (Bialystok, 2010). Several studies involving more than one culture—bilinguals and monolinguals in Canada and bilinguals in India (Bialystok & Viswanathan, 2009); American Korean-English bilinguals, Korean and English monolinguals in the USA, and Korean monolinguals in Korea (Yang, Yang, & Lust, 2011)—have clarified that across cultures, experiences with bilingualism offer an advantage in the control of attention.

Recent research has probed the independent effects of socioeconomic class and bilingualism on executive function. SES-related differences emerged in both language ability and EF between ethnically diverse middle class and working class children in Toronto (i.e., not extremes of wealth or poverty). Thus, even relatively small differences in family resources affected the development of children's skills. However, *within* each social class, bilingual children showed superior EF skills (working memory and attentional control) compared to monolingual children, despite lower English vocabulary scores (Calvo & Bialystok, 2014). In a study carried out in Luxembourg and Portugal, low-income bilingual immigrant children performed better than monolingual children matched on SES and ethnicity on EF tasks requiring selective attention and the suppression of interference from competing information, showing that "the bilingual advantage is neither confounded with nor limited by socioeconomic and cultural factors" (Engel de Abreu, Cruz-Santos, Tourinho, Martin, & Bialystok, 2012, p. 1364).

Cognitive Flexibility, Perspective Taking, and Mental State Understanding

At an earlier age than is typical for monolingual children, bilinguals succeed at tasks requiring cognitive flexibility (controlled, flexible attention shifting—Prior & MacWhinney, 2010) and begin to understand how other people's perspectives and beliefs might differ from their own. Compared to same-age monolingual children, bilinguals perform better on tests of the appearance-reality distinction, perspective taking tasks, and false belief tasks (Bialystok & Senman, 2004; Goetz, 2003; Kovacs, 2009). When children discussed objects that had different appearances and real identities (e.g., a sponge that looked like a rock), all answered an initial question ("What does this look like?"), but bilinguals surpassed monolinguals at correctly answering a follow-up question ("What is it really?") because the answer presents a conflict with their initial response that must be resolved through attention and inhibition (also see Berguno & Bowler, 2004). In another task requiring a resolution of cognitive conflict, bilingual children excelled at assigning a new interpretation to an already identified ambiguous figure such as the famous vase-faces picture (Bialystok & Shapero, 2005). Also, when asked to draw an object (e.g., a flower) that "doesn't exist," monolinguals tended to draw an object with a missing element (e.g., a flower without petals) whereas bilingual children flexibly coordinated conflicting concepts (e.g., drew a flower with teeth—Adi-Japha, Berberich-Artzi, & Libnawi, 2010).

Bilingual children passed standard "false belief" and perspective taking tasks (Goetz, 2003; Kovacs, 2009) that required understanding and attending to what different people knew about a situation. Besides needing to selectively focus attention on relevant information, bilingual children might have an advantage in understanding others' perspectives from experiences in their social lives—situations of miscommunication with speakers of only one of their languages (Akhtar & Menjivar, 2012; Goetz, 2003).

Bilingualism and Babies

Early exposure to multiple languages begins to shape brain function even before children begin to talk. When "crib bilinguals" are exposed to two languages from birth, it affects the tuning of the brain's representation of speech and has consequences for attention and language discrimination. Seven-month-old crib bilinguals already display better cognitive control abilities compared to monolingual infants— they were able to suppress looks to an initially rewarded location and redirect their anticipatory looks when a visual cue to the reward changed location (Kovacs & Mehler, 2009). Thus, merely processing two languages in the same environment and managing competing language representations may tune up attentional control. Additionally, bilingual 24-month-olds showed better inhibitory control on the Stroop Shape Task than monolingual same-age toddlers did (Poulin-Dubois, Blaye, Coutya, & Bialystok, 2011).

Exposure to two languages also has consequences for speech perception and for intermodal perception involving speech. Watching silent videos of a bilingual speaker switching between two unfamiliar languages, 8-month-old crib bilinguals (but not monolinguals) discerned when a speaker shifted between the unfamiliar languages (Sebastian-Galles, Albareda-Castellot, Weikum, & Werker, 2012). These results supported Sebastian-Galles et al.'s hypothesis that the ability to track one's native languages separately and learn about their distinct properties contributed to the bilingual advantage. On the other hand, juggling two languages can slow down acquisition of some aspects of speech perception. Four-year-olds learning English alone were better at discriminating a common English speech contrast (/d-th/) compared to children learning English and French at the same time (Sundara, Polka, & Genessee, 2006). However, early bilingual *adults* (who had simultaneously acquired English and French in childhood) better discriminated the English contrast than the 4-year-olds bilinguals did, showing that language experience over time facilitates speech perception and that development happens later when two languages are acquired together. However, experience was necessary for native speech perception: In the absence of

English exposure, the difficulty that French children and adults had in distinguishing this contrast remained unchanged across development.

Current research is aimed at exploring how bilinguals with different combinations of languages or degrees of exposure to the two languages differ from each other, and clarifying what language activities might relate to strengthening particular cognitive skills (Kroll et al., 2015). One possibility is that "code-switching"—going back and forth between languages—especially tunes up cognitive abilities needed to regulate competing languages. The timing of children's exposure to/acquisition of the two languages is undoubtedly important: whether the languages were acquired simultaneously or sequentially (Akhtar & Menjivar, 2012). For instance, adults who had become bilingual early in life showed a stronger advantage in inhibitory control than late bilinguals did (Luk, de Sa, & Bialystok, 2011). The relative level of proficiency in each language (is an individual a "balanced" bilingual and if not, how dominant is one of the languages) may play a crucial role in whether or not an EF advantage and other cognitive benefits are seen. Also, the settings in which the languages are acquired and used (e.g., in the home, at school) might distinguish different kinds of bilingual strengths and differences. In the infancy research, Kovacs and Mehler (2009) suggest that exposure to two languages from birth in the home context might call on EF abilities more than if the infant was exposed to the languages in different settings.

Linguistic and Metalinguistic Skills and Strategies

Akhtar and Menjivar (2012) provide a thorough review of the linguistic and metalinguistic skills of bilinguals and the strategies that bilingual children use to learn words. Research suggests that monolingual toddlers use a "mutual exclusivity bias," or initial assumption that two words cannot refer to the same object, to help them map between labels and referents by 16 months of age (Markman & Wachtel, 1988; Markman, Wasow, & Hansen, 2003). Bilingual toddlers do not seem to use this bias for word learning (Byers-Heinlein and Werker, 2009; Houston-Price, Caloghiris, & Raviglione, 2010). Instead, preschool-aged bilinguals are more likely than same-age monolinguals to accept two labels for the same referent (Au & Glusman, 1990; Bialystok, Barac, Blaye, & Poulin-Dubois, 2010; Davidson, Jergovic, Imami, & Theodos, 1997; Davidson & Tell, 2005).

The reason for this difference reflects the linguistic regularities that monolinguals and bilinguals abstract from their experiences. For monolinguals, the mutual exclusivity strategy is effective until they need to learn synonyms or go beyond basic-level object names (e.g., learn that a "dog" can also be called an "animal"). The strategy does not work for bilinguals, who are regularly confronted with multiple labels for the same object (e.g., Mom's "dog" is Dad's "perro"). As Akhtar and Menjivar (2012) note about young bilinguals, "their linguistic experience prepares them to be more flexible language learners" (p. 56). In Houston-Price et al.'s (2010) study, despite avoiding the mutual exclusivity strategy, bilingual children were efficient word learners with the same vocabulary size as the monolingual participants.

Evidence for efficiency of learning emerged in a study that included preschool-aged (4-year-old) bilinguals and non-bilingual children who had been substantially exposed to a second language (Menjivar & Akhtar, 2016). Compared to monolingual 4-year-olds, the bilingual and "exposed" children more easily learned labels for familiar and novel objects in a made-up language ("Nordish"), suggesting that exposure to two languages makes it easier for children to learn an additional language.

Besides learning words in their two languages, bilingual children may acquire *metalinguistic* knowledge: they may discover how languages work. For instance, bilingual school children (5–8 years of age and older) tend to have better "word awareness" than monolinguals do: knowing different labels for the same thing in their two languages, they better understand that words are arbitrary and conventional (Akhtar & Menjivar, 2012). Compared to children learning a single language, bilingual children will more easily follow an experimenter's requests to substitute a word in a sentence (e.g., replace "Airplane" with "Turtle" to create the sentence "Turtles can fly") and affirm the possibility of calling a dog "cow" and a cow "dog" (e.g., Ben-Zeev, 1977; Cromdal, 1999). Bialystok (1986) points out that demonstrating metalinguistic awareness may require cognitive control to ignore the familiar label, calling on children's enhanced EF as well as their insight about words.

Having Successful Conversations (Pragmatics)

Language pragmatics involves being able to communicate clearly and figure out the communicative intentions of others. Pragmatics develops along with other aspects of language during infancy and early childhood (Bates, 1976), regardless of the number of languages children are learning. However, bilingual children need to be especially aware of pragmatics during conversations: they must figure out what language a conversational partner speaks, how well they speak it, and how to communicate clearly to that person. They also must notice when their own communications are not understood.

Two-year-old bilinguals notice and repair communication breakdowns, and can switch languages to match the one spoken by the conversational partner (Comeau, Genesee, & Mendelson, 2007). They use both a speaker's *gaze direction* to infer communicative intentions (Yow & Markman, 2011a) and a speaker's *tone of voice* to judge the person's emotion (Yow & Markman, 2011b) better than same-age monolingual children do. Demonstrating their experience detecting speakers' intentions, 3- to 6-year-old bilinguals could detect violations of conversational principles (be truthful, relevant, polite, and informative—Grice, 1989) better than same-age monolinguals could (Siegal, Iozzi, & Surian, 2009; Siegal et al., 2010). Therefore, even very young bilingual children gain skill at navigating situations in which the conversational partners may have to work hard to understand each other.

Language Brokering in Bilingual Families

Related to bilingual children's facility with conversational pragmatics, part of their skill set develops from helping their parents navigate in a society that speaks a different language. To overcome language and cultural barriers in their new homeland, a common practice among immigrant communities is for children to become interpreters and translators between their parents and US society (McQuillan & Tse, 1995; Orellana, 2003; Tse, 1995). This kind of interaction is variously termed *paraphrasing, natural interpreting, family-interpreting*, or *language brokering* (Dorner, Orellana, & Li-Grining, 2007). Generally speaking, a broker (e.g., stockbroker) facilitates an interaction between two parties (e.g., a buyer and a seller). Child language brokers serve as go-betweens, using their developing knowledge of US culture and the English language to support their culturally and linguistically less-fluent family members (Katz, 2014).

Children of immigrants learn a second language for different reasons than are typical of children in families with more resources who "choose to learn a new language as part of their curriculum, whereas language brokers learn a language for their own and their family's survival" (Morales & Hanson, 2005, p. 473). Thus, child language brokers attempt to use their second language in highly motivating contexts with real-world consequences. According to research (predominately with Latino families in the USA), the majority of children and adolescents from immigrant families act as language brokers. Parents usually begin asking children to translate written material and interpret in social situations when they are between the ages of 8 and 12 (Morales & Hanson, 2005). Although children take on this responsibility to assist their families, the activity of going between languages may help them to learn more about both languages and cultures, as well as learning the pragmatics of conversing with a wide variety of people.

Brokering involves taking on the roles of "tutor" and "advocate" in the family (Valenzuela, 1999). Orellana, Dorner, and Pulido (2003) observed children and adolescents working with parents on parents' ESL homework, citizenship exams, and job applications. Children translated bank statements, balanced checkbooks, and tutored younger siblings. More tech-savvy than their parents, children helped the family purchase and use technology. They scheduled doctor appointments, mediated when parents needed to talk to landlords, and navigated complex situations in doctor's offices and social service agencies (Katz, 2014). Children used domain-specific vocabulary appropriate to the situation in both languages and sometimes could reflect on their efforts to choose language and frame situations to benefit and protect their families. Language brokering helped children to know more about the world, US culture, and the family's culture of origin, and to develop a trusting relationship with parents (McQuillan & Tse, 1995).

Orellana et al. (2003) note that child language brokers and their parents work as "performance teams" (Valdes, Chavez, & Angelelli, 2003) to help each other navigate challenging situations. Children alternately are guided or "scaffolded" by more experienced others, and become the "expert" tasked with explaining information to novices, putting language brokers in a challenging "zone of proximal development" (Vygotsky, 1978) that might promote their social and cognitive growth. For instance, parents scaffold children's understanding of their goals for communicating with an English speaker, the purpose of various documents, and aspects of interpersonal dynamics between the adults. While asking for their children's help, parents break up speech into smaller segments, provide linguistic knowledge (e.g., correct syntax and word forms) in Spanish and for the English vocabulary they know, push the child to find appropriate Spanish equivalents or definitions for other English words, and keep their child focused on the conversation's meaning. In turn, children are active brokers: even young children try to paraphrase, describe unknown words, use Spanish phonological pronunciation of English words, guess word meanings from context clues, and scaffold parents' understanding of American culture and values (Eksner & Orellana, 2012).

Thus, language brokering alters the typical "apprenticeship" (Rogoff, 1990) model of information transfer between adult and child, with the roles of expert and apprentice flowing back and forth (Eksner & Orellana, 2012). Older children become more comfortable speaking up, asking questions, and negotiating between adults based on cultural norms (Katz, 2014). However, this does not mean that parents lose their authority (Diaz-Lazaro, 2002). According to Katz, there is little evidence that parents become passive or that language brokering disrupts the family dynamic. Two (or more) adults and the child interpreter enter an interaction with varying levels of expertise regarding their different cultural expectations for the exchange, as well as the multiple languages involved. Thus, the parties must collaborate to successfully share information.

Parents use their children as translators even when another translator is available; relying on a family member helps parents feel confidence in their ability to survive what often feels like a hostile environment (Valdes et al., 2003). Parents report that the age of the broker is not a negative factor. Children present their family members in a positive way and protect them from embarrassment (Orellana et al., 2003). Because they are not professional interpreters or translators, child language brokers can influence the messages they convey (inadvertently or on purpose) or even act as decision makers during interactions with adults (Tse, 1995). For example, Katz (2014) describes a situation in which a Latino 16-year-old altered her parents' message to facilitate a better outcome. The doctor's office did not accept the family's health insurance; rather than literally interpret her parents' words of frustration toward the office staff, the daughter made clear that the blame lay with the insurance company. Staff members were more sympathetic and the end result benefited the family.

During brokered exchanges, parents report understanding more English than they thought they would, and using their understanding to correct the child's interpretation (Valdes et al., 2003). Thus, the parent co-learns English along with the child in highly motivating situations. For children, brokering allows them to practice both languages and feel competent in both; speaking Spanish made some children feel more connected to their cultural heritage.

Some evidence for positive academic effects of language brokering comes from an established Mexican immigrant community in Chicago where 90% of children interpreted language and cultural practices for their relatives, some of whom had been in the USA for a decade or more (Dorner et al., 2007). Children in the community varied in how often they engaged in language brokering. "Active" and "partial" language brokers tended to be first and second generation immigrants brought to the USA at a young age. They spoke Spanish at home and most had experienced some bilingual education when they entered school as Spanish monolinguals.

In a longitudinal study, Dorner and colleagues found that higher child-reported current levels of language brokering were significantly (with a large effect size) linked to better scores on fifth and sixth grade standardized reading tests, after controlling for earlier test scores (the average of children's first and second grade scores) to account for the possibility that early skill level promoted both language brokering and better academic outcomes. Active brokers tended to score lower on early achievement tests compared to partial brokers (possibly reflecting less parent English proficiency and the need for children to translate), but by fifth grade, the active brokers scored higher than partial- and non-brokers.

Many of the active language brokers entered school without much English and experienced a year or more of bilingual education (Dorner et al., 2007). These students may have gained multiple benefits from the opportunity to maintain their heritage language at school, including less stress and more skills for supporting their families, as well as assistance in their acquisition of English. As language brokers, children may develop cognitive, linguistic, and decision-making abilities due to their experiences as go-betweens. Several theorists propose that children who become competent are likely to develop their vocabulary, metalinguistic awareness, and interpreting/translating strategies that can support better school performance (Buriel, Perez, De Ment, Chavez, & Moran, 1998; Krashen, 1985; Heath, 1986; Malakoff & Hakuta, 1991). For instance, language brokering requires that children reconstruct and retell information while actively engaging with adults, which has been shown to increase oral language abilities (Morrow, 1985). Additionally, Jiménez et al. (2015) suggest that bilinguals' translation strategies are similar to strategies that highly proficient readers use to comprehend text and that activities that engage both languages can make explicit children's "tacit" knowledge about the structure of language. Thus, language brokering and translation hold promise for formal and informal learning, but further studies are needed of their effect on academic outcomes.

Challenges Facing Bilingual Students

Children from English-speaking homes develop English oral language skills by the time they enter formal schooling, acquiring thousands of words (Anglin, 1993) and learning the structure of English (Daniels, 1998). In contrast, preschool children acquiring two languages often have less developed vocabularies and grammar in each language than monolinguals, even when matched for SES (Hoff et al., 2012; Marchman, Fernald, & Hurtado, 2010; Vagh, Pan, & Mancilla-Martinez, 2009). However, measures that incorporate both languages indicate that bilingual children acquire both vocabulary and grammar at a faster rate than monolingual children (Hoff et al., 2012; Pearson, Fernández, & Oller, 1993). So the problem is not impaired learning, but not having early access to adequate English input.

Vocabulary knowledge among bilingual children is spread across two languages, each of which typically may be used in a different social context, such as speaking English at school (and building English vocabulary) while dealing with academic topics, and speaking Spanish (and building Spanish vocabulary) while carrying out daily activities at home (Mancilla-Martinez & McClain, 2017). Researchers are raising awareness that, by definition, single-language vocabulary measures cannot accurately reflect overall bilingual vocabulary knowledge (e.g., Bedore et al., 2005; Mancilla-Martinez & Vagh, 2013; Oller & Eilers, 2002; Pearson, Fernández, & Oller, 1995). An aggregate analysis that included language data from over 1500 monolingual and bilingual Canadian 3-to-10-year-olds revealed significantly lower (by 10 points) English language scores on the Peabody Picture Vocabulary Test (PPVT-III, Dunn & Dunn, 1997) for the bilingual compared to the monolingual children (Bialystok, Luk, Peets, & Yang, 2010). A closer look at the kinds of words children knew revealed no group differences in school category English vocabulary words. However, monolinguals outperformed bilinguals on *home* category English words (typically picked up when discussing events in the heritage language at home). It is important to note that the children included in this analysis were described by their parents as fluent in both languages and as using both languages on a daily basis. Children learning English as a second language (i.e., children of more recent immigrants) were not included.

Bilingualism itself is not a risk factor for academic difficulties (DeHouwer, 1999; Snow, 1992), but *poverty* is a well-established risk factor for a host of negative life outcomes, including comprised academic outcomes (Hart & Risley, 1995; Hindman, Wasik, & Snell, 2016; Hoff, 2003a, 2003b; Pearson, 2007; Ramey & Ramey, 2004; Weisleder & Fernald, 2013), and Latino children are now the largest group of poor children in the USA living in poverty (López & Velasco, 2011; Jiang, Granja, & Koball, 2017).

In a recent study, very early differences in language learning were reported between toddlers from low- and higher-SES families. Fernald, Marchman, and Weisleder (2013) followed English-learning infants from 18 to 24 months, tracking changes over development in real-time language processing efficiency and vocabulary learning. Fernald and her colleagues found that SES-related disparities in language processing efficiency and vocabulary development were already present at 18 months. By 24 months, toddlers from low SES families were 6 months behind their more advantaged peers in the processing skills needed for language development.

What causes this processing difference? Amount of language input seems central. Compared to lower-SES mothers, mothers with additional education and resources talk more to their children using more varied vocabulary (Hart & Risley, 1995; Hoff, 2003b; Rowe, 2012). Hart and Risley reported that welfare recipient families talked much less to their young children than professional class (high SES) families did, resulting in a "30 million word gap" in cumulative exposure by age 3. Critics of this work (e.g., Dudley-Marling & Lucas, 2009) point out methodological flaws (e.g., socioeconomic status was confabulated with race), but recent research has documented a similar gap in language input (e.g., Fernald et al., 2013; Schady et al., 2015). Differences in language input can be conceived of as *disparities in opportunity* to learn language (Carter & Welner, 2013). The resulting differences in children's vocabulary development contribute to an overall achievement gap during the school years (Farkas & Beron, 2004; Hoff, 2006, 2013; Huttenlocher, Waterfall, Vasilyeva, Vevea, & Hedges, 2010; Mancilla-Martinez & Lesaux, 2011; Rowe, 2008).

When talking with their children, high SES parents use longer utterances with more diverse words (Hoff, 2003a), and this quality of language mediates the relation between family SES and children's language development. For instance, in a study of Spanish–English bilingual (and English monolingual) children in Miami, language exposure at home and SES both contributed to children's English language skills (Oller & Eilers, 2002; see also Hernandez, 2004). Hoff (2006) reported that amount of child exposure to English, along with parent education, predicted children's language development. The reason for child-focused talk can also differ: parents with more education and resources asked their children more questions and used fewer utterances to direct and control their child's behavior than lower-SES parents did (Hoff, Laursen, & Tardif, 2002; Hoff-Ginsberg, 1991; Rowe, 2008).

Volume of parental language input can also differ between families that seem very similar in socioeconomic and cultural background. Using all-day audio recordings of family activities, Weisleder and Fernald (2013) found large differences in the amount of language Spanish-speaking families from low SES homes directed toward infants. These differences between families within a low SES population were almost as large as those found by Hart and Risley (1995) between wealthy and less advantaged families. Some families spoke to babies 18 times as much as others did. Those infants who experienced more daily speech were more efficient at processing words in real time, and they had larger expressive vocabularies at 24 months. Using mediation analysis, Weisleder and Fernald discovered that the effect of speech input volume on vocabulary development was explained by differential efficiency in language processing. The more speech that had been directed to babies, the faster they processed speech, which facilitated their language growth.

What might explain the disparity in language input across these low-SES families? The difference was not correlated with parent education. One possibility mentioned by Weisleder and Fernald is different levels of knowledge and beliefs about child development. Parents can be sensitive to changes in children's language development: In longitudinal research, parents varied the speech complexity and vocabulary diversity in response to children's language growth (Huttenlocher, Vasilyeva, Waterfall, Vevea, & Hedges, 2007). However, some parents may be more attuned to changes in their child's language than others are.

Parents challenge their children using varied vocabulary if they believe their children will understand (Rowe, 2000). Rowe (2008) collected naturalistic assessments of parents' child-directed speech at 30 months and vocabulary outcomes at 30 and

42 months. She found the typical positive relation between parent income/education and child language development. However, in further analyses of the data, the relation between parental SES and the amount and quality of child-directed speech was mediated by parents' *beliefs and knowledge about child development*. Rowe suggested that parents with more awareness of child development were better able to challenge children with sophisticated language just beyond their current developmental level. Thus, informing all parents about the value of talking to young children may be effective in building children's language development.

Beliefs about language predicted Spanish-speaking parents' language use at home (Hwang, Mancilla-Martinez, Flores, & McClain, 2017). Specifically, the belief that children can easily learn two languages was associated with more Spanish dominant home language use for Kindergarten-aged children and children with limited English proficiency. However, more use of Spanish did not directly relate to children's vocabulary outcomes. Rather, more use of *English* at home was related to higher conceptual vocabulary scores (wherein children were credited with knowledge of a concept if they knew the label in either language—Marchman & Martinez-Sussmann, 2002; Pearson & Fernández, 1994; Pearson et al., 1993). This somewhat surprising result suggests that the Spanish-speaking parents in this sample who used more English may have been more intentional in building their children's vocabularies.

A focus on building oral language in the preschool years is important for school success. Even before entering school, Latino children from low-income homes tend to have low vocabulary levels (August & Shanahan, 2006) that persist throughout the school years (García & Frede, 2010). In a longitudinal study of vocabulary growth, toddlers from Spanish-speaking families attending Head Start/Early Head Start were 24 months below national English and Spanish monolingual vocabulary norms (Mancilla-Martinez & Vagh, 2013). Rate of vocabulary growth was not sufficient for children to reach levels appropriate for their age by the time they were 3 years old. Over time, toddlers added more English than Spanish words to their lexicon, including the English equivalent of words known in Spanish as well as unique English words. Assessment of children's conceptual vocabulary (knowing a word for a concept in either language) still revealed a vocabulary and knowledge gap (somewhat attenuated) compared to monolinguals. This result differs from findings with middle-income bilingual toddlers who had conceptual vocabulary scores comparable to those of their Spanish-speaking monolingual peers (Patterson, 1998; Pearson & Fernández, 1994), suggesting the contribution of factors related to income status in the diverging outcomes.

The influence of developmental risk factors on vocabulary growth became apparent in a study that tracked the vocabularies of children enrolled in English-only preschools (Mancilla-Martinez, Christodoulou, & Shabaker, 2014). All children's English vocabularies grew across the school year. Risk factors that predicted less vocabulary growth included having a single parent and having a parent with limited English proficiency. Both parental English proficiency and cumulative risk (e.g., child prematurity, parental substance abuse, family mobility, etc.) had more effect on children who began with the least developed English vocabularies. In contrast, having multiple families living in the home was related to significantly higher vocabulary growth in English. As is the case for monolingual children, quality (or diversity) of language exposure predicts vocabulary growth among young bilingual learners (Aukrust & Rydland, 2011). For instance, in research by Place and Hoff (2011), exposure to multiple native English speakers (probably reflecting diversity of language exemplars) promoted acquisition, over and above the amount of English heard.

Bilingual Children and School

When they enter formal schooling, many bilingual children must become proficient in speaking English while simultaneously acquiring word-reading skills. Developing word-reading skills (such as decoding) is an important early step to reading. However, once these skills are acquired, the richness of a child's vocabulary places a limit on their ability to comprehend the text they read (García, 1991; Mancilla-Martinez & Lesaux, 2010, 2017; Verhoeven, 1990). While bilingual learners' word reading skills tend to be on par with national monolingual norms, their oral language skills and reading comprehension tend to remain significantly lower than the national average (Lesaux, 2006; Mancilla-Martinez & Lesaux, 2011, 2017). Of concern is that, although bilingual children acquire oral language skills at a rate that surpasses national norms, it is not enough for them to catch up to their peers.

Teachers in the early grades should devote sustained attention to early oral language, going beyond the simple language of conversation that is typical in classroom interactions (Bryant, Burchinal, Lau, & Sparling, 1994; Dickinson & Tabors, 2001; Scarcella, 2003; Wasik, Bond, & Hindman, 2006). Shared book reading is one of the most effective means of exposing young learners to new vocabulary words within a meaningful context (Bus, van Ijzendoorn, & Pellegrini, 1995; Dickinson & Smith, 1994), often with pictures illustrating word meanings (Ganea, Pickard, & DeLoache, 2008; Hindman et al., 2016). A comparison of the diversity of words in various input sources reveals much richer inclusion of unusual or rare words in children's books than in adult conversation (Cunningham & Stanovich, 1998; Montag, Jones, & Smith, 2015).

A focus on the sophisticated vocabulary of books and other written text helps English language learners to build conceptual networks of related words, important because *background knowledge* (and related vocabulary) predicts reading comprehension (Anderson & Pearson, 1984; Droop & Verhoeven, 1998; Jiménez, Garcia, & Pearson, 1996; Marzano, 2004). Giving children the rich oral vocabulary to sustain their reading comprehension is crucial, since research indicates that children learn most vocabulary words from reading in a "rich get richer" feedback loop (Fukkink & de Glopper, 1998; Stanovich & Cunningham, 1992, 1993; Cunningham & Stanovich, 1997, 1998). Additionally, syntax development can be accelerated through increased exposure to complex forms during book reading (Vasilyeva, Huttenlocher, & Waterfall, 2006). Evidence of a causal relation is the fact that preschool children's language growth reflects the quality of teacher language input during a school year (Dickinson & Porche, 2011; Huttenlocher, Vasilyeva, Cymerman, & Levine, 2002).

Innovations to Promote Bilingual Language Learning

In a review discussing interventions to overcome disparities in language input, Hindman et al. (2016) remark that:

> The success of interventions that aim to close the language stimulation gap rests largely on the degree to which they ultimately help families and educators talk more, using words that children will encounter in texts, in ways likely to help children learn. (p. 2).

To promote bilingual children's language learning and academic success, Konishi et al. (2014) recommend increasing English language input, capitalizing on child interests, using social interaction, prompts, and questions, and teaching more vocabulary. These principles can be difficult to implement when a family faces inadequate access to resources combined with language barriers. Because change is difficult, "interventions need to identify appealing, practical, and feasible strategies to retain families and educators over time" (Hindman et al., 2016, p. 3). Below we suggest some promising efforts to make these goals easier for families and teachers to achieve.

Hablame Bebe (Talk to Me, Baby)

Hablame Bebe (Baralt, Darcy Mahoney, & Brito, 2017) is a smartphone application for low-income immigrant Spanish-speaking families that builds on cultural strengths and beliefs to promote parent–infant talk. Daily reminders, tips, videos, and a word tracker (all in Spanish) build parents' knowledge of the benefits of bilingualism and encourage parents to use their heritage language to narrate everyday routines, in order to give their baby "language nutrition…the rich, back-and-forth interaction and loving words that are critical for the developing brain and for language acquisition" (Baralt et al., 2017). The app offers parents information about their child's development. It thereby builds confidence that parents are their baby's first and best teacher and can raise their child as a proud bilingual in the United States.

Language input to children is decreased when parents believe that they should switch from their native Spanish to a language in which they are less fluent (English) as a result of assimilation pressure (Hoff, 2013). Baralt and her colleagues discovered that local pediatricians were encouraging immigrant parents to switch to English, contrary to the evidence from research. Place and Hoff (2011) reported that in their research, Spanish-speaking parents' use of English was less beneficial for toddlers than input in parents' native language, which underscores the value of encouraging parents to continue to talk to their children in their most fluent language. In Weisleder and Fernald's (2013) study, the amount of Spanish input that parents directed to their toddlers affected children's speech processing and word learning. Therefore, evidence supports parents' use of the heritage language to increase language input to children.

Mothers' words and the number of questions they directed to their infant during play and book reading interactions rose significantly from pretest to posttest after the 2-month Hablame Bebe intervention. Parents' knowledge about language development and the benefits of bilingualism increased, and mothers reported greater pride and feeling safer using their heritage language.

The Hablame Bebe research team based their language intervention on research results and used parents' input to improve app design. These practices followed Hindman et al.'s (2016) suggestions that "interventions must be congruent with both scientific evidence and participants' cultural beliefs and expectations" and that people who take part "should have input during development and evaluation of programs" (p. 4).

Language Brokering During Shared eBook Reading

Interactive and responsive parent–child conversations, focused on topics of interest to the child, consistently emerge as key ingredients for language development in early childhood (e.g., Cristofaro & Tamis-LeMonda, 2012; Dieterich, Assel, Swank, Smith, & Landry, 2006; Hirsh-Pasek et al., 2015; Konishi et al., 2014; Pan, Rowe, Singer, & Snow, 2005; Tamis-LeMonda, Kuchirko, & Song, 2014; Weizman & Snow, 2001). Parents' uses of open-ended *wh-* questions typically require more complex responses from children, helping to build oral vocabulary (Rowe, Leech, & Cabrera, 2017). In low-income Spanish-speaking families, the number of words parents used in conversations with their children during play correlated with the children's language processing speed, or how efficiently they could take in and respond to language (Hurtado, Marchman, & Fernald, 2008). Processing speed was related to greater gains in children's vocabulary across time, showing that parent–child conversations are a powerful contributor to language development when children begin to talk.

As discussed earlier, parents in immigrant communities frequently ask school-aged "language brokers" questions in order to navigate in the English-speaking world. The typical Vygotskian roles of parent-expert and child-apprentice are altered, with the child sometimes being the one with knowledge answering questions for adults, and sometimes needing to ask adults for clarification as an interaction proceeds (Eksner & Orellana, 2012). Language brokering interactions usually involve topics more of interest to the adult than to the child, but the practice encompasses several of Konishi et al.' (2014) recommendations for improving oral language, including social interactivity, the use of prompts and questions, and a focus on the meaning of words. One possibility is that the interactive conversational style that parents and children achieve during language brokering might promote young children's language development if the interaction centered on the child's interests.

Parents usually begin asking children to translate written material and interpret in social situations when they are between the ages of 8 and 12 (Morales & Hanson, 2005). Flores (2017) explored whether younger bilingual children (5- to 8-year-olds) could interpret and answer questions about a story while reading a narrated digital picture book with a Spanish-speaking researcher. Parents reported that the children all had experience language brokering, although only a fifth had extensive (daily) experience. The rest participated in language brokering once a week or less. Most of the sample had at least some direct language brokering experience with multiple social partners, in line with results reported in Morales and Hanson's (2005) review. More than half of the participating children had watched a sibling interpret for the parents.

After the child and researcher listened to the English narration on each eBook page, the researcher asked, "Que dice?" ("What did it say?") to prompt the child to interpret from English to Spanish. Children were also asked the question, "Que es esa palabra?" ("What is that word?") about six challenging English target words (*shelter, insects, stream, predator, tunnel*, and *trail*). Participants could provide an equivalent Spanish word or a definition. Additionally, the researcher followed up on those pages with a *wh-* question (e.g., "What do you think Papa Mouse will do to escape?").

Despite their young age, participants could provide partial translations from English to Spanish of the eBook story and unusual target words (although with some errors). They did better at appropriately using and defining the difficult target words in the context of interpreting the story than when asked about word meanings in isolation. Children who were asked to translate used significantly more target words in their retelling of the story compared to children who read the book twice with the researcher but were not asked to translate (Flores, 2017). Actively engaging with the meaning of words during translation, answering challenging *wh-* questions about the story, and repeating rare words in a meaningful context during story retelling are likely to be powerful ways to build children's language over time during parent–child daily reading sessions.

A Digital Character to Train Parents in Dialogic Questioning

In Flores' (2017) language brokering study, a trained researcher asked questions aimed at getting children to engage with the contents of a storybook in ways that might promote language learning. The prompts and questions involved in language brokering are similar to "dialogic reading" techniques (Whitehurst et al., 1988), in which children are asked to answer open-ended questions about the story. In a meta-analysis of 16 experimental studies, dialogic reading was effective for vocabulary development (Mol, Bus, de Jong, & Smeets, 2008), particularly for younger children's expressive vocabulary, because this technique gets children to express themselves with oral language. In this meta-analysis, the effects were weaker for children from lower income homes and those at greater risk for school failure, although in individual studies, positive effects were found for children in these groups (Lonigan & Whitehurst, 1998; Opel, Ameer, & Aboud, 2009; Vally, Murray, Tomlinson, & Cooper, 2015; Whitehurst et al., 1994) as well as for English language learners (Brannon & Dauksas, 2014; Tsybina & Eriks-Brophy, 2010). Mol and colleagues highlight that not just the quantity, but the *quality* of book reading matters (e.g., active parent/teacher involvement that elicits children's verbal responses regarding the story).

This caveat brings to mind another of Hindman et al.'s (2016) suggestions about effective interventions to "bridge the word gap"—parents and teachers, particularly those with less education and resources, may need guidance both on how to talk with children and on how to effectively teach more uncommon words that are important for reading, as in observations they are less likely to define new words for children while reading (Evans, Reynolds, Shaw, & Pursoo, 2011) or to engage in reciprocal conversations that allow children to practice using vocabulary (Dickinson & Tabors, 2001).

Unfortunately, most school curricula provide little guidance regarding vocabulary instruction (Neuman & Dwyer, 2009) and classrooms that serve children from low-income families offer few opportunities for language and literacy development (Bryant et al., 1994; Dickinson & Tabors, 2001. Thus, training is required. In a study lasting an entire school year, Head Start teachers were trained in "dialogic questioning" strategies to increase opportunities for language and vocabulary development around stories (Wasik et al., 2006). At end of the year, children in the intervention classrooms performed significantly better on both receptive and expressive vocabulary tests. Teachers "were initially reluctant to ask questions of children and allow them to talk…concerned that children would become unruly and that talking would lead to chaos" (p. 72). Yet teachers became convinced through extensive training and experience to adopt strategies that promoted language development.

Hindman et al. (2016) point out that the few effective interventions for families and educators rely on fidelity of training, facilitated by intensive, ongoing, on-site support. However, scaling up this level of training is expensive, especially for communities with few resources. A potential solution is offering training in dialogic techniques by means of interactive digital media.

Strouse, O'Doherty, and Troseth (2013) demonstrated that dialogic questioning could be effectively administered by embedding a questioner in video storybooks. On each page of a lightly animated, English-narrated storybook, a preschool teacher appeared in the corner of the screen to ask children a variety of questions. English monolingual children first watched a video storybook for a week where the questioner asked simple questions, then switched to an identical storybook for another week in which the questioner asked more challenging questions. The next 2 weeks followed the same pattern with a different video (easy and harder question versions). Watching the story videos while being questioned by the embedded preschool teacher was not as effective as being questioned by their own trained parent, but children who were asked questions by the preschool teacher on video had somewhat better story vocabulary gains than children who watched the story videos without this support.

The next effort was to embed a dialogic questioning character in an eBook for children to read *with parents*. In a first version of the story, the character (Ramone) asked simple open-ended question, and in a second version of the same story, Ramone asked more challenging questions, including "distancing prompts" that called on children to connect between the story and their own lives, and *wh-* inference questions to get children reflecting on story characters' feeling and predicting what would happen next. On the title page, Ramone explained that parents were their child's best teacher, and that children learned best when parents talked to them and asked questions. In the second story version, Ramone prompted parents to take over questioning on later pages when he no longer appeared. While reading the two experimental story versions, parents and children talked significantly more with the character's encouragement and example than families did who read the unmodified eBook (without questioner) twice. Both low-income parents (Troseth, Strouse, & Russo-Johnson, 2017) and parents with more resources (Strouse, Flores, Stuckelman, Russo Johnson, & Troseth, 2017) uttered *more than three times as many words* as same-SES parents who read the eBook without the character modeling dialogic questioning.

When encouraged by the questioner's example, high SES *and* low SES parents also used significantly more unique words (a measure of language quality). More of their talk concerned the book contents, and less was aimed at controlling their children's behavior, compared to their SES-matched control group who read the book without Ramone. Children produced fewer words than their parent did, but the differences between the experimental and matched control groups within each SES were significant, and the content of children's talk went in the same direction as their parents' did. Of particular importance, parents in the experimental group began to adopt the dialogic questioning method, asking their own, original questions on the pages where Ramone did not appear. This very brief training in dialogic questioning was effective at helping vulnerable families begin to use the kind of conversational turn-taking, questioning style that has been shown to benefit expressive language development in a number of earlier studies (e.g., Mol et al., 2008; What Works Clearinghouse, 2007).

In a future study, families will take a tablet with the eBook (experimental book with Ramone or control book) home to read for 2 weeks. Pretest and posttest measures of vocabulary, posttest measures of story comprehension, and observations of parent–child reading will indicate whether the questioner's model is effective over time not only at inciting parent questioning and parent–child talk (with the trained eBook and other books), but also children's vocabulary learning and story comprehension.

An advantage of interactive digital technology is allowing parents to choose the language (e.g., English or Spanish) in which the avatar models questioning. Giving Spanish-speaking parents the option to change the language of the eBook narration and text is also possible. This adaptable version of the eBook is currently under development.

Conclusion

Growing up bilingual means actively navigating between two languages both internally, using one brain language system, and externally in the social world. Providing early rich language input, in the context of supportive social interaction, will help bilingual children reach their full potential.

Acknowledgements Part of the research reported here was supported by an HRSA Bridging the Word Gap Challenge Award from the Health Resources Services Administration to Georgene Troseth and by an NSF Graduate Research Fellowship (1445197) to Israel Flores.

References

Abutalebi, J., & Green, D. W. (2007). Bilingual language production: The neurocognition of language representation and control. *Journal of Neurolinguistics, 20*, 242–275.

Abutalebi, J., & Green, D. W. (2008). Control mechanisms in bilingual language production: Neural evidence from language switching studies. *Language & Cognitive Processes, 23*, 557–582.

Adesope, O. O., Lavin, T., Thompson, T., & Ungerleider, C. (2010). A systematic review and meta-analysis of the cognitive correlates of bilingualism. *Review of Educational Research, 80*, 207–245.

Adi-Japha, E., Berberich-Artzi, J., & Libnawi, A. (2010). Cognitive flexibility in drawings of bilingual children. *Child Development, 81*, 1356–1366.

Akhtar, N., & Menjivar, J. A. (2012). Cognitive and linguistic correlates of early exposure to more than one language. In J. B. Benson (Ed.), *Advances in child development and behavior* (Vol. 42). Mahwah, NJ: Elsevier.

Anderson, R. C., & Pearson, P. D. (1984). A schema-theoretic view of basic processes in reading comprehension. In P. D. Pearson, R. Barr, M. L. Kamil, & P. B. Mosenthal (Eds.), *Handbook of reading research* (pp. 255–291). New York, NY: Longman.

Anglin, J. M. (1993). Vocabulary development: A morphological analysis. *Monographs of the Society for Research in Child Development, 58*(10), Serial 238.

Au, T. K., & Glusman, M. (1990). The principle of mutual exclusivity in word learning: To honor or not to honor. *Child Development, 61*, 1474–1490.

August, D., & Shanahan, T. (Eds.). (2006). *Developing literacy in second-language learners: Report of the national literacy panel on language-minority children and youth*. Mahwah, NJ: Erlbaum.

Aukrust, V. G., & Rydland, V. (2011). Preschool classroom conversations as long-term resources for second language and literacy acquisition. *Journal of Applied Developmental Psychology, 32*(4), 198–207.

Barac, R., & Bialystok, E. (2011). Cognitive development in bilingual children. *Language Teaching, 44*(1), 36–54.

Baralt, M., Darcy Mahoney, A., & Brito, N. (2017). *Háblame Bebé is the first mobile application to promote Spanish-English bilingualism and reduce the Word Gap: Report to HRSA*. (HRSA Phase 3 Report). Bridging the Word Gap Challenge.

Bates, E. (1976). *Language and context: The acquisition of pragmatics*. New York, NY: Academic Press.

Bedore, L. M., Peña, E. D., García, M., & Cortez, C. (2005). Conceptual versus monolingual scoring: When does it make a difference? *Language, Speech, and Hearing Services in Schools, 36,* 188–200.

Ben-Zeev, S. (1977). The influence of bilingualism on cognitive strategy and cognitive development. *Child Development, 48,* 1009–1018.

Berguno, G., & Bowler, D. M. (2004). Communicative interactions, knowledge of a second language, and Theory of Mind in young children. *The Journal of Genetic Psychology: Research and Theory on Human Development, 165,* 289–309.

Bialystok, E. (1986). Children's concept of word. *Journal of Psycholinguistic Research, 15,* 13–32.

Bialystok, E. (1999). Cognitive complexity and attentional control in the bilingual mind. *Child Development, 70,* 636–644.

Bialystok, E. (2010). Global-local and trail-making tasks by monolingual and bilingual children: Beyond inhibition. *Developmental Psychology, 46,* 93–105.

Bialystok, E., Barac, R., Blaye, A., & Poulin-Dubois, D. (2010). Word mapping and executive functioning in young monolingual and bilingual children. *Journal of Cognition and Development, 11,* 485–508.

Bialystok, E., Luk, G., Peets, K. F., & Yang, S. (2010). Receptive vocabulary differences in monolingual and bilingual children. *Bilingualism: Language and Cognition, 13,* 525–531.

Bialystok, E., & Senman, L. (2004). Executive process in appearance-reality tasks: The role of inhibition of attention and symbolic representation. *Child Development, 75,* 562–579.

Bialystok, E., & Shapero, D. (2005). Ambiguous benefits: The effect of bilingualism on reversing ambiguous figures. *Developmental Science, 8,* 595–604.

Bialystok, E., & Viswanathan, M. (2009). Components of executive control with advantages for bilingual children in two cultures. *Cognition, 112,* 494–500.

Brannon, D., & Dauksas, L. (2014). The effectiveness of dialogic reading in increasing English language learning preschool children's expressive language. *International Research in Early Childhood Education, 5*(1), 1–10.

Bryant, D. M., Burchinal, M., Lau, L. B., & Sparling, J. J. (1994). Family and classroom correlates of Head Start children's developmental outcomes. *Early Childhood Research Quarterly, 9,* 289–309.

Buriel, R., Perez, W., De Ment, T. L., Chavez, D. V., & Moran, V. R. (1998). The relationship of language brokering to academic performance, biculturalism, and self-efficacy among Latino adolescents. *Hispanic Journal of Behavioral Sciences, 20*(3), 283–297.

Bus, A. G., van Ijzendoorn, M. H., & Pellegrini, A. D. (1995). Joint book reading makes for success in learning to read: A meta-analysis on intergenerational transmission of literacy. *Review of Educational Research, 65*(1), 1–21.

Byers-Heinlein, K. & Werker, J. F. (2009). Monolingual, bilingual, trilingual: Infants' language experience influences the development of a word-learning heuristic. *Developmental Science, 12,* 815–823.

Calvo, A., & Bialystok, E. (2014). Independent effects of bilingualism and socioeconomic status on language ability and executive functioning. *Cognition, 130*(3), 278–288. https://doi.org/10.1016/j.cognition.2013.11.015

Carlson, S. M. (2005). Developmentally sensitive measures of executive function in preschool children. *Developmental Neuropsychology, 28*(2), 592–616. https://doi.org/10.1207/s15326942dn2802_3

Carlson, S. M. & Meltzoff, A. N. (2008). Bilingual experience and executive functioning in young children. *Developmental Science, 11,* 282–298.

Carter, P. L., & Welner, K. G. (Eds.). (2013). *Closing the opportunity gap: What America must do to give all children an even chance.* New York, NY: Oxford University Press.

Comeau, L., Genesee, F., & Mendelson, M. (2007). Bilingual children's repairs of breakdowns in communication. *Journal of Child Language, 34,* 159–174.

Cristofaro, T. N., & Tamis-LeMonda, C. S. (2012). Mother–child conversations at 36 months and at pre-kindergarten: Relations to children's school readiness. *Journal of Early Childhood Literacy, 12*(1), 68–97. https://doi.org/10.1177/1468798411416879

Cromdal, J. (1999). Childhood bilingualism and metalinguistic skills: Analysis and control in young Swedish-English bilinguals. *Applied PsychoLinguistics, 20*, 1–20.

Cunningham, A. E., & Stanovich, K. E. (1997). Early reading acquisition and its relation to reading experience and ability 10 years later. *Developmental Psychology, 33*(6), 934–945.

Cunningham, A. E., & Stanovich, K. E. (1998). What reading does for the mind. *American Educator, 22*(1–2), 8–15.

Daniels, H. A. (1998). Nine ideas about language. In V. P. Clark, P. A. Eschholz, & A. F. Rosa (Eds.), *Language: Readings in language and culture* (pp. 43–60). New York, NY: St. Martin's Press.

Davidson, D., Jergovic, D., Imami, Z., & Theodos, V. (1997). Monolingual and bilingual children's use of the mutual exclusivity constraint. *Journal of Child Language, 24*, 3–24.

Davidson, D., & Tell, D. (2005). Monolingual and bilingual children's use of mutual exclusivity in the naming of whole objects. *Journal of Experimental Child Psychology, 92*, 24–45.

De Houwer, A. (1999). Environmental factors in early bilingual development: The role of parental beliefs and attitudes. In Extra, G. & Verhoeven, L. (Eds.), *Bilingualism and migration* (pp. 75–96). New York: Mouton de Gruyter.

Diaz-Lazaro, C. M. (2002). *The effects of language brokering on perceptions of family authority structure, problem solving abilities, and parental locus of control in Latino adolescents and their parents* (Unpublished doctoral dissertation), State University of New York, Buffalo, NY.

Dickinson, D. K., & Porche, M. V. (2011). Relation between language experiences in preschool classrooms and children's kindergarten and fourth-grade language and reading abilities. *Child Development, 82*(3), 870–886. https://doi.org/10.1111/j.1467-8624.2011.01576.x

Dickinson, D. K., & Smith, M. W. (1994). Long-term effects of preschool teachers' book readings on low-income children's vocabulary and story comprehension. *Reading Research Quarterly, 29*(2), 105–122.

Dickinson, D. K., & Tabors, P. O. (Eds.). (2001). *Beginning literacy with language: Young children learning at home and at school.* Baltimore, MD: Brookes.

Dieterich, S. E., Assel, M. A., Swank, P., Smith, K. E., & Landry, S. H. (2006). The impact of early maternal verbal scaffolding and child language abilities on later decoding and reading comprehension skills. *Journal of School Psychology, 43*(6), 481–494. https://doi.org/10.1016/j.jsp.2005.10.003

Dorner, L. M., Orellana, M. F., & Li-Grining, C. P. (2007). "I helped my mom," and it helped me: Translating the skills of language brokers into improved standardized test scores. *American Journal of Education, 113*, 451–478.

Droop, M., & Verhoeven, L. (1998). Background knowledge, linguistic complexity, and second-language reading comprehension. *Journal of Literacy Research, 30* (2), 253–271.

Dudley-Marling, C., & Lucas, K. (2009). Pathologizing the language and culture of poor children. *Language Arts, 86*, 362–370.

Dunn, L. M., & Dunn, D. M. (1999). *Peabody picture vocabulary test* (3rd ed.). Bloomington, MN: Pearson Assessments.

Eksner, H. J., & Orellana, M. F. (2012). Shifting in the zone: Latina/o child language brokers and the co-construction of knowledge. *Ethos, 40*(2), 196–220. https://doi.org/10.1111/j.1548-1352.2012.01246

Emmorey, K., Luk, G., Pyers, J. E., & Bialystok, E. (2008). The source of enhanced cognitive control in bilinguals. *Psychological Science, 19*, 1201–1206.

Engel de Abreu, P. M. J., Cruz-Santos, A., Tourinho, C. J., Martin, R., & Bialystok, E. (2012). Bilingualism enriches the poor: Enhanced cognitive control in low income minority children. *Psychological Science, 23*(11), 1364–1371. https://doi.org/10.1177/0956797612443836

Evans, M. A., Reynolds, K., Shaw, D., & Pursoo, T. (2011). Parental explanations of vocabulary during shared book reading: A missed opportunity. *First Language, 31*, 195–213. https://doi.org/10.1177/0142723710393795

Farkas, G., & Beron, K. (2004). The detailed age trajectory of oral vocabulary knowledge: Differences by class and race. *Social Science Research, 33*, 464–497. https://doi.org/10.1016/j.ssresearch.2003.08.001

Fernald, A., Marchman, V. A., & Weisleder, A. (2013). SES differences in language processing skill and vocabulary are evident at 18 months. *Developmental Science, 16*(2), 234–248. https://doi.org/10.1111/desc.12019

Flores, I. (2017). *Language brokering during shared ebook reading* (Unpublished Masters thesis). Vanderbilt University.

Fukkink, R. G., & de Glopper, K. (1998). Effects of instruction in deriving word meaning from context: A meta-analysis. *Review of Educational Research, 68*, 450–468.

Ganea, P. A., Pickard, M. B., & DeLoache, J. S. (2008). Transfer between picture books and the real world by very young children. *Journal of Cognition and Development, 9*, 44–66. https://doi.org/10.1080/15248370701836592

García, E. E., & Frede, E. C. (Eds.). (2010). *Young English language learners: Current research and emerging directions for practice and policy*. New York, NY: Teachers College Press.

García, G. E. (1991). Factors influencing the English Reading Test performance of Spanish-speaking Hispanic children. *Reading Research Quarterly, 26*(4), 371–392. http://www.jstor.org/stable/747894

Goetz, P. J. (2003). The effects of bilingualism on theory of mind development. *Bilingualism: Language and Cognition, 6*, 1–15.

Grice, H. P. (1989). *Studies in the way of words*. Cambridge, MA: Harvard University Press.

Hackman, D. A., & Farah, M. J. (2009). Socioeconomic status and the developing brain. *Trends in Cognitive Sciences, 13*, 65–73.

Hart, B., & Risley, T. (1995). *Meaningful differences in the everyday experience of young American children*. Baltimore, MD: Brookes.

Heath, S. B. (1986). Sociocultural contexts of language development. In California Department of Education (Ed.), *Beyond language: Social and cultural factors in schooling language minority students* (pp. 143–186). Los Angeles, CA: Evaluation, Dissemination, and Assessment Center, California State University.

Hernandez, D. J. (2004). Demographic change and the life circumstances of immigrant families. *Future of Children, 14*(2), 17–47. https://doi.org/10.2307/1602792

Hindman, A. H., Wasik, B. A., & Snell, E. K. (2016). Closing the 30 million word gap: Next steps in designing research to inform practice. *Child Development Perspectives, 10*, 134–139. https://doi.org/10.1111/cdep.12177

Hirsh-Pasek, K., Adamson, L. B., Bakeman, R., Owen, M. T., Golinkoff, R. M., Pace, A., … Suma, K. (2015). The contributions of early communication quality to low-income children's language success. *Psychological Science, 26*(7), 1–13.

Hoff, E. (2003a). Causes and consequences of SES-related differences in parent-to-child speech. In M. H. Bornstein & R. H. Bradley (Eds.), *Socioeconomic status, parenting, and child development* (pp. 147–160). Mahwah, NJ: Erlbaum.

Hoff, E. (2003b). The specificity of environmental influence: Socioeconomic status affects early vocabulary development via maternal speech. *Child Development, 74*, 1368–1378.

Hoff, E. (2006). How social contexts support and shape language development. *Developmental Review, 26*, 55–88. https://doi.org/10.1016/j.dr.2005.11.002

Hoff, E. (2013). Interpreting the early language trajectories of children from low-SES and language minority homes: Implications for closing achievement gaps. *Developmental Psychology, 49*(1), 4–14.

Hoff, E., Core, C., Place, S., Rumiche, R., Senor, M., & Parra, M. (2012). Dual language exposure and early bilingual development. *Journal of Child Language, 39*(1), 1–27.

Hoff, E., Laursen, B., & Tardif, T. (2002). Socioeconomic status and parenting. In M. H. Bornstein (Ed.), *Handbook of parenting. Ecology and biology of parenting* (Vol. II, pp. 161–188). Mahwah, NJ: Lawrence Erlbaum.

Hoff-Ginsberg, E. (1991). Mother-child conversation in different social classes and communicative settings. *Child Development, 62*, 782–796.

Houston-Price, C., Caloghiris, Z., & Raviglione, E. (2010). Language experience shapes the development of the mutual exclusivity bias. *Infancy, 15*, 125–150.

Hurtado, N., Marchman, V. A., & Fernald, A. (2008). Does input influence uptake? Links between maternal talk, processing speed and vocabulary size in Spanish-learning children. *Developmental Science, 11*, F31–F39. https://doi.org/10.1111/j.1467-7687.2008.00768.x

Huttenlocher, J., Vasilyeva, M., Cymerman, E., & Levine, S. (2002). Language input and child syntax. *Cognitive Psychology, 45*(3), 337–374.

Huttenlocher, J., Vasilyeva, M., Waterfall, H. R., Vevea, J. L., & Hedges, L. V. (2007). The varieties of speech to young children. *Developmental Psychology, 43*(5), 1062–1083.

Huttenlocher, J., Waterfall, H., Vasilyeva, M., Vevea, J., & Hedges, L. V. (2010). Sources of variability in children's language growth. *Cognitive Psychology, 61*(4), 343–365. https://doi.org/10.1016/j.cogpsych.2010.08.002

Hwang, J. K., Mancilla-Martinez, J., Flores, I., & McClain, J. (2017). *The interplay among parental beliefs home language use, and Spanish-speaking children's vocabulary*. Manuscript submitted for publication.

Jiang, Y., Granja, M. R., & Koball, H. (2017). *Basic facts about low-income children: Children under 18 years, 2015*. New York, NY: National Center for Children in Poverty, Columbia University Mailman School of Public Health.

Jiménez, R.T., David, S., Fagan, K., Risko, V.J., Pacheco, M., Pray, L., & Gonzales, M. (2015). Using translation to drive conceptual development for students becoming literate in English as an additional language. *Research in the Teaching of English, 49*(3), 248–271.

Jiménez, R. T., Garcia, G. E., & Pearson, P. D. (1996). The reading strategies of bilingual Latina/o students who are successful English readers: Opportunities and obstacles. *Reading Research Quarterly, 31*, 90–112.

Katz, V. (2014). Children as brokers of their immigrant families' health-care connections. *Social Problems, 61*(2), 194–215.

Konishi, H., Kanero, J., Freeman, M. R., Golinkoff, R. M., & Hirsh-Pasek, K. (2014). Six principles of language development: Implications for second language learners. *Developmental Neuropsychology, 39*(5), 404–420.

Kovacs, A. M. (2009). Early bilingualism enhances mechanisms of false-belief reasoning. *Developmental Science, 12*, 48–54.

Kovacs, A. M., & Mehler, J. (2009). Cognitive gains in 7-month-old bilingual infants. *Proceedings of the National Academy of Sciences, 106*(16), 6556–6560. https://doi.org/10.1073/pnas.0811323106

Krashen, S. D. (1985). *The input hypothesis: Issues and implications*. London, England: Longman.

Kroll, J. F., Dussias, P. E., Bice, K., & Perrotti, L. (2015). Bilingualism, mind, and brain. *Annual Review of Linguistics, 1*, 377–394.

Lesaux, N. (2006). The development of literacy. In D. August & T. Shanahan (Eds.), *Developing literacy in second-language learners: Report of the National Literacy Panel on Language-Minority Children and Youth* (pp. 75–122). Mahwah, NJ: Erlbaum.

Lonigan, C. J., & Whitehurst, G. J. (1998). Relative efficacy of parent and teacher involvement in a shared-reading intervention for preschool children from low income backgrounds. *Early Childhood Research Quarterly, 13*, 263–290. https://doi.org/10.1016/S0885-2006(99)80038-6

López, M. H., & Velasco, G. (2011). *The toll of the great recession: Childhood poverty among Hispanics sets record, leads nation*. Washington, DC: Pew Hispanic Center, Pew Research Center.

Luk, G., de Sa, E., & Bialystok, E. (2011). Is there a relation between onset age of bilingualism and enhancement of cognitive control? *Bilingualism: Language and Cognition, 14*, 588–595.

Malakoff, M., & Hakuta, K. (1991). Translation skill and metalinguistic awareness in bilinguals. In E. Bialystok (Ed.), *Language processing in bilingual children* (pp. 141–166). Cambridge, England: Cambridge University Press.

Mancilla-Martinez, J., Christodoulou, J. A., & Shabaker, M. M. (2014). Preschoolers' English vocabulary development: The influence of language proficiency and at risk factors. *Learning and Individual Differences, 35*, 79–86. https://doi.org/10.1016/j.lindif.2014.06.008

Mancilla-Martinez, J., & Lesaux, N. K. (2010). Predictors of reading comprehension for struggling readers: The case of Spanish-speaking language minority learners. *Journal of Educational Psychology, 102*(3), 701–711.

Mancilla-Martinez, J., & Lesaux, N. K. (2011). The gap between Spanish-speakers' word reading and word knowledge: A longitudinal study. *Child Development, 82*(5), 1544–1560. https://doi.org/10.1111/j.1467-8624.2011.01633.x

Mancilla-Martinez, J., & Lesaux, N. K. (2017). Early indicators of later reading comprehension outcomes among Spanish-speaking language minority learners. *Scientific Studies of Reading, 5*, 428–448.

Mancilla-Martinez, J., & McClain, J. (forthcoming, 2017). What do we know today about the complexity of vocabulary gaps and what do we not know? In E.B. Moje, P. Afflerbach, P. Enciso, & N.K. Lesaux (Eds.), *Handbook of reading research*, Vol. V.

Mancilla-Martinez, J., & Vagh, S. B. (2013). Growth in toddlers' Spanish, English, and conceptual vocabulary knowledge. *Early Childhood Research Quarterly, 28*, 555–567. https://doi.org/10.1016/j.ecresq.2013.03.004

Marchman, V. A., Fernald, A., & Hurtado, N. (2010). How vocabulary size in two languages relates to efficiency in spoken word recognition by young Spanish English bilinguals. *Journal of Child Language, 37*, 817–840.

Marchman, V. A., & Martinez-Sussmann, C. (2002). Concurrent validity of caregiver/ parent report measures of language for children who are learning both English and Spanish. *Journal of Speech, Language, and Hearing Research, 45*, 983–997.

Markman, E. M., & Wachtel, G. F. (1988). Children's use of mutual exclusivity to constrain the meaning of words. *Cognitive Psychology, 20*, 121–157.

Markman, E. M., Wasow, J. L., & Hansen, M. B. (2003). Use of the mutual exclusivity assumption by young word learners. *Cognitive Psychology, 47*, 241–275.

Martin-Rhee, M. M., & Bialystok, E. (2008). The development of two types of inhibitory control in monolingual and bilingual children. *Bilingualism: Language and Cognition, 11*, 81–93.

Marzano, R. J. (2004). *Building background knowledge for academic achievement: Research on what works in schools*. Alexandria, VA: Association for Supervision and Curriculum Development.

McQuillan, J., & Tse, L. (1995). Child language brokering in linguistic minority communities: Effects on cultural interaction, cognition, and literacy. *Language and Education, 9*(3), 195–215.

Menjivar, J. A., & Akhtar, N. (2016). Language experience and preschoolers' foreign word learning. *Bilingualism: Language and Cognition, 20*(3), 642–648. https://doi.org/10.1017/S1366728916001103

Mol, S. E., Bus, A. G., de Jong, M. T., & Smeets, D. J. H. (2008). Added value of dialogic parent-child book reading: A meta-analysis. *Early Education and Development, 19*(1), 7–26.

Montag, J. L., Jones, M. N., & Smith, L. B. (2015). The words children hear: Picture books and the statistics for language learning. *Psychological Science, 26*(9), 1489–1496. https://doi.org/10.1177/0956797615594361.

Morales, A., & Hanson, W. E. (2005). Language brokering: An integrative review of the literature. *Hispanic Journal of Behavioral Sciences, 27*(4), 471–450.

Morrow, L. M. (1985). Retelling stories: A strategy for improving young children's comprehension, concept of story structure, and oral language complexity. *The Elementary School Journal, 85*(5), 646. https://doi.org/10.1086/461427

Neuman, S. B., & Dwyer, J. (2009). Missing in action: Vocabulary instruction in pre-k. *The Reading Teacher, 62*, 384–392. https://doi.org/10.1598/RT.62.5.2

Oller, D. K., & Eilers, R. (Eds.). (2002). *Language and literacy in bilingual children.* Clevedon, England: Multilingual Matters.

Opel, A., Ameer, S. S., & Aboud, F. E. (2009). The effect of preschool dialogic reading on vocabulary among rural Bangladeshi children. *International Journal of Educational Research, 48*(1), 12–20. https://doi.org/10.1016/j.ijer.2009.02.008.

Orellana, M. F. (2003). Responsibilities of children in Latino immigrant homes. *New Directions for Youth Development: Understanding the Social Worlds of Immigrant Youth, 10*, 25–39.

Orellana, M. F., Dorner, L., & Pulido, L. (2003). Accessing assets: Immigrant youth's work as family translators or "para-phrasers.". *Social Problems, 50*(4), 505–524.

Pan, B. A., Rowe, M. L., Singer, J. D., & Snow, C. E. (2005). Maternal correlates of growth in toddler vocabulary production in low-income families. *Child Development, 76*(4), 763–782.

Patterson, J. L. (1998). Expressive vocabulary development and word combinations of Spanish–English bilingual toddlers. *American Journal of Speech and Language Pathology, 7*, 46–56.

Pearson, B. Z. (2007). Social factors in childhood bilingualism in the United States. *Applied PsychoLinguistics, 28*, 399–410.

Pearson, B. Z., & Fernández, S. C. (1994). Patterns of interaction in the lexical growth in two languages of bilingual infants and toddlers. *Language Learning, 44*, 617–653.

Pearson, B. Z., Fernández, S. C., & Oller, D. K. (1993). Lexical development in bilingual infants and toddlers: Comparison to monolingual norms. *Language Learning, 43*, 93–120.

Pearson, B. Z., Fernández, S. C., & Oller, D. K. (1995). Cross-language synonyms in the lexicons of bilingual infants: One language or two? *Journal of Child Language, 22*(2), 345–368.

Place, S., & Hoff, E. (2011). Properties of dual language exposure that influence 2-year olds' bilingual proficiency. *Child Development, 82*, 1834–1849.

Poulin-Dubois, D., Blaye, A., Coutya, J., & Bialystok, E. (2011). The effects of bilingualism on toddlers' executive functioning. *Journal of Experimental Child Psychology, 108*, 567–579.

Prior, A., & MacWhinney, B. (2010). A bilingual advantage in task switching. *Bilingualism: Language and Cognition, 13*, 253–262.

Ramey, C. T., & Ramey, S. L. (2004). Early learning and school readiness: Can early intervention make a difference? *Merrill-Palmer Quarterly, 50*, 471–491.

Rogoff, B. (1990). *Apprenticeship in thinking: Cognitive development in social context.* New York, NY: Oxford University Press.

Rowe, M. L. (2000). Pointing and talk by low-income mothers and their 14-month-old children. *First Language, 20*, 305–330.

Rowe, M. L. (2008). Child-directed speech: Relation to socioeconomic status, knowledge of child development and child vocabulary skill. *Journal of Child Language, 35*(1), 185–205. https://doi.org/10.1017/S0305000907008343

Rowe, M. L. (2012). A longitudinal investigation of the role of quantity and quality of child-directed speech in vocabulary development. *Child Development, 83*(1762), 1774. https://doi.org/10.1111/j.1467-8624.2012.01805.x

Rowe, M. L., Leech, K. A., & Cabrera, N. (2017). Going beyond input quantity: *Wh* questions matter for toddlers' language and cognitive development. *Cognitive Science, 41*, 162–179.

Sabbagh, M. A., Xu, F., Carlson, S. M., Moses, L. J., & Lee, K. (2006). The development of executive functioning and Theory of Mind: A comparison of Chinese and U.S. preschoolers. *Psychological Science, 17*, 74–81.

Scarcella R. (2003). *Academic English: A conceptual framework* (UC Berkeley Technical Report). https://escholarship.org/uc/item/6pd082d4

Schady, N., Behrman, J., Araujo, M. C., Azuero, R., Bernal, R., Bravo, D., … Vakis, R. (2015). Wealth gradients in early childhood cognitive development in five Latin American countries. *The Journal of Human Resources, 50*(2), 446–463.

Sebastian-Galles, N., Albareda-Castellot, B., Weikum, W. M., & Werker, J. F. (2012). A bilingual advantage in visual language discrimination in infancy. *Psychological Science, 23*(9), 994–999. https://doi.org/10.1177/0956797612436817

Siegal, M., Iozzi, L., & Surian, L. (2009). Bilingualism and conversational understanding in young children. *Cognition, 110*, 115–122.

Siegal, M., Surian, L., Matsuo, A., Geraci, A., Iozzi, L., Okumura, Y., et al. (2010). Bilingualism accentuates children's conversational understanding. *PLoS One, 5*(2), e9004.

Snow, C. (1992). Perspectives on second language development: Implications for bilingual education. *Educational Researcher: Special Issue on Bilingual Education, 21*, 16–19.

Stanovich, K. E., & Cunningham, A. E. (1992). Studying the consequences of literacy within a literate society: The cognitive correlates of print exposure. *Memory & Cognition, 20*, 51–68.

Stanovich, K. E., & Cunningham, A. E. (1993). Where does knowledge come from? Specific associations between print exposure and information acquisition. *Journal of Educational Psychology, 85*, 211–229.

Strouse, G.A., Flores, I., Stuckelman, Z., Russo Johnson, C., & Troseth, G. (2017, October). *Built-in questions support parent-child talk during shared reading of an electronic text.* Poster presented at the meetings of the Cognitive Development Society, Portland, OR.

Strouse, G. A., O'Doherty, K., & Troseth, G. L. (2013). Effective coviewing: Preschoolers' learning from video after a dialogic questioning intervention. *Developmental Psychology, 49*, 2368–2382.

Sundara, M., Polka, L., & Genessee, F. (2006). Language-experience facilitatesdiscrimination of /d-th/ in monolingual and bilingual acquisition of English. *Cognition, 100*(2), 369–388. https://doi.org/10.1016/j.cognition.2005.04.007

Tamis-LeMonda, C. S., Kuchirko, Y., & Song, L. (2014). Why is infant language learning facilitated by parental responsiveness? *Current Directions in Psychological Science, 23*, 121–126. https://doi.org/10.1177/0963721414522813

Troseth, G., Strouse, G., & Russo-Johnson, C. (2017, June). *Read to me, talk to me: An e-book app that incorporates dialogic questioning.* Paper presented in the symposium (Hassinger-Das, Dore, & Golinkoff, co-Chairs), Taming Technology: Making Evidence-Based Decisions Regarding Digital Media, at the meetings of the Jean Piaget Society, San Francisco.

Tse, L. (1995). Language brokering among Latino adolescents: Prevalence, attitudes, and school performance. *Hispanic Journal of Behavioral Sciences, 17*(2), 180–193.

Tsybina, I., & Eriks-Brophy, A. (2010). Bilingual dialogic book-reading intervention for preschoolers with slow expressive vocabulary development. *Journal of Communication Disorders, 43*(6), 538–556. https://doi.org/10.1016/j.jcomdis.2010.05.006.

Vagh, S. B., Pan, B. A., & Mancilla-Martinez, J. (2009). Measuring growth in bilingual and monolingual children's English productive vocabulary development: The utility of combining parent and teacher report. *Child Development, 80*, 1545–1563.

Valdes, G., Chavez, C., & Angelelli, C. (2003). A performance team: Young interpreters and their parents. In G. Valdes (Ed.), *Expanding definitions of giftedness: The case of young interpreters from immigrant countries* (pp. 63–97). Mahwah, NJ: Erlbaum.

Valenzuela, A. (1999). Gender roles and settlement activities among children and their immigrant families. *American Behavioral Scientist, 42*(4), 720–747.

Vally, Z., Murray, L., Tomlinson, M., & Cooper, P. J. (2015). The impact of dialogic book-sharing training on infant language and attention: a randomized controlled trial in a deprived South African community. *Journal of Child Psychology and Psychiatry, 56*(8), 865–873. https://doi.org/10.1111/jcpp.12352.

Vasilyeva, M., Huttenlocher, J., & Waterfall, H. (2006). Effects of language intervention on syntactic skill levels in preschoolers. *Developmental Psychology, 42*(1), 164–174.

Verhoeven, L. T. (1990). Acquisition of reading in a second language. *Reading Research Quarterly, 25*(2), 90–114.

Vygotsky, L. (1978). *Mind in society: The development of higher psychological processes.* Cambridge, MA: Harvard University Press.

Wasik, B. A., Bond, M. A., & Hindman, A. (2006). The effects of a language and literacy intevention on Head Start children and teachers. *Journal of Educational Psychology, 98*(1), 63–74.

Weisleder, A., & Fernald, A. (2013). Talking to children matters: Early language experience strengthens processing and builds vocabulary. *Psychological Science, 24*(11), 2143–2152.

Weizman, Z. O., & Snow, C. E. (2001). Lexical input as related to children's vocabulary acquisition: Effects of sophisticated exposure and support for meaning. *Developmental Psychology, 37*(2), 265–279. https://doi.org/10.1037/0012-1649.37.2.265

What Works Clearinghouse (2007). *Dialogic reading.* WWC Intervention Report. Institute of Education Sciences. U. S. Department of Education.

Whitehurst, G. J., Arnold, D. S., Epstein, J. N., Angell, A. L., Smith, M., & Fischel, J. E. (1994). A picture book reading intervention in day care and home for children from low-income families. *Developmental Psychology, 30*(5), 679–689.

Whitehurst, G. J., Lonigan, C. J., Falco, F. L., Valdez-Menchaca, M. C., Fischel, J. E., Debaryshe, B. D., … Caufield, M. (1988). Accelerating language development through picture book reading. *Developmental Psychology, 24*, 552–559. https://doi.org/10.1037/0012-1649.24.4.552

Yang, S., Yang, H., & Lust, B. (2011). Early childhood bilingualism leads to advances in executive attention: Dissociating culture and language. *Bilingualism: Language and Cognition, 14*, 412–422.

Yow, W. Q., & Markman, E. M. (2011a). Young bilingual children's heightened sensitivity to referential cues. *Journal of Cognition and Development, 12*, 12–31.

Yow, W. Q., & Markman, E. M. (2011b). Bilingualism and children's use of paralinguistic cues to interpret emotion in speech. *Bilingualism: Language and Cognition, 14*(562), 569.

Index

CPSIA information can be obtained
at www.ICGtesting.com
Printed in the USA
LVHW05*1625280518
578670LV00001B/67/P